Financial Instrument Pricing
Using C++

Wiley Finance Series

Financial Instrument Pricing Using C++

Daniel J. Duffy

John Wiley & Sons, Ltd

Published by   John Wiley & Sons Ltd, The Atrium, Southern Gate, Chichester,
West Sussex PO19 8SQ, England

Telephone (+44) 1243 779777

Email (for orders and customer service enquiries): cs-books@wiley.co.uk
Visit our Home Page on www.wileyeurope.com or www.wiley.com

Other Wiley Editorial Offices

John Wiley & Sons Inc., 111 River Street, Hoboken, NJ 07030, USA

Jossey-Bass, 989 Market Street, San Francisco, CA 94103-1741, USA

Wiley-VCH Verlag GmbH, Boschstr. 12, D-69469 Weinheim, Germany

John Wiley & Sons Australia Ltd, 33 Park Road, Milton, Queensland 4064, Australia

John Wiley & Sons (Asia) Pte Ltd, 2 Clementi Loop #02-01, Jin Xing Distripark, Singapore 129809

John Wiley & Sons Canada Ltd, 22 Worcester Road, Etobicoke, Ontario, Canada M9W 1L1

Wiley also publishes its books in a variety of electronic formats. Some content that appears
in print may not be available in electronic books.

Library of Congress Cataloging-in-Publication Data

Duffy, Daniel J.
   Designing and implementing financial instruments in C++ / Daniel J. Duffy.
     p. cm.
   ISBN 0-470-85509-6
  1. Investments – Mathematical models. 2. Financial engineering. 3. C++
(Computer program language) I. Title
   HG4515. 2. D85 2004
   332.6′0285′5133 – dc22

                            2004008925

British Library Cataloguing in Publication Data

A catalogue record for this book is available from the British Library

ISBN-13: 978-0-470-85509-6 (H/B)

Typeset in 10/12pt Times by Laserwords Private Limited, Chennai, India
Printed and bound in Great Britain by Antony Rowe Ltd, Chippenham, Wiltshire
This book is printed on acid-free paper responsibly manufactured from sustainable forestry
in which at least two trees are planted for each one used for paper production.

Contents

1
Executive Overview of this Book

1.1 WHAT IS THIS BOOK?

The goal of this book is to model financial instruments, such as options, bonds and interest-rate products by partial differential equations, finite differences and C++. It is intended for IT and quantitative finance professionals who know this material and wish to deepen their knowledge and for those readers who use techniques such as Monte Carlo, Fourier transform methods, stochastic differential equations and lattice methods (for example, the binomial method) for instrument pricing.

We integrate a number of well-known areas to create a traceable and maintainable path from when a financial engineer proposes a new model to when he or she codes the resulting equations in C++. When viewed as a black box, the core process in this book is to produce C++ classes and code for financial engineering applications. Furthermore, we give lots of examples of code that developers can use without much hassle. The accompanying CD contains all the source code in this book. We provide guidelines, algorithms and reusable code to help the reader to achieve these ends. The main activities that realise the core process are:

- Activity 1: Map the financial model to a partial differential equation (PDE)
- Activity 2: Approximate the PDE by the finite difference method (FDM)
- Activity 3: Implement the FDM using C++ and design patterns.

In this book we shall concentrate on Activities 2 and 3. Since this is a book on the application of C++ to financial engineering we concentrate on mapping the numerical algorithms from Activity 2 to robust and flexible C++ code and classes. However, we shall provide sufficient motivation and background information to help the reader to understand the complete 'instrument life cycle'. This life cycle describes the processes, activities, decisions and alternatives that describe how to program models for financial instruments in C++.

The topics in this book relate to finance, partial differential equations, numerical schemes and C++ code, and for this reason we use the term *Computational Finance* to sum up these related activities (see Seydel, 2003, where the same phrase is used). The foundations for partial differential equations and finite difference schemes for financial engineering applications are discussed in Duffy (2004b).

1.2 WHAT'S SPECIAL ABOUT THIS BOOK?

This book is part of a larger, ongoing project. It is the outcome of one part of this project and concentrates on showing how to program finite difference schemes in C++. Our approach is novel in a number of respects.

1. We use modern *object-oriented* and *generic* design patterns in C++ to solve a range of partial, stochastic and ordinary differential equations in financial engineering. Traditionally, engineers have used packages such as Matlab, Maple, the C language or

other specialised libraries. Each alternative solution has its own benefits of course, but using C++ means that your code is portable, flexible and future-proof (C++ will still be used 20 years from now). Using C++ means that you are not tied into one vendor or operating system.

2. We give a thorough introduction to finite difference methods, how to apply them to Black–Scholes type equations and how to map them to C++ code. We avoid glib recipe-type schemes that work well for toy problems but do not always scale to real-life problems. In particular, we show how to program the famous Crank–Nicolson scheme and discuss when it breaks down, especially in applications with small volatility, discontinuous payoff functions or non-linearities. We propose new schemes that overcome these problems and produce uniformly good approximations to the delta of an option. The book discusses finite difference schemes for both one-factor and two-factor problems.

3. Successful software always needs to be adapted and extended, and to this end we design our classes and applications so that they can easily be modified. Our book is novel in the sense that we apply the powerful and proven design patterns (see Gamma *et al.*, 1995; Buschmann *et al.*, 1996) to help us to produce applications that can be extended or adapted to different organisational, hardware and software contexts.

4. Last, but not least, it is vital that our software artefacts are well documented. We document these artefacts at the design level and, in particular, we use the *de-facto* Unified Modeling Language (UML) to visually display the structural, functional and behavioural relationships between the classes and objects in our applications.

In short, this book describes in a step-by-step manner how to create 'good' software for financial engineering applications; it also integrates established techniques from fluid mechanics, numerical analysis and software design to produce a coherent and seamless approach to the design and implementation of financial models in C++.

1.3   WHO IS THIS BOOK FOR?

This book is meant for IT and quantitative finance professionals (risk managers, product development and derivatives research groups) who work in financial institutions and software companies and are involved in designing and implementing pricing models in C++. This book deals with fundamental issues such as C++ design and implementation, design patterns, finite difference methods and advanced software environments. Thus, it is of value to financial engineers ('Quants'), software developers and financial modellers.

We feel that the book is useful for universities and other educational institutes that deliver financial courses. This is not a book on instrument theory as such, and we assume that the reader has knowledge of option theory as presented in books by Hull (2000) and Wilmott (1998), for example. We also assume that the reader has had some exposure to differential equations, differential and integral calculus and matrix algebra. Finally, the reader should have a working knowledge of C++.

As we have already mentioned in this chapter, the book is suited not only to those readers from a partial differential equation (PDE) background but also to those who use techniques such as Monte Carlo, Fourier transform methods, stochastic differential equations (SDEs) and the binomial method for instrument pricing. We do our best to show that finite differences compare well with, and even outperform, these former methods, especially for complex and non-linear one-factor and two-factor Black–Scholes models.

Finally, the real option theory is emerging and many of the techniques in this book can be used in decision support systems in the oil, gas and energy industries. Thus, the book is also of interest to engineers, scientists and financial engineers in these fields.

1.4   SOFTWARE REQUIREMENTS

We have written this book from a number of viewpoints that have to do with what we call *software quality*. In general, we adopt the ISO 9126 quality characteristics (see Kitchenham and Pfleeger, 1996) as our working model. ISO 9126 describes how good a software product is. It consists of six top-level characteristics:

- *Functionality*: The ability of the software to satisfy stated or implied customer needs.
- *Reliability*: Does the software maintain its level of performance for a stated period of time?
- *Usability*: Is the software easy to understand, learn or integrate with other applications?
- *Efficiency*: Describes the response times in the application and the corresponding resources that are needed.
- *Maintainability*: How easy is it to modify, adapt and test the application? How stable is the application under change?
- *Portability*: The ease with which the application can be adapted to work in some new software or hardware environment.

Any one (or all) of the above requirements may be important for *your* new or existing software project. In general, the more requirements your applications must satisfy the more time it will take to satisfy them. In this book we classify applications into three broad categories, depending on the level of flexibility that they must have:

- *Low flexibility*: These are either throwaway prototypes or simple programs in order to test a piece of code or check the validity of some new model
- *Medium flexibility*: The code and classes in this category can be customised (by changing its source code if necessary) and used in your own applications
- *High flexibility*: The code in this category can be used in your applications without any changes.

It is important to know at the outset how flexible our solutions must be; on the one hand, we do not want to 'over-engineer' our application, but nor do we want to produce code that is difficult to maintain, understand or falls apart when we modify it. This book will provide you with guidelines to help you to produce good designs for financial engineering applications.

We *layer* the software in this book by examining it at four different levels:

- *Foundation classes and building blocks*: Reusable components for vectors, lists, matrices and other containers. We make ample use of the Standard Template Library (STL).
- *Mechanisms*: Tightly coupled groups of generic functions that are related to a specific piece of functionality. An example is a set of functions for Date manipulations (cash flows, interest rate curves).
- *Half-products*: Ready-to-use libraries that you can use as part of your own applications. We can place these half-products in assemblies and DLLs.

- *Applications*: Dedicated applications for the user (not the developer). These applications are usually executables.

There are many advantages associated with taking this layered approach to software development, as we shall see in this book.

1.5   THE STRUCTURE OF THIS BOOK

This book is partitioned into six major parts, each of which deals with a major topic and consists of a number of chapters. These chapters deal with techniques that help to achieve the goals of each part.

Part I   This part is an introduction to C++ template classes. We define what templates are, how to create them and how to use them in financial engineering applications. We give an overview of the Standard Template Library (STL). This is a C++ library consisting of template classes for a wide range of data containers, algorithms and functionality for navigating in these containers. We develop a number of template classes based on STL that we can use in financial engineering applications.

Part II   In this part we create classes and code that will be used when approximating partial differential equations by finite difference methods. First, we create template classes for arrays, vectors and matrices as well as the corresponding mathematical operations on them. Furthermore, we introduce several classes that solve linear systems of equations. These classes implement direct and iterative matrix solvers in numerical linear algebra. Second, we create a number of other foundation classes that we need in numerical differentiation and integration. Finally, some useful classes for statistics are introduced.

Part III   This part represents the start of the book as far as the mathematical core is concerned. We motivate the finite difference method by applying it to a simple first-order ordinary differential equation in Chapter 11. This chapter discusses the most important ideas and schemes that will serve us well in later chapters. Continuing from Chapter 11, we introduce stochastic differential equations and the finite difference schemes needed in order to approximate them. We also propose several schemes to approximate two-point boundary value problems. Special attention is paid to the Crank–Nicolson scheme and why it fails to approximate the solution of the convection-diffusion equation in certain circumstances. It is in this part of the book that we introduce the class of exponentially fitted schemes and explain how they resolve the spurious oscillation problems associated with Crank–Nicolson.

Part IV   In this part we introduce the one-factor and two-factor Black–Scholes equations and devise appropriate finite difference schemes for them. Before we reach this level of Nirvana, we begin with the one-dimensional heat equation and discuss explicit and implicit finite difference schemes to approximate its solution. The schemes are extensions of the time-independent schemes that we introduced in Part III. Slightly increasing the level of difficulty, we discuss the Crank–Nicolson and fully implicit schemes for the one-dimensional convection-diffusion equation (and its specialisation, the Black–Scholes equation). We analyse the schemes in some detail, discussing why they work, when they do not work and how to produce fitted schemes that approximate the solution and the delta of the Black–Scholes equation.

Proceeding to two-factor problems, we propose Alternating Direction Implicit (ADI) and splitting methods and compare their relative merits.

Part V   In this part we give an introduction to design patterns. Design is about alternatives and we have many choices when designing a system as the choices are determined by the software requirements. We begin with an introduction to some general design principles. In particular, we focus on templates and inheritance and why they are competitors. We also introduce the important notion of *delegation* whose understanding is fundamental to design patterns.

The main objective in Part V is to show how the famous design patterns of GOF (see Gamma *et al.*, 1995) are applied to financial engineering applications. We pay special attention to choosing appropriate examples and to a discussion of the advantages of design patterns in this particular context. Three chapters are devoted to the Creational, Structural and Behavioural patterns.

Part VI   This part contains a number of chapters that are of particular interest to financial engineers and IT personnel who write financial engineering applications. First, we give an introduction to the Extensible Markup Language (XML), a W3C standard for interoperable data representation. We also describe how it is used in option pricing applications in this book. XML will become more important in the financial world in the coming years as evidenced by the work seen with FpML and FIX. We also discuss classes and code that allow C++ code to communicate with Excel. Finally, we introduce a number of design patterns that are very useful for the current work.

1.6   PEDAGOGICAL APPROACH

In general, our approach is incremental in the sense that we begin with simple examples to illustrate the theory and progress to larger problems and examples. This approach applies to the theory of finite differences for partial differential equations as well as the C++ code and design patterns. For example, our main objective is to model one-factor and two-factor Black–Scholes equations using finite differences. The main 'flow' in this case is:

- Finite differences for scalar, linear first-order ordinary differential equations (ODEs).
- Finite differences for stochastic differential equations (SDEs).
- Two-point boundary value problems (special case: stationary convection-diffusion).
- Explicit and implicit finite difference schemes for the heat equation.
- Crank–Nicolson and fitting schemes for the one-factor Black–Scholes equation.
- Approximating the Greeks.
- Alternating Direction Implicit (ADI) and splitting schemes for two-factor Black–Scholes equations.

In a similar vein, we build up C++ expertise as follows:

- The C++ template class.
- The Standard Template Library (STL) and its applications to financial engineering.

- The Property pattern and the modelling of financial instruments.
- C++ classes for ODEs and SDEs.
- C++ foundation classes: vectors, matrices and statistics.
- C++ classes for the heat equation.
- Modelling Black–Scholes with C++.
- C++ for ADI and splitting methods.

In short, we adopt the following rule-of-thumb:

1. Get it working.
2. Then get it right.
3. Then get it optimised.

One step at a time!

1.7   WHAT THIS BOOK IS NOT

First, this is not an introductory book on C++. We assume that the reader has a working knowledge of this language. Second, this book assumes that the reader knows what an option is, what Black–Scholes is, and so on. Finally, this is not a book on the theory of partial differential equations and their approximation using finite differences, but is rather a book that motivates finite difference schemes and applies them to financial engineering applications using C++.

1.8   SOURCE CODE ON THE CD

You can use the source code on the accompanying CD free of charge in your applications provided you acknowledge the author:

© Datasim Education BV 2004

Each source file has this copyright statement. Any questions or suggestions should be sent to Daniel Duffy at info@datasim.nl.

Part I

Template Programming in C++

A Gentle Introduction to Templates in C++

2.1 INTRODUCTION AND OBJECTIVES

This is the first chapter in Part I of this book. The main goal of Part I is to introduce the reader to generic programming in C++ by discussing template classes and function templates. We also give a fairly detailed introduction to the Standard Template Library (STL), which provides us with a ready-to-use set of data structures and algorithms that we can apply to financial applications. Furthermore, we define our own data structures that model European option attributes. In short, Part I is the foundation upon which we build all future classes and software systems in this book.

In Appendix 1 we give a review of the main features in C++ which you should read if your knowledge of C++ is a bit rusty, but experienced C++ developers can pass it.

In this chapter we give a detailed introduction to how C++ supports the notion of generic programming in the form of so-called *templates*. Just as a class can be seen as a factory or 'cookie-cutter' for objects, so too can we see a C++ template as a factory for normal C++ classes. This feature leads to massive reusability in C++ software applications. For example, the STL (see Musser and Saini, 1996) contains C++ templates for a wide range of data containers such as vectors, lists and sets as well as various kinds of algorithms that operate on these containers. For example, STL has a C++ template for vectors. A vector is an indexible array of objects to which new objects can be added. The objects in the vector are generic and the programmer can then 'instantiate' the generic underlying type by replacing it by a concrete type. Some examples of instantiated template classes are:

```
vector<double>            (an array of doubles)
vector<EuropeanOption>    (an array of European options)
vector <int>              (an array of integers)
```

Please note that each of the above examples represents a class and that no new member functions need to be written because they are generated as it were from the corresponding template. Thus, we only have to write the template once and we instantiate its generic underlying types to give us a class. The following example shows us how templates, classes and objects are related:

```
template <class Type> vector;       // Template declaration
typedef vector<double> DoubleVector; // A new class
DoubleVector myarr(10);             // An array object: 10 elements
```

In this case we create a new object called 'myarr' by calling the corresponding constructor that is defined in the code of the template. It is not necessary to write the code for this constructor in class `DoubleVector`. The conclusion is that we achieve large reusability gains that are not achievable with non-templated C++ code.

In this chapter we devote some attention to the most important aspects of C++ programming using templates and, in particular, we concentrate on the syntax issues that you need to master before progressing. Useful examples based on the financial domain will be discussed in some detail.

   The focus in this chapter is to show how to create your own simple template classes. In Chapter 3 we give an introduction to the C++ STL, a library of ready-to-use template classes.

2.2   MOTIVATION AND BACKGROUND

In Appendix 1 we create a class that models European options. In particular, we model the member data in the class as variables of type `double`. We then create instances of the class by initialising the data. In Appendix 1 the member data in the class is given by:

```
class EuropeanOption
{
  // Public member data for convenience only
  double r;          // Interest rate
  double sig;        // Volatility
  double K;          // Strike price
  double T;          // Expiry date
  double U;          // Current underlying price
  double b;          // Cost of carry

  string optType;    // Option type (call, put)

  // ...
};
```

But what if a programmer wishes to use this class in an application but would prefer to use `floats` or some other data types to represent the option's parameters? One option is to copy the header and code files for the original class and change the declarations of the parameters in the source and recompile. However, this is unacceptable because we would end up with two classes that are essentially identical but only differ in the types of their member data. It is easy to appreciate that this situation will lead to maintenance problems. Fortunately, there is an elegant solution to this problem and it is resolved by the use of the so-called *template mechanism* in C++. In this particular case we create a template class whose parameters belong to some generic type rather than a concrete type such as double or float. When creating the template class we are not worried about the parameter types but we declare the parameters as belonging to some abstract type. In the case of the Option class we show how this is done:

```
template <class ValueType> class EuropeanOption
{
  // Public member data for convenience only
  ValueType r;            // Interest rate
  ValueType sig;          // Volatility
  ValueType K;            // Strike price
  ValueType T;            // Expiry date
  ValueType U;            // Current underlying price
  ValueType b;            // Cost of carry

  string optType;    // Option name (call, put)

  // ...
};
```

In this case we have replaced the concrete type `double` by the generic data type 'Val-ueType'. Please note that this name is not a class but is just some easy-to-read name that represents the eventual real type that will be used in applications. We note that there is only one generic underlying type (namely `ValueType`) and this can be a restriction in practice. A solution is to define an Option class having several underlying types or creating classes that can contain heterogeneous data types.

What is the difference between a template class and a normal class? Strictly speaking, a template class is a *type* whose instances are classes in much the same way that objects are instances of classes. A template is a kind of *meta-class*.

How do we bring templates to life in an application? Basically, we replace the generic underlying abstract data type by a concrete type to produce a class from which we can create instances of that class, as the following code shows:

```
EuropeanOption<double> option1;      // Default constructor
EuropeanOption<float> option2;
option1.optType = "P";
option1.U = 19.0;
option1.K = 19.0;
option1.T = 0.75;
option1.r = 0.10;
option1.sig = 0.28;

// Similar code for option2 ...

cout << "Option price with doubles: " << option1.Price() << endl;
cout << "Option price with floats: " << option2.Price() << endl;
```

In this case we declare two instances of the *classes* for options with underlying types `double` and `float`, respectively! The added value is that we have created the code for the option template class only once. Depending on the context, a programmer can customise the class by replacing the generic data type `ValueType` by a specific type. This feature promotes reusability and reliability of the code; on the one hand, we only have to write the code once and, on the other hand, we only have to test and debug it once. We now give a step-by-step account of templates in C++ and give some examples for motivational purposes. We shall give more complex and practical examples as we progress in this book.

2.3 DEFINING A TEMPLATE

C++ supports two kinds of templates first, *template classes* (as motivated in section 2.2) and *function templates*. We concentrate on template classes in this and the next section, and section 2.5 will discuss function templates.

A template class is a type that uses one or more generic underlying data types. As we can see in Appendix 1, we partition the creation of a template class into two pieces, namely the creation of the *header file* (contains the declarations of the member data and member functions) and the creation of the *code file* (this contains the actual code for each member function that we have declared in the header file).

As far as the declaration of the template class is concerned, we need some way of telling the compiler that the underlying types are generic. To this end, we use the 'template' keyword in conjunction with the names of the underlying data types that will be used in the template class. We have already seen an example in section 2.2, where we defined a class for European options whose underlying type is generic:

```
template <class ValueType> class EuropeanOption
{
  // ...
};
```

It is possible to define a class with several underlying types. Later chapters will discuss this aspect in more detail but for the moment we are content to give some examples. The first example defines a so-called class that represents named properties:

```
template <class Name, class Type> class Property
{
private:
  Name nam;    // The name of the property
  Type con;    // The contents of the property
public:
  Property(); // Default constructor
  Property(const Name& name, const Type& t);

  // Other member function here ...
};
```

In this case a property has a name (for identification purposes) and a value. Both underlying types are generic and the programmer can replace them by specific types as in the following code snippet:

```
  Property<string, double> interestRate; // Use default constructor
  Property<string, double> T("Expiry date", 1.0);
```

Don't worry about the details of this class yet; we shall dissect it in great detail in Chapter 5.

Finally, to show what the possibilities are we give part of the definition of a class that represents points and entities in three-dimensional space. Each coordinate direction is generic, thus allowing customisation:

```
template <class First, class Second, class Third> class Point
{ // Three-dimensional point class
private:
  First f;
  Second s;
  Third t;
public:
  // Other member functions
};
```

Programmers can then use this class by instantiating the generic types by their own specific classes or even built-in types, for example (Spiegel, 1959):

```
Point<double, double, double> cartesianObject;
Point<double, Angle, double> cylindricalObject;
Point<double, Angle, Angle> sphericalObject;
```

Note that the instantiated types are either/or built-in types as the last example shows: `Angle` is a class representing degree or radian units.

2.3.1   An example

A good way to learn how templates work is to examine one example in detail. To this end, we give a self-contained account of a template class that we call `Range`. This class corresponds to a closed interval in one dimension. This is a useful 'utility' class and it contains functionality that is used by other applications in this book. In particular, the `Range` class (and in combination with other classes) models the following:

- Candlestick charts that model price movements (Lofton, 1997): commodity prices have a daily high and a daily low value; they also have opening and closing prices. When the closing price is higher than the opening price we speak of a *bullish day*, otherwise we speak of a *bearish day*. See Figure 2.1.
- Barrier option modelling: a double barrier option is knocked in or out if the underlying price touches a lower boundary L or an upper boundary U (Haug, 1998).
- Placing constraints on properties: a property should lie in a range; an exception or alert is triggered if its values fall outside the range.
- The range class is a part of other classes that model ordinary, stochastic and partial differential equations. In these cases it plays the role of an interval of stock prices, time or other financially relevant variable.

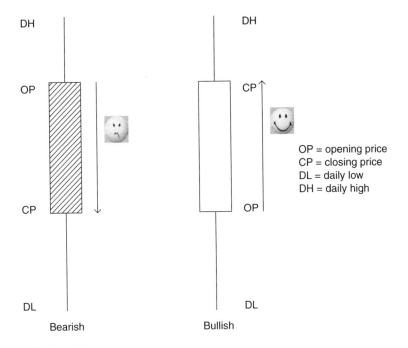

Figure 2.1   Candlestick charts

We first look at the header file for the `Range` class. We document this file by first looking at the member data and then the member functions. The declaration of the class and its member data is:

```
template <class Type> class Range
{ // A class for a one-dimensional interval
private:

  Type lo;
  Type hi;

public:

  // Member functions

};
```

Here we see that a range is identified by creating member data objects that represent the lower and upper values of the range, respectively. Once we have defined the structure of the template class we continue with a discussion of its member functions. We can group them into the following categories:

- Constructors and destructor.
- Member functions for setting and getting the high/low values of the range.
- Determining whether a given value is to the left, to the right or contained in a range.

The official class interface consisting of the member function is as follows:

```
template <class Type> class Range
{
private:

  Type lo;
  Type hi;

public:

  // Constructors
  Range();    // Default constructor
  Range(const Type& low, const Type& high); // Low and high value
  Range(const Range<Type>& ran2);// Copy constructor

  // Destructor
  virtual ~Range();

  // Modifier functions
  void low(const Type& t1); // Sets the low value of current range
  void high(const Type& t1);// Sets the high value of current range

  // Accessing functions
  Type low() const;       // Lowest value in range
  Type high() const;      // Highest value in the range

  Type spread() const;    // High - Low value

  // Boolean functions
  bool left(const Type& value) const; // Value to the left?
  bool right(const Type& value) const;// Value to the right?
  bool contains(const Type& value) const;// Contains value?
```

```
// Operator overloading
Range<Type>& operator = (const Range<Type>& ran2);
};
```

We shall now discuss how to implement the member functions for template classes. We shall show how this is done for three member functions in `Range`, namely the copy constructor, the function that calculates the extent of the range and the function that determines whether a given value is in the range.

```
template <class Type> Range<Type>::Range(const Range<Type>& r2)
{ // Copy constructor

  lo = r2.lo;
  hi = r2.hi;
}

template <class Type> Type Range<Type>::spread() const
{ // Returns the higher bound of the range

  return hi - lo;
}

template <class Type> bool Range<Type>::contains(const Type& t) const
{// Does range contain t?

  if((lo <= t) && (hi >= t))
    return true;

  return false;
}
```

Notice that the template specifier must be given in all cases. Failure to do so will result in compiler errors. Furthermore, if you look closely at the code you will see that the `Range` class has assumptions concerning what it should expect from the underlying type, in this case `Type`. Summing up, `Type` needs to implement the following:

The assignment operator $=$
The subtraction operator $-$
The operators $<=$ and $>=$

The built-in numeric types do indeed support these operators but you will get a compiler error if you instantiate the class with a type that does not support these operators. Thus, if you wish to use `Range` with your own types you must ensure that they satisfy the above requirements. This concept, called *policy*, describes what your template expects from its underlying generic types.

In general, `Range` is used for numerical underlying types.

2.4   TEMPLATE INSTANTIATION

The process of generating a normal class from a template class and a template argument is called *template instantiation* (Stroustrup, 1997). The generated classes are perfectly ordinary classes and can be used in your applications. For example, the following are all examples of classes:

```
Range<double>
Range<int>
Range<float>
```

You can then create instances of these classes in the usual way as the following code shows:

```
// Define a futures contract (simple data structure)
double closingPrice(45.7);
double openingPrice(60.0);
Range<double> bearish(closingPrice, openingPrice);

// Looking at some prices
double currentPrice = 50.0;

bool test1 = bearish.left(currentPrice);
bool test2 = bearish.right(currentPrice);
bool test3 = bearish.contains(currentPrice);

if (test1 == false && test2 == false && test3 == true)
   cout << "Everything OK\n";
```

In the same way we can instantiate a template class having multiple underlying values as follows:

```
Point<double, double, double> origin(0.0, 0.0, -10000.0);
```

2.5   FUNCTION TEMPLATES

Besides the ability to define and instantiate template classes we can also define so-called *function templates*. These are similar to procedural functions but with the additional property that they operate on generic data types or have template arguments. For example, here is a code that calculates the minimum of two generic numeric types:

```
template <class N> N min (const N& first, const N& second)
{ // Type 'N' is some generic numeric type

  if (first < second)
    return first;

  return second;
}
```

Another useful function that we can create is swap(); this swaps two objects:

```
template <class Any> void swap (Any& first, Any& second)
{ // Type 'Any' is any old type

  Any tmp = first;   // Make a temporary copy

  first = second;
  second = tmp;
}
```

Having defined how to program function templates, we shall now describe how to use them. In general, we use instantiate by just replacing the generic underlying type by a concrete type, as shown in the following sample code:

```
// Swap two integers
int i = 10;
int j = -1435;
swap (i, j);

// Swap two ranges, why not?
Range<double> r1(0.0, 1.0);
Range<double> r2(100.0, 150.0);
swap(r1, r2);
```

We can see that there are massive reusability gains to be had by defining and using template classes and function templates. Function templates will be used in this book to provide a set of mechanisms that provide services to higher-level classes and code. We use them to write essentially C-style functions having complex objects as arguments. We group related functionality in the form of function templates for the following areas of numerical analysis and statistics:

- Matrix manipulations, norms and other properties
- Statistics and statistical calculations
- Numerical interpolation and extrapolation
- Numerical integration

and many more. We shall discuss these mechanisms in more detail in later chapters.

2.5.1   An example

The Gaussian (normal) distribution is very important in financial engineering and option pricing. Furthermore, the probability density function (pdf) and cumulative normal distribution function (cdf) are used in many applications. We implement these functions as two function templates (see Haug, 1998):

```
template <class N> N NormalFunction(const N& x) const // pdf
{ // The type 'N' is some generic numeric type

  N A = 1.0/sqrt(2.0 * 3.1415);
  return A * exp(-x*x*0.5);

}

template <class N> N cdfNormal(double x) const        // cdf
{ // The approximation to the cumulative normal distribution

  N a1 = 0.4361836;
  N a2 = -0.1201676;
  N a3 = 0.9372980;

  N k = 1.0/(1.0 + (0.33267 * x));

  if (x >= 0.0)
  {
    return 1.0 - n(x)* (a1*k + (a2*k*k) + (a3*k*k*k));
  }
  else
  {
    return 1.0 - cdfNormal(-x);    // Recursive function
  }
}
```

The programmer can now use these functions with his or her own favourite underlying data type.

2.6   DEFAULT VALUES AND TYPEDEFS

C++ helps the programmer in a number of ways. For instance, it often happens that certain concrete types are used a lot and in this case we would like to create code without having to specify the concrete classes each time. For example, let us suppose that our properties have double values by default. Instead of having to write

```
Property<string, double> prop1("Rocky", 1.0);
```

we might prefer to write

```
Property<string> prop1("Rocky", 1.0);
```

This state of affairs can be achieved by defining so-called default values in the template class declaration:

```
template <class Name = string, class Type = double> class Property
{
  // Body
};
```

In fact, we see that the default name `type` is of class `string`, so it is possible to define a `Property` without having to use any parameters whatsoever; in that case the name will be a string and the value will be a double. Concluding, the following declarations are possible:

```
Property<string, double> s1("Rocky", 2.0);
Property<string> s2("Rocky", 3.0);
Property<> s3("Rocky", 4.0);  // Both types are default
```

The syntax for the case in which you use both defaults is a bit awkward and you should not forget the brackets as the third example above shows.

The use of default values is similar to supplying a *policy* through a template argument and then defaulting that argument to supply the most common policy. Template parameters used to express policies are called *traits* (see Stroustrup, 1997).

A useful trick to improve the readability of code that uses templates, and to help us to write less code, is to use a facility called `typedef` to create new data types. For example, we develop a shorthand notation for commonly used classes and other types, as the following examples show:

```
typedef int Length;
typedef Property<string, double> StandardProperty;
typedef BinaryDelegate<Key, Value> TObservers;
```

A `typedef` does not create a new type; it merely adds a new name for some existing type.

2.7   GUIDELINES WHEN IMPLEMENTING TEMPLATES

We shall now provide a number of tips to help you to eliminate annoying compiler errors. These can be very cryptic when working with templates.

Tip 1: When using templates you must include the code file that contains the bodies of the member functions in the template class. Otherwise, you will get a linker error.

Tip 2: Just because your template class compiles without error does not mean that your test program will work during template class instantiation. The template class expects the classes that instantiate the underlying types to support the member functions that are used in the code of the template class.

Tip 3: Ninety percent of the compiler errors associated with template class programming are caused by incorrect syntax.

Tip 4: Please use strings from the Standard Template Library (STL) instead of Stone Age char* (char pointers). Avoid using string classes from vendor-specific libraries. Include the following in your code:

```
#include <string>
using namespace std;     // Standard namespace for STL
```

We shall introduce STL in Chapter 3.

2.8   CONCLUSIONS AND SUMMARY

We have given an introduction to template programming in C++. A template class is a kind of meta-class as its underlying data types are generic and cannot be directly instantiated by objects. Instead, replacing the generic data types by concrete types in the template class leads to classes. This process is called *template instantiation*. The resulting classes can then be used to create objects.

Designing, programming and testing code written using templates can be a challenge for novices but with some forethought and perseverance many problems can be resolved. In particular, the compiler errors that are produced by syntactically incorrect template classes may be very difficult to resolve. The end-result will be a suite of generic code that can be used in many applications and satisfies a variety of software requirements. Template classes play an essential role in this book, as they do in many modern C++ applications, tools and libraries.

3

An Introduction to the Standard
Template Library

3.1 INTRODUCTION AND OBJECTIVES

In this chapter we introduce the reader to the Standard Template Library (STL) in C++. The library consists of a number of data containers, algorithms and so-called iterators for navigating in these data containers. STL is part of the standard C++ language and is portable between different C++ compilers and operating systems. Furthermore, STL allows you to reuse existing algorithms and data containers because they are *generic*; in general terms, we say that software is generic if it is not tied to any specific data structure or object type. In the case of STL the algorithms are as efficient as they would be if you had written them specifically for the task at hand. STL makes use of the C++ template mechanism and a reasonable understanding of templates (for example, the level attained in Chapter 2 of this book) is an essential prerequisite before you start using the classes in STL.

3.1.1 Why use STL?

First, for reusability reasons because it implements a number of generic template classes that you can use in your applications and as components of your own classes. In the past, each software or hardware vendor had its own proprietary set of reusable classes. We are thinking of organisations such as Borland, IBM, Microsoft, Rogue Wave and many others. Now we can just use STL. Second, STL is portable between C++ compilers and operating systems. For example, you can write and test your programs using your favourite C++ compiler under Windows and then port it to the Linux operating systems and compile it using the GNU compiler. Finally, once you learn the interfaces of two or three data containers and iterators you will also be able to use the other STL classes in applications.

This chapter forms the basis for many of the template classes in this book. We shall encounter STL directly and indirectly in later chapters. Investing in learning STL and how to apply it to financial engineering problems will repay itself handsomely. We motivate STL by giving quite a few examples and the corresponding output from each example. A good way to learn the syntax of STL is to look at the code and then at the output to see if you can match them up, as it were. In this way we hope that you will get a feeling for the syntax of the library.

As with Chapter 2, we provide lots of code examples to show how STL works. Looking at code and writing your own examples is the best way to learn in this particular context. The examples in this chapter are simple to enable you to grasp the essence of STL as quickly as possible and progress to more challenging problems.

3.2 A BIRD'S-EYE VIEW OF STL

In this section we give a high-level overview of STL. More detailed accounts can be found in many books on the subject (see, in particular, Musser and Saini, 1996; Breymann, 1998).

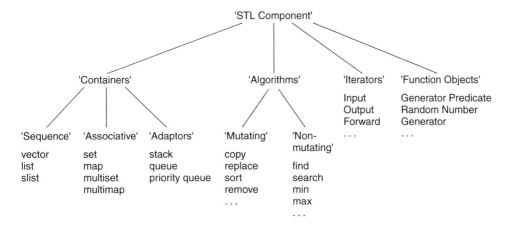

Figure 3.1   STL roadmap

Basically, STL provides functionality for data structures and algorithms that operate on those data structures as well as extra functionality that enables us to navigate in these data structures.

We discuss the following categories in STL (see Figure 3.1 for the STL roadmap):

Containers

Containers, which are collections of elements that have a logical relationship with each other, are essentially data structures. There are three subcategories of container:

- Sequence containers (list, vector, slist)
- Associative containers (set, multiset, map, multimap)
- Adaptors (stack, queue, priority queue).

A sequence container is one whose elements are arranged in a strictly linear order. Typical examples are lists, arrays and vectors. Elements in sequence containers are accessed in a sequential manner. An associative container, on the other hand, allows fast access to data by mean of some key. This key may or may not coincide with the data. For example, the telephone number of a person could be accessed by using the person's name as a key. In sets and multisets the key *is* the data whereas the key and data are different with maps and multimaps.

Finally, an adaptor is a container that changes the interface of an existing container. Examples of adaptors are stacks, queues and priority queues. These containers can be loosely called derivative containers because their member functions use the method of their base container by a technique called *delegation*. We shall discuss this topic in the chapters on design patterns.

Iterators

These tend to be difficult for novice programmers. An iterator is a mechanism for traversing a sequence container and it can be described as a 'glorified pointer': an iterator

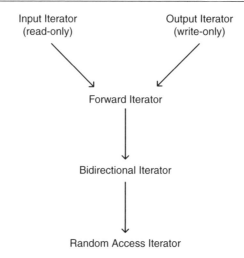

Figure 3.2 Hierarchy of iterator concepts

points to one specific element in a container at any one given time; thus, dereferencing the iterator gives you the element itself!

Iterators can be classified in a hierarchy of ever-increasing functionality, as shown in Figure 3.2. Input (read-only) and output (write-only) iterators are the most restricted types. They allow traversal in a range of elements in the forward direction only. They only accept single-pass algorithms. Forward iterators, on the other hand, can also traverse a range in the forward direction but they support more clever algorithms than the input and output iterators. A bidirectional iterator supports both forward and backward traversal. Finally, a random access iterator also supports arbitrary-sized jumps in a range.

Algorithms

These are classes that operate on containers. There are two important categories depending on the iterators that algorithms use. First, non-mutating (or *non-modifying*) algorithms use constant iterators and hence do not modify the elements of the underlying container while *mutating* algorithms use mutable iterators. Some examples of non-mutating algorithms are:

- Searching for specific values in a range of elements
- Counting the number of elements in a range that have a given value
- Applying a given function to each element in a range
- Comparing two ranges
- Finding the minimum and maximum of a range of elements.

In short, non-mutating algorithms can be loosely described as 'inspection' or read-only algorithms.

Some examples of mutating algorithms are:

- Copy a range of elements from one container to another container
- Swap two containers

- Transform a range of elements into another range
- Replace elements in some range
- Fill a range with elements
- Remove elements from a range
- Reverse a range in place.

The reader should take note that these algorithms exist in STL and that he or she does not have to reinvent the wheel when developing C++ applications: just reuse these algorithms. In short, mutating algorithms can be loosely described as 'modifier' or write-only algorithms.

Function objects

A function object (or *functor*) is any object that can be called using ordinary function call syntax. Each functor must overload the operator '()'. A simple example of a function object is the normal C function pointer. Examples of function objects are Generator, Unary Function and Binary Functions that can be called as $f()$, $f(x)$ and $f(x, y)$. A special function object that will interest financial engineers is the Random Number Generator. This generator uses the subtractive method for generating pseudo-random numbers based on the classic Knuth algorithms.

Final remark

One final remark concerning containers, algorithms and iterators. Most of the algorithms in STL operate on arbitrary containers and the algorithms have no knowledge of the container's internal structure because this problem is taken over by iterators. Iterators can be seen as the *mediators* between containers and algorithms. This promotes flexibility in the software.

3.3   SEQUENCE CONTAINERS

The elements in sequence containers are arranged in a strict linear order. They are variable-sized containers, which means that elements can be added or removed after the containers have been constructed. The most general representation of a sequence container is shown in Figure 3.3. Here we see that the container consists of a number of elements and that it

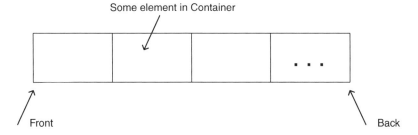

Figure 3.3   Sequence containers

has a front element and a back element. The main scenarios that have to do with container life cycle are:

- Creating instances of the container (constructor)
- Inserting elements (at front, back or in the interior of container)
- Erasing and removing elements
- Iterating over the elements of the sequence container
- Other possible operations depending on the type of container.

In this section we concentrate on the list template class because, first, we use it with many other classes in this book and, second, it embodies what we need to know if we wish to understand other STL containers. In other words, once you know how to use the list class in your applications you should not have many problems with the rest of the STL functionality.

Actually, there are two kinds of lists in STL: first, the 'slist' (singly linked list) template class where each element is linked to the next element but not to the previous element and the list template class where each element has a predecessor and a successor. The former class supports traversal in the forward direction only while the latter class supports both forward and backward traversal.

3.3.1   Programming lists

Let us look at how to create lists. In this first example we show how to create lists by using various constructors, how to use iterators in order to navigate in a list and how to add an element to the end of a list. To this end, the following code is complete and machine-readable:

```
// ch3list.cpp
//
// Examples to show how sequence containers (list) work.
//
// (C) Datasim Education BV 2003

#include <list>
#include <string>
#include <iostream.h>

using namespace std;    // You must use this to include STL!

int main()
{
  // Create list instances
  list<int> list1;              // Empty list

  size_t n = 10;
  double val = 3.14;
  list<double> list2(n, val);   // Create n copies of val

  list<double> list3(list2);    // Create a copy of list2

  cout << "Size of list1 " << list1.size() << endl;
  cout << "Size of list2 " << list2.size() << endl;
  cout << "Size of list3 " << list3.size() << endl;
```

```
  // We iterate over the elements of list 3 and print its elements
  // Create list iterator
  list<double>::const_iterator i;
  // Print every character in the list
  for (i = list2.begin(); i != list2.end(); ++i)
  {
    cout << *i << ",";
  }
  cout << endl;
  // Now populate a new list with the elements of list2
  list<double> list4;
  for (i = list2.begin(); i != list2.end(); ++i)
  {
    list4.push_back(*i);
  }
  // Print every character in the list
  for (i = list4.begin(); i != list4.end(); ++i)
  {
    cout << *i << ",";
  }
  cout << endl;
  return 0;
}
```

The output from this program is:

```
Size of list1 0
Size of list2 10
Size of list3 10
3.14,3.14,3.14,3.14,3.14,3.14,3.14,3.14,3.14,3.14,
3.14,3.14,3.14,3.14,3.14,3.14,3.14,3.14,3.14,3.14,
```

We note that if you use a given STL container in your code, you should first include its header and declare that you are using the STL namespace, as can be seen in the above example. As far as iterators are concerned, we paraphrase the code that prints the elements of list4 above: *set the iterator to point to the first element of list4, print the element, move to the next element and print it; print all elements until we come to the end of the list.* Finally, please note that we are using a so-called `const` iterator; it can read but not write the elements that it is traversing over.

3.3.2   Vectors and arrays in STL

The vector class in STL is similar to 'list' and many of the member functions are the same. In fact, we could replace all occurrences of the word 'list' by 'vector' in section 3.3.1, recompile and run the code. It works! However, with lists it is only possible to access an element by navigating from the begin or end in a linear fashion. Vectors do not have this problem because they have random access iterators defined for them. Further, it is possible to return the element in a vector at a specified position. The following code shows how the vector class is used:

```
// ch3vector.cpp
//
// Examples to show how sequence containers (vector) work.
//
```

```
// (C) Datasim Education BV 2003

#include <vector>
#include <string>
#include <iostream.h>

using namespace std;

template <class T> void print(const vector<T>& l)
{   // A generic print function for vectors

  cout << endl << "Size of vector is " << l.size() << "\n[";
  // Must use const iterator here, otherwise get a compiler error.
  vector<T>::const_iterator i;
  for (i = l.begin(); i != l.end(); ++i)
  {
    cout << *i << ",";
  }
  cout << "]\n";
}

int main()
{
  size_t n = 10;
  double val = 3.14;
  vector<double> vector2(n, val);      // Create n copies of val

  cout << "Size of vector2 " << vector2.size() << endl;

  print(vector2);

  // Access elements of vector by using the indexing operator []
  // Change some values here and there
  vector2[0] = 2.0;
  vector2[1] = 456.76;

  int last_element = vector2.size() - 1;
  vector2[last_element] = 55.66;

  print(vector2);

  return 0;
}
```

The output from this program is:

```
Size of vector2 10
Size of vector is 10
[3.14,3.14,3.14,3.14,3.14,3.14,3.14,3.14,3.14,3.14,]
Size of vector is 10
[2,456.76,3.14,3.14,3.14,3.14,3.14,3.14,3.14,55.66,]
```

In this example we first of all created a (reusable) function template to print the elements of a generic vector. The function is then called in the main program by instantiating it for double precision numbers. This reduces the amount of code in our tests. An important remark on indexing is in order; the vector class starts indexing at zero and hence a vector of length 10 will be accessed by indexes zero up to and including nine! This is an important point to remember when using the indexing operator with vector. We create more sophisticated vector classes in later chapters where the programmer can choose the start index. For example, he or she could choose zero, one or even a negative number as the start index. In this case we cater for different kinds of developers. This class `vector` is the 'building' block for the classes that we develop in later chapters for mathematical entities such as `Vector` and two-dimensional and three-dimensional `Matrix`. Thus, it is important to understand how it works and how it is used in applications. It will also be a useful class in your own applications.

3.4 ASSOCIATIVE CONTAINERS

Sequence containers do not impose any order; you can insert an element into a sequence container at any position. Associative containers are different because the elements are ordered on the basis of some special rule. We do not have to insert elements at a particular position because such details are hidden from us; you just insert the element and the associative container takes care of the rest. The main reason for this ploy is that lookup is quicker than with sequence containers. For example, we can use binary search instead of linear search; in this case the complexity is reduced from O(N) to O(log N). In general, associative containers allow efficient retrieval of elements based on *keys*. Each element has a key associated with it and it is possible to find that element based on the key. There are four associative containers in STL: `set`, `map`, `multiset` and `multimap`. In the case of `set` the key is the element while in the case of `map` and `multimap` the elements are associated with the keys. In essence, maps and multimaps are key:value pairs (similar to a telephone book of names and telephone numbers). In `set` and `map` the keys are unique, while with `multiset` and `multimap` duplicate keys are allowed.

3.4.1 Sets in STL

Sets are very important in general and for our financial applications in particular. Set theory is well established in mathematics and it can be applied to many domains. For the moment, we give an illustrative example of some sets containing descriptions of option attributes. We see how to create sets, add elements to sets, swap sets and print sets.

```
// ch3set1.cpp
//
// Creating sets. Simple functions for starters.
//
//          1. Create sets with string elements
//          2. Compare sets with '==' operator
//          3. Swap two sets using the swap() function
//          4. Assigning sets to each other
//
// (C) Datasim Education 2003

#include <set>
#include <iostream>
#include <string>

using namespace std;

template <class T> void print(const set<T>& mySet, const string& name)
{   // Print the contents of a set. Notice the presence of a const
    // iterator.

    cout << endl << name << ", size of set" << mySet.size() << "\n[";
```

```
  set<T>::const_iterator i;

  for (i = mySet.begin(); i != mySet.end(); ++i)
  {
    cout << (*i) << ",";
  }

  cout << "]\n";
}
int main()
{
  set<string> first;                       // Default constructor
  // Only unique (new elements) added
  first.insert("Interest rate");
  first.insert("Expiry date");
  first.insert("Volatility");

  cout << "First Size: " << first.size() << endl;
  set<string> second (first);    // Copy constructor

  // Add extra elements to second set
  second.insert("Interest rate");
  second.insert("Strike price");
  second.insert("Current underlying price");
  second.insert("Cost of carry");

  cout << "Second Size: " << second.size() << endl;

  // Are the sets the same?
  if (first == second)
    cout << "Sets have same elements\n";
  else
    cout << "Not same elements\n";

  // A bit of swapping
  swap(first, second);

  // Assignment
  set<string> third = first;

  // Now print the sets
  print(first, "First set");
  print(second, "Second set");
  print(third, "Third set");
}
```

The output from this program is:

```
First Size: 3
Second Size: 6
Not same elements

First set, size of set is 6
[K,S,T,b,r,sigma,]
Second set, size of set is 3
[T,r,sigma,]
Third set, size of set is 6
[K,S,T,b,r,sigma,]
An Executive Option, size of set is 7
[K,S,T,b,lambda,r,sigma,]
```

3.4.2   Maps in STL

In general, we can describe a `map` as a kind of dynamic associative array; 'dynamic' because we can add new elements at run-time and 'associative' because the values in the map are accessed by a key that is not necessarily of integer type. The following example shows what we mean. We create a `map` that models the attributes of a European option.

```
// ch3map1.cpp
//
// Test case for map container. Simple element-based operations.
//
// Important topics are:
//
//    1. The question of unique keys(when allowed/accepted)
//    2. Inserting pairs of object into map
//    3. Iterating over the elements of the map and using the current
//    pair's option and second elements.
//
// (C) Datasim Education 2003

#include <map>
#include <iostream>
#include <string>

using namespace std;

int main()
{

  map<string, double> option;

  // Using indexing to define the keys in the map
  option["r"] = 0.10;            // Interest rate
  option["sig"] = 0.28;          // Volatility
  option["K"] = 19.0;            // Strike price
  option["T"] = 0.75;            // Expiry date
  option["S"] = 19.0;            // Underlying asset

  cout << "Size of map: " << option.size() << endl;;

  // Iterating in the map
  map<string, double>::iterator i = option.begin();

  while (i != option.end())
  {
    cout << "Element pair [" << (*i).first << "," <<
      (*i).second << "]";
    i++;
  }

  return 0;

}
```

The output from this program is:

```
Size of map: 5
Element pair [K,19]
Element pair [S,19]
Element pair [T,0.75]
Element pair [r,0.1]
Element pair [sig,0.28]
```

We can already see some advantages of the map container in this example. Compared with the member data in the Option class in Chapter 1, we can group the attributes of an option into a single abstraction whose elements are accessed by meaningful keys, in this the string names representing the names of the different attributes of an option. We shall use this construction in later chapters as an embedded data structure for other higher-level classes.

Summarising, a map can be compared to a dictionary, hash table or telephone book.

3.5 ITERATORS IN STL

We have already discussed the iterator hierarchy (see Figure 3.2). Iterators are the life-blood of STL because without them we would not always be able to populate containers with data or retrieve information from these containers. They can be seen as a general-isation of pointers; they are in fact objects that point to other objects. With an iterator, you can navigate through a range of objects.

The main advantage of the iterator concept is that it decouples containers from the algorithms that operate on them. In STL, algorithms operate on a range of iterators rather than the containers themselves. All STL containers have iterators so you do not have to program them yourself. It is even possible to define iterators for user-defined types and classes and we shall discuss this topic in Chapter 5.

3.5.1 What kinds of iterators?

We have already discussed the iterator taxonomy in section 3.2. We now give an overview of how to use *some* of these iterators. We concentrate on the following useful types:

- Forward iterators that can read data
- Forward iterators that can write data
- Reverse iterators
- Random access iterators.

The following example makes heavy use of operator overloading in order to navigate in containers.

```
// ch3iterators.cpp
//
// Test program to test the following iterators;
// - Bidirectional random access iterators
// - Reverse iterators
// - Const iterators
//
// (C) Datasim Education BV 2003

#include <vector>
#include <iostream>

using namespace std;

vector<double> makevector(int size)
{ // Creates STL vector with doubles

  vector<double> result;  // Create empty vector
  for (int i=1; i<=size; i++)
  {
```

```
      result.push_back(double(i));
   }
   return result;
}

void print(const vector<double>& l)
{ // Print the vector

   cout << "Size of vector is: " << l.size() << endl;

   // Create vector iterator
   vector<double>::const_iterator i;

   // Print every character in the vector
   for (i=l.begin(); i!=l.end(); i++)
   {
      cout << (*i) << " ";
   }

   cout << endl;
}

void main()
{
   // Create a vector with characters
   vector<double> vector1=makevector(5);

   // Create bidirectional iterator
   vector<double>::iterator bi;

   // Traverse forward
   cout << "Traverse forward" << endl;
   bi=vector1.begin();              // Set iterator
   while (bi!=vector1.end()) cout << (*bi++) << " ";
   cout << endl << endl;;

   // Traverse backward
   cout << "Traverse backward" << endl;
   bi=(vector1.end());
   do
   {
      cout << (*--bi) << " ";
   }
   while (bi!=vector1.begin());
   cout << endl << endl;

   // Traverse random
   cout << "Traverse random" << endl;
   bi=vector1.begin();
   cout << *bi << " ";                      // First element
   cout << *(bi+=3) << " ";      // 1+3 is 4th element
   cout << *(bi-=1) << " ";      // 4-1 is third element
   cout << bi[-1] << " ";                   // 3-1 is second element
   cout << bi[1] << endl << endl;   // 3+1 is fourth element

   // Create bidirectional iterator
   vector<double>::reverse_iterator ri;

   // Traverse reverse forward
   cout << "Traverse reverse forward" << endl;
   ri=vector1.rbegin();            // Set iterator
   while (ri!=vector1.rend()) cout << (*ri++) << " ";
   cout << endl << endl;
```

```
// Traverse reverse backward
cout << "Traverse reverse backward" << endl;
ri=(vector1.rend());
do
{
   cout << (*--ri) << " ";
}
while (ri!=vector1.rbegin());
cout << endl << endl;

// Traverse reverse random
cout << "Traverse reverse random" << endl;
cout << *ri << " ";                 // First element
cout << *(ri+=3) << " ";            // 1+3 is 4th element
cout << *(ri-=1) << " ";            // 4-1 is third element
cout << ri[-1] << " ";             // 3-1 is second element
cout << ri[1] << endl << endl;     // 3+1 is fourth element

// Change element
cout << "Change first element with mutable iterator" << endl;
bi=vector1.begin();
*bi=double(99);
print(vector1);

// Change element with const iterator
cout << "Change first element with const iterator" << endl;
vector<double>::const_iterator ci;
ci=vector1.end();
ci--;
cout << *ci << endl;
}
```

The output from this program is:

```
Traverse forward
1 2 3 4 5
Traverse backward
5 4 3 2 1
Traverse random
1 4 3 2 4
Traverse reverse forward
5 4 3 2 1
Traverse reverse backward
1 2 3 4 5
Traverse reverse random
5 2 3 4 2
Change first element with mutable iterator
Size of vector is: 5
99 2 3 4 5
Change first element with const iterator
5
```

Some remarks on this code are:

- Random access iterators define operators +=, −+, + and − so that it is possible to 'jump' from one position in a vector to another position.
- Reverse iterators begin at the end of a vector (denoted by rend()) and they navigate in the vector until they reach the beginning of the vector (denoted by rbegin()).

• Iterators that read the elements of a vector and do not need to modify those elements should be implemented as `const` iterators.

3.6 ALGORITHMS

Most of the algorithms in STL are general in nature and there is no support for domain-specific functionality such as numerical analysis (in all its forms), statistics or matrix algebra. However, it is possible to create domain-specific libraries using STL components as 'building blocks'. In fact, this is what we do in this book, as we shall see in later chapters.

To give a taste of what STL offers in the area of algorithms, in this case we concentrate on the following:

• Creating `vectors` of random numbers
• Sorting a `vector`
• Merging two `vectors`
• Binary search in a `vector` for a particular value.

We take the `rand()` random function from a standard library. In real applications we should probably use specialised pseudo-random number generators. However, we should be suspicious of random number generators offered by the operating system. The algorithms can be used in applications for Monte Carlo simulations and the numerical solution of stochastic differential equations (SDEs).

For another approach to random number generation in quantitative finance, see Jäckel (2002).

```
// ch3alg.cpp
//
// Sample algorithms in STL.
//
// (C) Datasim Education BV 2003

#include <vector>
#include <iostream>
#include <algorithm>
#include <time.h>

using namespace std;

void print(const vector<int>& v)
{ // Print the vector

  // Create vector iterator
  vector<int>::const_iterator i;

  cout << "[";

  // Print every integer in the vector
  for (i=v.begin(); i!=v.end(); i++) cout << *i << ", ";
  cout << "]" << endl;
}

int main()
{
  // Create a 'seed' at the current time so that
```

```
// the random numbers will be different each time
// the generator is run
srand((unsigned) time (NULL));

int Size = 5;
// Create vectors and fill with random numbers
vector<int> v1, v2;
int i;
for (i=0; i<= Size; i++)
  v1.push_back(rand());
for (i=0; i< Size; i++)
  v2.push_back(rand());

cout << "Two random lists" << endl;
print(v1);
print(v2);

// Sort the lists
sort(v1.begin(), v1.end());
sort(v2.begin(), v2.end());

cout << "Two sorted lists" << endl;
print(v1);
print(v2);

// Merge the two lists to a third list
vector<int> v3(v1.size()+v2.size());
cout << endl << "Merge the two lists" << endl;
merge(v1.begin(), v1.end(), v2.begin(), v2.end(), v3.begin());
print(v3);

return 0;
}
```

The output from this program is:

```
Two random lists
[24251, 25008, 20095, 6266, 29955, 11496, ]
[26089, 32073, 682, 6132, 4099, ]

Two sorted lists
[6266, 11496, 20095, 24251, 25008, 29955, ]
[682, 4099, 6132, 26089, 32073, ]

Merge the two lists
[682, 4099, 6132, 6266, 11496, 20095, 24251, 25008, 26089, 29955, 32073, ]
```

Most of the code should be self-explanatory. However, we discuss the sort and binary search algorithms in some detail. The sort algorithm sorts a vector (in this case) between its beginning and end into ascending order. It is possible to sort the vector in some other way by using a so-called *comparison function*, but this topic is outside the scope of this chapter. The binary search algorithm takes three arguments: the start position, the end position and the value that we are looking for. Here is another example:

```
int arr[] = {1, 2, 3, 3, 5, 8};// Built-in sorted C-style array
const int N = sizeof(arr)/sizeof(int);

for (int j = 1; j <= 10; j++)
{
  cout << "\nSearching for: " << j << ":";
```

```
  if (binary_search(arr, arr+N, j) == true)
    cout << "present";
  else
    cout << "not present";
}
```

The output from this piece of code is:

```
Searching for: 1:present
Searching for: 2:present
Searching for: 3:present
Searching for: 4:not present
Searching for: 5:present
Searching for: 6:not present
Searching for: 7:not present
Searching for: 8:present
Searching for: 9:not present
Searching for: 10:not present
```

3.7   USING STL FOR FINANCIAL INSTRUMENTS

How much of STL do we use in this book? Of course, it is not possible to discuss all the possibilities (nor even desirable!) on how to apply STL to financial engineering applications but there is a suitable subset of the STL library that we use to build more complex and intelligent classes. These classes will be introduced piecemeal as we progress in the book.

3.8   CONCLUSIONS AND SUMMARY

We have given an overview of the functionality of the Standard Templates Library (STL). This is part of the official C++ language and hence code that uses STL is guaranteed to be portable and future-proof.

Our interest in this book is in *applying* STL to writing financial engineering applications. In particular, STL has support for containers, algorithms and iterators and we embed them in our own code and applications in the coming chapters.

4

STL for Financial Engineering Applications

4.1 INTRODUCTION AND OBJECTIVES

In this chapter we continue with our discussion of STL. In particular, we show how to use the STL classes in order to create new classes and containers. The possibilities are almost infinite but in this chapter we concentrate on several examples that lay the basis for many of the applications and classes in future chapters.

The main examples are:

- Creating classes for matrices
- How STL implements sets and set operations
- Numeric algorithms in STL
- Creating your own Property classes for option data modelling.

Once these new building blocks have been coded and tested they can be used in financial engineering applications such as:

- Creating tree data structures for the binomial and trinomial methods
- Band, tridiagonal and sparse matrix computation
- Numeric computation with statistical data
- Flexible attributes (member data) for many kinds of options.

There are many advantages to be gained from this manner of programming. The first advantage is reusability; once a class has been created it can then be applied and extended using the extension techniques that the object-oriented and generic programming paradigms offer. Second, it promotes reliability because we do not have to worry about low-level details. These details are encapsulated in other classes that we then use as black boxes. Finally, and possibly most important for financial engineers who use C++ in their applications, this approach promotes usability because we do not have to have knowledge of all the low-level details of a class when we are just using it. In short, encapsulating and hiding non-relevant detail in other classes reduces 'cognitive overload'.

The containers in this chapter (and indeed most of the chapters in this book) are time-independent. In order to rectify this situation somewhat we devote Appendix 2 to date and time classes that can be used in various financial engineering applications – for example, discount curves and cash flows.

4.2 CLEVER DATA STRUCTURES

STL supports nesting and recursive classes (Gamma *et al.*, 1995). Basically, this means that you can define container classes whose underlying types are also containers. There is an infinite number of possible combinations but our concern in this book is with defining

useful structures for financial engineering applications. For example, the following structures are all feasible in STL:

- Lists of vectors: `list<vector<T> >`
- Vectors of vectors: `vector<vector<T> >`
- Lists of sets: `list<set<T> >`
- List of vectors of vectors: `list<vector<vector<T> > >`(wow!)

Of course, one has to be reasonable and not get carried away by creating containers
and the corresponding code that is difficult to understand and difficult to maintain. In
this section we give some examples of creating matrices with various kinds of internal structure. This is a very important topic in numerical analysis and numerical linear
algebra and much research and effort has been devoted to the problem of constructing
memory-efficient matrix data structures, some of which are shown in Figure 4.1. The
main types are:

(a) General rectangular full matrices with n rows and m columns: this is a matrix with
    $n \times m$ elements in memory.
(b) Diagonal matrix: a matrix all of whose elements are zero except for the main diagonal.
(c) Tridiagonal matrix: a matrix all of whose elements are zero except for the main
    diagonal, the sub-diagonal and the super-diagonal. We shall need this type of matrix
    when we solve boundary value problems using finite differences.
(d) Block tridiagonal: a matrix whose diagonals are tridiagonal matrices.
(e) Lower triangular: a matrix whose element above the main diagonal are zero. An upper
    triangular matrix is one whose elements below the main diagonal are zero.

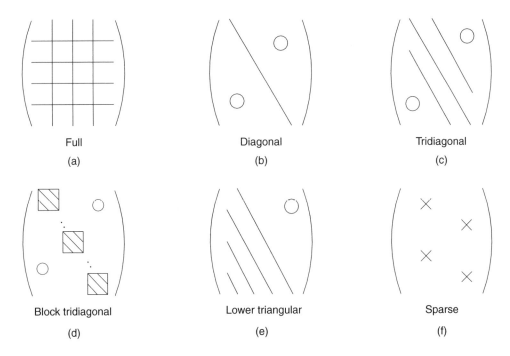

Full
(a)

Diagonal
(b)

Tridiagonal
(c)

Block tridiagonal
(d)

Lower triangular
(e)

Sparse
(f)

Figure 4.1   Matrix structures

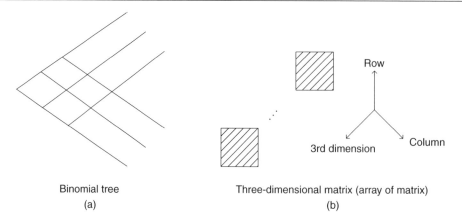

Binomial tree	Three-dimensional matrix (array of matrix)
(a)	(b)

Figure 4.2   Special matrix structures

(f) Sparse matrix: a matrix whose elements are mainly zero and that has a (small) percentage of non-zero elements. In general, there is no pattern to the position of the
non-zero elements. This is a special matrix category and is important for multidimensional problems

These matrix types will be used when we solve one-factor and multi-factor option
models with finite difference schemes. We choose the most appropriate matrix for the
problem at hand. Of course, we could use a full matrix (case (a) above) for all applications
but this approach would be wasteful of computer memory and would result in performance
degradation.

We mention two other very interesting structures in financial engineering: first, the data
structure that holds the data in the binomial method (see Figure 4.2(a)). This is a lattice
structure and is implemented as a vector of vectors in STL. Second, three-dimensional
matrices (or arrays of matrices) are useful when modelling portfolios (see Figure 4.2(b)).

We shall show how some useful matrix structures are defined in STL, but first we need
to create some simple functions for printing vectors and matrices. These functions are
useful when you are testing and debugging prototype code and applications.

4.2.1   A simple output mechanism

Since we shall often be working with vectors and matrices in this book we thought it
useful to provide a number of output mechanisms to enable the results of calculations to
be visualised. As a first attempt, we discuss how to output vectors and matrices using
the standard C++ iostream. (In later chapters we discuss how to display vectors and
matrices in a spreadsheet.) First, we print vectors using the following function template:

```
template <class V> void print(const vector<V>& v)
{
   cout << "\nV:[";

   vector<V>::const_iterator i;

   // Print every value in the vector
   for (i = v.begin(); i!=v.end(); i++)
```

```
{
   cout << (*i) << ",";
}
cout << "]";
}
```

Basically, we define a const iterator that navigates over the elements of a vector and prints the current element in that vector. The second step is to print a vector whose elements are themselves vectors. Again, this is achieved by iterating over the 'outer' vector and then calling the already-defined print function for 'simple' vectors. The resulting code is:

```
template <class V> void print (vector<vector<V> >& mat)
{ // This structure is really a matrix
  vector<vector<V> >::const_iterator i;

  // Print every vector in the matrix
  for (i = mat.begin(); i!=mat.end(); i++)
  {
    print (*i);
  }
  cout << endl;
}
```

We take an example to show how the print function works. To this end, we create a 5×5 'full' matrix as follows:

```
// Create a 'full' matrix
vector<vector<int> > myMat(5);        // 5 rows

myMat[0] = vector<int>(5,1);   // Size 5, value 1
myMat[1] = vector<int>(5,2);
myMat[2] = vector<int>(5,3);
myMat[3] = vector<int>(5,4);
myMat[4] = vector<int>(5,5);

print(myMat);
```

The output from this code is:

```
V:[1,1,1,1,1,]
V:[2,2,2,2,2,]
V:[3,3,3,3,3,]
V:[4,4,4,4,4,]
V:[5,5,5,5,5,]
```

Another example is the case where we create a matrix containing character data. Each 'inner' vector contains one less element than its predecessor:

```
// Matrices with character values
vector<vector<char> > myCharMat(5); // 5 rows

myCharMat[0] = vector<char>(5,'A'); // Elements with value 'A'
myCharMat[1] = vector<char>(4,'B');
myCharMat[2] = vector<char>(3,'C');
myCharMat[3] = vector<char>(2,'D');
myCharMat[4] = vector<char>(1,'E');

print(myCharMat);
```

The output from this code is:

```
V:[A,A,A,A,A,]
V:[B,B,B,B,]
V:[C,C,C,]
V:[D,D,]
V:[E,]
```

The moral of this story is that you can create simple yet effective printing functions for your code and applications before integrating them with more sophisticated output software such as Excel and other graphics packages.

4.3 SET THEORY AND STL

STL support the notion of a set. This has powerful ramifications because many applications use sets as high-level data structures. We are interested in creating sets, adding elements to and removing elements from a set, and comparing two sets. The main functions are:

- Is set *A* a subset of set *B* (includes())?
- The union of *A* and *B* (set_union())

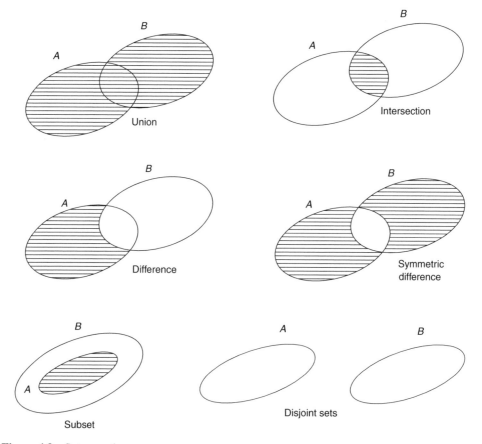

Figure 4.3   Set operations

- The intersection of *A* and *B* (set_intersection())
- The difference of *A* and *B* A\B (set_difference())
- The symmetric difference of *A* and *B* (set_symmetric_difference())

These functions and relationships are shown in Figure 4.3. They are supported by STL although you have to write your own function to test if two sets are disjoint.

In our first example we give some code to show how to create sets, copy sets and insert elements into sets.

```cpp
// ch4set1.cpp
//
// Creating sets. Simple functions for starters.
//
//          1. Create sets with string elements
//          2. Compare sets with '==' operator
//          3. Swap two sets using the swap() function
//          4. Assigning sets to each other
//
// (C) Datasim Education 2003

#include <set>
#include <iostream>
#include <string>

using namespace std;

template <class T> void print(const set<T>& mySet, const string& name)
{  // Print the contents of a set.

  cout << endl << name << ",size of set" << mySet.size() << "\n[";

  set<T>::const_iterator i;

  for (i = mySet.begin(); i != mySet.end(); ++i)
  {
    cout << (*i) << ",";
  }
  cout << "]\n";
}

int main()
{
  set<string> first;                    // Default constructor

  // Only unique (new elements) added
  first.insert("r");
  first.insert("T");
  first.insert("sigma");

  cout << "First Size: " << first.size() << endl;

  set<string> second (first);    // Copy constructor

  // Add extra elements to second set
  second.insert("r");        // "Interest rate"
  second.insert("K");        // "Strike price"
  second.insert("S");        // "Current underlying price"
  second.insert("b");        // "Cost of carry"

  cout << "Second Size: " << second.size() << endl;
```

```
// Are the sets the same?
if (first == second)
   cout << "Sets have same elements\n";
else
   cout << "Not same elements\n";

// A bit of swapping
swap(first, second);

// Assignment
set<string> third = first;

// Now print the sets
print(first, "First set");
print(second, "Second set");
print(third, "Third set");

// Now create a set representing Executive options
set<string> execOption(first);
execOption.insert("lambda");   // The jump rate, see Haug (1998)

   print(execOption, "An Executive Option");
}
```

The output from this code is:

```
First Size: 3
Second Size: 6
Not same elements

First set, size of set is 6
[K,S,T,b,r,sigma,]

Second set, size of set is 3
[T,r,sigma,]

Third set, size of set is 6
[K,S,T,b,r,sigma,]

An Executive Option, size of set is 7
[K,S,T,b,lambda,r,sigma,]
```

Note that there is no predefined order in a set, in contrast to vectors and lists. You insert an element in the set and for the rest you do not (need to) know how the element is stored. That is the beauty of encapsulation and information hiding.

We now discuss how sets are related to each other by applying the STL functions that implement the operations in Figure 4.3. Most of this theory should be well known and to this end we concentrate on the STL function that gives the intersection of two sets s1 and s2. To this end, we must define a so-called insert_iterator. This is officially an STL adaptor and its function is to insert objects into a container, in this case a set.

```
int main()
{
   set<int> first;                          // Default constructor

   // Only unique (new elements) added
   first.insert(1);
   first.insert(2);
   first.insert(3);
   print (first, "First set");
```

```
set<int> second (first);

second.erase(3);
second.insert(999);
print (second, "Second set");

// Intersection of two sets
set<int> myintersect;
set<int>::iterator i = myintersect.begin();
insert_iterator<set<int> > insertiter2(myintersect, i);

set_intersection(first.begin(), first.end(), second.begin(),
    second.end(), insertiter2);

print(myintersect, "Intersection");

return 0;
}
```

The output from this code snippet is:

```
First set, size of set is 3
[ 1 2 3 ]

Second set, size of set is 3
[ 1 2 999 ]

Intersection, size of set is 2
[ 1 2 ]
```

We can use sets as management classes in financial engineering applications. To give an example, we could compare two portfolios p_1 and p_2 (when viewed as sets) by asking the following questions:

- What have p_1 and p_2 in common?
- What are the differences between $p_1 \backslash p_2$ and $p_2 \backslash p_1$?

The outcomes will then be used in the application. In this sense the sets are a kind of repository containing vital or configuration information.

4.4   USEFUL ALGORITHMS

STL has support for a number of numeric algorithms. The offering is meager and the algorithms that we discuss in this section are:

- Carry out an operation on the elements of a vector (add, product)
- The inner product of two containers (for example, vectors)
- Partial summation functions
- Calculate the difference between consecutive elements of a container.

The following code shows how STL implements these numeric algorithms:

```
// STLNumericAlgorithms.cpp
//
// Some of the numeric algorithms in STL. This library has
```

```cpp
// minimal support for numerical analysis.
//
// (C) Datasim Education BV 2003

#include <vector>
#include <iostream>
#include <numeric>               // For numeric algorithms

using namespace std;

int main()
{

  // Create the containers for the algorithms
  vector<double> vec1(4, 2.0);   // Length 4, all values == 2.0
  vector<double> vec2(4, 4.0);   // Length 4, all values == 4.0

  // The accumulate is a generalisation of summation
  double init = 0.0;
  double summation = accumulate (vec1.begin(), vec1.end(), init);

  cout << "Sum of elements in vector 1: " << summation << endl;

  // Inner product of two vectors
  double ip = inner_product(vec1.begin(), vec1.end(),
      vec2.begin(), init);
  cout << "Inner product of vec1 and vec2: " << ip << endl;

  // Now calculate the partial sum of a vector; result is also a
  // vector
  int size = 6;
  int seed_value = 2;
  vector<int> vec3(size, seed_value);
  vector<int> result(size);
  partial_sum(vec3.begin(), vec3.end(), result.begin());

  cout << "The partial sum of the vector vec3\n";
  print(result);

  // Compute difference between consequence elements of a vector
  int sz = 10;
  int value = 2;
  vector<int> vec4(sz);

  vector<int>::iterator it;
  for (it = vec4.begin(); it != vec4.end(); it++)
  {
    (*it) = value;
    value += 1;
  }
  vector<int> result2(vec4.size());
  adjacent_difference(vec4.begin(), vec4.end(), result2.begin());
  cout << "The adjacent difference of the vector vec4\n";

  print(result2);

  return 0;
}
```

In later chapters we shall present many more numeric algorithms for numerical analysis problems.

4.5   STL ADAPTOR CONTAINERS

STL has functionality for stack, queue and priority queue abstractions. These are called adaptors because they adapt or modify the interfaces of other containers (Gamma *et al.*, 1995). We discuss the stack and priority queue by looking at some source code.

A stack has two major functions, pop (remove an element from the top of the stack) and push (place an element on the top of the stack). The strategy is First In Last Out (FILO) for element addition and removal. Here is some code:

```
stack<int, vector<int> > s1;

cout << "Size of a stack " << s1.size() << endl;

for (int i = 0; i < 10; i++)
{
  s1.push(i);
}

cout << "Size of a stack " << s1.size() << endl;

// Non-destructive pop
cout << "Top element is: " << s1.top() << endl;

// Destructive pop (stack has no begin() or end())
while (!s1.empty())
{
  s1.pop();
}
cout << "Size of a stack " << s1.size() << endl;
```

A queue is a container where elements join and leave on a First In First Out (FIFO) basis. A priority queue is a variation of the queue because elements are placed in the queue on the basis of some priority. Here is some code (note the presence of the *comparitor function* which determines the placing of elements in the priority queue):

```
priority_queue<int, vector<int>, less<int> > myque;

myque.push(20);
myque.push(21);
myque.push(22);
myque.push(23);

cout << "Size of first queue " << myque.size() << endl;

while (!myque.empty())
{
  cout << myque.top() << " ";
  myque.pop();
}

cout << "Size of first queue " << myque.size() << endl;
```

The output from this code is:

```
Size of queue 4
23 22 21 20
Size of queue 0
```

You may be able to find useful applications for these adaptor containers, in simulations, for example. We admit that vectors and matrices are the most important classes in your daily work.

4.6 CONCLUSIONS AND SUMMARY

This chapter examines STL from the viewpoint of extensibility; can we create new classes and containers based on the building blocks that STL offers? The answer is a definite 'Yes' and we have shown, by a number of relevant examples, how to create specific classes for financial engineering and other applications. The productivity gains are measurable and no longer do we have to build low-level utility classes before getting to the real issue of designing and implementing robust C++ applications for financial instrument modelling.

5
The Property Pattern in Financial Engineering

5.1 INTRODUCTION AND OBJECTIVES

In this chapter we develop a number of reusable classes that will be used in the construction of models for options and other financial products. In particular, we introduce the Property pattern that encapsulates an option's attributes. A property is a template class that has a name and a value. Furthermore, it has a number of member functions, two of which are functions to set and get the encapsulated value. The underlying types of the name and value are generic, which means that programmers can instantiate these types with their own specific types. In short, the Property pattern leads to high levels of reusability.

An important point to make when using the Property pattern to model attributes of option models is that it leads to a general risk engine framework. For a trader it is desirable to calculate the sensitivities (that is, the partial derivatives) of an option with respect to its parameters. Once the Property pattern is in place, it is straightforward to write code that runs through the attributes, perturbs them and calculates a new option model value and also approximates these sensitivities by a finite difference scheme. This code is usually placed in a Visitor pattern (see Gamma *et al.*, 1995, and Part V of the current book).

Once we have created the Property pattern it is then possible to use it in many different applications. For example, it can be seamlessly used with the classes in the STL and as a mechanism for defining flexible attributes in other classes. We do not (yet) investigate all the possibilities at this stage; instead, we focus on creating a class that represents a list of properties. This is the SimplePropertySet class and it is possible to add properties to and remove properties from this class (even at run-time!). Having defined this class, we shall show how to use it to construct the properties of several plain and exotic option types.

In general, application of the Property patterns will improve the overall quality of C++ code and promote programmer productivity. When we talk in this chapter about the Property pattern, we implicitly mean the two classes Property and SimplePropertySet that it subsumes. In our production environment, the pattern contains more classes than just those discussed here.

5.2 THE PROPERTY PATTERN

Object-oriented technology takes the view of a class as having public member functions and private member data. The functions and data are tightly coupled (this is called *encapsulation*) and the data cannot be accessed directly by client objects. Instead, a class must expose its member data by providing clients with member functions to set and get the member data as the following piece of code shows:

```
class Point
{ // Two-dimensional point in Cartesian space
```

```
private:

  double x;
  double y;

public:

  // ...
  double getX() const;
  void setX(double d);
  // ...
};
```

In this case we define a `Point` class containing two private member data of type `double`. Public member functions for retrieving and modifying these data are available in the form of so-called `set` and `get` functions. The use of these functions is relatively easy, as the following code shows:

```
Point pnt(1.0, 2.0);    // Create a point instance
cout << pnt.getX();     // Print the x-coordinate of the point
pnt.setX(3.3);          // Change the x-coordinate
```

This is perfectly acceptable C++ code but this style of programming has a number of disadvantages that surface when creating code for Option classes. Some of the problems are:

- The underlying data type of the member data is double; if you wish to create a `Point` class with integer coordinates you must edit and recompile the code. What we would like is to create template `Point` classes whose underlying data types are generic.
- For every private member data we must create the corresponding `set` and `get` member functions. This is an extremely laborious and error-prone process and it leads to classes with many 'junk' functions, that is, functions that do nothing more than access the member data. Of course, we could create public member data but this approach destroys encapsulation, one of the cornerstones of the object-oriented paradigm.
- Each programmer has his or her own favourite naming convention for member functions. For example, the following names are legitimate candidates for a member function to set the *x*-variable of a `Point` instance:

```
void setX(double d);        // Copy of d used
void setX(const double& d); // Const reference
void setX(double* d);       // Pointer to a double

// and many more possibilities ...
```

Clients of the `Point` class need to be aware of the precise signature (function name, input parameters and return type) when they use the class. What we would like to have in fact is a standard syntax for all `set` and `get` functions irrespective of the class used or the underlying data types.
- It is not possible to configure the `Point` class with three coordinates (*x*, *y*, *z*) without editing and compiling the source code. In other words, the data is hard-coded.
- It is not possible to determine the member data of a `Point` instance at run-time without having prior, hard-wired knowledge. The current `Point` is not *self-aware*.

5.2.1 Requirements for a Property pattern

Having motivated why standard approaches to implementation of member data in C++ is not always satisfactory for all situations, we now discuss some of the requirements that a

Property pattern should fulfil and we motivate why we should go to the effort of writing and using the patterns.

Some reasons for creating and using the Property pattern are:

- *Usability*: It is easy to learn how to use the pattern. We use operator overloading (the operator '()') to implement `set` and `get` member functions. This means that all instantiated property classes will be accessed in a uniform manner. This will also improve communication between developers.
- *Functionality*: It should be possible, for example, to add new properties to an object at run-time and it should be possible to remove a property from an object at configuration-time or run-time. For example, a property set containing standard properties for a plain option can be extended to a property set for executive options (see Haug, 1998) by just adding a new property that represents the so-called jump rate per year property.
- *Maintainability*: A class now uses public properties and property sets and clients know how to access these in a uniform way. For example, we could enforce standardisation by defining the member functions for properties with the same signature in all cases. Each class would then have the following entry:

```
SimplePropertySet<Name, Value> properties; // Properties in Entity
```

Each client would then access the properties of the class using the above. Furthermore, changes to the property of a class or an object occur in one place. In short, local changes to the C++ code have local impact on the stability of that code.

- *Efficiency*: This characteristic relates to how well properties perform as far as response time is concerned, and how much memory is needed in order to store a property. To this end, we can design property sets using STL sequence containers and associative containers depending on our performance requirements. For example, a class with very many properties (a quite unusual situation!) could be designed using an STL map while classes with, at most, seven or eight properties (which is the case with Option classes) will be implemented using an STL `list` container for our present purposes. As far as memory usage is concerned, a property object will always consume more resources than the object it encapsulates. This may be a problem for real-time embedded systems but we do not think that memory problems will occur for most applications.
- *Reliability*: The Property pattern can be made robust by extending it with functionality that saves the property values before they are modified. In fact, we shall show in a later chapter how design patterns (see Gamma *et al.*, 1995) are applied to create mature, fault-tolerant properties and properties that can be recovered after a system crash or an incorrect modification.
- *Portability*: This quality characteristic relates to effort that is needed to transfer software from one environment to another. In this particular case, we may wish to save properties in a database (such as Access, SQL Server or Oracle) or we may even wish to export these properties to Excel or to OpenGL. All these wishes come true by the application of design patterns (see Gamma *et al.*, 1995) to the Property pattern. These topics will be discussed in later chapters.

Another advantage of the Property pattern is that it can be specialised to many different kinds of value types. For example, some clients may be unhappy with double precision numbers because of rounding errors, in which case the value could be defined using a class that represents infinite-dimension precision:

```
Property<string, PrecisionType> myProp("Large", 34438563946.927365353);
```

Now for the big moment! We introduce the Property pattern by first defining a template class that models named values. This is thus a class having two underlying data types and is defined as follows:

```
template <class Name = string, class Type = double> class Property
```

Notice the presence of default data types; in this case the default value type is `double` (quite common) and the default ID or reference type is `string` (also quite common). As a programmer you are free to choose how to specialise this template class. For example, the following statements are equivalent:

```
Property<string, double> first("r", 0.06);
Property<string> first("r", 0.06);
Property<> first("r", 0.06);        // N.B. funny syntax!
```

We now describe the interface of the `Property` class. First, we define constructors to define instances of the class. They are:

- Default constructor (uses default constructors of the underlying types)
- Constructor using a name only
- Constructor using a name and type (value)
- Copy constructor.

Once a property has been created we can get its values by the use of the overloaded operator '()' as the following illustrative code shows:

```
Property<string, double> K("Strike Price", 65.0);
Property<string, double> T("Expiry date", 0.25);
Property<string, double> U("Underlying Asset", 60.0);
Property<string, double> sig("Volatility",0.30);

double tmp = sig() * sqrt(T());
double d1 = (log(U()/K()) + (b()+(sig()*sig())*0.5) * T())/ tmp;

// Changing the values in the properties
sig = Property<string,double>(0.20);
K = Property<string,double>(66.0);
T = Property<string,double>(1.0);
U = Property<string,double>(63.0);
```

Finally, we have defined a specific equality operator: *Two properties are equal if and only if their names are the same.*

The source code on the CD contains a class for a *heterogeneous* `PropertySet` and an example is that of a person having a name, address, age and date of birth; the properties and their types look something like the following:

Name	`string`
Address	`string`
Age	`int`
Date of birth	`Date`

In this chapter, however, each property has the same (homogeneous) underlying data type.

The full interface for the `Property` class is given as follows:

```
// property.hpp
//
// Base class for Properties. This is a concrete class.
//
// (C) Datasim Education BV 2001-2003

#ifndef PROPERTY_HPP
#define PROPERTY_HPP

#include <string>

template <class Name = string, class Type = double> class Property
{ // Property with a name and a value (notice default types)
private:
  Name nam;
  Type con;

  // Assignment: we do not want client to use this!
  Property<Name, Type>& operator = (const Property<Name, Type>& source);
public:
  // Constructors and destructor
  Property();
  Property(const Name& name);
  Property(const Name& name, const Type& t);
  Property(const Property<Name, Type>& source);

  virtual ~Property();

  // Accessing function operators
  virtual Type operator()() const;
  virtual void operator()(const Type& t);

  virtual Name name() const;
  virtual void name(const Name& new_name);

  bool operator == (const Property<Name, Type>& prop2);
};
```

5.3   AN EXAMPLE

Since this is a book about C++ for financial engineering it is useful to give some relevant examples from this domain. As a warm-up, we discuss how we would model the attributes of a plain option using the Property pattern. You can see that we modelled these attributes as hard-coded built-in doubles in Appendix 1. First, we discuss how to create properties and, second, we can now define a class representing plain options by defining option attributes in terms of properties:

```
class ExactEuropeanOption
{
private:
  // ...
```

```
public:
  Property<string, double> r;         // Interest rate
  Property<string, double> sig;       // Volatility
  Property<string, double> K;         // Strike price
  Property<string, double> T;         // Expiry date
  Property<string, double> U;         // Current underlying price
  Property<string, double> b;         // Cost of carry

  // ...

  // Functions that calculate option price and sensitivities
  double Price() const;
  double Delta() const;
  double Gamma() const;
  double Vega() const;
  double Theta() const;
  double Rho() const;
  double Coc() const;                          // Cost of carry
  double Elasticity(double percentageMovement) const;
};
```

The formulae for the option price and its sensitivities now use the properties, as the following code shows in the case of `Price()` for a call option:

```
double ExactEuropeanOption::Price() const
{
  double tmp = sig() * sqrt(T());

  double d1 = (log(U()/K())+ (b() + (sig()*sig())*0.5) * T())/ tmp;
  double d2 = d1 - tmp;

  return (U()*exp((b()-r())*T())*N(d1))-(K()*exp(-r()*T())* N(d2));
}
```

The full source code is to be found on the accompanying CD.

5.4   EXTENDING THE PROPERTY PATTERN: PROPERTY SETS AND PROPERTY LISTS

We would like to cluster or amalgamate the properties of some object into a single object so that we can access this new object as one entity. To this end, we create an aggregate class (see Buschmann *et al.*, 1996) called `SimplePropertySet`. Each instance of this class consists of a number of `Property` instances as shown in the UML diagrams in Figure 5.1. Officially, an instance of class `SimplePropertySet` (called the *Whole*) consists of zero or more instances of class `Property` (the so-called *Parts*). It is possible to add and remove parts from the Whole at run-time. In the particular implementation that we discuss here, we assume that each property occurs only once in the property set and we are able to give the set a name. This latter is feasible because we can access the property set by a unique reference ID.

The general requirements of a class for a property set are:

- It must be possible to create sets with an arbitrary number of properties
- It must be possible to add properties and other sets to the set
- It must be possible to remove properties from the set

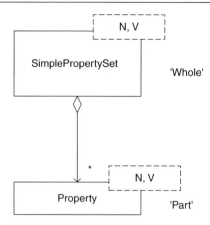

Figure 5.1   Properties and property sets

- It must be possible to iterate in the set (from beginning to end, for example)
- It must be possible to query if the set contains a given property
- There must be efficient access to the members of the property set.

We have designed and implemented this class using the STL list class as a basis. All functions in our new property set delegate to other functions in the list. The class interface is given by:

```
// SimplePropertySet.hpp
//
// Class that represents a list of named properties. This is simply
// a list of Property objects. Each property is a name/value pair.
// This kind of structure occurs in many applications, for
// example relational database theory.
//
// (C) Datasim Education BV 2002-2003

#ifndef SimplePropertySet_hpp
#define SimplePropertySet_hpp

#include "property.cpp"
#include <list>
#include <set>

using namespace std;

template <class N, class V> class SimplePropertySet
{
private:
  N nam;                // The name of the set

  // The SimplePropertySet list using the STL list
  list<Property<N,V> > sl;

public:
  // User can use the STL iterator
  typedef typename list<Property<N,V> >::iterator iterator;
  typedef typename list<Property<N,V> >::const_iterator const_iterator;

  // Constructors and destructor
```

```
SimplePropertySet();              // Default constructor
SimplePropertySet(const N& name);         // Named property set
SimplePropertySet(const SimplePropertySet<N,V>& source);

virtual ~SimplePropertySet(); // Destructor

// Iterator functions
iterator Begin();         // Return iterator at begin of composite
const_iterator Begin() const; // Return const iterator
iterator End();                 // Return iterator after end
const_iterator End() const;   // Return const iterator after end

// Selectors
int Count() const;        // The number of properties in the list
N operator ()() const;   // The name of the property set
bool hasProperty(const N& search_name) const;    // In list?

// Modifiers
void operator () (const N& name);     // Change the name of PSet
Property<N,V> value(const N& name) const; // Get the Property

// Add and remove functions (sort of mixin or embedded
// inheritance)
void add(const Property<N,V>& p);
void add(const SimplePropertySet<N,V>& p);
void remove(const N& value);   // Remove all elements with 'value'

// Operators
SimplePropertySet<N,V>& operator = (const SimplePropertySet<N,V>&
    source);
};

#endif      // SimplePropertySet_hpp
```

Note that we have provided two kinds of iterators (const and non-const versions) that allow you to navigate in the set. In some cases you may just wish to read the properties (const iterator) while in other cases you may wish to modify the property values in some way (in that case you can use the non-const iterator).

The full source code is on the CD. However, it is not a bad idea to show how one of the member functions (removing an element from the list) has been implemented:

```
template <class N, class V> void SimplePropertySet<N,V>::remove(const
    N& value)
{ // Remove all elements with 'value' O(N)

  // We iterate over the list until we find the value
  iterator it;

  for (it=sl.begin(); it!=sl.end(); it++)
  {
    if ((*it)() == value)
    {
      erase(it);
    }
  }
}
```

The SimplePropertySet will be used in very many classes and applications through-out the rest of this book. Don't leave home without it!

5.4.1   An example

Going back to the example in section 5.3 we show how clients can access *all* the properties in an Option class without having to go to the bother of accessing each property individually. To this end, we create a public member function that adds all the properties to a property set and returns it to the client. The interface functions is defined as follows:

```
// The option's defining parameters
SimplePropertySet<string, double> properties() const;
```

The body of this function is given as follows (notice that we are only interested in the names of the properties and not in their values):

```
// The option's defining parameters
SimplePropertySet<string, double> ExactEuropeanOption::properties()
const
{
  SimplePropertySet<string, double> result;

  result.add (Property<string, double> (r.name(), r() ) );
  result.add (Property<string, double> (sig.name(), sig() ) );
  result.add (Property<string, double> (K.name(), K() ) );
  result.add (Property<string, double> (T.name(), T() ) );
  result.add (Property<string, double> (U.name(), U() ) );
  result.add (Property<string, double> (b.name(), b() ) );

  return result;
}
```

We can then iterate over result in order to determine the *kinds* of properties the option contains.

Finally, it is sometimes very useful to have a 'snapshot' of an option by computing an option price along with its sensitivities in one simple function (simple for the client):

```
// Now give all values and sensitivities in a propertyset
SimplePropertySet<string, double> propertylist() const;
```

The source code for this function is:

```
SimplePropertySet<string, double> ExactEuropeanOption::propertylist()
const
{
  SimplePropertySet<string, double> result;

  result.add (Property<string, double> ("Option Value", Price()));
  result.add (Property<string, double> ("Delta",Delta()));
  result.add (Property<string, double> ("Gamma",Gamma()));
  result.add (Property<string, double> ("Vega",Vega()));
  result.add (Property<string, double> ("Theta",Theta()));
  result.add (Property<string, double> ("Rho",Rho()));
  result.add (Property<string, double> ("Cost of Carry",Coc()));

  return result;
}
```

It is useful to have a look at some code that creates a future option call, initialises its attributes and computes the price and sensitivity values for those attribute values. We then 'toggle' the option so that it becomes a put and we carry out the exercise again.

```
// tstOptionSensitivities.cpp
// Test program for the sensitivities for European options.
// Input taken from Haug 1998.
//
// (C) Datasim Component Technology BV 2003

#include "EOptionExact.hpp"
#include <iostream>

int main()
{ // All options are European

  ExactEuropeanOption futureOption("C", "Future Option");
  futureOption.U(105.0);
  futureOption.K(100.0);
  futureOption.T(0.5);
  futureOption.r(0.10);
  futureOption.sig(0.36);
  futureOption.b( 0.0);

  // Calculate all interesting values
  SimplePropertySet<string,double> r = futureOption.propertylist();

  // Iterate over the result and print the values
  SimplePropertySet<string,double>::const_iterator it;

  cout << "\nDump the parameters, call prices ... \n";
  for (it=r.Begin(); it!=r.End(); it++)
  {
    cout << (*it).name() << ", " << (*it)() << endl;
  }

  // We now examine the values when the option is a put
  futureOption.toggle();

  // !! Recalculate the prices again
  r = futureOption.propertylist();

  cout << "\nPut prices ...\n";
  for (it=r.Begin(); it!=r.End(); it++)
  {
    cout << (*it).name() << ", " << (*it)() << endl;
  }
  return 0;
}
```

The output from this program is:

```
Dump the parameters, call prices ...
Option Value, 12.4317
Delta, 0.59462
Gamma, 0.0134938
Vega, 26.7785
Theta, -8.39709
Rho, -6.21587
Cost of Carry, 31.2176
```

```
Put prices  ...
Option Value, 7.67559
Delta, -0.356609
Gamma, 0.0134938
Vega, 26.7785
Theta, -8.87271
Rho, -3.83779
Cost of Carry, -18.722
```

5.5 PROPERTIES AND EXOTIC OPTIONS

We have discussed how to model attributes of plain options. Our aim in this section is to investigate how to model a number of exotic options by examining their attributes and modelling them using the Property pattern (Haug, 1998). In particular, the attributes of an exotic option are extensions of the attributes of plain options in some way. For example, an executive option has all the properties of a plain option plus a property that models the jump rate per year (λ). It would be nice to append this extra property to the property set for the corresponding plain option.

Some examples of exotic options and their properties are:

Forward start options
   α: scaling factor $K = \alpha_S$ at time t
   t: the elapsed time at which $K = \alpha_S$

Options on options
   All properties of the 'underlying' option (as before)
   T_1: the time to maturity of the option on the option
   K_1: strike price of the option on the option.

Chooser option
   All properties of the 'underlying' option (as before)
   T_1: At this stage decide if option is a call or put.

Let us take an example.

5.5.1 Example: Executive options

We show how to 'extend' plain options to support an exotic variant by examining how to create a class for executive options. The technique used is called *composition* in conjunction with a so-called delegation mechanism. In short, we create a class for executive options that has its own specific properties (such as the jump rate) as well as having an 'embedded' plain option. In fact we can see an executive option as a wrapper for a plain option. Furthermore, the formula for pricing an executive option is found by multiplying the price of the corresponding plain option by an exponential factor, as shown in Haug (1998). The UML diagram depicting the structural relationship between the two options is shown in Figure 5.2.

The class interface for executive options is now shown. Note the presence of the embedded plain option as member data, the constructors and a new member function for

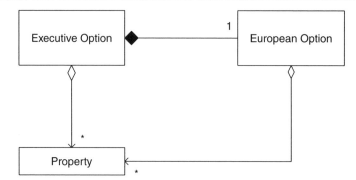

Figure 5.2 Creating an Executive Option class from a European Option class

calculating the price of the executive option:

```
class ExecutiveOption
{
private:
  // 'Kernel' functions for option calculations
  double CallPrice() const;
  double PutPrice() const;

public:     // Properties
  Property<string, double> jrate;          // Jump rate
  Property<string, ExactEuropeanOption> base; // Object inheritance

public:     // Public functions
  ExecutiveOption();                       // Default call option
  ExecutiveOption(const ExecutiveOption& option2);
  ExecutiveOption (double jump_rate, const ExactEuropeanOption&
      base_option);
  virtual ~ExecutiveOption();

  ExecutiveOption& operator = (const ExecutiveOption& option2);

  // Functions that calculate option price and sensitivities
  double Price() const;

  // Modifier functions
  void toggle();          // Change option type (C/P, P/C)
};
```

Most of the code for this class is straightforward but it is useful to show how the `Price()`
member function has been implemented. Notice how the pricing formula for an executive
option uses the pricing formula for a plain option:

```
double ExecutiveOption::Price() const
{
  double expT = base().T();

  return exp(-jrate() * expT) * (base().Price());
}
```

Indeed we see delegation at work: part of the price calculation is delegated to the plain
option where it has been implemented and tested.

What does a main program look like? In short, we create a plain option and embed it in an executive option:

```
int main()
{ // All options are European

    // Executive options

    // Put option on a stock
    ExactEuropeanOption stockOption("C", "Common Stock Option");
    stockOption.U(60.0);
    stockOption.K(64.0);
    stockOption.T(2.0);             // 2 years
    stockOption.r(0.07);
    stockOption.sig(0.38);

    double q = 0.03;          // Dividend yield
    stockOption.b( stockOption.r() - q );

    cout << "Call Option on Stock: " << stockOption.Price() << endl;

    // Now define an executive option based on stock option. We clone
    // the base stock option (copy all properties) and then delegate
    ExecutiveOption eo(0.15, stockOption);

    cout << "Executive Call Option on Stock: " << eo.Price() << endl;

    return 0;
}
```

The output from this file is:

```
Call Option on Stock: 12.3161
Executive Call Option on Stock: 9.12396
```

These results are consistent with those in Haug (1998).

One final remark: Delegation and composition will play a major role in the chapters to come. They are powerful mechanisms that allow us to create flexible software components and will form the basis of the design patterns that appear later in this book (see Gamma *et al.*, 1995). Watch this space.

5.6 CONCLUSIONS AND SUMMARY

There are fundamental reasons why we prefer to use properties instead of 'naked' member data in C++ applications, some of which we enumerate here:

- Classes for options, bonds and other derivative products can be modelled as lists of properties, thus making it easier to understand and extend these classes.
- Properties and the classes that use them become self-aware or *reflective*; we can ask the name of a property and we can ask an option if it contains a given property. This is a form of run-time type identification (RTTI) that is necessary in certain applications. Furthermore, it is possible to add properties to or remove them from an object at run-time.
- Properties support *serialisation*: we can save the data in a list of properties to XML, Excel and relational database formats in a seamless way. We come back to this topic after we have given an introduction to STL.

- Developers can create new Option classes by customising the properties that are appropriate to the current application. This is no need to use hard-coded member data or to create class hierarchies that are difficult to maintain.
- We can configure new kinds of options using properties without having to use static C++ inheritance. This adds both to application flexibility and programmer productivity.
- Since `Property` is a class, we can apply the creational, structural and behavioural design patterns to it in order to produce highly adaptable software (see Gamma *et al.*, 1995, for a definitive account of design patterns).

Part II

Building Block Classes

6

Arrays, Vectors and Matrices

6.1 INTRODUCTION AND OBJECTIVES

In Part II of the book we create several *foundation class categories* that will serve as building blocks for future chapters. These classes build on STL and in general we are interested in classes for several kinds of arrays, vectors and matrices. Furthermore, we create generic functions for some intrinsic properties of these classes (such as their maximum and minimum values, inner products and norms). We also discuss how to solve linear systems of equations using *LU* decomposition. Chapter 9 shows how we have defined C++ classes for various categories of mathematical functions: scalar functions, real-valued functions, vector functions and vector-valued functions. Finally, we discuss how to model continuous and discrete probability distributions using C++.

In this chapter we design and implement flexible data structures for arrays and matrices. We extend the STL classes to include support for numerical analysis and financial engineering applications. We concentrate on one-dimensional and two-dimensional data structures. In later chapters we shall extend this basic functionality to suit different contexts. To this end, we introduce basic *foundation* classes, namely:

- `Array`: sequential, indexible container containing arbitrary data types
- `Vector`: array class that contains numeric data
- `Matrix`: sequential, indexible container containing arbitrary data types
- `NumericMatrix`: matrix class that contains numeric data.

Of course, the classes `Array` and `Vector` are one-dimensional containers whose elements we access using a single index while `Matrix` and `NumericMatrix` are two-dimensional containers whose elements we access using two indices. Furthermore, we can introduce structure into these classes as introduced in Chapter 4:

- 'Full' arrays and matrices
- Banded arrays and matrices
- ... and many more.

Patterned matrices are important when solving linear systems of equations. This topic will be discussed in more detail in Chapters 7 and 8.

The structure of this chapter is as follows: in section 6.2 we discuss the rationale behind creating `Array` and `Matrix` classes. Section 6.3 is an introduction to the high-level design of these classes and the member functions they expose to clients, while section 6.4 describes the detailed design. Section 6.5 gives some useful examples to show how easy it is to use the `Array` and `Matrix` classes in applications. Section 6.6 introduces *associative arrays*.

6.2   MOTIVATION AND BACKGROUND

In this section we discuss the reasons why we have created a class hierarchy for arrays and matrices. First, at the moment of writing there is no C++ ISO or ANSI standard for such classes and the chances of one being written and accepted would seem to be small. However, there are many commercial and free matrix libraries in the marketplace and it is useful to investigate what is on offer. Most libraries tend to be highly specialised and geared to scientific and engineering applications. They may have a degree of overkill for financial applications but, personally speaking, I find that *less is more*. Most software systems are over-engineered and offer functionality that we hardly ever need or use.

In this chapter we introduce a number of classes that we shall use when solving financial engineering applications. These classes can be used as they are and the reader can easily extend them to suit his or her own specific needs. We have designed the software using object-oriented design principles and patterns.

A major problem with numerical algorithms in general (and with financial engineering applications in particular) is that the code that implements them tends to be difficult to understand, modify and adapt. The author has witnessed this problem when using C, C++ and Visual Basic in applications.

We have drawn up a list of requirements that we would like the current class library to satisfy. If we are successful, we shall hopefully be more productive in our daily work. We shall discuss the requirements detailed below.

Usability

Developers should be able to understand the class interfaces and use them in their applications, for example in the numerical solution of differential equations resulting from finite difference methods for the Black–Scholes equation. In a sense, we would like to use the classes as 'black boxes' without having to worry about their internal structure or implementation details.

The classes in this chapter are easy to learn and use. The classes have similar interfaces and once you learn one class it is not difficult to learn the interfaces of the other classes. A lot of detail has been hidden from the client such as memory management, array indexing and other annoying details that make us so unhappy. An added feature in this chapter is that we document the relationships between classes using UML (Unified Modeling Language) class diagrams. UML is the *de-facto* standard for documenting object-oriented software systems.

Suitability

The classes will be used in financial engineering applications and should be highly relevant to this domain. There is not much point creating classes that are not going to be used. As we shall see, we have created a useful set of classes for vectors and matrices and the corresponding mathematical operations such as multiplication and addition. You can do all the things you did before in Visual Basic, IMSL, Maple and other products and, in some cases, we offer more specialised functionality that is not always found in standard software packages.

Interoperability

We wish to export the data in arrays and matrices to the popular spreadsheet package Microsoft Excel. Furthermore, we may wish to export the data to XML (Extensible Markup Language) as this language is becoming more important as a lingua franca between diverse financial systems. Finally, importing data from Excel into a vector or matrix may also be a requirement.

Efficiency

It is not possible to create a 'one size fits all' matrix class that is going to please all customers. Some clients work with matrices all of whose elements (at the intersection of a row and a column) must be allocated and utilised while other clients may wish to define sparsely populated matrices where only a small fraction of the elements are needed. We must thus be able to conserve memory by creating the correct matrix structure for the problem at hand. This issue is called *resource efficiency*. Furthermore, we may require that mathematical operations on arrays and matrices be as efficient as possible. In this case we speak of *time efficiency*.

Maintainability

This is a requirement that tends to get 'lost in action' as it were. Its absence in software projects manifests itself by C++ code that is very difficult to understand and modify. Another resulting problem is that once some part of the software has been changed, new errors and bugs may enter the system. Instability then sets in.

We resolve possible maintainability problems by structuring and layering the classes into well-defined units having clear responsibilities.

Reliability

This requirement has to do with fault tolerance and maturity of the software. In the specific case of arrays and matrices we wish to avoid memory leaks and exceptions (for example, accessing an element in an array that is outside the array's bounds). To this end, we design and implement our classes as templates, thus ensuring that we only have to worry about memory allocation and deallocation once, while we can use the exception handling mechanisms in C++ to handle out-of-bounds indexing problems.

Portability

This requirement has to do with the effort that is required to transfer the code from one environment to another. An example is to transfer code from a Windows environment to Linux. This is not a problem in practice unless you embed Windows-specific code in the array and matrix (which we have not done). Furthermore, we recommend using STL whenever possible because this library is part of the C++ standard and portability problems should not arise.

In the rest of this chapter we shall show how we have realised these requirements with our own array and matrix class library.

6.3   A LAYERED APPROACH

In this section we give an overview of the design principles underpinning the library. This section has been written from the perspective of the developer who *uses* the library. We partition the library into several layers:

- Layer 1: General data structure classes (for arbitrary data types)
- Layer 2: Data structure classes containing numeric data
- Layer 3: Specialised operations (for example, inner products of vectors)
- Layer 4: Matrix algebra and specific mechanisms.

We discuss the classes in Layers 3 and 4 in Chapters 7 and 8. In this book we discuss the classes Array and Matrix in Layer 1 while the classes Vector and NumericMatrix are the two main classes in Layer 2. The classes in Layer 2 use the services in Layer 1.

We pay special attention to defining matrices with a predefined structure as we saw in Chapter 4. For example, it is possible to define full, sparse, banded and tridiagonal matrices. In general, we model the life cycle of instances of classes in the library. To this end, we can list the following function categories:

- Constructors: Creating arrays and matrices with given dimensions
- Accessing: Selector(get) and modifier(set) functions
- Mathematical Operations (for example, multiplication)

We give some remarks. First, C programmers prefer to index the elements of an array starting at position 0 while Fortran programmers prefer to start with the value 1. Our classes can accommodate both styles; in fact, it is even possible to have negative indices! Second, it is not possible to increase or decrease the size of an instance once it has been constructed. This is in contrast to STL where the class `vector` can be extended. Finally, we iterate through the elements of arrays and matrices using standard looping techniques in C++. We have not created customised iterators although it is certainly an interesting option.

6.4   THE ARRAY AND MATRIX CLASSES IN DETAIL

We start with the class `Array`. This is the most fundamental class in the library and its represents a sequential collection of values. This template class, which we denote by `Array<V, I, S>`, has three generic parameters:

- V: The data type of the underlying values in the array
- I: The data type used for indexing the values in the array
- S: The so-called storage class for the array.

The storage class is in fact an encapsulation of the STL vector class and it is here that the data in the array is actually initialised. At the moment there are specific storage classes, namely `FullArray<V>` and `BandArray<V>` that store a full array and a banded array of values, respectively.

Please note that it is **not** possible to change the size of an `Array` instance once it has been constructed. This is in contrast to the STL `vector` class in which it is possible to let it grow.

The declaration of the class `Array` is given by:

```
template <class V, class I=int, class S=FullArray<V>  >
class Array
{
private:
  S m_structure;          // The array structure
  I m_start;              // The start index
};
```

We see that `Array` has an embedded storage object of type S and a start index. The default storage is `FullArray<V>` and the default index type is `int`. This means that if we work with these types on a regular basis we do not have to include them in the template declaration. Thus, the following three declarations are the same:

```
  Array<double, int, FullArray<double> > arr1;
  Array<double, int> arr1;
  Array<double> arr1;
```

You may choose the data types that are most suitable for your needs. The constructors in `Array` allow us to create instances based on size of the array, start index and so on. The constructors are:

```
Array();                // Default constructor
Array(size_t size);     // Give length start index == 1
Array(size_t size, I start);            // Length and start index
Array(size_t size, I start, const V& value); // Size, start, value
Array(const Array<V, I, S>& source);    // Copy constructor
```

Once we have created an array, we may wish to navigate in the array, access the elements in the array and modify these elements. The member functions to help you in this case are:

```
  // Selectors
  I MinIndex() const;                 // Return the minimum index
  I MaxIndex() const;                 // Return the maximum index
  size_t Size() const;                // The size of the array
  const V& Element(I index) const;    // Element at position

  // Modifiers
  void Element(I index, const V& val); // Change element at position
  void StartIndex(I index);            // Change the start index

  // Operators
  virtual V& operator [] (I index);    // Subscripting operator
  virtual const V& operator [] (I index) const;
```

This completes the description of the `Array` class. We do not describe the class that actually stores the data in the array. The reader can find the source code on the accompanying media kit.

The UML class diagram that describes the design of `Array` is shown in Figure 6.1. Here we see that `Array` is a client of storage classes such as `FullArray` and

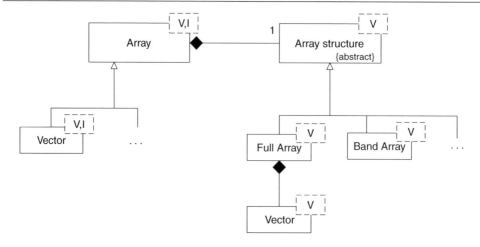

Figure 6.1   Array and Vector classes

`BandArray`. We now turn our attention to the class `Matrix`, which is defined as follows:

```
template <class V, class I=int, class S=FullMatrix<V> >
class Matrix
{
private:
  S m_structure;          // The array structure
  I m_rowstart;           // The row start index
  I m_columnstart;        // The column start index

  // Redundant data
  size_t nr, nc;          // Number of rows and columns
};
```

Referring to Figure 6.2 we see that `Matrix` uses the services of storage classes, for example `FullMatrix`. The main constructors in `Matrix` are:

```
// Default constructor
Matrix();

// Matrix with r rows, c columns, and given start indices
Matrix(size_t r, size_t c);

// Matrix with r rows, c columns, and given start indices
Matrix(size_t r, size_t c, I rowStart, I columnStart);

// Copy constructor
Matrix(const Matrix<V, I, S>& source);
```

The following four functions are selectors that give the minimum and maximum index values along the row and column directions:

```
// Selectors
I MinRowIndex() const;       // Return the minimum row index
I MaxRowIndex() const;       // Return the maximum row index
I MinColumnIndex() const;    // Return the minimum column index
I MaxColumnIndex() const;    // Return the maximum column index
```

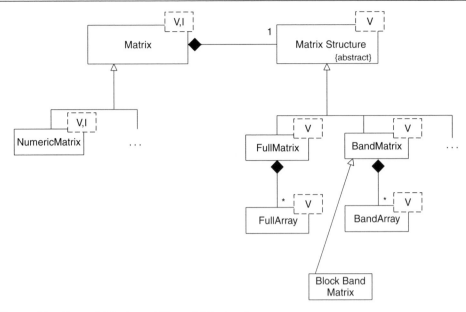

Figure 6.2   General Matrix and NumericMatrix classes

The next two functions tell us about the number of rows and columns in the matrix:

```
size_t Rows() const;          // The number of rows
size_t Columns() const;       // The number of columns
```

The following two useful functions allow us to replace the elements in a row or column by another array of elements:

```
void Row(I row, const Array<V, I>& val);          // Replace row
void Column(I column, const Array<V, I>& val);   // Replace column
```

Finally, we have used operator overloading to allow us to access elements in a given row and column in the matrix:

```
const V& operator () (I row, I column) const; // Get element
V& operator () (I row, I column);
```

The next three sub-sections show how to use the above member functions.

6.4.1   Simple print functions

We present simple code to show how to print arrays and matrices. You can use these functions in many places in this book as a simple debugging and visualisation tool. The code also shows how you can use the member functions in these classes. The simple print function for `Array` is:

```
template <class V, class I> void print(const Array<V,I>& v)
{
  cout << "\n\nMinIndex: " << v.MinIndex() << " , MaxIndex: " <<
      v.MaxIndex() << endl;
```

```
cout << "\nARR:[";
for (I j = v.MinIndex(); j <= v.MaxIndex(); j++)
{
  cout << v[j] << ",";
}
cout << "]";
}
```

The simple print function for `Matrix` is:

```
template <class V, class I> void print(const Matrix<V,I>& m)
{
cout << "\n\nMinRowIndex: " << m.MinRowIndex() << " , MaxRowIndex: " <<
    m.MaxRowIndex() << endl;

cout << "MinColumnIndex: " << m.MinColumnIndex() << " , MaxColumnIndex: " <<
    m.MaxColumnIndex() << endl;
cout << "\nMAT:[";
for (I i = m.MinRowIndex(); i <= m.MaxRowIndex(); i++)
{
  cout << "\nRow" << i << "(";
  for (I j = m.MinColumnIndex(); j <= m.MaxColumnIndex(); j++)
  {
    cout << m(i, j) << ",";
  }
  cout << ")";
}
cout << "]";
}
```

Of course, it will be necessary to provide more sophisticated display and output functionality in later chapters, but the present functions are useful when you are writing new classes and code and when you wish to test and run your code as efficiently and effectively as possible. The objective at this stage is to get the code working.

6.4.2 Array example

We construct three arrays with various start indices and values.

```
// Create some arrays
Array<double, int> arr1(10);              // Start index = 1
Array<double, int> arr2(10, -1);          // Start index = -1

// An array with 10 elements, starting at 0 and all values == 3.14
Array<double, int> arr3(10, 0, 3.14);

print (arr1);
print (arr2);
print (arr3);
```

The output from the print function is:

```
MinIndex: 1 , MaxIndex: 10
ARR:[0,0,0,0,0,0,0,0,0,0,]

MinIndex: -1 , MaxIndex: 8
ARR:[0,0,0,0,0,0,0,0,0,0,]
```

```
MinIndex: 0 , MaxIndex: 9
ARR:[3.14,3.14,3.14,3.14,3.14,3.14,3.14,3.14,3.14,3.14,]
```

6.4.3   Matrix example

We construct a default matrix with 10 rows and 10 columns. The default start index is 1 and the default value in each cell is 0.0. The second matrix has 10 rows and 10 columns. However, the start row is −2 and the start column is 0.

```
// Matrices
Matrix<double, int> m1(10, 10);
Matrix<double, int> m2(10, 10, -2, 0);

print (m1);
print (m2);
```

The output is:

```
MinRowIndex: 1 , MaxRowIndex: 10
MinColumnIndex: 1 , MaxColumnIndex: 10

MAT:[
Row 1  (0,0,0,0,0,0,0,0,0,0,)
Row 2  (0,0,0,0,0,0,0,0,0,0,)
Row 3  (0,0,0,0,0,0,0,0,0,0,)
Row 4  (0,0,0,0,0,0,0,0,0,0,)
Row 5  (0,0,0,0,0,0,0,0,0,0,)
Row 6  (0,0,0,0,0,0,0,0,0,0,)
Row 7  (0,0,0,0,0,0,0,0,0,0,)
Row 8  (0,0,0,0,0,0,0,0,0,0,)
Row 9  (0,0,0,0,0,0,0,0,0,0,)
Row 10 (0,0,0,0,0,0,0,0,0,0,)]

MinRowIndex: -2 , MaxRowIndex: 7
MinColumnIndex: 0 , MaxColumnIndex: 9

MAT:[
Row -2 (0,0,0,0,0,0,0,0,0,0,)
Row -1 (0,0,0,0,0,0,0,0,0,0,)
Row 0  (0,0,0,0,0,0,0,0,0,0,)
Row 1  (0,0,0,0,0,0,0,0,0,0,)
Row 2  (0,0,0,0,0,0,0,0,0,0,)
Row 3  (0,0,0,0,0,0,0,0,0,0,)
Row 4  (0,0,0,0,0,0,0,0,0,0,)
Row 5  (0,0,0,0,0,0,0,0,0,0,)
Row 6  (0,0,0,0,0,0,0,0,0,0,)
Row 7  (0,0,0,0,0,0,0,0,0,0,)]
```

Finally, we create a matrix and we use operator overloading to set the value of each row−column intersection:

```
// 10 rows and 2 columns, values = 3.14
Matrix<double, int> m3(10, 10);
for (int i = m3.MinRowIndex(); i <= m3.MaxRowIndex(); i++)
{
   for (int j = m3.MinColumnIndex(); j <= m3.MaxColumnIndex();
       j++)
```

```
      {
        m3(i,j)  = 3.14;
      }
  }

  print (m3);
```

The output for matrix m3 is:

```
MinRowIndex: 1 , MaxRowIndex: 10
MinColumnIndex: 1 , MaxColumnIndex: 10

MAT:[
Row 1  (3.14,3.14,3.14,3.14,3.14,3.14,3.14,3.14,3.14,3.14,)
Row 2  (3.14,3.14,3.14,3.14,3.14,3.14,3.14,3.14,3.14,3.14,)
Row 3  (3.14,3.14,3.14,3.14,3.14,3.14,3.14,3.14,3.14,3.14,)
Row 4  (3.14,3.14,3.14,3.14,3.14,3.14,3.14,3.14,3.14,3.14,)
Row 5  (3.14,3.14,3.14,3.14,3.14,3.14,3.14,3.14,3.14,3.14,)
Row 6  (3.14,3.14,3.14,3.14,3.14,3.14,3.14,3.14,3.14,3.14,)
Row 7  (3.14,3.14,3.14,3.14,3.14,3.14,3.14,3.14,3.14,3.14,)
Row 8  (3.14,3.14,3.14,3.14,3.14,3.14,3.14,3.14,3.14,3.14,)
Row 9  (3.14,3.14,3.14,3.14,3.14,3.14,3.14,3.14,3.14,3.14,)
Row 10 (3.14,3.14,3.14,3.14,3.14,3.14,3.14,3.14,3.14,3.14,)]
```

6.5   THE VECTOR AND NUMERICMATRIX CLASSES IN DETAIL

These classes are derived from `Array` and `Matrix`, respectively (see Figures 6.1 and 6.2). Thus all the functionality that we have described in the previous section remains valid for these new classes, including the useful print functions in section 6.4.1. Furthermore, we have created constructors for `Vector` and `NumericMatrix` classes as well. So what do these classes have that their base classes do not have? The general answer is that `Vector` and `NumericMatrix` assume that their underlying types are numeric. We thus model these classes as implementations of the corresponding mathematical structures, namely *vector space* and *inner product spaces* (see Ayres, 1965; Bronson, 1989; Varga, 1962).

We have implemented `Vector` and `NumericMatrix` as approximations to a vector space. In some cases we have added functionality to suit our needs. However, we have simplified things a little because we assume that the data types in a vector space are of the same types as the underlying field. This is for convenience only and it satisfies our needs for most applications in financial engineering.

Referring to Figure 6.1 again we see that `Vector` is derived from `Array`. Its definition in C++ is:

```
template <class V, class I=int, class S=FullArray<V> >
class Vector: public Array<V, I, S>
{
private:
  // No member data
};
```

We give the prototypes for some of the mathematical operations in `Vector`. The first is a straight implementation of a vector space; notice that we have applied operator overloading in C++:

```
Vector<V, I, S> operator - () const;
Vector<V, I, S> operator + (const Vector<V, I, S>& v) const;
Vector<V, I, S> operator - (const Vector<V, I, S>& v) const;
```

The second group of functions is useful because it provides functionality for offsetting the values in a vector:

```
Vector<V, I, S> operator + (const V& v) const;
Vector<V, I, S> operator - (const V& v) const;
Vector<V, I, S> operator * (const V& v) const;
```

The first function adds an element to each element in the vector and returns a new vector. The second and third functions are similar except that we apply subtraction and multiplication operators.

Referring to Figure 6.2 again, we see that `NumericMatrix` is derived from `Vector`. Its definition in C++ is:

```
template <class V, class I=int, class S=FullMatrix<V> >
class NumericMatrix: public Matrix<V, I, S>
{
private:
  // No member data
};
```

The constructors in `NumericMatrix` are the same as for `Matrix`. We may also wish to manipulate the rows and columns of matrices and we provide 'set/get' functionality. Notice that we return vectors for selectors but that modifiers accept `Array` instances (and instances of any derived class!):

```
// Selectors
Vector<V, I> Row(I row) const;
Vector<V, I> Column(I column) const;

// Modifiers
void Row(I row, const Array<V, I> val);
void Column(I column, const Array<V, I> val);
```

Since we shall be solving linear systems of equations in later chapters we must provide functionality for multiplying matrices with vectors and with other matrices:

- Multiply a matrix and a vector
- Multiply a (transpose of a) vector and a matrix
- Multiply two matrices.

Of course, we must abide by compatibility rules between matrices and vectors when performing these operations:

```
NumericMatrix<V, I, S> operator * (const NumericMatrix<V, I, S>& m)
    const;

friend Vector<V, I, S> operator * (const NumericMatrix<V, I, S>& m,
    const Vector<V, I, S>& v);

friend Vector<V, I, S> operator * (const Vector<V, I, S>& v, const
    NumericMatrix<V, I, S>& m);
```

Notice that the last two functions are not members of `NumericMatrix` but are non-member friends. This ploy allows us to multiply a matrix by a vector or vice versa.

6.5.1   Vector example

We give some simple examples showing how to create vectors and how to perform some mathematical operations on the vectors.

```
// Create some vectors
Vector<double, int> vec1(10, 1, 2.0); // Start = 1, value 2.0
Vector<double, int> vec2(10, 1, 3.0); // Start = 1, value 3.0

Vector<double, int> vec3 = vec1 + vec2;
Vector<double, int> vec4 = vec1 - vec2;
Vector<double, int> vec5 = vec1 - 3.14;
```

6.5.2   NumericMatrix example

We give an example to show how to use numeric matrices. The code is:

```
int rowstart = 1;
int colstart = 1;
NumericMatrix<double, int> m3(3, 3, rowstart, colstart);
for (int i = m3.MinRowIndex(); i <= m3.MaxRowIndex(); i++)
{
   for (int j = m3.MinColumnIndex(); j <= m3.MaxColumnIndex();
      j++)
   {
     m3(i, j) = 1.0 /(i + j -1.0);
   }
}

print (m3);
```

The output from this code is:

```
MinRowIndex: 1 , MaxRowIndex: 3
MinColumnIndex: 1 , MaxColumnIndex: 3
MAT:[
Row 1 (1,0.5,0.333333,)
Row 2 (0.5,0.333333,0.25,)
Row 3 (0.333333,0.25,0.2,)]
```

6.6   ASSOCIATIVE ARRAYS AND MATRICES

One of the disadvantages of the classes in this chapter is that elements in vectors and matrices must be accessed by integral indices. This is because the STL uses `int` as the index type. In many applications we would like to have strings as subscripts. This feature is seen in the SNOBOL4 language and the AWK language (see Aho *et al.*, 1988). Furthermore, Excel's data structures (ranges, cells and sheets) are essentially associative structures. Thus, it is important to show how to create associative vectors and matrices in C++.

We create a class that encapsulates an `Array` instance but also has a map of key values to the internal integer values. Clients access elements in the array by using the associative index (for example, a string) while the code maps this index to an integral index. The header for this basic class is:

```
template <class V,class AI = string,class I=int,class S=FullArray<V> >
  class AssocArray
{
private:
  map<AI,I> internal_array;      // The list of associative value

public: // N.B. for convenience only
  Array<V, I, S> contents;       // The numeric values

public:
  // Constructors & destructor
  AssocArray(const list<AI>& names, const Array<V, I, S>& source);

  // New overloaded indexing operator for subscripting
  virtual V& operator [] (const AI& index);
  virtual const V& operator [] (const AI& index) const;

  typedef std::map<AI,I>::iterator iterator;
  typedef std::map<AI,I>::const_iterator const_iterator;

  // Iterator functions
  iterator Begin();
  const_iterator Begin() const;
  iterator End();
  const_iterator End() const;
};
```

We see that we create an associative array by giving a list of keys or names and an array. The code for this constructor is:

```
template <class V, class AI, class I, class S>
  AssocArray<V, AI, I, S>::AssocArray(const list<AI>& names,
      const Array<V, I, S>& source)
{
  I curr = source.MinIndex();
  list<AI>::const_iterator it;
  for (it = names.begin(); it != names.end(); it++)
  {
    internal_array.insert(pair<AI,I>(*it, curr));
    curr++;
  }
  contents = source;
}
```

We also see that there is functionality for navigating in the associative array and we have the facility for accessing elements by the '[]' operator.

We have created a useful function to print associative arrays. Here we see that a map consists essentially of pairs of elements:

```
void print (const AssocArray<double, string>& assArr)
{
  // Iterating in the map
  AssocArray<double, string>::const_iterator i = assArr.Begin();
```

```
    while (i != assArr.End())
    {
      cout << "Element pair [" << (*i).first << "," <<
        (*i).second << "]\n";
      i++;
    }
}
```

The following is a test program:

```
int main()
{
  list<string> names;
  names.push_back("A1");
  names.push_back("A2");
  names.push_back("A3");
  names.push_back("A4");

  Array<double> myArr(4);
  myArr[1] = 2.0;
  myArr[2] = 3.0;
  myArr[3] = 4.0;
  myArr[4] = 5.0;

  AssocArray<double, string> myAssocArray(names, myArr);

  // Iterating in the map
  print(myAssocArray);
  print(myAssocArray.contents);

  myAssocArray["A4"] = 99.99;

  print(myAssocArray.contents);

  return 1;
}
```

The output from the program is:

```
Element pair [A1,1]
Element pair [A2,2]
Element pair [A3,3]
Element pair [A4,4]

MinIndex: 1 , MaxIndex: 4
ARR:[2,3,4,5,]
MinIndex: 1 , MaxIndex: 4
ARR:[2,3,4,99.99,]
```

We see that it is possible to create sophisticated data structures using STL. In this case we created an associative array class that essentially wraps or decorates a 'normal' array class (see Gamma *et al.*, 1995, for a discussion of the *Decorator* pattern). We see many applications of this class for financial engineering, for example decision tables and Excel, to mention just two.

6.7 CONCLUSIONS AND SUMMARY

We have presented the classes `Array` and `Matrix` in this chapter. These classes and their specialisations will play a vital role in later chapters and applications. In particular, we use them in numerical linear algebra and when we solve linear systems of equations. They are tuned to a numerical analysis world and this is why we have created them. Of course, there are many other matrix libraries (many of which are certainly more complete and possibly more efficient) but our classes are good enough for future work. At this stage, we are of the opinion that *less is more*.

Arrays and Matrix Properties

7.1 INTRODUCTION AND OBJECTIVES

In Chapter 6 we introduced the classes `Array`, `Matrix`, `Vector` and `NumericMa-trix`. In that chapter we concentrated on how to create instances of these classes using various constructors and how to access the elements in these instances after they have been created. Furthermore, we have discussed how to print arrays and matrices using the standard output stream in C++.

In this chapter we extend the functionality of arrays and matrices. In particular, we create new functions that implement vector and matrix operations. These functions will be needed in later chapters. To this end, we introduce reusable functions and classes that can be applied over and over again in your applications. In this sense we have created a so-called BLAS (Basic Linear Algebra Subprograms) in much the same way as can be found in commercial Fortran and C/C++ libraries.

7.2 AN OVERVIEW OF THE FUNCTIONALITY

When working in numerical analysis we often need to work with arrays, vectors, matrices and other containers. There are many areas of numerical analysis where we need to perform operations on these containers. Some major areas are:

- Numerical linear algebra (solution of matrix equations, eigenvalue analysis)
- Using vectors and matrices in statistics
- Inequality relationships in operations research
- Curve fitting and extrapolation

... and many more.

In this chapter we discuss a set of functions that serve as useful building blocks for the above applications. In particular, we shall use them in later chapters of this book when we propose finite difference schemes for parabolic partial differential equations and the related one-factor and two-factor Black–Scholes equations. To this end, we have created functions that we group into the following categories:

- Sums, averages and means of vectors
- Extremum operations on vectors
- Vector and matrix norms
- Measures of dispersion (in statistics)
- Moments, skewness and kurtosis (in statistics)
- Inequality operations with vectors and matrices ($<$, $<=$, $==$ and so on)
- Some utility functions (for example, printing vectors and matrices with `cout`).

We are unable to deal with all the underlying mathematics of the functions in these categories as this book is, after all, devoted to C++ programming. On the other hand, we feel that we must motivate how we produced our code and where the basic ideas came from. To this end, we give the mathematics for those functions that calculate vector and matrix norms and the mathematics is mapped or transformed to C++ code. The mapping should be as transparent and as easy to understand as possible. To this end, we give a detailed description of the activities in section 7.4.

7.3 SOFTWARE REQUIREMENTS

We must define the efficiency of our software library. They say that beauty is in the eye of the beholder, but we must define the software requirements that our library should satisfy. In general, customers are interested in both functional and non-functional requirements and we, as software developers, should know what these requirements are before we start programming. In this chapter we shall discuss some requirements that our software satisfies and then show how we realise these requirements in C++.

7.3.1 Accuracy

Accuracy is a functional requirement and it states that the software should perform its duties as expected or as agreed. In this case we state that the algorithms that implement vector and matrix operations should be correct and should be correctly programmed in C++. An algorithm (or its implementation) that is incorrect is at best useless and at worst disastrous.

In order to reduce the cognitive gap between mathematical algorithms and C++ code we try to use the same variables and variable names in the code as in the corresponding algorithms.

7.3.2 Efficiency

This is a non-functional requirement that relates to the time and resource behaviour of the software. In general, we are interested in how long it takes to perform a calculation (response time) and how much memory resources are needed to perform that calculation. Most of the algorithms in this chapter navigate sequentially in vectors and matrices; thus, the performance depends on the number of elements in the container. As far as resources are concerned, in some applications we create temporary *workspace containers* to store intermediate results. This trick can improve response time at the expense of some extra memory usage. These days, however, computer memory is not so expensive so it can be a wise choice to sacrifice some computer memory (which is renewable) for the benefit of customer satisfaction.

7.3.3 Reliability

This is a non-functional requirement that refers to properties of the software such as fault-tolerance, the ability of the software to recover from an exception and the maturity of the software in general. The functions in this chapter expect input to certain properties. If the input has the necessary properties then the function can perform its duties. If not, the deal is off as it were and the function *should* throw an exception to the calling code stating what the problem was. In this chapter the following exceptional situations can arise:

- We attempt to divide by zero in some calculation
- We attempt to access an array/vector element outside its legal bounds
- Two vectors have mutually incompatible sizes
- In general, two containers cannot work together because of some mathematical contradiction.

We shall see in a later section how these exceptions are designed and implemented in C++ and how they are handled if a run-time error does occur.

7.3.4 Understandability

Understandability is a non-functional requirement that has to do with how easy it is to understand the C++ code and how easily the functions can be used in other applications. In fact, the current requirement is one of a triad in the Usability ISO 9126 (Kitchenham and Pfleeger, 1996) characteristic:

- *Understandability*: How easy is it to understand the code at a 'user' level? (level 1)
- *Learnability*: How easy is it to learn the major workflow in the software and to use it as a client? (level 2)
- *Operability*: How easy is it to learn the internals of the software, extend and customise it and apply it to your own applications? (level 3)

In this book we hope to get the reader up to level 3 by giving enough examples of use so that he or she can apply the functions in various financial engineering applications.

7.4 THE CORE PROCESSES

We now describe how we designed and implemented the C++ code for the function categories in section 7.2. To this end, we focus on the category of functions that calculate the norms of vectors and matrices. A norm is a precise mathematical concept (see Bronson, 1989) and we define it now in order to motivate the code. First, a *semi-norm* for vector x is a mapping $x \rightarrow p(x)$ from the space of vectors to the real line such that

$$(1) \ p(x) \geq 0$$

$$(2) \ p(\lambda x) = |\lambda| p(x), \ \lambda \ \text{real number} \qquad (7.1)$$

$$(3) \ p(x + y) \leq p(x) + p(y)$$

for any vectors x and y. If, in addition, the following holds:

$$(4) \ p(x) = 0 \Leftrightarrow x = 0 \qquad (7.2)$$

then we say that p is a *norm*.

We now turn our attention to defining specific norms for vectors and matrices, starting with vectors. We define the following four vector norms:

$$\text{Euclidean } (l_2) \text{ norm:} \quad \|\mathbf{x}\|_2 = \left(\sum_{j=1}^{n} x_j^2 \right)^{\frac{1}{2}}$$

$$l_1 \text{ norm:} \quad \|\mathbf{x}\|_1 = \sum_{j=1}^{n} |x_j| \tag{7.3}$$

$$l_\infty \text{ norm:} \quad \|\mathbf{x}\|_\infty = \max_{1 \le j \le n} |x_j|$$

$$l_p \text{ norm:} \quad \|\mathbf{x}\|_p = \left(\sum_{j=1}^{n} |x_j|^p \right)^{\frac{1}{p}}$$

The next challenge is to map this mathematical notation to C++ code. We wish to keep everything generic so we need two generic underlying types:

V: the data type of the elements of the vector
I: the index set in the vector.

Thus, each function in the 'Norm' category accepts a vector as input and produces a value (the norm itself) as output. The function prototypes for the formulae in (7.3) now become:

```
template <class V, class I>
  V innerProduct(const Vector<V,I>& x, const Vector<V,I>& y);
template <class V, class I>
  V l1Norm(const Vector<V,I>& x);
template <class V, class I>
  V l2Norm(const Vector<V,I>& x);
template <class V, class I>
  V lpNorm(const Vector<V,I>& x, const I& p);
template <class V, class I>
  V lInfinityNorm(const Vector<V,I>& x);
```

These are just normal C/C++ procedural functions that accept instances of class Vector as argument. We have not tried to wrap them in some static class or attempted to force them into an object-oriented framework.

The code for the inner product of two vectors is:

```
template <class V, class I>
  V innerProduct(const Vector<V,I>& x, const Vector<V,I>& y)
{
    // PREC: x and y have same size
    V ans = V(0.0);
    for (I j = x.MinIndex(); j <= x.MaxIndex(); j++)
    {
      ans += x[j] * y[j];
    }
    return ans / vector.Size();
}
```

Notice how we have applied the Information Hiding principle; the function for the inner product of two vectors does not know about the internal structure or indexing scheme used. All it needs to know is how to access the elements of the vectors.

For completeness, we now give the full source code for the function for the l_2 norm. We have increased the level of reusability because the value of the l_2 norm is the square root of the sum of squares of the elements and we have created a dedicated function for the latter operation. This function can then be used by many other client functions.

```
template <class V, class I> V sumSquares(const Vector<V,I>& x)
{
    V ans = V(0.0);
    for (I j = x.MinIndex(); j <= x.MaxIndex(); j++)
    {
      ans += (x[j] * x[j]);
    }
    return ans;
}
```

We now use this function as a reusable module in the following function:

```
template <class V, class I> V l2Norm(const Vector<V,I>& x)
{
  return sqrt(sumSquares(x));
}
```

We have also developed many functions that calculate norms of the difference of two vectors. To take one example:

```
template <class V, class I> V l2Norm(const Vector<V,I>& vectorA, const
    Vector<V,I>& vectorB)
{
  Vector vecDiff = vectorA - vectorB;
  return l2Norm(vecDiff);
}
```

It should be obvious that this code is relatively easy to understand and to debug. In fact, we have built the software up in a layered fashion. Software at the higher levels use tested and correct software at the lower layers.

We now turn our attention to matrix norms:

$$L_1 \text{ norm:} \quad \|A\|_1 = \max_{j=1,...,n} \left(\sum_{i=1}^{n} |a_{ij}| \right) \quad \text{(largest column sum)}$$

$$(7.4)$$

$$L_\infty \text{ norm:} \quad \|A\|_\infty = \max_{i=1,...,n} \left(\sum_{j=1}^{n} |a_{ij}| \right) \quad \text{(largest row sum)}$$

The function prototypes for the corresponding implementation are:

```
  template <class V, class I>
    V L1Norm(const NumericMatrix<V,I>& matrix);
  template <class V, class I>
    V FrobeniusNorm(const NumericMatrix<V,I>& matrix);
```

```
template <class V, class I>
  V LInfinity1Norm(const NumericMatrix<V,I>& matrix);
```

and the source code for the Frobenius (L2) norm is:

```
template <class V, class I>
  V FrobeniusNorm(const NumericMatrix<V,I>& matrix)
{
  V ans = V(0.0);
  for (I i=matrix.MinRowIndex();i<=matrix.MaxRowIndex(); i++)
  {
    for (I j=matrix.MinColIndex(); j<=matrix.MaxColIndex(); j++)
    {
      tmp = matrix(i, j);
      ans += tmp * tmp;
    }
  }
  return sqrt(ans);
}
```

There are lots more C++ code on the CD that shows how the other functions have been implemented.

7.4.1 Interactions between matrices and vectors

We conclude this section with a discussion of a number of formulae and functions that involve both matrices and vectors as input. In this particular case we look at two specific functions. These have applications in numerical linear algebra and eigenvalue analysis:

$$\text{Quadratic form:} \qquad \sum_{i=1}^{n}\sum_{j=1}^{n} a_{ij}x_i x_j$$

$$\text{Rayleigh quotient:} \qquad R(x) = (Ax, x)/(x, x) \qquad (7.5)$$

$$L_2 \text{ norm (Frobenius)}: \quad \|A\|_{\mathrm{F}} = \left(\sum_{i=1}^{n}\sum_{j=1}^{n} |a_{ij}|^2\right)^{\frac{1}{2}}$$

The formula for the quadratic form is often used to test the definiteness of a matrix (in particular, if a matrix has an inverse) and the Rayleigh quotient gives an indication of the size of the eigenvalues of a matrix (see Bronson, 1989).

The corresponding code for these two functions is:

```
template <class V, class I>
  V quadraticForm(const NumericMatrix<V,I>& matrix, const
  Vector<V,I>& x)
{
  V ans = V(0.0);
  for (I i=matrix.MinRowIndex();i<=matrix.MaxRowIndex(); i++)
  {
    for (I j=matrix.MinColIndex();j<=matrix.MaxColIndex(); j++)
    {
      ans += matrix(i,j) * x[i] * x[j];
```

```
    }
  }
  return sqrt(ans);
}
template <class V, class I>
  V RayleighQuotient(const NumericMatrix<V,I>& A, const
  Vector<V,I>& x)
{
  // PREC: Compatibility, number of cols of A == number of rows of x
  // PREC: inner product does not evaluate to 0.0
  Vector y = A * x;
  return innerProduct(y, x) / innerProduct (x,x);
}
```

Notice that we have not carried out any range checking or compatibility checks in this code. It is the responsibility of the client code (in this case) to ensure that the number of columns in a matrix is the same as the number of rows in a vector if we wish to multiply them. We shall see in a later section how this kind of problem can be identified and resolved by using the *exception handling* mechanism in C++.

7.4.2 Some examples

We give some code to show how to use the functions in the 'Norm' category. For testing purposes we have created a function

```
template <class V, class I>
  SimplePropertySet<string, double> allNorms(const Vector<V,I>& x);
```

This is a handy function because you can call it and it calculates all relevant properties of a vector and places the results in a property set. The source code for this function is:

```
template <class V, class I> SimplePropertySet<string, double>
allNorms(const Vector<V,I>& x)
{
  SimplePropertySet<string, double> result; // Empty list
  result.add(Property<string, V> ("l1", l1Norm(x)));
  result.add(Property<string, V> ("l2", l2Norm(x)));
  result.add(Property<string, V> ("linf", lInfinityNorm(x)));

  return result;
}
```

We now give

```
  Vector<double, int> myVector2(4);   // Length 4, start index == 1
  myVector2[1] = 1.0;
  myVector2[2] = -10.0;
  myVector2[3] = 9.0;
  myVector2[4] = 2.0;
  ans = allNorms(myVector2);
  print(ans);
```

The output from this piece of code is:

```
l1: 22
l2: 13.6382
linf: 10
```

7.5   OTHER FUNCTION CATEGORIES

We give a global overview of the functionality in the other categories. The function prototypes are easy to understand and the structure of the source code is similar to that in section 7.4. The functions have to do with statistics (see Spiegel, 1992) and you can use them as reusable models in financial engineering and risk management applications.

7.5.1   Measures of central tendency

These are functions that we need in statistics and they are concerned mainly with various kinds of averages of vectors. An average is a value that is typical, or representative of a set of data. Since such typical values tend to lie centrally within a set of data arranged according to magnitude, averages are also called *measures of central tendency*.

Sum $$\sum_{j=1}^{n} x_j$$

Sum of reciprocals $$\sum_{j=1}^{n} (1/x_j)$$

Sum of squares $$\sum_{j=1}^{n} x_j^2$$

(Arithmetic) mean $$\overline{X} = \sum_{j=1}^{n} (x_j/n)$$

Weighted arithmetic mean $$\sum_{j=1}^{n} w_j x_j \bigg/ \sum_{j=1}^{n} w_j \qquad (7.6)$$

Geometric mean $$\sqrt[n]{x_1 x_2 \dots x_n} = \sqrt[n]{\prod_{j=1}^{n} x_j}$$

Harmonic mean $$n \bigg/ \left(\sum_{j=1}^{n} (1/x_j) \right)$$

Quadratic (mean) (root mean square) $$\sqrt{\sum_{j=1}^{n} (x_j^2/n)}$$

The function prototypes are:

```
template <class V, class I>
  V mean(const Vector<V,I>& x);
template <class V, class I>
  V weightedArithMean(const Vector<V,I>& x, const Vector<V,I>& w);
template <class V, class I>
  V geometricMean(const Vector<V,I>& x);
template <class V, class I>
  V harmonicMean(const Vector<V,I>& x);
template <class V, class I>
  V quadraticMean(const Vector<V,I>& x);
```

7.5.2 Measures of dispersion

The degree to which numerical data tend to spread about an average value is called the *dispersion* or *variation* of the data. There are several measures of this dispersion and we shall discuss most of them in this section. These functions describe deviations from the mean of a vector quantity.

$$\text{Mean (average) deviation} \qquad \frac{\displaystyle\sum_{j=1}^{n} |x_j - \overline{X}|}{n}$$

$$\text{Standard deviation} \qquad s = \sqrt{\frac{\displaystyle\sum_{j=1}^{n} (x_j - \overline{X})^2}{n}} \tag{7.7}$$

$$\text{Variance} \qquad \frac{\displaystyle\sum_{j=1}^{n} (x_j - \overline{X})^2}{n}$$

The function prototypes are:

```
template <class V, class I>
  V deviationFromMean(const Vector<V,I>& x);
template <class V, class I>
  V standardDeviation(const Vector<V,I>& x);
template <class V, class I>
  V variance(const Vector<V,I>& x);
template <class V, class I>
  SimplePropertySet<string, double> allDispersions(const Vector<V,I>& x);
```

7.5.3 Moments, skewness, kurtosis

These are useful functions that indicate the 'centre' of the distribution of some random variable. An example is the mean() function described above. The current functions are generalisations of this concept.

$$r\text{th moment} \qquad \left(\sum_{j=1}^{n} x_j^r \right) \Big/ n$$

$$r\text{th moment with respect to origin } A \qquad \left(\sum_{j=1}^{n} (x_j - A)^r \right) \Big/ n$$

$$r\text{th moment with frequencies and origin } A \qquad m_r = \left(\sum_{j=1}^{n} f_j(x_j - A)^r \right) \Big/ n$$

Skewness   (mean-mode)/standard derivation

Moment coefficient of kurtosis m_4/S^2 (7.8)

The function prototypes are:

```
template <class V, class I>
  V rthMoment(const Vector<V,I>& x, const I& r);
template <class V, class I>
  V rthMomentMean(const Vector<V,I>& x, const I& r);
template <class V, class I>
  V rthMoment(const Vector<V,I>& x, const I& r, const V& A);
template <class V, class I>
  V rthMoment(const Vector<V,I>& x, const Vector<V,I>& freq, const
      I& r, const V& A);
template <class V, class I>
  V median(const Vector<V,I>& x);
template <class V, class I>
  V mode(const Vector<V,I>& x);
template <class V, class I>
  V skewness(const Vector<V,I>& x);
template <class V, class I>
  V momentCoeffKurtosis(const Vector<V,I>& x);
```

For more information on these and other formulae, see Spiegel (1992).

7.5.4 Inequalities

We have included a number of functions that are useful in optimisation theory. For example, we can compare two vectors v1 and v2 in order to determine if all the elements in v1 are greater than all the elements in v2. Some function prototypes are:

```
template <class V, class I>
  bool positive(const Vector<V,I>& x);
template <class V, class I>
  bool negative(const Vector<V,I>& x);
template <class V, class I>
  bool positive(const NumericMatrix<V,I>& x);
```

A subset of the functionality is:

```
template <class V, class I>
  bool operator < (const Vector<V,I>& v1, const Vector<V,I>& v2);
template <class V, class I>
  bool operator <= (const Vector<V,I>& v1, const Vector<V,I>& v2);
```

For further information, please see the source code on the CD.

7.6 USING THE FUNCTIONS

We now give two examples on how to use the library functions. The examples are not very difficult but our aim is to show that use of these functions leads to reliable, understandable and maintainable code.

7.6.1   Calculating historical volatility

We give a short overview of a technique for calculating the historical volatility of stock. In order to estimate the volatility of the price of stock empirically we can observe the stock price at fixed intervals of time, for example every day (see Hull, 2000). Let

$$n + 1 = \text{Number of observations}$$

$$S_j = \text{Stock price of end of } j\text{th interval}, \quad j = 0, \ldots, n \tag{7.9a}$$

$$\tau = \text{Length of time interval in years}$$

Let

$$u_j = \ln(S_j/S_{j-1}), \quad j = 1, \ldots, n \tag{7.9b}$$

The standard deviation of the u values is given by

$$s = \sqrt{\frac{1}{n-1} \sum_{j=1}^{n} u_j^2 - \frac{1}{n(n-1)} \left(\sum_{j=1}^{n} u_j \right)^2} \tag{7.9c}$$

In Hull (2000) it is shown that

$$\sigma = s^* = \frac{s}{\sqrt{\tau}} \tag{7.9d}$$

We now have an estimate for the volatility.

7.6.2   Variance of return of a portfolio

Portfolio theory describes how investors allocate their funds between various assets in order to construct a basket ('portfolio') of assets that are held simultaneously. Let us assume that we have a portfolio of n assets. Let us define the following notation:

$$x = \text{Weights for assets}$$

$$\sigma_{ii} = \text{Variance for } i\text{th asset} \tag{7.10}$$

$$\sigma_{ij} = \text{Covariance of expected returns on assets } i \text{ and } j$$

An important problem in portfolio theory is calculating the variance of a portfolio:

$$\text{var}(\tau_p) = \sum_{j=1}^{n} x_j^2 \sigma_{jj} + \sum_{i=1}^{n} \sum_{j=1}^{n} \sigma_{ij} a_{ij} x_i x_j \tag{7.11}$$

7.7   AN INTRODUCTION TO EXCEPTION HANDLING

We now turn our attention to the things that can go wrong when clients call functions. In order to reduce the scope, let us re-examine the source code for one of the functions:

```
template <class V, class I>
V sumReciprocals(const Vector<V,I>& x)
```

```
{ // Sum of reciprocals
    V ans = V(0.0);
    for (I j = x.MinIndex(); j <= x.MaxIndex(); j++)
    {
      ans += 1.0/x[j];
    }
    return ans;
}
```

We see that if any one of the elements in the vector is zero we shall get a run-time error and your program will crash. This is not what the doctor ordered! To circumvent this problem we use the exception handling mechanism in C++ which provides the client with software with a 'net', as it were, that will save the client if he or she falls off the trampoline. We now discuss the fine details of this mechanism.

7.7.1 Try, throw and catch: A bit like tennis

In order to understand exception handling we must discuss the concept of a *contract* between *client code* (the calling function) and the *server code* (the function being called). Each party has its rights and responsibilities. The server states what the conditions and rules are and the client should abide by these rules. If not, then there is no guarantee that the results are correct (or indeed that a result is returned at all). So, the client defines a block of code that captures any run-time errors, should they occur. The client calls a server function in this block. If the server discovers an error it will throw a newly created exception object back to the client.

In general, the steps at run-time are:

1. Client calls a server function in a *try block*.
2. Server function checks if contract has been honoured.
3. If contract has been honoured, the server's *postconditions* are executed and control is returned to the client.
4. If the contract has not been honoured, the server code throws exception object back to the client which then catches it in its *catch block*.

The main challenges for the developer are:

- Determining what is and is not an exception.
- Deciding where to place the *precondition* code that checks for a break of contract in the server.
- Determining the data that should be placed in the exception object to help the client to figure out what he or she did wrong.

In general, we design exception classes so that they contain enough data to help the client code in order to make decisions on what to do if an exception does occur at run-time. Essential information includes the following:

- The type of exception thrown (e.g. `DivideByZero`, `InvalidRange`).
- The message text in the exception (this can be displayed on the client screen).
- The source of the exception (the server function in which the exception occurred).

It is important to realise that software should be as reliable as possible and steps should be taken to ensure that our code can recover from incorrect input or calculations.

7.8   CONCLUSIONS AND SUMMARY

We have given an overview of some added-value functionality for vectors and matrices. The functionality has been implemented as functions that take vectors and matrices as input arguments. Included is functionality for statistics, norms, inequalities, extremum properties and some utility properties (for example, printing vectors and matrices using the standard stream library).

The functions are in fact modules that can be used in larger examples and applications. The advantage of this function library is that you do not have to program it yourself.

Numerical Linear Algebra

8.1 INTRODUCTION AND OBJECTIVES

In this important chapter we introduce a number of methods that allow us to solve linear systems of equations. This particular area of numerical analysis is called Numerical Linear Algebra. It is a vast subject on which many books have been written. We are concerned with an important subset, namely solving a matrix system by direct techniques. By 'direct', we mean that the solution of a linear system of equations can be found in a finite, predetermined number of steps. Furthermore, we introduce several matrix solvers that are of relevance to financial engineering and option pricing (see, for example, Wilmott, 1998). For example, we shall use finite difference methods to discretise the one-factor Black–Scholes equation and the resulting scheme is cast as a matrix system that we solve at each time step. Furthermore, multi-factor models will also be solved as a sequence of simpler equations which, in their turn, are solved by matrix solvers.

The structure of this chapter is as follows: in section 8.2 we give an introduction to numerical linear algebra and the type of problems we are trying to solve. It may be skipped if the reader has had some exposure to the subject. We discuss two competing strategies for solving matrix systems in this book: first, direct methods produce the solution to the problem in a finite number of arithmetic steps; second, iterative methods start with an arbitrary initial approximation and an iterative scheme is devised that hopefully converges to the exact solution. In this latter case we need to define a so-called stopping criterion that indicates that the current solution is close enough to the exact solution. Having completed with the motivation in section 8.3 we introduce specific direct methods (iterative methods are discussed in further detail in Chapter 14). To this end, we introduce *LU* decomposition as a means of breaking up a matrix problem into two simpler sub-problems. This is the subject of section 8.3. An important special case is when the matrix is tridiagonal, and here we give two efficient solvers.

Section 8.4 deals with an extension of *LU* decomposition for block triangular matrices. These structures are found when finite difference methods are applied to systems of partial differential equations – for example, if we reduce the Black–Scholes equation to a first-order system that we then approximate using the Keller box scheme (see Keller, 1971). Finally, section 8.5 discusses some necessary and sufficient conditions for a matrix system to have a unique solution. In particular, we dwell on certain intrinsic properties of matrices that ensure this uniqueness.

Matrix solvers and their applications to finance are discussed in Wilmott (1998) and Tavella and Randall (2000). You should be able to incorporate the matrix solvers in your C++ applications without too much hassle. You use them as 'black boxes'.

8.2 AN INTRODUCTION TO NUMERICAL LINEAR ALGEBRA

We now give a very general overview of Numerical Linear Algebra. There is a *vast* literature on this subject, which is one of the cornerstones of numerical analysis. In fact, many problems can be reduced to a system of linear equations.

Our interest in this chapter is focused on the following problem: Given a vector F of length n and a *square matrix* A (that is, one with n rows and n columns), find the unique vector U that satisfies the linear system:

$$AU = F \tag{8.1}$$

In general, we say that U is the solution of equation (8.1) and write it formally as

$$U = A^{-1}F \tag{8.2}$$

In general, we do not calculate the inverse of A directly because this is too cumbersome. Instead we use so-called matrix solvers to compute the solution U. There are more efficient and less resource-intensive techniques than using a sledgehammer algorithm to invert the matrix A, but we shall discuss this in more detail in later sections.

Writing an equation in the form of (8.1) is not difficult in general (although, as we shall see in later chapters, working out the equations involves a lot of basic and somewhat tedious arithmetic) but there are a number of issues to be addressed:

- Does (8.1) have a solution in the first place?
- Can we find sufficient conditions on matrix A to produce a solution to (8.1)?
- How sensitive is the solution U to small perturbations in the matrix A?
- What are the different kinds of structures that A might have?
- Can we find efficient, reliable and accurate matrix solvers for (8.1)?

We shall discuss these topics in the course of this chapter, but first let us draw a distinction between the zero and non-zero elements of the matrix A. If we know that some elements of A are zero, and if the distribution of zeros follows a recognisable pattern, then we might hope to develop matrix solvers that take these structures into account. Furthermore, we do not need to store the zero elements in memory, thus adding to good resource utilisation.

We are exposed to various kinds of matrix structures in numerical analysis. Related to this issue is how to store the matrices in memory, how to access the matrix elements (read and write) and how to solve systems of equations in which these matrices play the role of the matrix A in equation (8.1). Some possible matrix structures are:

- Full matrix
- Sparse matrix
- Patterned matrix.

In a *full matrix*, all the elements must be stored in memory. Such matrices are common in some applications (for example, solving integral equations) but they are not so common in the finite difference method. In general, a full matrix with n rows and m columns will require nm memory locations. A *sparse matrix* is one in which the majority of elements has the value zero. This implies that we only have to store a small percentage of the elements in memory. One of the challenges associated with the choice of data structure is the problem of accessing the non-zero elements in the matrix. Sparse matrices occur when modelling multidimensional problems using finite differences or the Finite Element Method (FEM) and, again, there is a vast literature on the subject. A *patterned matrix* is one in which the zero and non-zero elements bear a well-defined structural relationship to each other. There are many kinds of patterns in the literature, some of which we have discussed in Part I of this book, and we have presented some examples in Figure 4.1 of this text. In general, a *band matrix* is one whose diagonal element and $2K$ off-diagonal elements are non-zero. An important special case is when $K = 1$; this is the class of *tridiagonal matrices*. Thus, a tridiagonal matrix is one with three non-zero diagonal elements. These matrices are very important when we come to the chapters on finite differences methods for ordinary and partial differential equations when we employ three-point difference schemes to discretise the space variable. A more general kind of tridiagonal matrix is the so-called block *tridiagonal matrix* (see Isaacson, 1966). This type of matrix is needed when we approximate *systems* of partial differential equations by finite differences (for example, chooser options, see Wilmott, 1998) or when we reduce a second-order parabolic partial differential equation to a first-order system in order to get good approximation to the solution and its first derivative.

A *lower triangular* matrix is one whose non-zero elements are all on or below the main diagonal while an *upper triangular* matrix is one whose non-zero elements are all on or above the main diagonal.

We now discuss two major categories of methods for solving linear systems of the form (8.1).

8.2.1 Direct methods

By a direct method for solving a system of linear equations (8.1), we mean a method that gives the exact solution U after a certain finite number of steps. We mention some common methods:

- Gaussian elimination for full matrices
- *LU* decomposition techniques
- Crout's method

... and many more. In this book we are interested in solving systems (8.1) where the matrix A is tridiagonal. We propose two schemes, one of which is a direct specialisation of *LU* decomposition.

8.2.2 Iterative methods

An iterative scheme starts from a first approximation that is then successively improved until a sufficiently accurate solution is obtained (Varga, 1962; Dahlquist, 1974). The big question is: Does the algorithm implementing the iterative scheme converge, how efficient is the algorithm and how many iterations are needed before the desired accuracy is achieved? We shall devote some attention to these issues in Chapter 14, where we discuss:

- The Jacobi method
- The Gauss–Seidel method
- Successive Overrelaxation (SOR)
- The Conjugate Gradient method
- The Projected SOR method and its relationship with American option pricing.

In general, iterative methods are suitable for sparse matrix systems. We mention them in this chapter as a resource for future work and because we need to understand the theory underlying the Projected SOR method (Cryer, 1979; Wilmott, 1993) that is used when we discretise the Black–Scholes equation for American options. In this case we get a system of matrix inequalities having the general form:

$$(U - c) \cdot (AU - b) = 0 \tag{8.3}$$

where $AU \geq b$, $U \geq c$, c is a vector and the dot '.' denotes the inner product of two vectors.

8.3 TRIDIAGONAL SYSTEMS

We discuss two direct methods for solving systems of the form (8.1) in which the matrix A is tridiagonal. This is a very important case in practice because when we apply three-point difference schemes to the one-factor Black–Scholes equation we get a system of the form (8.1) that must be solved at each time level. Furthermore, we shall need to solve tridiagonal systems when we discuss Alternating Direction Implicit (ADI) and splitting methods for two-factor and multi-factor Black–Scholes equations (see Thomas, 1998).

8.3.1 *LU* decomposition

This is a technique to decompose a matrix into the product of two simpler matrices (see Keller, 1968). *LU* decomposition can be applied to general full matrices (see Dahlquist, 1974) but this is too general for our needs at the moment. Our focus is on tridiagonal matrices and to this end we write A as the product of a lower triangular matrix L and an upper triangular matrix U (we use a slight change of notation when compared with earlier sections; in this section U is a matrix when u is the solution of the original system $Au = r$)

$$A = LU$$

Then the matrix problem $Au = r$ can be decomposed into (hopefully) two simpler sub-problems

$$Lz = r \quad \text{and} \quad Uu = z$$

where z is some intermediate vector having the same size as the final solution u. To achieve this end, we must first of all find the coefficients of the matrices L and U and second we must also devise the algorithms for solving $Lz = r$ and $Uu = z$.

We assume a structure for the matrices L and U as follows:

$$L = \begin{pmatrix} \beta_1 & & & \\ a_2 & \ddots & 0 & \\ & \ddots & \ddots & \\ 0 & & \ddots & \ddots \\ & & & a_J & \beta_J \end{pmatrix} \tag{8.4}$$

$$U = \begin{pmatrix} 1 & \gamma_1 & & 0 \\ & \ddots & \ddots & \\ & & \ddots & \gamma_{J-1} \\ 0 & & & 1 \end{pmatrix} \tag{8.5}$$

We see that L is lower triangular and U is upper triangular and some simple (if sometimes tricky/tedious) arithmetic shows that

$$\beta_1 = b_1, \qquad \gamma_1 = c_1/\beta_1$$
$$\beta_j = b_j - a_j \quad \gamma_{j-1}, j = 2, 3, \ldots, J \qquad (8.6)$$
$$\gamma_j = c_j/\beta_j, \quad j = 2, 3, \ldots, J - 1$$

You can convince yourself that these results are true by working out the equality $A = LU$. Incidentally, designing and implementing algorithms involving matrices (and even finite difference schemes) can be difficult because we have to worry about things like start and end index values of vectors when working with discrete systems. These problems demand that you work in a precise manner.

The matrix solver is a combination of two simpler problems:

$$Lz = r \qquad (8.7)$$

and

$$Uu = z \qquad (8.8)$$

Simple arithmetic shows how to calculate the vector z:

$$\beta_1 z_1 = r_1 \Longrightarrow z_1 = r_1/\beta_1$$
$$a_j z_{j-1} + \beta_j z_j = r_j \Longrightarrow z_j = \beta_j^{-1}(r_j - a_j z_{j-1}), \quad j = 2, \ldots, J \qquad (8.9)$$

This is called the *forward sweep*. The *backward sweep* for $Uu = r$ is given by the algorithm

$$u_J = z_J$$
$$1.u_j + \gamma_j u_{j+1} = z_j \Longrightarrow u_j = z_j - \gamma_j u_{j+1}, \quad j = J - 1, \ldots, 2, 1 \qquad (8.10)$$

And now C++ for LU decomposition

```
template <class V, class I> class LUTridiagonalSolver
{ // Solve tridiagonal matrix equation

private:

    // Defining arrays (input)
    Vector<V,I> a;      // The lower-diagonal array [2..J]
    Vector<V,I> b;      // The diagonal array [1..J] "baseline array"
    Vector<V,I> c;      // The upper-diagonal array [1..J-1]
    Vector<V,I> r;      // Right-hand side of equation Au = r [1..J]

    // Work arrays
    // Coefficients of Lower and Upper matrices: A = LU
    Vector<V,I> beta;        // Range [1..J]
    Vector<V,I> gamma;       // Range [2..J-1]
    // Solutions of temporary and final problems
    Vector<V,I> z;           // Range [1..J]
    Vector<V,I> u;           // Range [1..J]

    I J;  // Largest index
    void calculateBetaGamma();        // Calculate beta and gamma
    void calculateZU();               // Calculate z and u

public: (partial)
```

```cpp
  // other stuff
  LUTridiagonalSolver(const Vector<V,I>& lower_A,
    const Vector<V,I>& diagonal_B, const Vector<V,I>& upper_C,
    const Vector<V,I>& rhs_R);

  // Integrity checks
  bool validIndices() const;      // Indices and size bound OK?
  bool diagonallyDominant() const;

  // Calculate the (final) solution to Au = r
  Vector<V,I> solve();
};
template <class V, class I> void
LUTridiagonalSolver<V,I>::calculateBetaGamma()
{ // Calculate beta and gamma

  // Constructor derived from Array (size, startIndex [,value])
  beta = Vector<V,I> (J, 1);
  gamma = Vector<V,I> (J - 1, 1);

  beta[1] = b[1];
  gamma[1] = c[1] / beta[1];

  for (I j = 2; j <= J - 1; j++)
  {
    beta[j] = b[j] - (a[j] * gamma[j-1]);
    gamma[j] = c[j]/beta[j];
  }
  beta[J] = b[J] - (a[J] * gamma[J-1]);
}

template <class V, class I> void
LUTridiagonalSolver<V,I>::calculateZU()
{ // Calculate z and u

  z = Vector<V,I> (J, 1);
  u = Vector<V,I> (J, 1);

  // Forward direction
  z[1] = r[1] / beta[1];

  for (I j = 2; j <= J; j++)
  {
    z[j] = (r[j] - (a[j]*z[j-1]) ) / beta[j];
  }

  // Backward direction
  u[J] = z[J];

  for (I i = J - 1; i >= 1; i--)
  {
    u[i] = z[i] - (gamma[i]*u[i+1]);
  }
}

template <class V, class I> Vector<V,I>
LUTridiagonalSolver<V,I>::solve()
{
  calculateBetaGamma();            // Calculate beta and gamma
  calculateZU();                   // Calculate z and u

  return u;
}
```

Examples

```
size_t J = 10;
// First test case, trivial solution == 1 (the sanity check)
// Constructors with size, start index, value (diagonals)
Vector<double, int> a(J-1,2,0.0);    // Size J -1, start index 2
Vector<double, int> b(J,1 ,1.0);
Vector<double, int> c(J-1, 1, 0.0);
Vector<double, int> r(J, 1, 1.0);    // Right-hand side
LUTridiagonalSolver<double, int> mySolver(a, b, c, r);
Vector<double, int> result = mySolver.solve();
cout << "Solution for LU:\n"; print(result);

// Matrix for boundary value problem u" + u = 0,u(0) = 0,u(1) = 1
double h =   1.0 / double(J);
Vector<double, int> A(J-1,2,1.0);    // Size J -1, start index == 2
Vector<double, int> B(J,1,-2.0 + (h*h));
Vector<double, int> C(J-1,1,1.0);

Vector<double, int> R(J, 1, 0.0);    // Right-hand side
R[R.MaxIndex()] = - 1.0;

LUTridiagonalSolver<double, int> secondSolver(A, B, C, R);
Vector<double, int> Result = secondSolver.solve();
cout << "Solution" << endl;    print(Result);

Vector<double, int> exact(Result);
double d = ::sin(1.0);
double x = h;
for (int i = exact.MinIndex(); i <= exact.MaxIndex(); i++)
{
   exact[i] = ::sin(x) / d;
   x += h;
}
print(exact);

// Norm of difference
cout << "l2 norm of difference: " << l2Norm(Result, exact);
cout << "l1 norm of difference: " << l1Norm(Result, exact);
cout << "linf norm of difference: " << lInfinityNorm(Result, exact);
```

8.3.2   Godunov's Double Sweep method

We shall now discuss a scheme that is used to solve systems of linear equations that originate from finite difference discretisations of two-point value problems with Dirichlet boundary conditions (Godunov, 1987). Note that we shall introduce boundary value problems and their finite difference discretisations in Chapter 13.

We shall now discuss Godunov's scheme, which is typically used for solving linear two-point value problems with Dirichlet boundary condition. Consider the problem

$$\left.\begin{array}{l} a_j u_{j-1} + b_j u_j + c_j u_{j+1} = f_j, \quad 1 \le j \le J-1 \\ u_0 = \varphi, \qquad u_J = \psi \end{array}\right\} \tag{8.11}$$

where φ and ψ are constants.

All constants, vectors and coefficients in (8.11) are known with the exception of the vector u which must be found. To this end, Godunov employs a recurrence relationship consisting of two sweeps. It requires some arithmetical juggling to convince yourself that the algorithms are correct. We define the solution as follows:

$$u_j = L_{j+\frac{1}{2}} u_{j+1} + K_{j+\frac{1}{2}} \tag{8.12}$$

where

$$
\left.
\begin{aligned}
L_{j+\frac{1}{2}} &= \frac{-c_j}{b_j + a_j L_{j-\frac{1}{2}}} \\
K_{j+\frac{1}{2}} &= \frac{f_j - a_j K_{j-\frac{1}{2}}}{b_j + a_j L_{j-\frac{1}{2}}}
\end{aligned}
\right\} \text{Recurrence Relation}
$$

and the 'initial' values for the vectors K and L are given by

$$u_0 = L_{\frac{1}{2}} u_1 + K_{\frac{1}{2}} \implies L_{\frac{1}{2}} = 0, \qquad K_{\frac{1}{2}} = \varphi$$

$$u_1 = L_{\frac{3}{2}} u_2 + K_{\frac{3}{2}} \implies L_{\frac{3}{2}} = \frac{-c_1}{b_1}, \qquad K_{\frac{3}{2}} = \frac{f - a_1\varphi}{b_1} \tag{8.13}$$

We now show how we coded parts of the algorithms in (8.13) and in (8.14) below:

```
template <class V, class I>
class DoubleSweep
{ // The Balayage method from Godunov

private:
  // The vectors
  Vector<V,I> a, b, c, f;
  V left;       // Left boundary condition
  V right;      // Right boundary condition

public:
  // all the public stuff
  DoubleSweep(const Vector<V,I>& lower,
     const Vector<V,I>& diagonal, const Vector<V,I>& upper,
     const Vector<V,I>& RHS, const V& bc_left,
     const V& bc_right);
};
```

Summarising, the Godunov scheme is given by:

$$u_J = \psi$$

$$u_j = L_{j+\frac{1}{2}} u_{j+1} + K_{j+\frac{1}{2}}, \qquad j = J-1, \dots, 1 \tag{8.14}$$

```
template <class V, class I, class AS>
Vector<V,I> DoubleSweep<V,I>::solve()
{ // Code to actually create the solution to the tridiagonal system

  size_t N =  a.Size() + 1;

  Vector<V,I> U( N + 1, 0 ); // start index = 0; this vector will
                             // 'contain' the result
  U[0] = left;
  U[N] = right;
```

```
Vector<V,I> L(N, 0);      // [0, N-1]
L[0] = 0.0;

for (I   j = L.MinIndex() + 1; j <=  L.MaxIndex(); j++ )
{ // L
  L[j] = ( -c[j] ) / ( b[j] + ( a[j] * L[j-1] ) ) );
}

Vector<V,I> K(N, 0);      // [0, N-1]
K[0] = left;

for (j = K.MinIndex() + 1; j <= K.MaxIndex(); j++ )
{// K
  K[j] = ( f[j] - ( a[j] * K[j-1] ) ) / ( b[j] + ( a[j] * L[j-1] ) ) );
}

for (j = N - 1; j >= 1; j-- )
{ // U
  U[j] = ( L[j] * U[j + 1] ) + K[j];
}

return U;
}
  J = 10;
  h =  1.0 / double(J);
  Vector<double, int> A2(J-1,   1,1.0);      // Size J, start == 1
  Vector<double, int> B2(J-1,   1,-2.0 + (h*h));
  Vector<double, int> C2(J-1,   1,1.0);
  Vector<double, int> R2(J-1, 1, 0.0); // Right-hand side
  R2[R2.MaxIndex()] = - 1.0;

  LHS = 0.0;
  RHS = 1.0;
  DoubleSweep<double, int>
    doubleSweepSolver(A2, B2, C2, R2, LHS, RHS);
  Vector<double, int> ResultDS = doubleSweepSolver.solve();
  print(ResultDS);
```

8.3.3   Designing and implementing tridiagonal schemes

We have tried to keep the cognitive distance between the mathematical notation and the eventual C++ code as small as possible. There are three main reasons for this approach. First, it helps the person writing the code because he or she is forced (in a nice way of course) to work in a disciplined manner by mapping each variable in the mathematical algorithm to a C++ object or class. Second, the resulting code is hopefully easier to understand and to deploy in other applications. (We have learned from experience that writing C++ spaghetti code is almost impossible to understand and to debug.) Finally, code written in this way is usable and easy to maintain.

8.4   BLOCK TRIDIAGONAL SYSTEMS

The *LU* decomposition technique can be applied to block tridiagonal systems (recall the definition from section 8.2. This is needed when we model first-order systems, partial differential equations and integral equations (Keller, 1968, 1971). Consider the block tridiagonal matrix

$$
A = \begin{pmatrix}
A_1 & C_1 & & & \\
B_2 & A_2 & \ddots & & 0 \\
& \ddots & \ddots & \ddots & \\
& & \ddots & \ddots & \ddots \\
0 & & & & C_{n-1} \\
& & & B_n & A_n
\end{pmatrix}
\tag{8.15}
$$

where A_j = square matrix of order m_j
B_j, C_j = rectangular matrices that fit into the 'pattern'.

Thus, B_j has m_j rows and m_{j-1} columns and C_j has m_j rows and m_{j+1} columns. A specials case is where $m_j = m$, then all submatrices are square of order m.
We seek a factorisation in the form $A = LU$, where

$$
L = \begin{pmatrix}
\tilde{A}_1 & & & \\
B_2 & \tilde{A}_2 & & 0 \\
& \ddots & \ddots & \\
& & \ddots & \ddots \\
0 & & B_n & \tilde{A}_n
\end{pmatrix}
\tag{8.16}
$$

and

$$
U = \begin{pmatrix}
I_2 & \Gamma_2 & & \\
& \ddots & \ddots & 0 \\
0 & & \ddots & \ddots \\
& & I_n & \Gamma_{n-1}
\end{pmatrix}
\tag{8.17}
$$

where I_j = identity matrices of order m_j
$\tilde{A}_j$ = square matrix of order m_j
Γ_j = rectangular matrices with m_j rows, m_{j+1} columns.

Formally, the equality $A = LU$ can be decomposed as follows:

$$
\tilde{A}_1 = A_1; \qquad \Gamma_1 = A_1^{-1} C_1
$$
$$
\tilde{A}_j = A_j - B_j \Gamma_{j-1}, \quad j = 2, \ldots, n
\tag{8.18}
$$
$$
\Gamma_j = \tilde{A}_j^{-1} C_j, \quad j = 2, 3, \ldots
$$

This algorithm is a generalisation of the 'scalar' LU decomposition algorithm. However, the details of the algorithms will be slightly more complicated because we are solving linear systems with 'embedded' vectors. What does this mean? It means that we are solving a system of equations similar to (8.1) except that each component of U is not a scalar quantity but is in fact a vector itself. From a C++ point of view we speak of a *composite* or *nested* vector. In general, we wish to solve the system

$$Ax = f, \qquad x = \begin{pmatrix} \mathbf{x}^{(1)} \\ \vdots \\ \mathbf{x}^{(n)} \end{pmatrix} \quad f = \begin{pmatrix} \mathbf{f}^{(1)} \\ \vdots \\ \mathbf{f}^{(n)} \end{pmatrix} \tag{8.19}$$

The vectors are now calculated by the following scheme:

$$\left. \begin{aligned} L\mathbf{y} &= \mathbf{f}, \qquad U\mathbf{x} = \mathbf{y} \\ \mathbf{y}^{(1)} &= \tilde{A}_1^{-1}\mathbf{f}^{(1)} \\ \mathbf{y}^{(j)} &= \tilde{A}_j^{-1}\left(\mathbf{f}^{(j)} - \beta_1\mathbf{y}^{(j-1)}\right), \quad j = 1, 2, \ldots, n \end{aligned} \right\} \tag{8.20}$$

$$\left. \begin{aligned} \mathbf{x}^{(n)} &= \mathbf{y}^{(n)} \\ \mathbf{x}^{(j)} &= \mathbf{y}^{(j)} - \Gamma_j\mathbf{x}^{(j+1)}, \quad j = n-1, n-2, \ldots, 1 \end{aligned} \right\} \tag{8.21}$$

This completes the algorithm for solving this problem.

8.5   WHAT REQUIREMENTS SHOULD OUR MATRIX SATISFY?

The matrix A in equation (8.1) should satisfy certain properties if the equation is to have a solution. To this end, we give a short discussion of some necessary and sufficient conditions for (8.1) to have a unique solution. We shall deal with specific examples and cases in later chapters when we model parabolic partial differential equations by finite differences. Furthermore, the concepts will be needed in Chapter 14 when we introduce the Projected SOR method.

8.5.1   Positive-definite matrices and diagonal dominance

A matrix A is said to be *positive definite* if

$$^t v.A.v > 0 \tag{8.22}$$

for any vector. This is equivalent to saying that the quadratic form is positive. We have programmed this as a function in the `ArrayMechanisms` package that we discussed in Chapter 7. Recall the prototype for this function:

```
template <class V, class I>
  V quadraticForm(const NumericMatrix<V,I>& A,
    const Vector<V,I>& x);
```

In general, it is difficult to prove that a matrix is positive definite so we need other conditions. One useful criterion is that of *diagonal dominance*. A matrix A is said to be diagonally dominant if for each row the absolute value of the diagonal element is greater than or equal to the sum of the absolute values of its non-diagonal elements for that row:

$$\left. \begin{aligned} A &= (a_{ij})_{i,j=1,\ldots,n} \\ |a_{ii}| &\geq \sum_{\substack{j=1 \\ i \neq j}}^{n} |a_{ij}| \quad \text{for} \quad j = 1, \ldots, , n \end{aligned} \right\} \tag{8.23}$$

In the case where the matrix A is tridiagonal, this inequality takes on the form:

$$|b_j| \geq |a_j| + |c_j|, \quad j = 1, \ldots, n \tag{8.24}$$

where we have used the same notation for the vectors a, b and c as in section 8.3.

Diagonally dominant matrices will be very important in later chapters. In particular, we see diagonal dominance as a very desirable property in a matrix. If it is not satisfied, all sorts of strange things start to happen, for example oscillating solutions, non-physical solutions and other anomalies.

8.5.2 M-Matrices

We introduce another very important class of matrices that arises when modelling convection-diffusion equations and other difficult boundary-layer and singular perturbation problems (see Duffy, 1980; Morton, 1996; Farrell *et al.*, 2000). An M-matrix is very attractive, as we shall see in later chapters. For example, the *exponentially fitted schemes* (Duffy, 1980) for the Black–Scholes equation produce schemes of the form (8.1) where A is an M-matrix, whereas some traditional finite differences schemes (such as Crank–Nicolson) produce matrices that are not M-matrices. In the latter case the matrix will have complex eigenvalues that lead to the famous *spurious oscillation problem* associated with the Crank–Nicolson method.

We say that a square matrix A is an M-matrix if it is non-singular, its inverse is non-negative and its off-diagonal elements are less than or equal to 0

$$\left.\begin{array}{l} A^{-1} \geq 0 \\ a_{ij} \leq 0, \quad i \neq j, \quad \forall\, 1 \leq i, \quad j \leq n \end{array}\right\} \tag{8.25}$$

Sufficient conditions for the inverse of a matrix to be non-negative are given in Farrell *et al.* (2000) and Varga (1962). We restate the major result:

Lemma : *Suppose that the matrix A is irreducibly diagonally dominant and*

$$\left.\begin{array}{l} a_{ij} \leq 0, \quad i \neq j \\ a_{ii} > 0 \end{array}\right\} \forall\, 1 \leq i, \quad j \leq n$$

Then A is non-singular and its inverse is strictly positive.

8.6   CONCLUSIONS AND SUMMARY

We have introduced the topic of Numerical Linear Algebra. This area is one of the cornerstones of numerical analysis and is essential when we approximate differential equations using finite differences. In particular, in Part IV we apply *LU* decomposition to solve linear systems of equations arising from discretisation of the Black–Scholes equations.

We shall continue our discussion of matrices in Chapter 14 when we consider *matrix inequalities* and how to solve them as well as their applications to American option pricing.

9

Modelling Functions in C++

9.1 INTRODUCTION AND OBJECTIVES

In this chapter we deal with the problem of modelling various kinds of mathematical functions as classes and objects. Instead of using naked function pointers we model functions as *first-class objects* in C++. Having done that, we shall have the full power of encapsulation, inheritance and polymorphism at our disposal as well as the spectrum of creational, structural and behavioural design patterns (Gamma *et al.*, 1995). These features promote flexibility in our applications. In later chapters we shall use these new classes in financial engineering applications.

Much of mathematics can be described as functions or mappings between different spaces. To this end, it is vital that we can model them in C++. In this chapter we offer the reader three choices:

- Using normal function pointers in C++
- Function objects (functors) in STL
- Creating your own template classes to model scalar, vector, vector-valued and real-valued functions.

You can choose the option that is most suitable to the current situation. Function pointers, for example, are simple to define and use but they lack flexibility. They are not *first-class objects*.

Scalar functions (sometimes called univariate functions) accept a single real parameter as input and produce a single real value as output. Although scalar functions get the lion's share of the attention, we shall give some guidelines on approximating functions in two dimensions – that is, functions that have two input arguments and produce a real value as output.

9.2 FUNCTION POINTERS IN C++

C++ can be seen as a 'better C' and it is possible to use it without applying any object-oriented features at all. In particular, every feature in classic C can be used directly in C++ applications. To this end, what interests us in this chapter is how to model mathematical functions using C++. There are different ways of achieving this end and the choice depends on the level of flexibility that you desire in your application. In this chapter we discuss three ways to model functions in C++:

- Traditional function pointers in C/C++
- Function objects in STL
- Creating your own classes that model functions.

In this section we discuss function pointers and give an example to show how they work. In general, pointers to functions can be assigned, placed in arrays, passed to functions, returned by functions, and so on.

We declare a function pointer by defining its input arguments, return type and its name by using pointer arithmetic. We now give an example of a function declaration with an embedded function pointer:

```
void genericFunction (double myX, double myY, double (*f) (double x,
    double y))
{
  // Call the function f with arguments myX and myY
  double result = (*f)(myX, myY);

  cout << "Result is: " << result << endl;
}
```

This is the declaration of a function called genericFunction. It accepts two arguments myX and myY that will be passed to the function pointer f. You can then call generic-Function by giving any two arguments and a specific function that has two arguments of type double and whose return type is a double, as in the following example:

```
double add(double x, double y)
{
  cout << "** Adding two numbers: " << x << ", " << y << endl;
  return x + y;

}

double multiply(double x, double y)

{
  cout << "** Multiplying two numbers: " << x << ", " << y << endl;

  return x * y;
}

double subtract(double x, double y)

{
  cout << "** Subtracting two numbers: " << x << ", " << y << endl;

  return x - y;
}
```

The advantage of using function pointers is that functions using them are not hard-wired into specific functions but a primitive form of polymorphism is offered.

Continuing with the above example, we define the basic operations for addition, multiplication and subtraction and these functions will be called from genericFunction that accepts a function pointer, calls it and then prints the answer. We now show how this is done by giving the source code for the individual operations. We call generic-Function three times from the main() program:

```
int main()
{
  double x = 3.0;
  double y = 2.0;

  genericFunction(x, y, add);
  genericFunction(x, y, multiply);
  genericFunction(x, y, subtract);

  return 0;
}
```

The output from this program is:

```
** Adding two numbers: 3, 2
Result is: 5
** Multiplying two numbers: 3, 2
Result is: 6
** Subtracting two numbers: 3, 2
Result is: 1
```

There is nothing inherently wrong with this code except that the function calls are hard-coded into the main program and the design *may not* be flexible enough for certain applications. In general, a function pointer is not a *first-class object* in the object-oriented sense. We shall see in section 9.4 how to resolve some practical limitations of the function pointer mechanism. In particular, we define classes that encapsulate function pointers as member data, thus opening the possibility for application of all the powerful features of the object-oriented paradigm such as encapsulation, inheritance, polymorphism and the ability to integrate function classes with design patterns (we devote Part V of this book to design patterns).

We shall see in later chapters how to embed function pointers as member data in classes. For example, in Chapters 11 and 12 we shall look at ordinary differential equations (ODEs) and stochastic differential equations (SDEs). For example, the interface specification for an ODE is:

```
template <class V> class ScalarIVP  // du/dt + a(t)u = f(t), u(0) = A
{ // Scalar initial value problem (first order). Mainly for test cases
  // and illustration of theory and models.
private:
  V ic;               // Initial condition
  Range<V> ran;       // The interval that we are interested in

  V (*rhs)(const V& t);   // Forcing term f(t),
  V (*a)(const V& t);     // Coefficient zero order term
public:
  // Other public stuff

  // Choosing functions in equation
  void Rhs(V (*fp)(const V& x));      // f(t)
  void Coeff(V (*fp)(const V& x));    // a(t)

  // Calculate the values of the functions
  V RhsCalc(const V& t) const;        // f(t)
  V CoeffCalc(const V& t) const;      // a(t)
};
```

In this example we embed two function pointers as private member data and we must create set/get member functions because other client classes will need access to them. Each programmer has his or her own way of conjuring up names for these set/get functions. The situation is just about tenable for this simple equation, but what about a two-factor Black–Scholes model where we might have up to 10 coefficients that must be modelled as function pointers? This leads to code that is difficult to understand and to maintain. In short, this solution does not scale well. There must be a better way. The next two sections hope to throw some light on this problem.

9.3   FUNCTION OBJECTS IN STL

A *function object* (or *functor*) in STL is an object that can be called using an ordinary function call syntax. Function objects contain function pointers as a special case; put another way, a function pointer is a function object. Furthermore, any class that implements `operator()` can be used as a function object. In fact, a function object is an entity that you execute, and in this sense it is similar to a Command design pattern (see Gamma *et al.*, 1995).

Functors are objects that behave like functions but have all the properties of objects. In particular, they can be generalised, passed as parameters or have their state modified – something that is not possible with normal function pointers (Breymann, 1998).

STL provides a number of templated functions, but we shall concentrate on two main groups. The first group has to do with functions taking zero, one or two arguments having the names:

- Zero argument: Generator
- One argument: Unary function
- Two arguments: Binary function

In practice STL has this level of functionality because its algorithms do not require function objects that have more than two arguments. *Generator* is a function object that is called with no arguments. A *Unary* is a function object that is called with a single argument while a *Binary* is a function object that is called with two arguments.

In order to write your own unary functions, you should derive your class from the empty base class `unary_function`:

```
template<class Arg, class Result>
  struct unary_function
  {
    typedef Arg argument_type;
    typedef Result result_type;
  };
```

The following simple example shows how to define your own unary function class called `Greater` and apply it in an example. In this case, we iterate through the elements of a vector and apply the predicate function that we have just created to each element in the container.

```
class Greater: public unary_function<int, bool>
{ // A sledgehammer to ... but it works nonetheless

public:
  // You must overload operator '()'
  result_type operator () (argument_type k)
  {
    if (k > 10)
      return true;
    else
      return false;
  }
};
```

The test program is:

```
vector<int> v1;
for (int i = 0; i <= 5; i++)
{
  v1.push_back(5*i);
}
// Print the values in the vector
vector<int>::iterator it;
for (it = v1.begin(); it != v1.end(); it++)
{
  cout << (*it) << ", ";
}

// Count number of elements whose value > 10 from start to end
int result = count_if(v1.begin(), v1.end(), Greater());
cout << "\nNumber of elements greater than 10: " << result;
```

The output from this program is:

```
0, 5, 10, 15, 20, 25,
Number of elements greater than 10: 3
```

In order to write your own binary functions, you should derive your class from the empty base class binary_function:

```
template<class Arg1, class Arg2, class Result>
  struct binary_function
  {
    typedef Arg1 first_argument_type;
    typedef Arg2 second_argument_type;
    typedef Result result_type;
  };
```

The following simple example shows how to define your own binary function class that averages two values and we then apply it to an example where we iterate through the elements of two vectors to calculate the element-wise averages.

```
template <class Type> class Average : binary_function<Type, Type, Type>
{
public:
  result_type operator () (first_argument_type a,
  second_argument_type b)
  {
    return (a + b) * 0.5;
  }
};
```

A test program is:

```
// Now calculate the element-wise averages of vectors v1 and v2
// and place them in a vector v3
vector<double> v1(10, 2.1);    // Size 10, value 2.1
vector<double> v2(v1);         // Copy (for convenience)
vector<double> v3(v1.size());

transform(v1.begin(), v1.end(), v2.begin(),
    v3.begin(), Average<double>());
```

```
cout << "Elements of averaged vector\n";

vector<double>::iterator itd;

for (itd = v3.begin(); itd != v3.end(); itd++)
{
   cout << (*itd) << ", ";
}
```

The output from this program is:

```
Elements of averaged vector
2.1, 2.1, 2.1, 2.1, 2.1, 2.1, 2.1, 2.1, 2.1, 2.1,
```

9.3.1 Comparison functions

STL provides a large number of template classes for comparisons. These comparison functions are binary functions and are thus derived from `binary_function`. Most of the functions have to do with equality, inequality, greater than, less than and so on. For example, the `equal_to()` class is defined as follows:

```
template<class Type>
  struct equal_to : public binary_function<Type, Type, bool>
  {
    bool operator()(
    const Type& left, const Type& right) const;
  };
```

An example of use: in this case we iterate over two vectors and test if the values (element-wise) are equal:

```
// We now mutate one element in v2 and test if its elements are
// pairwise equal with those of v1 (v2 is above)
v2[3] = 4.5;
vector<double> resultArr(10);
transform(v2.begin(), v2.end(), v3.begin(),
    resultArr.begin(), equal_to<double>());
cout << "\nResult of pairwise comparison \n";
for (itd = resultArr.begin(); itd != resultArr.end(); itd++)
{
   cout << (*itd) << ", ";
}
```

The output from this program is:

```
Result of pairwise comparison
1, 1, 1, 0, 1, 1, 1, 1, 1, 1,
```

9.3.2 STL and financial engineering

STL is a useful library for many low-level operations in C++. The function objects in STL are not powerful enough for what we wish to do in our financial engineering applications. In particular, we would like to create classes for modelling functions that we meet in mathematics, numerical analysis and finance. Some requirements on these classes are:

- We wish to access functions by some identifier, for example a string. In this case we speak of named functions.
- Create a hierarchy of functions; scalar functions, vector functions, vector-valued functions and functions of a real variable. In general, we wish to model the functions that are used in mathematics.
- The ability to create C++ classes for deterministic, random (stochastic) and other kinds of functions (for example, Brownian motion and fuzzy sets).
- The ability to explicitly model inherent properties of functions such as points of discontinuity, calculating function values, inverse functions and so on.
- We can apply the GOF creational, structural and behavioural design patterns (Gamma *et al.*, 1995) to function classes. This will improve the flexibility of our applications. Such flexibility is not possible with function pointers or STL function objects.

You can survive in C++ land without needing to define or use function classes in your financial engineering applications but experience has shown that the resulting code becomes very messy and difficult to maintain. Thus, we show how to create user-defined function classes and the reader can choose if it is worth the effort to use them or just stick with good old function pointers.

9.4   SOME FUNCTION TYPES

A *function* (or *mapping*) f between elements of a space D (called the *domain* of f) and a space R (called the *range* of f) is an association in which each value of a variable x in D is mapped to one and only one variable y in R. See Figure 9.1 for a pictorial representation of a function where we are given the impression that it is a mapping from one space D to another space R.

A function is a particular kind of *relation* and we can then view the function as a set of ordered pairs (x, y) with x in D and y in R.

A common notation for a function f from D to R is

$$f : D \rightarrow R \tag{9.1}$$

Functions can be composed. For example, suppose f is a mapping from D to R_1 and g is a mapping from R_1 to R_2 then the composition of g and f is defined by

$$(gf)(x) = g(f(x)) \quad \text{for all } x \text{ in } D \tag{9.2}$$

Notice that the range of the composed mapping gf is R_2.

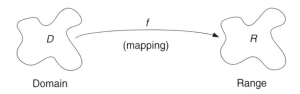

Figure 9.1   Functions as mappings

In equation (9.1) we have said nothing about the structure or 'texture' of the spaces D and R. For example, these spaces may be continuous or discrete, deterministic, fuzzy and so on. We concentrate in this chapter on deterministic functions only and the possible kinds of mappings are:

G1: Continuous to continuous
G2: Continuous to discrete
G3: Discrete to continuous
G4: Discrete to discrete.

In order to reduce the scope even further, we distinguish the following kinds of functions:

- Scalar-valued function (maps a double to a double, for example)
- Vector function (maps a double into a vector)
- Real-valued function (maps a vector into a double)
- Vector-valued function (maps a vector into a vector).

See Figure 9.2 for a pictorial representation of these four function categories.

A *scalar-valued function* takes a single scalar argument as input and produces a single scalar result as output. A *vector function* takes a scalar as input and produces a vector as output. Thus, a vector function can be seen as an array of scalar-valued functions. A *real-valued function* accepts a vector as input and produces a scalar result as output. Finally, a *vector-valued function* accepts a vector as input and produces a vector result as output. A summary of the properties of the various categories is given in Figure 9.3.

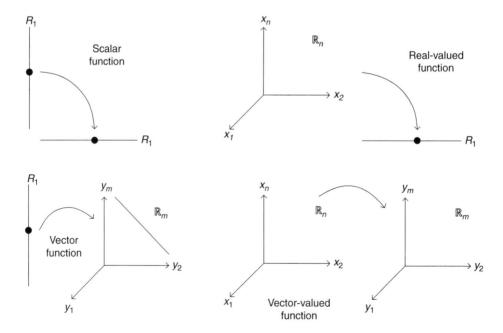

Figure 9.2   Function universe

	Domain	Range
Scalar	Scalar	Scalar
Vector	Scalar	Vector
Real-valued	Vector	Scalar
Vector-valued	Vector	Vector

Figure 9.3 Summary

9.4.1   Applications in numerical analysis and financial engineering

There are many areas of numerical analysis and financial engineering where function classes can be used:

- *Interpolation*: Approximating a function based on its values at a discrete set of points.
- *Numerical Integration*: Methods for calculating the approximate value of the integral of some function.
- *Numerical Differentiation*: Numerical techniques for approximating the derivatives of a given function.

9.4.2   An example: Functions in option pricing

We return to the specific example that we discuss in Appendix 1. Here we are interested in calculating the price of an option (and possibly its sensitivities) based on the option's parameters. This is nothing shocking but we can view this problem as a vector-valued function that maps *n*-dimensional space as represented by the interest rate, volatility and other option parameters into *m*-dimensional space as represented by the following functions (which, of course, will be calculated at a specific point):

```
// Functions that calculate option price and sensitivities
double Price() const;
double Delta() const;
double Gamma() const;
double Vega() const;
double Theta() const;
double Rho() const;
double Coc() const;
// Cost of carry
double Elasticity(double percentageMovement) const;
```

This insight has consequences for the flexibility of our designs because we can then tailor a vector-valued function to suit the kinds of parameters (this is the domain space) and the kinds of functions that we wish to calculate (the range space). The object-oriented paradigm allows us to configure our software to suit different needs.

A special case of a vector-valued function is a real-valued function. In this case the range is a scalar. An example relating to options is when we are only interested in calculating the price of an option without needing to know what its sensitivities are.

9.5   CREATING YOUR OWN FUNCTION CLASSES

We wish to create a hierarchy of classes that model the mathematical functions in section 9.4. There is not enough flexibility in STL for our applications and to this end we

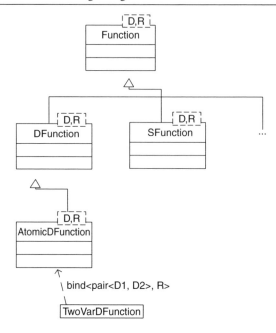

Figure 9.4 Function class hierarchy

build highly generic classes for functions. See Figure 9.4 where the following template classes are introduced:

- `Function<D,R>` base class for all functions with domain D and range R
- `DFunction<D,R>` deterministic functions
- `AtomicDFunction<D,R>` essentially scalar functions from D to R
- `SFunction<D,R>` stochastic functions (not implemented, *futureware*)
- `TwoVarDFunction<D,R>` function of two variables.

In later chapters we shall concoct even more sophisticated classes, but here we concentrate on the classes `AtomicDFunction` and `TwoVarDFunction`. The first class can be used to approximate functions for ordinary differential equations while the second class will be used to model functions of the form $a(S, t)$ in the Black–Scholes equation, for example. In this case S is the value of the underlying stock while t represents time. The advantage of classes for functions is that they not only become *first-class entities* but also become amenable to the application of all the powerful features in the object-oriented and generic programming paradigms, for instance polymorphism, encapsulation, delegation and run-time switching. We shall return to these topics in Part V when we discuss design patterns.

We shall now discuss the two major classes and give some preliminary examples to motivate how to use them. The header files are:

```
template <class D, class R> class AtomicDFunction : public DFunction<D, R>
{

private:
   R (*f)(const D& x);              // Hidden C-type function
```

```
public:
  AtomicDFunction();
  AtomicDFunction (R (*fp)(const D& x));       // Function pointer
  AtomicDFunction(const AtomicDFunction<D, R>& f2);
  virtual ~AtomicDFunction();
  AtomicDFunction<D, R>& operator=(const AtomicDFunction<D, R>& f2);

  virtual R calculate(const D& x) const;

  // Choosing a new function
  void function(R (*fp)(const D& x));
};
```

This class is essentially an encapsulation of a function pointer. Note the presence of set/get functions to access the embedded function pointer and the function `calculate()`. This is a well-known universal name for all kinds of function classes. The reader has only to remember one name!

The interface for a class having two input parameters is:

```
template <class D1, class D2, class R>
  class TwoVarDFunction : public AtomicDFunction<pair<D1, D2>, R>
{ // A class representing a function of two variables.

private:

public:
  // Constructors
  TwoVarDFunction();

  TwoVarDFunction (R (*fp)(const pair<D1,D2>&));

  TwoVarDFunction(const TwoVarDFunction<D1,D2,R>& f2);
  virtual ~TwoVarDFunction();

  TwoVarDFunction<D1, D2, R>& operator = (
      const TwoVarDFunction<D1, D2,R>& f2);

  // We need to instantiate both d1 and d2 and give an R!
  R calculate(const D1& d1, const D2& d2) const;
};
```

We give some examples of using the function class `TwoVarDFunction`. First, we define two 'normal' C-type functions:

```
int addition(const pair<double, double>& p)
{
  return (int) (p.first + p.second);
}

int multiplication(const pair<double, double>& p)
{
  return (int) (p.first * p.second);
}
```

We now show how to encapsulate these functions in function classes.

```
int main()
{
  // A two-variable function representing addition
  TwoVarDFunction<double, double, int> myfun;
```

```
    myfun.function(addition);
    cout << "Call addition: " << myfun.calculate(1.0, 2.0) << endl;

    // A two-variable function representing multiplication
    TwoVarDFunction<double, double, int> myfun2;
    myfun2.function(multiplication);
    cout << "Call multiplication: " << myfun2.calculate(20.0, 2.0);
    return 0;
}
```

The output from this program is:

```
Add 1 and 2: 3
Multiply 20 and 2: 40
```

In the following sections we give some examples of function classes to show how they can be used. We instantiate all underlying generic data types and we avoid creating new classes because, first, they make the code more difficult to understand and, second, it is not always necessary to create a new class in order to get new functionality! In fact, we combine template classes by nesting, for example:

- Arrays and matrices of atomic and two-variable functions
- Atomic functions having arrays as domain and/or range
- Property sets of functions.

There is a lot of opportunity to extend and modify the code to suit your own needs. In order to be concrete we assume that all values have the type double and indexing uses int.

9.6   ARRAYS OF FUNCTIONS

This is a fairly straightforward case of defining an array whose elements are functions. Why not? In this case we concentrate on functions of two variables. Template classes (and in particular, nested template classes) can be a bit difficult to read so we use a common shorthand notation as follows:

```
    typedef Array<TwoVarDFunction<double, double, double>, int>
       FunctionArray;
```

We can use the new name in all future code, for example the function to calculate the value of the array of functions for a specific value:

```
Array<double, int> calculate(const FunctionArray& funArr, double first,
double second)
{
  Array<double, int> result(funArr.Size());
  for (int i=funArr.MinIndex(); i<=funArr.MaxIndex(); i++)
  {
    result[i] - funArr[i].calculate(first, second);
  }
  return result;
}
```

Notice that this function returns an array of doubles. A simple test program is as follows:

```
// Array of functions; myfun and myfun2 are as in section 9.5
FunctionArray myFunArr(2);
myFunArr[1] = myfun;
myFunArr[2] = myfun2;

Array<double, int> arr = calculate(myFunArr, 1.0, 2.0);

print (arr);
```

9.7   VECTOR FUNCTIONS

A vector function maps a double to an array and is in fact an array of scalar functions. We model this class as a property set in this case and we access elements in the set using a string (of course, other implementations are possible):

```
typedef SimplePropertySet<string, AtomicDFunction<double, double> >
    VectorFunction;
```

We see the power of generic programming in this code. We take the cognitive leap by saying that a vector function is a set of atomic functions. We can then navigate in the vector function class by using iterators in the property set. The following code shows how this is done; please note that an array of doubles is returned:

```
Array<double, int> calculate(const VectorFunction& vvfun, double d)
{
  VectorFunction::const_iterator it;

  Array<double, int> result(vvfun.Count());
  int j = result.MinIndex();

  for (it = vvfun.Begin(); it != vvfun.End(); it++, j++)
  {// Optimise this loop
    Property<string, AtomicDFunction<double, double> >
    tmp = (*it);
    result[j] = tmp().calculate(d);
  }
  return result;
}
```

9.8   REAL-VALUED FUNCTIONS

These are functions that map an array to a double. In essence we define a scalar function whose domain is n-dimensional space:

```
double realValuedFunction(const Vector<double, int>& arr)
{
  // Simple test case; return sum of the elements
  return sum(arr); // 'sum' is in ArrayMechanisms
}
```

Here is a test case that shows how to apply the concept:

```
// Real-valued functions
AtomicDFunction<Vector<double, int>, double> rvFun;
```

```
rvFun.function(realValuedFunction);

// Create vector: length 10, start index 1, value 2.0
Vector<double, int> myArr(10, 1, 2.0);
print(myArr);
cout << "Value of RVF: " << rvFun.calculate(myArr) << endl;
```

9.9   VECTOR-VALUED FUNCTIONS

These are functions that map points in n-dimensional space to an array of functions. We leave this case as an exercise for the reader.

9.10   CONCLUSIONS AND SUMMARY

We have given an introduction to the problem of modelling functions in C++. Our ultimate objective in this book is to create C++ classes for scalar, vector, vector-valued and real-valued functions. We chose between function pointers, STL function objects and user-defined classes. In the latter case we speak of first-class entities and these are amenable to multiple rounds of design patterns (see Gamma *et al.*, 1995). We discuss this topic in Part V.

We shall use the function classes from this chapter in later chapters when we approximate boundary value problems and initial boundary value problems by the finite difference method.

C++ Classes for Statistical Distributions

10.1 INTRODUCTION AND OBJECTIVES

In this chapter we develop C++ classes that model continuous and discrete probability distributions. For each distribution type, we encapsulate essential information about it in a single class. Clients can then instantiate the class to produce objects that can be used in various applications. In fact, we have created a reusable class library of C++ classes. You can use these classes in your applications without having to worry about how they were implemented. This promotes understandability of the resulting code.

This chapter discusses a number of traditional aspects of object-oriented programming in C++:

- Encapsulation and information hiding
- Single inheritance hierarchies
- Polymorphism (pure virtual and default virtual functions)
- Run-time switching.

These topics are discussed in many C++ books. In this chapter we apply the above techniques in combination with the template mechanism to produce highly reusable classes.

For an introduction to probability and statistics, see Meyer (1970) and Spiegel (1992).

10.2 DISCRETE AND CONTINUOUS PROBABILITY DISTRIBUTION FUNCTIONS

We model each probability distribution as a C++ class. Furthermore, we distinguish between discrete and continuous distributions. In Chapter 12 we shall give a more detailed discussion of these categories but the focus at the moment is on the object-oriented programming aspects. We do not wish to mix the maths and the C++ too much at this stage.

We create the initial class hierarchy as shown in Figure 10.1. We distinguish between discrete and continuous categories. Each class in Figure 10.1 is abstract because it will have a number of abstract (pure virtual) member functions. Of course, we must carry out an analysis to discover what these functions are and what their *full signature* (input parameters, name and return type) are. In general, we must model two very important functions for each kind of distribution, for example:

- Probability distribution function (we call it pdf)
- Cumulative distribution functions (we call it cdf).

Furthermore, each distribution, whether it be discrete or continuous, has an expected value and a variance function.

Discrete probability distributions are easier to program than continuous distributions mainly because we are working with discrete variables while, in the latter case, we

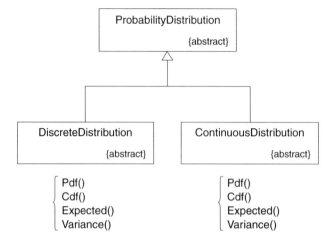

Figure 10.1 Initial class hierarchy

are often confronted with integrals that must be evaluated using numerical integration techniques or by using some approximate analytical formula.

The interface for the discrete probability base class is:

```
template <class T, class I>
  class DiscreteDistribution : public ProbabilityDistribution<T>
{ // T is the range set, I the index set

private:

public :
  DiscreteDistribution();
  virtual T pdf(const I& k) const = 0;
  virtual T cdf(const I& k) const;

  virtual T expected() = 0;             // Expectation
  virtual T variance() = 0;             // Variance

  T probability (const I& k) const;     // Prob(RV has value k)
};
```

The interface for the continuous probability base class is:

```
template <class Domain, class Range>
  class ContinuousDistribution
    : public ProbabilityDistribution<Domain, Range>
{ // Abstract base class for continuous probability distributions

private:
  // ...

public:
  // Constructors
  ContinuousDistribution();
  ContinuousDistribution(const ContinuousDistribution<Domain,
  Range>& d2);

  virtual ~ContinuousDistribution();
```

```
// Selector member functions
virtual Range pdf(const Domain& x) const = 0;
virtual Range cdf(const Domain& x) const;

// Selectors
virtual Range expected() const = 0;
virtual Range variance() const = 0;
virtual Range std() const { return ::sqrt(variance()); }

// Calculating probabilities
virtual Range probability (const Domain& a, const Domain& b)
const;
};
```

In the continuous case we witness a combination of *pure virtual* and *default virtual* functions. You *must* define and implement pure virtual functions in derived classes while you *may* implement default virtual functions in derived classes.

10.3 CONTINUOUS DISTRIBUTIONS

The class hierarchy for a number of important continuous probability distributions is shown in Figure 10.2. The hierarchy is quite shallow except in the case of the Gamma distribution. This is a generalisation of the exponential and chi-squared distributions. We now discuss each distribution in some detail in the following sub-sections.

10.3.1 Uniform (rectangular) distribution

A random experiment in which all outcomes are equally likely is said to have a uniform distribution. We consider the one-dimensional case on an interval (a, b) and give formulae for the probability density function $f(x)$, cumulative distribution function $F(x)$, expected

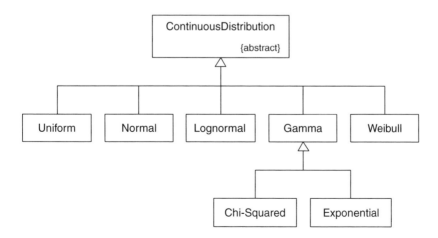

Figure 10.2   Continuous distribution

value $E(x)$ and variance $V(x)$:

$$f(x) = \begin{cases} 1/(b-a), & a \le x \le b \\ 0, & \text{elsewhere} \end{cases}$$

$$F(x) = P(x \le x) = \int_{-\infty}^{x} f(x) \mathrm{d}x$$

$$= (x-a)/(b-a) \text{ if } a \le x < b \tag{10.1}$$

$$= 0 \text{ if } x < a$$

$$= 1 \text{ if } x \ge b$$

$$E(x) = (a+b)/2$$

$$V(X) = E(x^2) - [E(x)]^2 = (b-a)^2/12$$

The difference $(b-a)$ is sometimes called the *scale parameter*.
   The C++ interface is:

```
template <class T>
class Uniform : public ContinuousDistribution<T, T>
{ //  Uniform distribution in one dimension).

private:
  T a;  // Lower end of interval
  T b;  // Upper

public:
  // Constructors
  Uniform();                      // On unit interval [0,1]
  Uniform(const T& left, const T& right); // Interval [left, right]

  // Selector member functions
  T expected(const Uniform<T>& u);
  T variance(const Uniform<T>& u);

  T pdf(const T& x) const;
  T cdf(const T& x) const;

  // Calculating probabilities
  T probability (const T& upper, const T& lower) const;
};
```

We examine some of the code for the member functions that implement the formulae in equation (10.1).

```
template <class T> T Uniform<T>::expected()const
{
  return(a + b) * 0.5;
}

template <class T> T Uniform<T>::variance()const
{
  double t = a - b;
  return((t*t)/12.0);
}
```

```
template <class T> T Uniform<T>::pdf(const T& x) const
{ // The density function

  return (1.0/(b - a));
}

template <class T> T Uniform<T>::cdf(const T& x) const
{ // The cdf function

  return (x - a) / (b - a);
}

// Calculating probabilities
template <class T> T Uniform<T>::probability (const T& xUpp,
    const T& xLow) const
{
  return (xUpp - xLow) / (b - a);
}
```

10.3.2 Normal distribution

This distribution is probably (no pun intended) one of the most important distributions. It is so important that it was depicted on the old 10 Deutschemark bank notes. The formula is due to the famous German mathematician Gauss.

The probability function, expected value and variance are given by:

$$f(x) = \frac{1}{\sqrt{2\pi}\sigma} \exp\left(-\frac{1}{2}\left[\frac{x-\mu}{\sigma}\right]^2\right) \quad -\infty < x < \infty$$

$$E(x) = \mu \quad\quad\quad\quad (10.2)$$

$$V(x) = \sigma^2$$

A closed-form solution for the cdf is not available and some kind of approximation must be used; see, for example, Haug (1998). The basic code in C++ is:

```
double N(double x)
{ // The approximation to the cumulative normal distribution

  double a1 =  0.4361836;
  double a2 = -0.1201676;
  double a3 =  0.9372980;

  double k = 1.0/(1.0 + (0.33267 * x));

  if (x >= 0.0)
  {
    return 1.0 - n(x)* (a1*k + (a2*k*k) + (a3*k*k*k));
  }
  else
  {
    return 1.0 - N(-x);
  }
}
```

We can embed this code in the function Normal::cdf(). Please see the accompanying CD for the source code.

A special case of the normal distribution with mean equal to 0 and standard deviation equation equal to 1:

$$f(x) = \varphi(x) = \frac{1}{\sqrt{2\pi}} e^{-x^2/2} \tag{10.3}$$

10.3.3 Lognormal distribution

This is an important distribution in finance because it is used to model stock price behaviour (see, for example, Hull, 2000). The probability function, expected value and variance are given by:

$$f(x) = \frac{1}{x\sigma\sqrt{2\pi}} \exp\left\{ \frac{-[\log x/m]^2}{2\sigma^2} \right\}, \quad 0 \le x \le \infty$$

$$E(x) = m \exp\left(\frac{1}{2}\sigma^2 \right) \tag{10.4}$$

$$V(x) = m^2 w(w-1), \quad w = \exp(\sigma^2)$$

In this case the parameter m is called the *scale factor*.

10.3.4 Gamma distribution and its specialisations

We now discuss the Gamma distribution and some of its specialisations. The approach taken here leads to some reusability gains. In short, the Gamma distribution is very general and its specialisations are generated by some kind of *value restriction*. The probability function, expected value and variance are given by:

$$f(x) = \begin{cases} \dfrac{\alpha}{\Gamma(r)} (\alpha x)^{r-1} e^{-\alpha x}, & x > 0 \\ 0, & \text{elsewhere} \end{cases}$$

$$E(X) = r/\alpha \tag{10.5}$$

$$V(X) = r/\alpha^2, \quad \begin{array}{ll} 0 < r & \text{shape parameter} \\ 0 < \alpha & \text{scale parameter} \end{array}$$

where the gamma function is given by the integral

$$\Gamma(p) = \int_0^\infty x^{p-1} e^{-x} \, dx, \quad p > 0, \quad p = n, \text{ a positive integer} \tag{10.6}$$

When p is an integer ($p = n$) the gamma integral reduces to a simpler form:

$$\Gamma(n) = (n-1)! \tag{10.7}$$

```
template <class T>
class Gamma : public ContinuousDistribution<T, T>
{
protected:

    T   r;
    T   a;
```

```
public :
  // Constructors
  Gamma();                                // r == 1, a == 1
  Gamma(const Gamma<T>& distrib2);        // Copy constructor
  Gamma(const T& alpha, const T& rr);     // Two parameters

  // Accessing the parameters
  T alpha() const;
  T rcoeff() const;

  T pdf(const T& x) const;                // Probability density
  T cdf(const T& x) const;

  T expected() const;     // Expected value
  T variance() const;     // Variance
};
```

The cdf for this class is (see Meyer, 1970)

$$F(x) = 1 - \int_{\alpha x}^{\infty} \frac{u^{r-1}e^{-u}}{(r-1)!} du, \quad u \equiv \alpha s$$

$$= 1 - \sum_{k=0}^{r-1} e^{-\alpha x}(\alpha x)^k / k!, \quad x > 0$$

(10.8)

```
template <class T> T Gamma<T,I>::cdf(const T&  x) const
{ // Meyer, p. 195; the cdf of Gamma can be written as a sum of pdfs of
  // the Poisson distribution. Note that this is valid only when the
  // parameter r is a positive integer.

  T   res = 0.0;
  T   t = a * x;
  Poisson<T, int> pois_dist(t);        // int is 'dummy'

  // Take into account that r needs to be integral; what we
  // do is convert it to an integer and use this value.
  int ir = int(r);
  for (int k = 0; k <= ir-1; k++)
    res += pois_dist.pdf(k);

  return 1.0 - res;
}
```

We thus see that the cumulative distribution function for the Gamma distribution may be expressed in terms of the Poisson distribution (which we discuss in the next section). We now discuss the exponential distribution and why we see it as a specialisation of the gamma distribution:

$$f(x) = \begin{cases} \alpha\, e^{-\alpha x}, & x > 0 \\ 0, & \text{otherwise} \end{cases} \qquad F(x) = \begin{cases} 1 - e^{\alpha x}, & x \geq 0 \\ 0, & \text{otherwise} \end{cases}$$

$$E(X) = 1/\alpha$$

$$V(X) = 1/\alpha^2$$

(10.9)

How do we implement this class? Basically we demand that the parameter r in the Gamma distribution has the value 1. Of course, we have to redefine constructors but the other member functions are 'free'. Some code now follows:

```
template <class T> Exponential<T>::Exponential(const T& par)  : Gamma<T>
(par, 1)
{

}

template <class T> T Exponential<T>::cdf(const T& x) const
{ // We redefine the cdf() here because it is simpler than the
  // inheritance from the gamma distribution

  if (x > T(0.0))
    return 1.0 - exp(-alpha() * x);

  return T(0.0);
}
```

We have redefined `cdf()` for readability reasons but we have not redefined `pdf()` because it is inherited from the class `Gamma`.

10.4   DISCRETE DISTRIBUTIONS

The class hierarchy for a number of important discrete probability distributions is shown in Figure 10.3. We now discuss each distribution in some detail in the following sub-sections.

10.4.1   Poisson distribution

This is an important distribution in financial engineering because it models the following kinds of events:

- Jumps in the spot price of commodity futures
- Spikes in energy, oil and gas spot prices (Pilipović, 1998)
- Real option theory (Mun, 2002)

The details are:

$$P(X = k) = \frac{e^{-\alpha}\alpha^k}{k!}, \quad k = 0, 1, \ldots, n$$

$$E(X) = \alpha, \quad \alpha > 0 \tag{10.10}$$

$$V(X) = \alpha$$

To give an example, we see that start-up ventures and other R&D initiatives usually follow a jump-diffusion process. Business operations continues with its ups and downs for a few years, after which a product or initiative becomes highly successful and then takes off (Mun, 2002). In general, we assume that the probability of jumps follows a Poisson distribution and we then get a process of the form:

$$dX = f(X, t)dt + g(X, t)dq$$

where f and g are known and where the probability function is given by

$$dq = 0 \quad \text{with probability } 1 - \lambda\, dt$$

$$dq = 1 \quad \text{with probability } \lambda\, dt$$

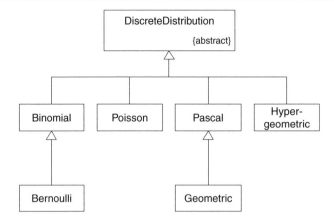

Figure 10.3   Discrete distribution

10.4.2   Binomial and Bernoulli distributions

The Bernoulli distribution is one that has only two discrete values. Let us call them A and B and the probability of occurrence is

$$P(A) = p, \quad P(B) = q,$$

where $q = 1 - p$. Notice that the probabilities add up to 1.

Repeating a Bernoulli experiment n times and examining the number of occurrences k of a given value generate the binomial distribution. The formulae are:

$$P(X = k) = \binom{n}{k} p^k (1 - p)^{n-k}, \quad k = 0, 1, \ldots$$

$$E(X) = np \qquad\qquad\qquad\qquad\qquad (10.11)$$

$$V(X) = npq$$

The C++ interface for the binomial distribution is given by:

```
template <class T, class I>
  class Binomial : public DiscreteDistribution<T, I>
{
private:

  T p;  // Probability of success on each trial
  I N;  // The number of trials(N repetitions of an experiment)

public :

  // Constructor
  Binomial(const T& prob, const I& ntrial);

  // Selector
  T pdf(int k) const; // Probability that an event occurs k times
  T expected() const;
  T variance() const;
};
```

It is interesting to examine how we have implemented the combinatorial function in equation (10.11). To this end, we have to create a class called `MISCFUN` containing static functions, one of which satisfies our current needs:

```
template <class T, class I> T Binomial<T, I>::pdf(int k) const
{
    double tmp = MISCFUN::combination(N,k);   // n!/(k!(n-k)!)
    return (tmp * pow(p,k) * pow(1.0 - p, N - k));
}
```

The actual code for calculating $n!/k!(n-k)!$ is given by:

```
double MISCFUN::fact(int n)
{ // The n-factorial; by default 0! == 1! == 1. Note the use of
  // the recursive function call (this feature is not present in
  // all languages). For example, it Fortran it is necessary to use
  // an internal array to simulate the stack mechanisms in recursion.
  // Precondition: n cannot be negative
  if (n < 0)
    return 0.0;

  if ((n == 0) || (n == 1))
    return 1.0;

  return (double (n) * fact(n-1));
}

double MISCFUN::combination(int n, int k)
{ // The binomial coefficient. This is equivalent to the number of ways
  // of choosing k out of n different objects, disregarding order.

  // Precondition: n > 0 and 0 <= k <= n
  if (n <= 0 || k < 0 || k > n)
    return 0.0;

  // At this stage we are assured that the fact function is
  // never zero, so division by zero is not possible.
  double t1 = fact(n);
  double t2 = fact(n-k) * fact(k);
  return(t1/t2);
}
```

10.4.3 Pascal and geometric distributions

The Pascal distribution has to do with the following kinds of experiment: continue an experiment until a particular event A occurs for the rth time. If

$$P(A) = p, \quad P(\text{not } A) = q = 1 - p$$

on each repetition then we define the random variable X as being the number of repetitions needed in order to have A occur exactly r times. Then

$$P(X = k) = \binom{k-1}{r-1} p^r q^{k-r}, \quad k = r, r+1, \ldots$$

$$E(X) = r/p, \quad V(X) = rq/p^2, \quad q = 1 - p$$

(10.12)

The geometric distribution is a specialisation of the Pascal distribution. Let us define a random variable as the number of repetitions required up to and including the first occurrence of A. Let us assume that X takes the values $1, 2, \ldots$ Then $X = k$ if and only if the first $(k - 1)$ repetitions of an experiment are not(A) we have

$$P(X = k) = q^{k-1}p, \quad k = 1, 2, \ldots, \quad q = 1 - p \tag{10.13}$$

while the expectation and variance are given by

$$E(X) = 1/p$$
$$V(X) = q/p^2 \tag{10.14}$$

10.5   TESTS

We give two very simple examples to show how to use the classes for continuous and discrete probability distributions.

10.5.1   Continuous distributions

In this example we show how to define Uniform variables.

```
#include "unifdist.cxx"
#include <iostream>
using namespace std;

int main()
{
  // Uniform distribution
  Uniform<double> linseg(0.0, 2.0);    // Interval of interest
  cout << "Mean value: " << linseg.expected() << endl;
  cout << "Variance: " << linseg.variance();

  return 0;
}
```

10.5.2   Discrete distributions

In this example we show how to define Poisson variables.

```
#include "poisdist.cxx"
#include <iostream>
using namespace std;

int main()
{
  Poisson<double, int> p(1.2);
  cout << p.expected();

  return 0;
}
```

10.6   CONCLUSIONS AND SUMMARY

In this chapter we have created a C++ class hierarchy for a number of discrete and continuous probability distribution functions. This library is reusable and you can use it in your financial engineering applications without having to know the mathematical formulae that implement the probability distribution function, cumulative distribution functions, expectation or variance.

We have designed the library along traditional object-oriented lines. We make use of pure virtual and default virtual member functions and the classes have been templated so that clients can choose their own specific data types for specific applications.

Part III
Ordinary and Stochastic Differential Equations

Numerical Solution of Initial Value Problems: Fundamentals

'Tus maith leath na hoibre (a good start is half the work)'

11.1 INTRODUCTION AND OBJECTIVES

Part III deals with the problem of approximating ordinary and stochastic differential equations by the finite difference method (FDM). The chapters in this part are very important because they discuss FDM for readers who do not necessarily have any background in this area. Furthermore, having understood the basics for ordinary differential equations, it is then a relatively small step in motivating FDM for partial differential equations in Part IV of this book.

The main reason for the selection of the chapters in this part is that they have only one independent variable.

Part III is concerned with finding approximations to the solution of ordinary differential equations (ODEs) and stochastic differential equations (SDEs) with special emphasis on financial engineering. In this book we concentrate on finite difference schemes and methods (FDMs). To this end, Chapter 11 is the first chapter in a series that introduces and elaborates the finite difference method. In particular, we shall show how to construct simple and effective finite difference schemes for first-order differential equations. In short, Chapter 11 has three objectives:

- We wish to introduce the reader to finite differences by discussing a well-defined and tractable problem. In this case we introduce schemes for linear scalar problems in one dimension. In many cases we can find an exact or analytic solution to the so-called *continuous problem* and can benchmark various finite difference schemes against this exact solution. We pay attention to how well the solution to the finite difference scheme approximates the solution of the continuous problem. In general, we want the two solutions to be close in some sense.
- We are interested in applying our results to financial engineering problems. Studying the equations in this chapter will help us to understand interest-rate modelling problems, stochastic behaviour of assets, interest rates and other basic quantities. Furthermore, the schemes in this chapter will be extended to the approximation of the Black–Scholes equation and its generalisations. These and other relevant topics will be discussed in due course.
- We shall develop algorithms and pseudo-code based on the finite difference schemes; the algorithms will then be programmed in C++. We emphasise reusability and to this end we shall use a number of the classes that we developed in Parts I and II, in particular Range, Vector and other related template classes from the STL.

Summarising, this chapter introduces several fundamental concepts and techniques that will be needed in later chapters. You can consider this chapter to be a self-contained overview of the finite difference method.

11.2 A MODEL PROBLEM

Consider a bounded interval $[0, T]$, where $T > 0$. This interval could represent time or distance, for example, but in most cases we shall view this interval as representing time values. In the interval we define the initial value problem (IVP)

$$\left. \begin{array}{l} Lu \equiv u'(t) + a(t)u(t) = f(t), \quad t \in [0, T] \quad \text{with} \\ u(0) = A \qquad\qquad\qquad\qquad\qquad\quad a(t) \geq \alpha > 0, \quad \forall\, t \in [0, T] \end{array} \right\} \quad (11.1)$$

where L is a first-order linear operator involving the derivative with respect to the time variable and $a = a(t)$ is a strictly positive function in $[0, T]$. The term $f(t)$ is sometimes called the inhomogeneous forcing term and is independent of u. Finally, the solution to the IVP must be specified at $t = 0$; this is the so-called initial condition.

In general, the problem (11.1) has a unique solution given by

$$u(t) = I_1(t) + I_2(t)$$

$$I_1(t) = A \exp\left(-\int_0^t a(s)\, ds \right) \qquad\qquad\qquad (11.2)$$

$$I_2(t) = \exp\left(-\int_0^t a(s)\, ds \right) \int_0^t \exp\left(-\int_0^x a(s)\, ds \right) f(x)\, dx$$

(see Hochstadt, 1964, where the so-called *integration* factor is used to determine a solution).

A special case of (11.1) is when the right-hand term $f(t)$ is zero and $a(t)$ is constant; in this case the solution becomes a simple exponential term without any integrals and this will be used later in this chapter when we examine difference schemes to determine their feasibility. In particular, a scheme that behaves badly for the above special case will be unsuitable for more general or more complex problems unless some modifications are introduced.

11.2.1 Qualitative properties of the solution

Before we introduce difference schemes for (11.1) we discuss a number of results that allow us to describe how the solution u behaves. First, we wish to conclude that if the initial value A and inhomogeneous term $f(t)$ are positive, then the solution $u(t)$ should also be positive for any value t in $[0, T]$. This so-called positivity result should be reflected in our difference schemes (unfortunately, not all schemes possess this property). Second, we wish to know how the solution $u(t)$ grows or decreases as a function of time. The following two results deal with these issues.

Lemma 11.1 (Positivity): *Let w be a well-behaved function satisfying the inequalities*

$$\begin{array}{c} L\omega\,(t) \geq 0, \quad \forall\, t \in [0, T] \\ \omega\,(0) \geq 0 \end{array} \qquad\qquad (11.3)$$

Then the following results holds true:

$$\omega(t) \geq 0, \quad \forall\, t \in [0, T] \qquad\qquad (11.4)$$

Roughly speaking, this lemma, which states that you cannot get a negative solution from positive input, has been proved in Duffy (1980); you can verify this by examining equations (11.2) because all terms are positive.

The following results gives bounds on the growth of $u(t)$.

Theorem 11.1: *Let $u(t)$ be the solution of (11.1). Then*

$$|u(t)| \leq (N/\alpha) + |A|, \quad \forall\, t \in [0, T] \tag{11.5}$$

where $|f(t)| \leq N, \quad \forall\, t \in [0, T].$

This result states that the value of the solution is bounded by the input data. We wish to replicate these properties in our difference schemes for (11.1).

11.3 DISCRETISATION

The interval or range where the solution of (11.1) is defined is $[0, T]$. When approximating the solution using finite difference equations we use a discrete set of points in $[0, T]$ where the discrete solution will be calculated. To this end, we divide $[0, T]$ into N equal intervals of length k, where k is a positive number called the *step size*. We number these discrete points as shown in Figure 11.1. In general all coefficients and discrete functions will be defined at these so-called *mesh points*. We must draw a distinction between those functions that are known at the mesh points and the solution of the corresponding difference scheme. We adopt the following notation:

$$a^n = a(t_n), \qquad f^n = f(t_n)$$
$$a^{n,\theta} = a(\theta t_n + (1-\theta)t_{n+1}), \qquad 0 \leq \theta \leq 1, \quad 0 \leq n \leq N-1 \tag{11.6}$$
$$u^{n,\theta} = \theta u^n + (1-\theta)u^{n+1}, \quad 0 \leq n \leq N-1$$

Not only do we have to approximate functions at mesh point but we also have to come up with a scheme to approximate the derivative appearing in (11.1). There are several possibilities and they are based on *divided differences*. For example, the following divided differences approximate the first derivative of u at the mesh point $t = n * k$;

$$\left. \begin{array}{c} D_+ u^n \equiv \dfrac{u^{n+1} - u^n}{k} \\[2mm] D_- u^n \equiv \dfrac{u^n - u^{n-1}}{k} \\[2mm] D_0 u^n \equiv \dfrac{u^{n+1} - u^{n-1}}{2k} \end{array} \right\} \tag{11.7}$$

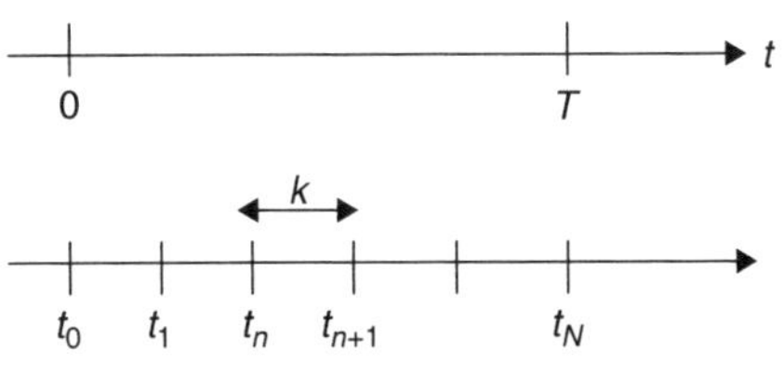

Figure 11.1 Continuous and discrete spaces

The first two divided differences are called one-sided differences and give us first-order accuracy to the derivative, while the last divided difference is called a centred approximation to the derivative. In fact, by using a Taylor's expansion (assuming sufficient smoothness of u) we can prove the following:

$$\left.\begin{array}{ll} |D_{\pm}u(t_n) - u'(t_n)| \leq Mk, & n = 0, 1, \ldots \\ |D_0u(t_n) - u'(t_n)| \leq Mk^2, & n = 0, 1, \ldots \end{array}\right\} \tag{11.8}$$

We now decide on how to approximate (11.1) using finite differences. To this end, we need to introduce two new concepts:

- One-step and multi-step methods
- Explicit and implicit schemes.

A *one-step method* is a finite difference scheme that calculates the solution at time-level $n + 1$ in terms of the solution at time-level n. No information at levels $n - 1, n - 2, \ldots$, is needed in order to calculate the solution at level $n + 1$. To draw an analogy, we could view a one-step scheme as a Markov chain because the future value (that is, at level $n + 1$) of the difference scheme depends only on the present state and not on the past history (see Hsu, 1997). A *multi-step method*, on the other hand is a difference scheme where the solution at level $n + 1$ is determined by values at levels $n, n - 1$ and previous time-levels. Multi-step methods are of course more complicated than one-step methods and we concentrate solely on the latter methods in this book.

An *explicit difference scheme* is one where the solution at time $n + 1$ can be calculated from the information at level n directly. No extra arithmetic is needed, for example, when using division or matrix inversion. An *implicit finite difference scheme* is one in which the terms involving the approximate solution at level $n + 1$ are grouped together and only then can the solution at this level be found. Obviously, implicit methods are slightly more difficult to program than explicit methods.

11.4 COMMON SCHEMES

We now introduce a number of important and useful difference schemes that approximate the solution of (11.1). These schemes will pop up all over the place in later chapters. Understanding how the schemes work in a simpler context will help you to appreciate them when we tackle partial differential equations based on the Black–Scholes model. The main schemes are:

- Explicit Euler
- Implicit Euler
- Crank–Nicolson (or Box scheme)
- The trapezoidal method

The explicit Euler method is given by:

$$\frac{u^{n+1} - u^n}{k} + a^n u^n = f^n, \quad n = 0, \ldots, N - 1$$
$$u^0 = A \tag{11.9}$$

whereas the implicit Euler method is given by:

$$\frac{u^{n+1} - u^n}{k} + a^{n+1}u^{n+1} = f^{n+1}, \quad n = 0, \ldots, N - 1$$

$$u^0 = A$$

(11.10)

Notice the difference: in (11.9) the solution at level $n + 1$ can be directly calculated in terms of the solution at level n while in (11.10) we must rearrange terms in order to calculate the solution at level $n + 1$.

The next scheme is called the Crank–Nicolson, or Box, scheme and it can be seen as an average of explicit and implicit Euler schemes. It is given as:

$$\frac{u^{n+1} - u^n}{k} + a^{n,\frac{1}{2}}u^{n,\frac{1}{2}} = f^{n,\frac{1}{2}}, \quad n = 0, \ldots, N - 1$$

$$u^0 = A \quad \text{where} \quad u^{n,\frac{1}{2}} \equiv \tfrac{1}{2}(u^n + u^{n+1})$$

(11.11)

It is useful to know that the three schemes can be merged into one generic scheme as it were by introducing a parameter θ:

$$\frac{u^{n+1} - u^n}{k} + a^{n,\theta}u^{n,\theta} = f^{n,\theta}$$

$$u^{n,\theta} \equiv \theta u^n + (1 - \theta)u^{n+1}, \quad 0 \le \theta \le 1$$

$$f^{n,\theta} \equiv f(\theta t_n + (1 - \theta)t_{n+1})$$

(11.12)

and the special cases are given by

$$\theta = 0, \quad \text{explicit Euler}$$

$$\theta = 1, \quad \text{implicit Euler}$$

$$\theta = \tfrac{1}{2}, \quad \text{Crank–Nicolson}$$

(11.13)

The solution of (11.12) is given by

$$u^{n+1} = \frac{(1 - k\theta a^{n,\theta})u^n + kf^{n,\theta}}{1 + k(1 - \theta)a^{n,\theta}}$$

(11.14)

This equation is useful because it can be mapped to C++ code and will be used in other schemes by defining the appropriate value of the parameter θ.

Finally, the trapezoidal method is similar to Crank–Nicolson but takes a slightly different averaging mechanism:

$$\frac{u^{n+1} - u^n}{k} + \tfrac{1}{2}(a^n u_n + a^{n+1}u_{n+1}) = \tfrac{1}{2}(f^n + f^{n+1}), \quad n = 0, \ldots, N - 1$$

$$u^0 = A$$

(11.15)

11.5 SOME THEORETICAL ISSUES

Having developed some difference schemes we would like to have some way of determining if the discrete solution is a good approximation to the exact solution. Although we do not deal with this issue in great detail (for more, see Dahlquist, 1974), we do look at stability and convergence issues.

Definition 11.1: The one-step difference scheme $L(k)$ is said to be positive if

$$L(k)w_j \geq 0, \qquad j = 0, \ldots, N-1, \quad w_j \geq 0 \tag{11.16}$$

implies that $w_j \geq 0$, $\forall j = 0, \ldots, N$.

Based on this definition we see that the implicit Euler scheme is always positive while the explicit Euler scheme is positive if the term

$$1 - ka^n \geq 0 \quad \text{or} \quad k \leq (1/a^n), \quad n \geq 0 \tag{11.17}$$

is positive. Thus, if the function $a(t)$ achieves large values (and this happens in practice) we shall have to make k very small indeed in order to produce good results. Even worse, if k does not satisfy the inequality in (11.17) the discrete solution looks nothing like the exact solutions and so-called *spurious oscillations* occur. This phenomenon occurs in other finite difference schemes and we propose a number of remedies for them later in this book.

Definition 11.2: A difference scheme is stable if its solution is bounded in much the same way as the solution of the continuous problem (11.1) (see Theorem 11.1), that is

$$|u^n| \leq \frac{N}{\alpha} + |A|, \quad n \geq 0 \tag{11.18}$$

where

$$a(t_n) \geq \alpha, \quad n \geq 0$$
$$|f(t_n)| \leq N, \quad n \geq 0$$

and

$$u^0 = A$$

Based on the fact that a scheme is stable and consistent (see Dahlquist, 1974) we can state in general that the error between the exact and discrete solutions is bounded by some polynomial power of the step-size k:

$$|u^n - u(t_n)| \leq Mk^p, \quad p = 1, 2, \ldots \tag{11.19}$$

where M is a constant that is *independent* of k. For example, in the case of some of the above schemes we have:

Implicit Euler $\qquad |u^n - u(t_n)| \leq Mk, \quad n = 0, \ldots, N$

Crank–Nicolson (Box) $\quad |u^n - u(t_n)| \leq Mk^2, \quad n = 0, \ldots, N$

Explicit Euler $\qquad |u^n - u(t_n)| \leq Mk, \quad n = 0, \ldots, N$

if $\qquad 1 - a^n k > 0.$

$$\tag{11.20}$$

Thus, we see that the Box method is second-order accurate and is better than the implicit Euler scheme, which is only first-order accurate.

11.6 FITTING: SPECIAL SCHEMES FOR DIFFICULT PROBLEMS

We now introduce a special class of schemes with desirable properties. These are schemes that are suitable for problems with rapidly increasing or decreasing solutions. In the literature these are called *stiff* or *singular perturbation* problems (see Duffy, 1980). We can motivate these schemes in the present context. Let us take the problem (11.1) when $a(t)$ is constant and $f(t)$ is zero. The solution is given by a special case of (11.2), namely:

$$u(t) = A \exp(-at) \tag{11.21}$$

If a is large then the derivatives of $u(t)$ tend to increase; in fact, at $t = 0$, the derivatives are given by:

$$\frac{d^k u(0)}{dt^k} = A(-a)^k, \quad k = 0, 1, 2, \ldots \tag{11.22}$$

The physical interpretation of this fact is that a boundary layer exists near $t = 0$ where u is changing rapidly and it has been shown that classical finite difference schemes fail to give acceptable answers when a is large (typically values between 1000 and 10 000). We get so-called *spurious oscillations* and this problem is also encountered when solving one-factor and multi-factor Black–Scholes equations using finite difference methods. We have resolved this problem using so-called *exponentially fitted schemes*. We motivate the scheme in the present context and later chapters describe how to apply it to more complicated cases.

In order to motivate the fitted scheme, consider the problem of constant $a(t)$ and $f(t) = 0$. We wish to produce a difference scheme in such a way that the discrete solution is equal to the exact solution at the mesh points. We introduce a so-called fitting factor σ in the new scheme:

$$\begin{cases} \sigma \left(\dfrac{u^{n+1} - u^n}{k} \right) + a^{n,\theta} u^{n,\theta} = f^{n,\theta}, & n = 0, \ldots, N - 1, \quad 0 \le \theta \le 1 \\ u^0 = A, \end{cases} \tag{11.23}$$

The motivation for finding the fitting factor is to demand that the exact solution (which is known) has the same values as the discrete solution at the mesh points.

Plugging the exact solution (11.21) into (11.23) and doing some simple arithmetic we get the following representation for the fitting factor:

$$\sigma = \frac{ak(\theta + (1 - \theta)e^{-ak})}{1 - e^{-ak}} \tag{11.24}$$

Having found the fitting factor for the constant coefficient case we generalise to a scheme for the case (11.12) as follows:

$$\sigma^{n,\theta}\frac{u^{n+1} - u^n}{k} + a^{n,\theta}u^{n,\theta} = f^{n,\theta}, \qquad n = 0, \dots, N-1, \quad 0 \le \theta \le 1$$

$$u^0 = A \qquad\qquad (11.25)$$

$$\sigma^{n,\theta} = \frac{a^{n,\theta}k(\theta + (1-\theta)\exp(-a^{n,\theta}k))}{1 - \exp(-a^{n,\theta}k)}$$

In practice we work with a number of special cases:

$$
\left.
\begin{aligned}
&\theta = 0 \qquad\qquad\qquad\qquad\text{(implicit)}\\
&\sigma^{n,o} = a^{n+1}k/[\exp(a^{n+1}k) - 1]\\
&\theta = \tfrac{1}{2} \qquad\qquad\qquad\qquad\text{(fitted Box)}\\
&\theta^{n,\frac{1}{2}} = \frac{a^{n,\frac{1}{2}}k}{2}\left(\frac{1 + \exp(-a^{n,\frac{1}{2}}k)}{1 - \exp(-a^{n,\frac{1}{2}}k)}\right)\\
&\quad = \frac{a^{n,\frac{1}{2}}k}{2}\coth\frac{a^{n,\frac{1}{2}}k}{2} \qquad\text{(Il'in)}
\end{aligned}
\right\} \qquad (11.26)
$$

In the final case $\coth(x)$ is the hyperbolic tangent function.

In Duffy (1980) we have proved that the implicit fitted method in (11.26) has first-order accuracy irrespective of the size of a. In other words, the inequality (11.19) holds with $p = 1$ and the constant factor M is independent of both k *and* the coefficient a. Thus we can say that the fitted scheme is insensitive to a. This is a remarkable property of the scheme! We say that the scheme is *uniformly convergent*, a property that traditional finite difference schemes do not share.

In later chapters we shall apply the fitting scheme to the one-factor and multi-factor Black–Scholes equations and we shall show that we get good approximations to the option price and its delta in all regions of (S, t), where S is the underlying asset and t is time (up to maturity T). This is in stark contrast to the Crank–Nicolson scheme where the infamous spurious oscillations are seen, especially when the underlying S is near the strike price K or when the payoff function is discontinuous.

11.7 NON-LINEAR SCALAR PROBLEMS AND PREDICTOR–CORRECTOR METHODS

Real-life problem are very seldom linear. In general, we model physical and financial applications using non-linear IVPs:

$$
\begin{cases}
u' \equiv \dfrac{du}{dt} = f(t, u), & t \in (0, T]\\[2mm]
u(0) = A
\end{cases}
\qquad (11.27)
$$

Here $f(t, u)$ is a non-linear function of u in general. Of course, equation (11.27) contains equation (11.1) as a special case. However, it is not possible to come up with an exact solution for (11.27) in general and we must resort to some numerical techniques. Approximating (11.27) poses challenges because the resulting difference schemes may also be non-linear, thus forcing us to solve the discrete system at each time level by Newton's method or some other non-linear solver. For example, consider applying the trapezoidal method to (11.27):

$$u_{n+1} = u_n + \frac{k}{2}[f(t_n u_n) + f(t_{n+1}, u_{n+1})], \quad n = 0, \ldots, N - 1 \tag{11.28}$$

where $f(t, u)$ is non-linear. Here see that the unknown term u is on both the left- and right-hand sides of the equation and hence it is not possible to solve the problem in the way that we did for the linear case. However, all is not lost and to this end we introduce the predictor–corrector method, which consists of a set of two difference schemes; the first equation uses the explicit Euler to produce an intermediate solution that is then used in what could be called a modified trapezoidal rule.

Predictor: $\bar{u}_{n+1} = u_n + k \ f \ (t_n, u_n)$

$$\tag{11.29}$$

Corrector: $u_{n+1} = u_n + \frac{k}{2}[f(t_n, u_n) + f \ (t_{n+1}\bar{u}_{n+1})]$

or

$$u_{n+1} = u_n + \frac{k}{2}\{f(t_n, u_n) + f(t_{n+1}, u_n + k \ f \ (t_n, u_n))\}$$

The predictor–corrector is used in practice, and can be used with non-linear systems and stochastic differential equations (SDEs).

11.8   EXTRAPOLATION TECHNIQUES

We now give an introduction to a technique that allows us to improve the accuracy of finite difference schemes. This is called Richardson extrapolation in general. We take a specific case to show the essence of the method, namely the implicit Euler method (11.10). We know that it is first-order accurate and that it has excellent stability properties. We now apply the method on meshes of size k and $k/2$ and can show that the approximate solutions can be represented as:

$$v^k = u + mk + 0(k^2)$$

$$v^{k/2} = u + m\left(\frac{k}{2}\right) + 0(k^2) \tag{11.30}$$

Then

$$2v^{k/2} - v^k = u + 0(k^2)$$

The constant m is independent of k and this is why we can eliminate it in the first equations to get a scheme that is second-order accurate. The same trick can be employed with the Crank–Nicolson scheme to get a fourth-order accurate scheme as follows:

$$v^k = u + mk^2 + 0(k^4)$$

$$v^{k/2} = u + m\left(\frac{k}{2}\right) + 0(k^4) \tag{11.31}$$

Then

$$\tfrac{4}{3}v^{k/2} - \tfrac{1}{3}v^k = u + 0(k^4)$$

In general, with extrapolation methods we say what accuracy we desire and the code divides the interval $[0, T]$ into smaller sub-intervals until the difference between the solutions on consecutive meshes is less than a given tolerance.

A thorough introduction to extrapolation techniques for ordinary and partial differential equations (including one-factor and multi-factor parabolic equations) can be found in Marchuk and Shaidurov (1983).

11.9   C++ DESIGN AND IMPLEMENTATION

We now need to develop the steps for the C++ code that implements one-step finite difference schemes for initial value problems. In particular, we need to unambiguously describe the following:

A1: The input to the continuous problem
A2: The input to the discrete problem
A3: The output from the discrete problem
A4: The activities to be executed in order to produce output from input.

These four activities allow us to describe the problem correctly and completely. In order to motivate this section we concentrate on the scalar linear problem (11.1).

The code that realises the finite difference schemes for (11.1) has been kept simple so that we can understand the essential details without being bogged down in irrelevant detail. To this end, we model (11.1) as a class called ScalarIVP. If we look at equation (11.1) we see that we must design and implement the following elements:

- The linear coefficients $a(t)$ and $f(t)$
- The initial condition A
- The range of integration $[0, T]$.

We model functions as normal C function pointers (this is acceptable for the moment) and the range of integration as a Range instance. Of course, we use template classes for extra reusability. The interface is as follows:

```
template <class V> class ScalarIVP  // du/dt + a(t)u = f(t), u(0) = A
{ // Scalar initial value problem (first order). Mainly for test cases
  // and illustration of theory and models.
private:
  V ic;                   // Initial condition
  Range<V> ran;           // The integration interval

  V (*rhs)(const V& t);   // Forcing term f(t)
  V (*a)(const V& t);     // Coefficient of zero order term
public:
  ScalarIVP();
  ScalarIVP(const Range<V> range, const V& initialCond);
  ScalarIVP(const ScalarIVP<V>& source);

  virtual ~ScalarIVP();

  ScalarIVP<V>& operator = (const ScalarIVP<V>& source);

  // Choosing functions in equation
```

```
  void Rhs(V (*fp)(const V& x));       // Choose function f(t)
  void Coeff(V (*fp)(const V& x));     // Choose function a(t)

  // Selector functions
  Range<V> range() const;              // Interval of interest
  V startValue() const;                // Give initial value
  V RhsCalc(const V& t) const;         // Calculate f(t)
  V CoeffCalc(const V& t) const;       // Calculate a(t)
};
```

A major advantage of modelling the IVP in this way is that all logically related entities are brought together in one place. We can then access the IVP as a single entity.

Let us now take an example. We first of all define the needed functions:

```
double RHS(const double& d)
{ // Define the RHS f(t) in IVP

  return 0.0;
}
double a(const double& d)
{ // Define the coefficient a(t) in IVP

  return 1.0;
}
```

Now we are ready to define an instance of the class:

```
  ScalarIVP<double> ivp1(Range<double>(0.0, 1.0), 1.0);

  ivp1.Rhs(RHS);
  ivp1.Coeff(a);
```

We now must decide on how to model finite difference schemes in C++. In this case we create a new class `ScalarIVPSolver` that is a client of `ScalarIVP` and encapsulates the specific difference schemes that we discuss in this book. To this end, we define an enumeration to reflect the schemes:

```
  enum FDMType {EEuler, IEuler, Box, Trap,
       Fitted, FittedBox, ExtrapEuler, PC};
```

The public interface for `ScalarIVPSolver` is:

```
template <class V, class I> class  ScalarIVPSolver
{ // Set of finite difference to solve scalar linear IVP

private:
  ScalarIVP<V>* ivp;      // Pointer to 'parent' IVP
  FDMType typ;            // Which scheme?

  I N;                    // The number of subdivisions

  V k;                    // Calculated step length
  Vector<V, I> res;       // Results of calculation

  // private functions
  void eeuler();
  void fitted();
  void predictorCorrector();
  // etc.
```

```
public:
  ScalarIVPSolver();
  ScalarIVPSolver(ScalarIVP<V>& source, FDMType type);

  virtual ~ScalarIVPSolver();

  // Modifier functions
  void steps(const I& Nsteps);
  void setType(FDMType type);

  // Output
  V stepSize() const;
  Vector<V, I> result();          // The result of the calculation
};
```

We have thus applied the separation of concerns techniques; in one class we define the parameters of the continuous problem and in the other class we have defined the parameters of the discrete problem. The latter class uses the interface functions of the former class. Furthermore, the output of the finite difference calculation is placed in a Vector instance. For each kind of scheme in the enumeration FDMType we have defined a private function to do the job. For example, the code for the explicit Euler scheme in equation (11.9) is:

```
template <class V, class I> void ScalarIVPSolver<V,I>::eeuler()
{
  for (I i = res.MinIndex() + 1; i <= res.MaxIndex(); i++)
  {
    res[i] = res[i-1]*(1.0 - (k* ivp->CoeffCalc((i-1)*k)) )
      + (k* ivp->RhsCalc((i-1)*k));
  }
}
```

The C++ code for the fitted scheme in equation (11.26) is given by:

```
template <class V, class I> void ScalarIVPSolver<V,I>::fitted()
{ // Exponentially fitted scheme

  V f, coeff;
  for (I i = res.MinIndex() + 1; i <= res.MaxIndex(); i++)
  {
    if (ivp->CoeffCalc(i*k) == 0.0) // An extreme case
      f = 1.0;
    else
    {
      coeff = (ivp->CoeffCalc(i*k)) * k;
      f = coeff / (::exp(coeff) - 1.0);
    }

    res[i]=(f*res[i-1]+k*ivp->RhsCalc(i*k)))
      /(f+(k*ivp->CoeffCalc(i*k)) );
  }
}
```

The code for the predictor–corrector method (11.29) is interesting because it combines explicit Euler and trapezoidal methods:

```
template <class V, class I>   void
ScalarIVPSolver<V,I>::predictorCorrector()
```

```
{ // Predictor-corrector method

   for (I i = res.MinIndex() + 1; i <= res.MaxIndex(); i++)
   {

     // First get the predictor (Explicit Euler)
     V predictor = res[i-1]*(1.0 - (k*ivp->CoeffCalc((i-1)*k)) )
       + (k* ivp->RhsCalc((i-1)*k));

     // Corrector (this IS the solution)
     V vup = 1.0 - ( k * 0.5 *ivp->CoeffCalc((i-1)*k) );
     V pTerm = (k * 0.5 * ivp->CoeffCalc(i*k) ) * predictor;

     V favg = k*0.5*(ivp->RhsCalc(i*k)+ivp->RhsCalc((i-1)*k) );

     res[i] = (res[i-1] * vup - pTerm + favg) ;
   }
}
```

Having discussed the internal of `ScalarIVPSolver` in some detail we finish this section by giving an example of use:

```
ScalarIVPSolver<double, int> ivpSol(ivp1, EEuler);
ivpSol.steps(10);

res = ivpSol.result();
print(res);
```

11.10   GENERALISATIONS

The theory and examples in this chapter were chosen in order to explain the essential features of finite difference methods and their mapping to C++ code. Of course, real-life is more complex than just modelling linear scalar initial-value problems but the schemes in this chapter will reappear and resurface throughout the rest of this book. In particular, we shall apply these schemes when we approximate one-factor and multi-factor Black–Scholes equations and extensions. By taking time to understand this chapter you will be in a good position to appreciate the numerical methods in the rest of this book. In particular, the theory will be extended to more complex non-linear systems of ODEs. Recalling the linear IVP

$$u : \mathbf{R}^1 \to \mathbf{R}^1$$

$$\begin{cases} \dfrac{du}{dt} + a(t)u = f(t), & t \in (0, T] \\ u(0) = A \end{cases} \tag{11.32}$$

we generalise it to *non-linear systems*

$$u : \mathbf{R}^n \to \mathbf{R}^1, \quad u(t) = (u(t), \dots, u_n(t))$$

$$\begin{cases} \dfrac{dU}{dt} = f(t, U), & t \in (0, T) \\ U(0) = A \end{cases} \tag{11.33}$$

Here U is a *vector function* by which we mean a function mapping time to an array of scalar functions. A special and common case of (11.33) is when we discretise linear parabolic differential equations by the *Method of Lines (MOL)* to produce a linear system of ODEs as follows:

$$U : \mathbf{R}^1 \to \mathbf{R}^n, \quad U(t) = (u_1(t), \ldots, u_n(t))$$

$$\frac{du}{dt} + M(t)U = F(t), \quad t \in (0, T] \tag{11.34}$$

$$U(0) = A$$

In this case $F = F(t)$ is a vector function, $M = M(t)$ is a matrix of scalar functions and A is a vector that represents the initial condition in the IVP.

Later chapters will discuss numerical schemes and C++ code for problems (11.33) and (11.34).

11.11   CONCLUSIONS AND SUMMARY

This chapter is a concise and compact introduction to the Finite Difference Method (FDM) applied to the simplest differential equation in the differential equation galaxy, namely first-order, scalar, linear initial value problems (IVP). We have chosen this example because it is easy to understand and can also be extrapolated to more complex equations and applications. We shall see in later chapters how useful this experience has been. For example, in Chapter 12 we introduce finite difference schemes for stochastic differential equations (SDEs). A SDE is like an extension to an ODE with a random process added on, and we shall see that many of the schemes can also be used in this case albeit with calculations using random variables.

We took the following approach in this chapter:

- Examination of the continuous problem
- Introduction to FDMs and suitable schemes that approximate the solution of the continuous problem
- How 'good' is the approximate solution?
- Developing C++ classes and code to model finite difference schemes.

In this chapter we have tried to adopt an object-oriented approach by grouping similar structure and behaviour into classes that correspond to the continuous and discrete parts of the problem.

12

Stochastic Processes and Stochastic Differential Equations

12.1 INTRODUCTION AND OBJECTIVES

In this chapter we introduce stochastic differential equations (SDEs) and show how to apply the finite difference method to produce approximations to them. To this end, we define what we mean by random variables and random (or stochastic) processes because these are part of an SDE. In general, we can say that an SDE is an ODE with some additional noise terms. These noise terms are Wiener processes in this chapter. We focus on scalar, linear SDEs and do not discuss non-linear systems of SDEs. Most of the finite difference schemes will be familiar to you if you have studied Chapter 11. In fact, the schemes in this chapter have the same form as those in Chapter 11 except that we need to take care of the noise terms.

12.2 RANDOM VARIABLES AND RANDOM PROCESSES

We introduce a number of concepts and definitions that are needed if we wish to understand stochastic differential equations. In probability, any process of observation is called an *experiment*, and the results of an experiment are called the *outcome* of the experiment. A *random experiment* is one whose outcomes cannot be predicted. The set of all possible outcomes of a random experiment is called the *sample space* and is usually denoted by S. An element in S is called a *sample point*. Thus, each outcome of a random experiment corresponds to a sample point.

We shall give a simple example. Consider the experiment of tossing a coin twice. We get either heads (H) or tails (T) and there are four possible outcomes given by the sample space {HH, HT, TH, TT}.

A sample space is called *discrete* if it consists of a finite number of sample points while it is called *continuous* if the sample points constitute a continuum. Any subset of the sample space is called an *event* while a sample point is called an *elementary event*. For instance, in the above example the set of outcomes containing heads {HH, HT, TH} is an event while the outcome that always gives heads {HH} is an elementary event.

12.2.1 Random variables

A *random variable* $X(s)$ is a real-valued function that assigns a real number (called the value) to each sample point s in S. Thus, a random variable is in fact a function and not a variable. The sample space is called the *domain* of the random variable and the real line is called the *range* of the random variable. For example, in tossing a coin once, we could define the random variable X as follows:

$$X(H) = 1, \qquad X(T) = 0$$

There is nothing magical about this function and we could have defined other variables on this sample space as follows:

$$Z(H) = 0, \qquad Z(T) = 1$$
$$Z(H) = 1, \qquad Z(T) = 0$$

If X is a random variable and x is a fixed number we define the event $\{X = x\}$ as

$$\{X = x\} = \{s \colon X(s) = x\}$$

Similarly, we can define other events in which equality is replaced by some inequality, for example:

$$\{X \le x\} = \{s \colon X(s) \le x\}$$

Events have probabilities, for example:

$$P(X = x) = P\{s \colon X(s) = x\}$$
$$P(X \le x) = P\{s \colon X(s) \le x\}$$

Having defined random variables, we move on to a discussion of distribution functions. The *distribution function* (or *cumulative distribution* function, cdf) is defined as:

$$F_X(x) = P(X \le x), \quad -\infty < x < \infty \tag{12.1}$$

The cdf determines much of the behaviour about a random experiment defined by the random variable X. From definition (12.1) we can compute different probabilities as follows:

$$P(a < X \le b) = F_X(b) - F_X(a)$$
$$P(X > a) = 1 - F_X(a) \tag{12.2}$$
$$P(X < b) = F_X(b^-), \qquad b^- = \lim_{0 < \epsilon \to 0} b - \epsilon$$

We are interested in two kinds of probability function, called *discrete* and *continuous* functions. First, suppose that the jumps occur at the points x_1, x_2 and let us assume that $x_i < x_j$ for $i < j$. Then

$$F_X(x_i) - F_X(x_{i-1}) = P(X \le x_i) - P(X \le x_{i-1}) = P(X = x_i) \tag{12.3}$$

Let

$$P_X(x) = P(X = x) \tag{12.4}$$

then $P_X(x)$ is called the probability mass function (pmf) of the discrete random variable X. The cdf and pmf are related by the formula

$$F_X(x) = P(X \le x) = \sum_{x_k \le x} P_X(x_k) \tag{12.5}$$

An important example of a discrete random variable is the Poisson random variable with parameter $\lambda > 0$, whose pmf is given by:

$$P_X(k) = P(X = k) = e^{-\lambda}\frac{\lambda^k}{k!}, \quad k = 0, 1, \ldots \tag{12.6}$$

and the corresponding cdf is:

$$F_X(x) = e^{-\lambda}\sum_{k=0}^{n}\frac{\lambda^k}{k!}, \quad n \le x < n + 1 \tag{12.7}$$

We now turn our attention to continuous random variables and we define the pdf as:

$$f_X(x) = \frac{dF_X(x)}{dx} \tag{12.8}$$

We are interested in two special cases, namely the Uniform distribution and the Normal distribution. For the Uniform distribution on an interval (a, b) we have the following formulae:

$$f_X(x) = \begin{cases} \dfrac{1}{b-a}, & a < x < b \\ 0, & \text{otherwise} \end{cases}$$

$$F_X(x) = \begin{cases} 0, & x \le a \\ \dfrac{x-a}{b-a}, & a < x < b \\ 1, & x \ge b \end{cases} \tag{12.9}$$

The Normal (or Gaussian) distribution has the following pdf and cdf:

$$\begin{cases} f_X(x) = \dfrac{1}{\sqrt{2\pi}\sigma}e^{-(x-\mu)^2/2\sigma^2} \\ F_X(x) = \dfrac{1}{\sqrt{2\pi}}\displaystyle\int_{-\infty}^{(x-\mu)/\sigma} e^{-y^2/2}dy \end{cases} \tag{12.10}$$

The source code for the formulae in (12.10) can be found in the *StatisticsMechanisms* package.

This completes our short introduction to random variables. For a more detailed discussion on random variables, we refer the reader to Hsu (1997), for example.

12.2.2 Generating random variables

When approximating the solutions of stochastic differential equations we often have to come up with some techniques for generating random numbers on a computer. True randomness is impossible on a computer because random number generation occurs in a deterministic and entirely predictable way on such machines. For this reason, we prefer to use the term *pseudo-random* when we wish to stress the difference.

In general, pseudo-random numbers are generated by so-called linear congruential generators (this topic is a part of Number Theory; see Ayres, 1965, or Hunter, 1964, for example). These are defined by the recursion

$$X_{j+1} = aX_j + b(\text{mod } M), \quad j = 1, 2, \ldots \tag{12.11}$$

where a and M are positive integers and b is non-negative. For an initial value (or *seed*) for X_j when $j = 0$, scheme (12.11) generates a pseudo-random sequence. When a, b and M are chosen properly, the numbers

$$U_j = X_j/M \tag{12.12}$$

often seem to be uniformly distributed in the interval [0, 1].

In practice, most computers and operating systems provide some kind of random number generators and many commercial generators are available. For this book, we used generators under both Linux and Windows. For Linux, we use `drand48()` to generate uniform random numbers in [0, 1] and on Windows we have used the function `rand()` as the basis for a uniform random number generator. In general, each function supplies specific values for a, b and M in the recursion relation (12.11).

Our main objective is in generating Gaussian random variables because we need them when working with SDEs. To this end, we discuss two techniques for generating such numbers from uniformly distributed numbers:

- The Box–Muller method
- The Polar–Marsaglia method (see Kloeden, Platen and Schurz, 1994)

Each method accepts two uniform variables as input and produces two Gaussian variables as output. The formula for the Box–Muller is:

$$\begin{cases} \theta = 2\pi U_2, & \rho = \sqrt{-2 \log U_1} \\ Z_1 = \rho \cos \theta, & Z_2 = \rho \sin \theta \end{cases} \tag{12.13}$$

and the formula for Polar–Marsaglia is:

$$\begin{cases} V_j = 2U_j - 1(W = V_1^2 + V_2^2 < 1) \\ Z_1 = V_1\sqrt{-2\log(W)/W} \\ Z_2 = V_2\sqrt{-2\log(W)/W} \end{cases} \tag{12.14}$$

Polar–Marsaglia is a variation of Box–Muller but it avoids the time-consuming calculation of trigonometric functions. We use it in applications and show how it has been programmed as a 'flat' function in C++ (Linux version):

```
void PolarMarsaglia (double & N1, double & N2)
{
   double W;
   double V1, V2;

   do
   {
      double U1 = drand48();   // Uniform (0,1) random variables
```

```
  double U2 = drand48();

  V1 = 2 * U1 - 1;         // Uniform (-1,1) random variables
  V2 = 2 * U2 - 1;

  W = V1*V1 + V2*V2;
} while( W>1 );

double W_function = sqrt( -2 * log(W) / W );

N1 = V1 * W_function;
N2 = V2 * W_function;

return;
}
```

In later experiments we shall generate arrays of normally distributed numbers. The C++
code uses the Polar–Marsaglia formula and places the results in a `Vector` object:

```
void Random::Normal (Vector<double,int> & v,  const int & iNumber,
   const double & Mu, const double & Var)
{
  int size = iNumber + (iNumber%2);   // Add 1 if odd

  Vector<double, int> tmp(size, 1);   // Temporary vector

  double Sd = sqrt(Var);              // Standard deviation

  for( int i=1; i<=size; i+=2 )
  {
    double N1;
    double N2;

    PolarMarsaglia (N1,N2); // Uniform U1 and U2

    tmp[i] = N1 * Sd + Mu;
    tmp[i+1] = N2 * Sd + Mu;
  }

  v = tmp;

  return;
}
```

On Windows, we have used the following code:

```
  double(rand()) / double(RAND_MAX) ;
```

as an estimate, where RAND_MAX is the maximum value that can be returned by the
rand() function. This information can be used in order to write your own uniform
random number generator under Windows.

We give an example of how to generate uniformly distributed numbers under Windows.

```
// tstrandom.cpp
//
// Random number stuff
//
// (C) Datasim Education BV 2003

#include <stdlib.h>
#include <time.h>
```

```
#include <iostream.h>

int main()
{
  srand ((unsigned) time (NULL)); // Define seed for generator
  cout << "\nFirst bunch\n";

  for (int i = 1; i <= 10; i++)
  {
    cout << double(rand()) / double(RAND_MAX) << ", ";
  }

  cout << "\nNext bunch\n";
  for (i = 1; i <= 10; i++)
  {
    cout << double(rand()) / double(RAND_MAX) << ", ";
  }
  return 0;
}
```

The output from this program is:

```
First bunch
0.378216, 0.172918, 0.204382, 0.0794397, 0.397015, 0.562822, 0.36961,
0.557573, 0.105808, 0.813807,

Next bunch
0.0647298, 0.388043, 0.0874966, 0.786981, 0.376598, 0.799158, 0.691275,
0.833857, 0.554155, 0.634297,
```

A more detailed discussion on generating random numbers from a computational finance point of view is given in Seydel (2003). You might consider purchasing a commercial random number generator.

12.2.3 Random (stochastic) processes

A *random* or *stochastic process* is a family of random variables $\{X(t)\}$ defined on a given probability space and indexed by the parameter t that we assume to be in a set T. A random process is really a function of two variables $\{X(t, s)\}$ where t is in T and s is in the sample space S. For a fixed t, X is a random variable while for a fixed s in the sample space it is a function of t only. In the latter case it is called a *realisation* or *path* of X. The index set T is called the *parameter set* of the random process. The values assumed by $X(t)$ are called *states* and the set of all possible values forms the *state space* E of the random process. If the set T is discrete then the process is called a discrete-parameter or *discrete-time* process. If T is continuous then we have a continuous-parameter or *continuous-time* process. If the state space E is discrete the process is called a *discrete-state* process while if E is continuous the process is called a *continuous-state* process. It is possible to classify random processes (see Hsu, 1997):

- Stationary process
- Wide-sense stationary process
- Independent process
- Process with stationary independent increments
- Markov process

- Normal process
- Ergodic process

A full discussion of these processes is, however, beyond the scope of this book. We are interested in the so-called *Wiener process* and we shall explain it because it is important for SDEs. The rest of this section dwells on defining the essentials of the Wiener process.

A random process $\{X(t): t \geq 0\}$ is said to have *independent increments* if whenever

$$0 < t_1 < t_2 < \ldots < t_n \tag{12.15}$$

the differences

$$X(0), X(t_1) - X(0), X(t_2) - X(t_1), \ldots, X(t_n) - X(t_{n-1}) \tag{12.16}$$

are independent. Furthermore, if $\{X(t), t \geq 0\}$ has independent increments and $X(t) - X(s)$ has the same distribution as $X(t+h) - X(s+h)$ for non-negative s, t and h with $s < t$, then the process $X(t)$ is said to have *stationary independent increments*.

Definition 12.1 (Wiener process): A random process $\{X(t), t \geq 0\}$ is called a Wiener process if

- $X(t)$ has stationary independent increments
- The increments $X(t) - X(s)$ (when $t > s$) are *normally distributed*
- $E[X(t)] = 0$ (the mean or expected value)
- $X(0) = 0$.

The importance of the Wiener process in finance is that it models the behaviour of stock prices and other underlying assets (see Hull, 2000). It is not the only model in the world but it has been (almost) universally accepted as a good approximation to stock price behaviour. We usually use the notation $W(t)$ to denote the Wiener process. We note that $\text{var}(W(t) - W(s)) = t - s$ (see Kloeden, Platen and Schurz, 1994) and hence $W(t) - W(s)$ is a normal $N(0, t - s)$ Gaussian distribution.

The Wiener process is similar to the concept of *Brownian motion*. The British botanist Brown first noticed the perpetual motion of small particles of colloidal size immersed in a fluid in 1826. The chaotic behaviour of a typical particle is called Brownian motion and this motion is caused by collisions with the molecules of the surrounding fluid (Schuss, 1980). This model has been applied to modelling the random changes in a stock's price.

12.3   AN INTRODUCTION TO STOCHASTIC DIFFERENTIAL EQUATIONS

In this section we give a very basic introduction to SDEs. We do not try to provide rigour but our goal is to give enough background to help us to understand what an SDE is so that we can then approximate it using finite difference schemes. For the moment, we concentrate on scalar problems. To this end, we examine the general scalar SDE

$$\begin{cases} dX = a(t, X) \, dt + b(t, X) \, dW \\ X(0) = X_0 \end{cases} \tag{12.17}$$

In fact, equation (12.17) is meaningless in a mathematical sense because we should really write it as an integral equation

$$X_t(w) = \int_{t_0}^{t} a(s, X_s(w))\, ds + \int_{t_0}^{t} b(s, X_s(w))\, dW_s(w) \tag{12.18}$$

The theory of SDEs can be found in many books, for example Schuss (1980), Steele (2001). However, we view (12.17) as a differential equation with a random term defined by the Wiener process tagged onto it.

Some special cases of equation (12.17) are found by instantiating the coefficients $a(t, X)$ and $b(t, X)$ by specific functions:

Geometric Brownian motion:

$$dX_t = A(t)X_t\, dt + B(t)X_t\, dW_t \tag{12.19a}$$

Square root process:

$$dX_t = aX_t\, dt + b\sqrt{X_t}\, dW_t \tag{12.19b}$$

Many underlying assets in financial applications are determined by one of these forms; for example, stock, interest rates and commodities. It can be said that (12.17) is a *generalised Wiener process*. For example, in order to model the term structure of interest rates we employ the model

$$dr = m(r)\, dt + s(r)\, dW \tag{12.20}$$

where r is the short-term rate, m is the instantaneous drift and s is the instantaneous standard deviation (Hull, 2000). Notice that these coefficients are independent of t. There are many special cases of (12.20), for example the Vasicek model

$$dr = a(b - r)\, dt + r\, dW \tag{12.21}$$

We now describe how to approximate the solution of these one-factor models using finite difference schemes, starting with the easiest and the one that is most unstable. The test equation is (12.17).

12.4   SOME FINITE DIFFERENCE SCHEMES

We have laid the foundation for finite difference schemes for SDEs because of the equivalence:

$$\text{SDE} = \text{ODE} + \text{Random process}$$

Thus, when approximating SDEs by finite differences we use the results for ODEs (as discussed in Chapter 11) and we must examine how to approximate the Wiener process at discrete times. To this end, the *explicit Euler* scheme is given by:

$$Y_{n+1} = Y_n + a(t_n, Y_n)k + b(t_n, Y_n)\left\{ \underbrace{W_{t_{n+1}} - W_{t_n}}_{\Delta W_n} \right\}$$

$$k = t_{n+1} - t_n, \quad \forall n \geq 0$$

$$Y_0 = X_0 \tag{12.22}$$

Here we use a divided difference to approximate the Wiener process. The increments of the Wiener process are generated by Polar–Marsaglia (for example) at each time level n. The step-length k in equation (12.22) must be chosen small enough, otherwise the discrete solution will oscillate wildly (as was seen in the ODE case). This stability problem is resolved by employing the *implicit Euler* scheme as follows:

$$Y_{n+1} = Y_n + a(t_{n+1}, Y_{n+1})k + b(t_{n+1}, Y_{n+1})\Delta W_n$$
$$Y_0 = X_0 \tag{12.23}$$

The only problem is that this scheme is non-linear if the term $b(t, X)$ is non-linear; for example, the square root process in equations (12.19). The situation can be rectified by using the *Predictor–Corrector* scheme

Predictor: $\qquad \overline{Y}_{n+1} = Y_n + a(t_n, Y_n)k + b(t_n, Y_n)\Delta W_n \tag{12.24a}$

Corrector: $\qquad Y_{n+1} = Y_n + \{\alpha\overline{a}_\eta(t_{n+1}, \overline{Y}_{n+1}) + (1-\alpha)\overline{a}_\eta(t_n, Y_n)\}k$

$$+ \{\eta b(t_{n+1}, \overline{Y}_{n+1}) + (1-\eta)b(t_n, Y_n)\}\Delta W_n \tag{12.24b}$$

with $\alpha \in [0, 1]$, $\eta \in [0, 1]$ and $\overline{a}_\eta = a - \eta b(\partial b/\partial X)$. (See Kloeden, Platen and Schurz, 1994.)

A new-fangled scheme is the so-called *Milstein scheme*

$$Y_{n+1} = Y_n + a(t_n, Y_n)k + b(t_n, Y_n)\Delta W_n + \tfrac{1}{2}bb'\{(\Delta W_n)^2 - k\}$$
$$b' = \frac{\partial b(t, X)}{\partial X} \tag{12.25}$$

Of course, the Predictor–Corrector and Milstein schemes become easier to understand and to program if $b(t, X)$ is a linear function of X only.

12.4.1 Improving the accuracy: Richardson extrapolation

Although the Euler scheme is not always what we would expect, we can apply extrapolation techniques in order to achieve second-order accuracy. We have already discussed this topic in Chapter 11. The steps are:

$$Y_N(k) = X_t + e(T)k + 0(k^2)$$
$$Y_{2N}(k/2) = X_t + \tfrac{1}{2}e(T)k + 0(k^2) \tag{12.26}$$
$$Z_N(k) = 2Y_{2N}(k/2) - Y_N(k)$$

where $e(T)$ is the error associated with the difference scheme.

12.5   WHICH SCHEME TO USE?

We now discuss the stability and accuracy of the different schemes in section 12.4 and base our conclusions on our own experiments. The reader can carry out his or her own experiments by using the code provided on the CD. Here are our conclusions:

- Explicit Euler is easy to program but does not converge very quickly.
- Implicit Euler is always stable but is difficult to apply to non-linear equations.

- The Milstein scheme provides no real advantages when compared to explicit Euler. This is strange because it is often referred to in the literature (see, for example, Jäckel, 2002).
- The Predictor–Corrector scheme converges consistently (and quickly) and performs well under most conditions. It can be scaled to non-linear systems of SDEs.
- Richardson extrapolation is another excellent scheme, but coding this scheme can be a bit tricky.

We stress that these are only guidelines but they should help you to determine the most suitable scheme for your particular problem.

12.6   SYSTEMS OF SDEs

The discussion in this chapter was restricted to scalar problems. In general, we can define systems of SDEs (see Kloeden, Plateu and Schurz, 1994). A treatment of finite difference schemes for such problems is outside the scope of this book.

12.7   CONCLUSIONS AND SUMMARY

We have given an introduction to finite difference methods for approximating stochastic differential equations. Several good and not-so-good schemes were proposed for linear scalar problems. We have tried to demystify this area of mathematics by a gradual build-up from random variables to random processes up to SDEs. Many of the schemes should be familiar at this stage because they are 'perturbations' of similar schemes for ODEs. The only (big) difference is that a white noise term has been added to the equation and in order to solve the equations we must use random number generators (for example, Polar–Marsaglia or Box–Muller).

13

Two-Point Boundary Value Problems

13.1 INTRODUCTION AND OBJECTIVES

In this pivotal chapter we introduce the finite difference method for solving a class of second-order ordinary differential equations on a finite interval. In general, we must provide two extra *boundary conditions* (one at each end of the interval) in order to specify a unique solution. We discuss different ways of specifying a boundary condition that must then be approximated numerically.

This chapter is important for two main reasons. First, it deals with several non-trivial topics that the reader must master if he or she wishes to progress to finite difference schemes for the Black–Scholes equation. In particular, we discuss the following fundamental issues:

- Discretising boundary value problems by finite difference schemes
- Centred difference schemes and when/why they break down
- Exponentially fitted schemes for problems with a large convection term (Il'in, 1969; Duffy, 1980; Farrell *et al.*, 2000; Morton, 1996)
- How to approximate Dirichlet, Neumann, Robin and linearity boundary conditions by one-sided differences and 'ghost points'.

These are important issues to be addressed and we have included them in one chapter for easy access. Second, the C++ classes that we develop in this class use results from previous chapters. In this way we achieve a high level of reusability and usability because we build on what has gone before and hide low-level detail in other classes. We use these classes in new code and applications. We (re)use of the following classes:

- `Vector` and `NumericMatrix`
- Classes that model scalar functions (`AtomicDFunction`)
- Classes to solve tridiagonal systems of equations (for example, `LUTridiagonal-Solver`)
- The functionality in the `ArrayMechanisms` package.

For an excellent introduction to the theory of boundary value problems and their numerical approximation using finite differences, we refer the reader to Herbert Keller's monograph (Keller, 1968).

This chapter provides basic training in finite difference schemes for boundary value problems. It is not very difficult, especially if you have studied and understood Chapter 11 where we introduced finite difference schemes for first-order equations.

13.2 DESCRIPTION OF PROBLEM

We introduce the two-point boundary value problem (TPBVP) by formulating the most general case. Consider a bounded interval (a, b) with $a < b$ and let f be some non-linear function that depends on three variables. The exercise is to find a function $u = u(x)$ in the interval (a, b) that satisfies the second-order equation

$$u'' = f(x, u, u') \qquad \text{on } (a, b) \tag{13.1}$$

in conjunction with the boundary conditions

$$\alpha_0 u(a) + \alpha_1 u'(a) = \alpha \quad |\alpha_0| + |\alpha_1| \neq 0$$
$$\beta_0 u(b) + \beta_1 u'(b) = \beta \quad |\beta_0| + |\beta_1| \neq 0 \tag{13.2}$$

In this latter equation all parameters are known with the exception of the (unknown) solution u and its derivative.

Equation (13.1) is non-linear and in general we say that devising robust numerical schemes for such equations in combination with the boundary conditions (13.2) is a real challenge. The problem may have no solution or it may even have multiple solutions. Fortunately, the situation is simpler in this book as we use a class of *linear* TPBVP that is general enough to model problems in financial engineering. Nonetheless, it is still a challenge to devise robust schemes for such problems, as we shall see later in this chapter.

In general, we can state the following result:

$$f = f(x, u_1, u_2) \tag{13.3}$$

Let

$$\frac{\partial f}{\partial u_1} > 0, \quad \left| \frac{\partial f}{\partial u_2} \right| \leq M$$

and

$$\alpha_0 \alpha_1 \leq 0, \beta_0 \beta_1 \geq 0, \quad |\alpha_0| + |\beta_0| \neq 0$$

Then problem (13.1), (13.2) has the unique solution.

In this chapter we examine a special case of (13.1)

$$Lu \equiv -u'' + p(x)u' + q(x)u = r(x) \tag{13.4}$$

This is a linear equation that is general enough for most of the work in this book. If we take the special case of $p(x) = q(x) = r(x) = 0$ and if we then integrate the equation $u'' = 0$ twice, we see that the solution has the form:

$$u(x) = Ax + B$$

where A and B are integration constants. We conclude that we must be given two extra conditions in order to specify a unique solution. To this end, we usually specify one constraint at $x = a$ and another constraint at $x = b$. There are four main possibilities:

Dirichlet boundary conditions

$$u(a) = \alpha, \qquad u(b) = \beta \tag{13.5}$$

Neumann conditions

$$u'(a) = \alpha, \qquad u'(b) = \beta \tag{13.6}$$

Robin conditions (these have already been discussed – see equation (13.2)).

Linearity boundary condition (see Tavella and Randall, 2000, p. 122)

$$u''(a) = 0, \qquad u''(b) = 0 \tag{13.7}$$

Of course, we can give combinations of the above boundary conditions. For example, we can give a Dirichlet condition at $x = a$ and a Neumann condition at $x = b$ and so on. Equation (13.7) is used when a derivative quantity has a payoff that is at most linear in the underlying (see Wilmott, 1998, p. 642). We are in fact saying that the option value is nearly linear with respect to the spot price. Note that the pure Neumann boundary conditions (13.6) do not always produce a solution to the corresponding boundary value problem.

13.3   (TRADITIONAL) CENTRED-DIFFERENCE SCHEMES

We divide the interval (a, b) into J equal sub-intervals and let h be the length of each sub-interval. Thus, we set up a finite difference scheme on a uniform mesh by approximating the first and second derivatives of u at each mesh point:

$$
\begin{aligned}
L_h u_j &\equiv - \left(\frac{u_{j+1} - 2u_j + u_{j-1}}{h^2} \right) + p(x_j) \left(\frac{u_{j+1} - u_{j-1}}{2h} \right) + q(x_j) u_j \\
&= r(x_j), \quad 1 \le j \le J - 1
\end{aligned}
\tag{13.8}
$$

$$u_0 = \alpha, \quad u_J = \alpha$$

where we have taken Dirichlet conditions for the moment. Grouping terms in (13.8) we can then write the equations as a matrix system (as shown in Chapter 8):

$$A\mathbf{U} = \mathbf{r}$$

$$
A = \begin{pmatrix}
b_1 & c_1 & & & & \\
a_2 & \ddots & \ddots & & 0 & \\
& \ddots & \ddots & \ddots & & \\
& 0 & & \ddots & & c_{J-1} \\
& & & \ddots & \ddots & \\
& & & & a_J & b_J
\end{pmatrix}
\tag{13.9}
$$

where the coefficients of the matrix A are given by

$$
\begin{aligned}
a_j &\equiv -\tfrac{1}{2} \left[1 + \tfrac{1}{2} h \cdot p(x_j) \right] \\
b_j &\equiv \left[1 + \tfrac{1}{2} h^2 \cdot q(x_j) \right] \\
c_j &\equiv -\tfrac{1}{2} \left[1 - \tfrac{1}{2} h \cdot p(x_j) \right]
\end{aligned}
\tag{13.10}
$$

with $1 \le j \le J - 1$, and the vectors are given by:

$$\mathbf{U} = {}^t(u_1, \ldots, u_{J-1})$$

$$
\mathbf{r} = \begin{pmatrix} r_1 \\ \vdots \\ r_{J-1} \end{pmatrix} = \frac{h^2}{2} \begin{pmatrix} r(x_1) \\ \vdots \\ r(x_{J-1}) \end{pmatrix} - \begin{pmatrix} a_1 \alpha \\ \vdots \\ c_J \beta \end{pmatrix}
\tag{13.11}
$$

Incidentally, the reader can check how the boundary conditions have been incorporated into the vector **r** in (13.11).

We call scheme (13.8) a standard difference scheme because it approximates the coefficients and derivatives using conventional divided difference schemes. We shall see that the numerical solution shows *oscillatory behaviour* precisely because we approximate the first derivative by *centred divided differences*. Unfortunately, this approach is used in financial engineering literature and authors tend to use workarounds to avoid spurious oscillations.

Another sufficient condition for (13.8) to have a unique solution is that the matrix in (13.9) is diagonally dominant, that is:

$$|b_j| > |a_j| + |c_j|, \quad j = 1, 2, \ldots, J \quad (a_1 \equiv c_1 \equiv 0) \tag{13.12}$$

In this case the matrix A is non-singular and (13.8) will have a unique solution.

13.3.1   Does the discrete system have a solution?

Can we give sufficient conditions for the system (13.8) to have a unique solution and can we bound the solution by its input? We can state the following:
Assume $|p(x)| \leq P^*$, and

$$0 < Q_* \leq q(x) \leq Q^*, \quad a \leq x \leq b \tag{13.13}$$

Let $h < 2/P^*$. Then scheme (13.8) has a unique solution.

We see that the coefficient of the first derivative plays an important role. If it has large values then the mesh-size h must be chosen small. It turns out in practice that if this is not so then spurious oscillations arise in the numerical solution and its divided differences occur, as is borne out in the engineering and financial engineering literature. In fact, the reader can take a test case and experiment with different values of h and $p(x)$ using *LU* decomposition (see Chapter 8) in order to solve the system of equations. The results speak for themselves. For some other counter-examples, see Farrell *et al.* (2000).

13.3.2   Extrapolation

The scheme (13.8) is second-order accurate when the mesh-size h is constant (otherwise it is only first-order accurate!) and if the conditions in (13.13) are true. As in Chapter 11, we can apply extrapolation techniques to improve the accuracy of the solution to fourth-order. To this end, we must create meshes of size h and $h/2$ and solve the finite difference equations on each one. The result is:

$$u_j(h) - u(x_j) = h^2 e(x_j) + O(h^4)$$
$$\overline{u}_j \equiv \tfrac{4}{3} u_{2j}(h/2) - \tfrac{1}{3} u_j(h) \tag{13.14}$$

13.4   APPROXIMATION OF THE BOUNDARY CONDITIONS

The financial literature tends to be a bit fuzzy when it comes to discussing boundary conditions for Black–Scholes equations and their numerical approximations.

We now discuss how to approximate boundary conditions using finite differences. The main challenge lies in deciding how to approximate the first and possibly second derivatives of the unknown solution at the end-points. We concentrate on the general Robin boundary conditions for the moment (notice that it includes the Dirichlet and Neumann conditions as special cases). Furthermore, we look at the problem at the left-hand boundary $x = a$. There are two main techniques for approximating the Robin boundary condition:

- Taking one-sided differences to approximate the first derivative.
- Defining 'ghost points' and using centred differences to approximate the first derivative at the boundary point (Thomas, 1998).

Let us be specific by looking at the boundary condition

$$\alpha_0 u(a) + \alpha_1 u'(a) = \alpha \tag{13.15}$$

We take a one-sided approximation to the first derivative to get the discrete Robin boundary condition:

$$\begin{cases} \alpha_0 u_0 + \dfrac{\alpha_1}{h}(u_1 - u_0) = \alpha & \text{or} \\ (\alpha_0 h - \alpha_1)u_0 + \alpha_1 \mu_1 = \alpha h \end{cases} \tag{13.16}$$

This is a first-order approximation and it destroys the second-order accuracy of scheme (13.8). In short, the first-order accuracy that we achieved at the boundary percolates as it were into the interior of the interval (a, b). In order to preserve second-order accuracy at the boundary we introduce so-called ghost or fictitious points. These are points that fall outside the interval (a, b). Then we approximate the boundary condition (13.15) at $x = a$ by the following scheme:

$$\begin{cases} \alpha_0 u_0 + \dfrac{\alpha_1}{2h}(u_1 - u_{-1}) = \alpha & \text{or} \\ 2h\alpha_0 u_0 + \alpha_1 (u_1 - u_{-1}) = 2h\alpha \end{cases} \tag{13.17}$$

We now eliminate the value at the ghost point from (13.17) by assuming that the difference scheme in (13.8) is satisfied at $j = 0$. This leads to the difference equation

$$-\left(\frac{u_1 - 2u_0 + u_{-1}}{h^2}\right) + p(x_0)\left(\frac{u_1 - u_{-1}}{2h}\right) + q(x_0)u_0 = r(x_0) \tag{13.18}$$

We then use the expression for the value at the ghost point from (13.17) in (13.18), thus eliminating the ghost point entirely from the system of equations while at the same time preserving second-order accuracy. This technique can be applied to parabolic partial differential equations in general and to the Black–Scholes equation in particular (see Thomas, 1998, p. 15).

13.4.1 Linearity boundary condition

We now discuss how to approximate the boundary conditions (13.7). These are quite common but I have not been able to find a mathematical argument in their favour. Anyway, we use ghost points. The approach is similar to that taken for Robin boundary conditions and in this case we have:

$$\frac{u_1 - 2u_0 + u_{-1}}{h^2} = \alpha \qquad (13.19)$$

Again, we eliminate the value at the ghost point from the two equations (13.19) and (13.18).

13.5   EXPONENTIALLY FITTED SCHEMES AND CONVECTION–DIFFUSION

Let's go back to the result in section 13.3.1 where there are restrictions on the size of h if we wish to have a stable and unique approximate solution to the boundary value problem by the traditional centred difference scheme (13.8). In other words, if the coefficient $p(x)$ is large (and we are talking value of the order of 10 000 for example) we will need to choose h to be very small. It is then time to go for coffee, go to the gym for a workout and then come back to your workstation because the calculations will be very time-consuming. In this case we speak of *convection-dominated problems* (see Morton, 1996) or *singular perturbation problems*. It has been known for more than 50 years that traditional finite difference methods are not up to the job and many solutions have been found that can handle such problems (an early solution can be found in de Allen and Southwell, 1955). This has relevance to financial engineering because similar problems arise in these cases, especially when the volatility is small or when we wish to calculate option sensitivities (delta, gamma).

Concluding, the exponentially fitted method produces a uniformly stable and convergent scheme of order h. We can improve convergence by use of extrapolation techniques. We shall extend the scheme to the Black–Scholes equation in a later chapter based on the schemes in Duffy (1980).

13.6   APPROXIMATING THE DERIVATIVES

The difference scheme (13.8) gives terrible results if the first and second derivatives are defined by the following divided differences:

$$\begin{aligned} u'(x_j) &\sim \frac{u_{j+1} - u_{j-1}}{2h} \\[2mm] u''(x_j) &\sim \frac{u_{j+1} - 2u_j + u_{j-1}}{h^2} \end{aligned} \qquad (13.20)$$

We can show mathematically and by computer experiment that these approximations exhibit *spurious oscillations*. Similar problems are noted in Tavella and Randall (2000, p. 191). In this case the solution itself exhibits spike behaviour so there is little chance that approximation of the sensitivities will be much better (in fact, they are worse!).

So, how do we proceed? There are various solutions. For example, the exponentially fitted method gives good approximation to the delta while the approximation to the gamma tends to be a bit 'flat' when compared to the exact solution (see Cooney, 1999). Another solution is to reformulate the problem (13.4) as a two-by-two system of first-order equations consisting of the solution u and its first derivative. We then approximate this system by a so-called exponentially fitted Box scheme, the scalar version of which we introduced in Chapter 11. We discuss this briefly here and base the discussion on Emel'yanov (1975, 1978).

Consider the Dirichlet boundary value problem

$$\epsilon u'' + a(x)u' - b(x)u = f(x), \quad x \in (0, 1) \tag{13.21}$$

$$u(0) = \mu_0, \quad u(1) = \mu_1$$

$$\epsilon > 0 \text{ small parameter}$$

$$a(x) \geq \alpha > 0, \quad b(x) \geq 0$$

We transform this problem into a first-order system as follows:

$$L_1(u_1 v) \equiv \epsilon v' + av - \epsilon bu = \epsilon f$$

$$L_2(u_1 v) \equiv v - \epsilon u' = 0 \tag{13.22}$$

$$u(0) = \mu_0, \quad u(1) = \mu_1$$

We now approximate (13.22) by the fitted Box scheme:

$$\begin{cases} L_1(u^h, v^h) \equiv \gamma \dfrac{v_{j+1}^h - v_j^h}{h} + a_{j+\frac{1}{2}} \left(\dfrac{v_{j+1}^h + v_j^h}{2} \right) \\[2mm] - \gamma b_{j+\frac{1}{2}} \left(\dfrac{u_{j+1}^h + u_j^h}{2} \right) = \gamma f_{j+\frac{1}{2}}^h \\[2mm] L_2(u^h, v^h) = \dfrac{v_{j+1}^h + v_j^h}{2} - \gamma \left(\dfrac{u_{j+1}^h - u_j^h}{h} \right) = 0 \end{cases} \tag{13.23}$$

where

$$\gamma \equiv \gamma_{j+\frac{1}{2}} = \frac{a_{j+\frac{1}{2}} h}{2} \coth \frac{a_{j+\frac{1}{2}} h}{2\epsilon} \tag{13.24}$$

Then, the major convergence result is:

$$\|u - u^h\|_\infty + \|\epsilon u' - v^h\|_\infty \leq Mh \tag{13.25}$$

This result states that we get uniform convergence of u and its derivative v always. Thus, there are no spurious oscillations.

In a later chapter we examine the time-dependent version of this problem when we introduce the Keller Box scheme for the Black–Scholes equation. Again, we get good results for the option price and its delta.

13.7   DESIGN ISSUES

Having defined the continuous problem and the discrete problem for BVP we must now make a shot at a design that will eventually be implemented in C++. It is possible to design a system that is very malleable and flexible. However, the solution may be over-engineered, by which we mean that it contains so many whistles and bells that the customer is never going to use. On the other hand, we do not wish to hard-wire data structures or algorithms in C-like functions because we may wish to extend the software in the future. Finally, it is not our objective in this book to deliver production code and executable systems but we are interested in analysing and designing difficult numerical problems and showing how they are implemented in C++.

In the current chapter we approximate the solution of two-point boundary value problems using finite difference schemes. The core process is to produce an array of values that approximates the exact solution on some meshes. The main activities that we need to execute in order to realise this process are:

1. Set up the coefficients of the BVP (equation (13.4)).
2. Determine the type of boundary condition for the BVP.
3. Approximate the BVP by centred-difference, fitted or one-sided schemes.
4. Approximate the boundary conditions in step 2 by one-sided differences or by using ghost points.
5. Assemble and build the discrete scheme.
6. Solve the system of equations by LU decomposition or by the Double Sweep method, for example.
7. Present the results to clients (for example, as an output function that writes to Excel).

In order to reduce the scope in this chapter we must make some assumptions and take certain standpoints. The main requirements and restrictions are:

• Use the Datasim function classes.
• Examine Dirichlet conditions only.
• There must be flexibility in switching between different kinds of finite difference schemes.
• We use LU decomposition to solve systems of equations.
• Use classes and code from previous chapters.
• Make tradeoffs: we have a limited amount of time to get results (*gold-plating* comes later).

The UML class diagram is shown in Figure 13.1. Here we see the classes:

• BVP: encapsulates the essence of the continuous problem.

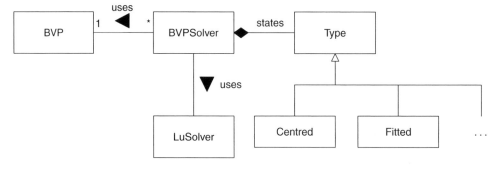

Figure 13.1   Class diagram for finite difference solution

- BVPSolver: central coordinator class for all finite difference schemes that approximate the continuous problem.
- Type: base class for all different kinds of difference schemes.

13.8   CONCLUSIONS AND SUMMARY

We have given a compact introduction to finite difference schemes for two-point boundary value problems. We considered both centred-difference schemes and a new class of exponentially fitted schemes that avoid some of the spurious oscillation problems that we encounter with traditional finite difference schemes. We also introduced Dirichlet, von Neumann and Robin boundary conditions and we proposed both first-order and second-order accurate approximation to them. Finally, we discussed the steps to be taken when actually setting up the C++ code for solving this class of problems.

The knowledge built up in this chapter will be invaluable when we come to discuss parabolic initial boundary value problems and the Black–Scholes equation in later chapters.

Matrix Iterative Methods

14.1 INTRODUCTION AND OBJECTIVES

This chapter discusses how to solve linear systems of equations using iterative methods and it may be skipped on a first reading of this book without loss in continuity. We have included this chapter because iterative methods are an alternative to the direct methods that we introduced in Chapter 8.

In Chapter 8 we showed how *LU* decomposition is used to solve matrix systems. We restricted our attention to tridiagonal and block tridiagonal matrices. We employed *direct methods* to find a solution to the system of linear equations in a finite number of steps. In this chapter we take a completely different approach. Here we start with some initial approximation to the solution of the matrix system and we then construct a sequence of estimates to the solution where each estimate is closer to the exact solution than the previous one. We are thus in the realm of *iterative methods* for solving systems of linear equations. The main methods of interest are:

- The Jacobi method
- The Gauss–Seidel method
- Successive Overrelaxation (SOR)
- The Conjugate Gradient method
- Projected SOR method (for matrix inequalities).

These methods are particularly suitable for sparse matrices. Furthermore, we generalise these methods to solve Linear Complementarity Problems (LCP) of the form

$$Ax \geq b, \quad x \geq c$$
$$(x - c) \cdot (Ax - b) = 0 \tag{14.1}$$

Here A is a square positive-definite matrix, b and c are given vectors and we seek a solution x that satisfies the conditions in (14.1). Here we speak of vector inequality; by definition, a vector v_1 is greater than a vector v_2 if each element in v_1 is greater than the corresponding element in v_2. Please recall that C++ functions that test inequality relationships between vectors are discussed in Chapter 7 and you should use the `ArrayMechanisms` package if you plan to write your own LCP programs. It saves you having to reinvent the wheel.

We propose an algorithm for solving (14.1). The method was invented by C.W. Cryer (1979) and has gained wide acceptance in the financial engineering world (see Wilmott *et al.*, 1993). This algorithm is called the Projected SOR method, which we shall discuss in section 14.7.

We now give a general introduction to solving linear systems of equations using iterative methods.

14.2   ITERATIVE METHODS

In general we wish to find the solution of the linear system written in matrix form:

$$Ax = b \tag{14.2}$$

We give some motivation on finding iterative methods to solve (14.2) and show how they work. For a definitive and very clear discussion, see Varga (1962). Let us rewrite matrix A in the following equivalent form

$$A = D(L + I + U) \tag{14.3}$$

where D is the diagonal matrix with value zero everywhere except on the main diagonal where the values are equal to the diagonal elements of A. The matrix I is the identity matrix, U is upper triangular and L is lower triangular. We can then rewrite the matrix equation $Ax = b$ in the equivalent form

$$x = -Lx - Ux + D^{-1}b \quad \text{or} \quad x = Bx + c \tag{14.4}$$

where $B = -(L + U)$ and $c = D^{-1}b$.

This equation contains the unknown x on both left- and right-hand sides. Now is the crux: we define a 'one-step' sequence of vectors as follows:

$$x^{(k+1)} = Bx^{(k)} + c, \quad k = 0, 1, 2, \ldots \tag{14.5}$$

Starting with some initial approximation to the solution we hope that the sequence will converge to the exact solution x as k increases. As mathematicians we must prove that the sequence does converge; for more information, we refer again to Varga (1962).

There are a number of ways to choose the iteration in (14.4), and we shall discuss each one in turn.

14.3   THE JACOBI METHOD

This is the simplest iterative method. The terms Lx and Ux in (14.4) are both evaluated at level k and the Jacobi scheme in matrix form is given by:

$$x^{(k+1)} = -(L + U)x^{(k)} + D^{-1}b \tag{14.6}$$

or in component form:

$$x_j^{(k+1)} = \frac{-\sum_{\substack{i=1 \\ i \neq j}}^{n} a_{ji} x_i^{(k)} + b_j}{a_{jj}} \quad j = 1, \ldots, n \tag{14.7}$$

We usually take the initial approximation to be that vector all of whose values are zero. With this method we do not use the improved values until after a complete iteration.

14.4   GAUSS–SEIDEL METHOD

This method is similar to the Jacobi method except that the term Lx is evaluated at the level $k + 1$:

$$x^{(k+1)} = -Lx^{(k+1)} - Ux^{(k)} + D^{-1}b \qquad (14.8)$$

In component form, Gauss–Seidel is:

$$x_j^{(k+1)} = \frac{-\sum_{i=1}^{j-1} a_{ji}x_i^{(k+1)} - \sum_{i=j+1}^{n} a_{ji}x_i^{(k)} + b_j}{a_{jj}} \qquad j = 1,\ldots,n \qquad (14.9)$$

We can rewrite (14.9) to produce a more algorithmic depiction that is suitable for C++ development:

$$x_j^{(k+1)} = x_j^{(k)} + r_j^{(k)}$$

$$r_j^{(k)} = \frac{-\sum_{i=1}^{j-1} a_{ji}x_i^{(k+1)} - \sum_{i=j+1}^{n} a_{ji}x_i^{(k)} + b_j}{a_{jj}} \qquad j = 1,\ldots,n \qquad (14.10)$$

STOP? $\|r_j^{(k)}\| \leq$ TOL

Notice that, in contrast to the Jacobi method, the Gauss–Seidel method uses the improved values as soon as they are computed. This is reflected in equation (14.10).

14.5   SUCCESSIVE OVERRELAXATION (SOR)

By a simple modification of the Gauss–Seidel method it is often possible to make a substantial improvement in the rate of convergence, by which we mean the speed with which the sequence of approximations converges to the exact solution x of (14.2). To this end, we modify (14.10) by introducing a so-called *relaxation parameter* ω as a coefficient of the *residual* term:

$$x_j^{(k+1)} = x_j^{(k)} + \omega r_j^{(k)}, \quad j = 1,\ldots,n \qquad (14.11)$$

For $\omega = 1$ we get the Gauss–Seidel method as a special case. A major result is

SOR converges if $0 < \omega < 2$

Furthermore, it has also been shown by experiment that for a suitably chosen ω the number of approximations needing to be computed may be reduced by a factor of 100 in some cases. Indeed for certain classes of matrices this optimal value is known. See Dahlquist (1974) or Varga (1962) for more information.

14.6   OTHER METHODS

We discuss two methods that are related to the current discussion.

14.6.1 The conjugate gradient method

This is a direct method that is useful in practice. We assume that A is positive definite having n rows and n columns. We start with an initial vector U_0. Then for $j = 1, 2, 3, \ldots,$ n compute

$$\left.\begin{matrix} r_0 = F - AU_0 \\ p_0 = r_0 \end{matrix}\right\} \qquad (14.12a)$$

For $j = 1, \ldots, n$ compute:

$$a_j = \|r_j\|_2^2 / (tp_j Ap_j)$$

$$U_{j+1} = U_j + a_j p_j$$

$$r_{j+1} = r_j - a_j Ap_j \qquad (14.12b)$$

$$b_j = \frac{\|r_{j+1}\|_2^2}{\|r_i\|_2^2}$$

$$p_{j+1} = r_{j+1} + b_j p_j$$

Then U_n will be the solution of the linear system $AU = F$ if rounding errors are neglected.

14.6.2 Block SOR

We can generalise the SOR method to the case where the matrix A is partitioned into sub-matrices

$$A = (A_{ij}), A_{ii} \text{ square}, \quad x = (X_i), \quad b = (B_j) \qquad (14.13)$$

For example, A could be a block tridiagonal matrix (recall that we discussed this problem in Chapter 8). We thus propose the following *block SOR* method (see Cryer, 1979):

$$\begin{cases} R_i^{(k)} = B_i - \sum_{j<i} A_{ij} X_j^{(k+1)} - \sum_{j>i} A_{ij} X_j^{(k)} \\ A_{ii} X_i^{(k+1/2)} = A_{ii} X_i^{(k)} + R_i^{(k)} \\ X_i^{(k+1)} = X_i^{(k)} + \omega(X_i^{(k+1/2)} - X_i^{(k)}) \end{cases} \qquad (14.14)$$

A special case is when A is a block tridiagonal matrix. We can then combine LU decomposition with the block SOR because the intermediate vector in (14.14) is a candidate for LU decomposition.

14.6.3 Solving sparse systems of equations

When approximating multidimensional partial differential equations by finite difference methods the resulting matrices are often sparse. An example is when we discretise the Black–Scholes equation for an option based on the maximum of two assets. When the matrix is sparse we can resort to sparse matrix solvers. There is a vast literature on this subject and a full treatment is outside the scope of this book. For applications to financial engineering, see Tavella and Randall (2000). It is possible to use both direct methods and iterative methods to solve such systems although iterative methods are possibly more popular. For an introduction to direct methods for sparse systems, see Duff *et al.* (1990). In general, if you discretise a multidimensional problem directly in all directions, an iterative solver is more flexible; on the other hand, if you use Alternating Direction Implicit (ADI) or some other splitting method, a direct method is more flexible because we solve the problem as a sequence of tridiagonal systems for which we use *LU* decomposition.

14.7 THE LINEAR COMPLEMENTARITY PROBLEM

We now give an introduction to solving problems as shown in (14.1). These are the so-called Linear Complementarity Problem (LCP) methods and they arise in financial engineering applications when we discretise Black–Scholes equations with an early exercise option. For the moment, we present the Projected SOR algorithm (PSOR) that solves (14.1) (see Wilmott *et al.*, 1993):

1. Choose: $x^{(0)} \geq c$

2. $y_j^{(k+1)} = \dfrac{1}{a_{jj}} \left(b_j - \displaystyle\sum_{i=1}^{j-1} a_{ji} x_i^{(k+1)} - \sum_{i=j+1}^{n} a_{ji} x_i^{(k)} \right)$

$x_j^{(k+1)} = \max(c_j, x_j^{(k)} + w(y_j^{(k+1)} - x_j^{(k)}))$

3. Check: $\|x^{(k+1)} - x^{(k)}\| \leq \text{TOL}$

The interface for the class that implements the PSOR method is:

```
template <class V, class I> class ProjectedSOR
{ // The Projected SOR method

private:
  // Ingredient of problem, this is
  //
  //     Ax >= b,  x >= c
  //     (x - c).(Ax - b)  == 0 (inner product)

  NumericMatrix<V, I>* A;        // The matrix
  Vector<V, I>* b;               // The right-hand side vector
  Vector<V, I>* c;               // The lower-bound on the solution

  // Temporary work space
  Vector<V, I> OldVec;           // The solution at level k
  Vector<V,I> NewVec;            // The solution at level k+1
  Vector<V,I> InterVec;          // The intermediate vector

  V tol;                         // Determines how many iterations

public:
  // For you my friend
};
```

We leave it as an exercise to write the code for this class. It is a simple extension of the code for the Gauss–Seidel method.

14.8   IMPLEMENTATION

The header file for the iterative scheme is:

```
enum MatrixIterativeType {Jacobi, GaussSeidel};

template <class V, class I>
  class MatrixIterativeSolver
{
private:
    // Input to class
    NumericMatrix<V, I>* A;        // The matrix to be inverted
    Vector<V, I>* b;               // The right-hand side vector
    V tol;                         // Tolerance for convergence
    MatrixIterativeType itype;
    MatrixIterativeSolver();
    MatrixIterativeSolver (const MatrixIterativeSolver<V,I>& s2);
    MatrixIterativeSolver<V,I>& operator =
         (const MatrixIterativeSolver<V,I>& i2);

    // Temporary work space
    Vector<V, I> OldVec;           // The solution at level k
    Vector<V,I> NewVec;            // The solution at level k+1

    // Nitty-gritty functions
    void calcJacobi();
    void calcGaussSeidel();
public:
    // Constructors and destructor
    MatrixIterativeSolver(NumericMatrix<V,I>& MyA,
        Vector<V,I>& myRHS);
    virtual ~MatrixIterativeSolver();
    void setTolerance(const V& tolerance);
    void setIterationType(MatrixIterativeType type);
    // Result; note that this vector INCLUDES BOTH end conditions
    Vector<V,I> solve();
};
```

The essential code for Jacobi and Gauss–Seidel is:

```
template <class V, class I>
void MatrixIterativeSolver<V,I>::calcJacobi()
{
  V tmp;
  for (I  j = (*A).MinRowIndex(); j <= (*A).MaxRowIndex(); j++)
  {
    tmp = V(0.0);
    for (I i = (*A).MinColumnIndex();
      i <= (*A).MaxColumnIndex(); i++)
    {
      if (i != j)
      {
        tmp += (*A)(j,i) * OldVec[i];
      }
    }
    NewVec[j] = (-tmp + (*b)[j]) / (*A)(j, j);
  }
```

```
}
template <class V, class I>
void MatrixIterativeSolver<V,I>::calcGaussSeidel()
{
  V tmp1, tmp2;

  for (I j = (*A).MinRowIndex(); j <= (*A).MaxRowIndex(); j++)
  {
    tmp1 = tmp2 = V(0.0);
    for (I i = (*A).MinColumnIndex(); i <= j-1; i++)
    {
      tmp1 += (*A)(j,i) * NewVec[i];
    }

    for (i = j+1; i <= (*A).MaxColumnIndex(); i++)
    {
      tmp2 += (*A)(j,i) * OldVec[i];
    }

    NewVec[j] = (-tmp1 -tmp2 + (*b)[j]) / (*A)(j, j);
  }
}
```

The reader can check the above code with the algorithms in (14.7) and (14.9). We have done our best to make the relationship as clear as possible.

Sample code is to be found on the CD. Here is a snippet:

```
// A matrix corresponding to boundary value problem u" + u = 0, u(0) = 0,
u(1) = 1
  J = 10;
  double h =  1.0 / double(J);
  Vector<double, int> A(J-1, 2, 1.0); // J-1 els, start == 2
  Vector<double, int> B(J, 1, -2.0 + (h*h));
  Vector<double, int> C(J-1, 1, 1.0);

  Vector<double, int> R(J, 1, 0.0);    // Right-hand side
  R[R.MaxIndex()] = -1.0;

  NumericMatrix<double, int> A3 = createMatrix(A,B,C);
  print(A3);

  MatrixIterativeSolver<double, int> secondSolver(A3, R);
  secondSolver.setTolerance(0.0001);
  secondSolver.setIterationType(Jacobi);

  Vector<double, int> Result4 = secondSolver.solve();
  cout << "\nSolution" << endl; print(Result4);

  Vector<double, int> exact(Result4);
  double d = ::sin(1.0);
  double x = h;
  for (int i = exact.MinIndex(); i <= exact.MaxIndex(); i++)
  {
    exact[i] = ::sin(x) / d;
    x += h;
  }
  print(exact);
```

The output from this program is:

```
MAT: [
Row 1 (-1.99, 1, 0, 0, 0, 0, 0, 0, 0, 0, )
Row 2 (1, -1.99, 1, 0, 0, 0, 0, 0, 0, 0, )
Row 3 (0, 1, -1.99, 1, 0, 0, 0, 0, 0, 0, )
Row 4 (0, 0, 1, -1.99, 1, 0, 0, 0, 0, 0, )
Row 5 (0, 0, 0, 1, -1.99, 1, 0, 0, 0, 0, )
Row 6 (0, 0, 0, 0, 1, -1.99, 1, 0, 0, 0, )
Row 7 (0, 0, 0, 0, 0, 1, -1.99, 1, 0, 0, )
Row 8 (0, 0, 0, 0, 0, 0, 1, -1.99, 1, 0, )
Row 9 (0, 0, 0, 0, 0, 0, 0, 1, -1.99, 1, )
Row 10 (0, 0, 0, 0, 0, 0, 0, 0, 1, -1.99, )]

Solution
[Vector: size 10, Min/Max indices: 1, 10
0.111809,0.222533,0.331031,0.436305,0.537217,0.63287,0.722194,0.8044,
0.878562, 0.944001,]

[Vector: size 10, Min/Max indices: 1, 10
0.118642,0.236098]
```

14.9   CONCLUSIONS AND SUMMARY

We have given an introduction to iterative methods for solving linear systems of equations. We looked at the Jacobi, Gauss–Seidel and Successive Overrelaxation (SOR) methods. All of these methods start with an initial guess to the solution of the matrix problem and a sequence of improved estimates is calculated that hopefully converge to the exact solution. An important point is the speed or rate of convergence and to this end it is possible to choose an optimal overrelaxation parameter that improves the convergence rate.

Having built up the theory of iterative methods we then introduce the Linear Complementarity Problem (LCP). This has to do with matrix inequalities and we discuss the Projected SOR method to solve this problem. LCP solvers are needed when we discretise the Black–Scholes equation by finite differences and they are needed primarily because of the early exercise feature of American options.

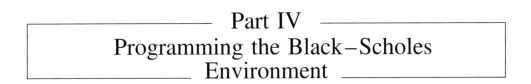

Part IV
Programming the Black–Scholes Environment

15
An Overview of Computational Finance

15.1 INTRODUCTION AND OBJECTIVES

In Part IV we build on chapters from Part III by extending the finite difference method for ordinary differential equations to partial differential equations. We pay particular attention to the one-factor and two-factor Black–Scholes equations.

In this chapter we give an overview of the models and techniques that are needed in order to produce C++ code for instrument pricing. We take a holistic view and sketch the *instrument life cycle* from the moment that a financial engineer conceives a new derivative product to when a software product is up and running on his or her workstation. Thus, the core process is to create the appropriate C++ code for the problem at hand. We realise this by a number of major activities that we will describe in more detail in section 15.2.

This chapter gives an overview of the major concepts pertaining to the numerical approximation of partial differential equations (PDEs) (in particular, the one-factor and two-factor Black–Scholes equation). In this book we use the finite difference method (FDM) to approximate the solution of partial differential equations. In general, exact solutions of PDEs cannot be found or are too unwieldy to be of use in practice. The topics in this chapter are for the benefit of those readers who do not necessarily have an applied mathematics or numerical analysis or physics background. We are thinking of economists, statisticians and other financial engineers for whom the theory of partial differential equations and numerical analysis is new. We are thinking of quantitative engineers who have a background in statistic, econometrics and those who use Monte Carlo methods for option pricing. For the benefit of this latter group of readers we have included a number of references on the theory of partial differential equations and numerical analysis in order to provide some guidelines.

15.2 THE DEVELOPMENT LIFE CYCLE

The core process in this book is to produce C++ classes and code that model the behaviour of financial instruments in general and options in particular. Thus, the input is a specification of a financial model while the output is C++ code that implements the model and satisfies customer requirements. To this end, we identify three major activities:

A1: Create a PDE based on the financial model
A2: Approximate the PDE by FDM
A3: Map the FDM to C++ code.

Each activity has clearly defined input and output and this improves maintainability. In software terms we say that each activity is a black box that delivers value to the next activity in the supply chain, but other activities do not know about its internal structure or how it actually performed its duties. This is another example of the Information Hiding principle. Its application will have major maintainability advantages during the C++ development phase. The UML activity diagram for the current process is shown in

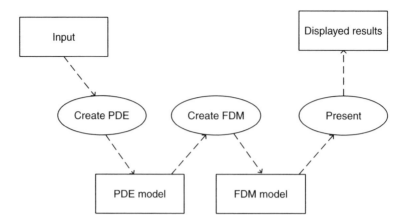

Figure 15.1   Development life cycle

Figure 15.1. Each oval represents an activity while each rectangular box is a data structure. Each data structure is unambiguously defined and its composition can be described using an UML class diagram.

We mention that Figure 15.1 can be modified to work with other kinds of numerical schemes, for example the finite element method (FEM). In this case the second activity in Figure 15.1 should be replaced by a finite element solver.

15.3   PARTIAL DIFFERENTIAL EQUATIONS

PDEs have been around for about 200 years now and a vast literature has been written on the subject. They have been applied in the past (and at present) to model many natural phenomena such as fluid and heat flow, magnetohydrodynamics, stresses in buildings, semiconductor devices and many more (see Morton, 1996). Many pure and applied mathematicians have studied these equations in great detail and much is known about how to formulate them and prove existence and uniqueness theorems for them. Furthermore, engineers, scientists and numerical analysts have developed numerical schemes that solve the equations of PDEs numerically on digital computers.

All kinds of PDEs are available, but our interest in this book is in a particular class of PDE that models options. Before we discuss this class it is useful to determine the different ways of viewing PDEs; in other words, we wish to determine the essential dimensions of all PDEs:

- Time-dependent or time-independent
- The number of space dimensions in the PDE (one, two, three, ...)
- Scalar equation or systems of equations
- PDE type (parabolic, elliptic, hyperbolic)
- Boundary value problem or initial value problem
- Type of boundary (Dirichlet, Neumann, Robins, radiation type)
- Linear or non-linear equations.

It is not possible to discuss all of these dimensions in this book but we shall certainly discuss them in the chapters in Part IV when they have relevance to PDEs for financial engineering.

The classification of PDEs into elliptic, parabolic and hyperbolic types is standard. Each of these classes has special subclasses and specific examples. It is also useful to study special cases in great detail in order to gain insights in solving more complicated equations in the same class. Our main interest is in parabolic equations and we devise several finite difference schemes to approximate their solution. Finite difference schemes for hyperbolic, elliptic or mixed problems is outside the scope of this book, although we shall give some mention of schemes for first-order hyperbolic equations because these can be seen as the limiting case of the Black–Scholes equation when the volatility term in that equation approaches zero.

Some classes of options and derivatives can be modelled by partial integral differential equations (PIDEs). These are equations in which an integral term containing the unknown solution is appended to a parabolic differential equation (see Tavella and Randall, 2000, for an example of a PIDE).

15.4   NUMERICAL APPROXIMATION OF PDEs

In general it is not possible or even desirable to attempt to find the exact solution of parabolic initial boundary value problems (IBVP). We then resort to some numerical techniques. In general, the *continuous space* of (x, t) values must be replaced by a *discrete space* represented by a finite set of points in (x, t) space. Furthermore, derivatives, function values, boundary and initial conditions also need to be approximated in some way. In general, we need to address the following issues:

- Choosing a suitable discretisation of (x, t) space
- Approximating derivatives and coefficients appearing in the IBVP
- Approximating the boundary conditions
- Approximating the initial condition.

Once these activities have been executed we shall be able to construct the approximate solution at the discrete mesh points. These values are rolled into a linear system of equations and we then solve this system using some kind of direct or iterative matrix solver (recall that we discussed these issues in Chapters 8 and 14).

There are very many ways to approximate IBVPs. We shall give a list of the major contenders and a brief description of each one.

Finite element method

This is a well-established theory in engineering. FEM is ideally suited to calculating stresses in buildings and other static problems. It has been applied to PDE (in particular, parabolic equations) and is a powerful tool for problems with irregular boundaries and/or discontinuous coefficients.

In general, the FEM process takes place in two steps. First, the space direction is discretised by using polynomials with compact support. This results in a first-order system of ordinary differential equations that are then solved by one of the integration techniques that we introduced in Chapter 11.

Be warned: Finite element theory demands a certain amount of mathematical sophistications and, furthermore, the author is not convinced that this method is suitable for financial engineering. It may be overkill.

Spectral and pseudo-spectral methods

These are similar to FEM except that we seek an approximate solution as a sum of trigonometric polynomials. These methods are only suitable for well-behaved problems with no discontinuous coefficients. I doubt if the methods are general and robust enough for real-life and nasty initial boundary value problems.

Finite difference method

In this case we replace derivatives in x and t by divided differences at discrete mesh points. We then obtain a linear system of equations that we solve with a matrix solver. The chapters in Part IV expand on that work to show how to apply finite differences to time-dependent problems.

Finite volume method

This method has its roots in fluid dynamics and conversation laws. In contrast to FDM where we work with values of discrete functions at mesh points, we use the finite volume method to integrate over some so-called volume to compute a discrete value. The finite volume method is similar to FDM and gives the same discrete set of equations in the one-dimensional case. However, some schemes lead to *non-linear* systems of equations and this complicates computations because we need to solve the system of equations by Newton's method, for example. On the other hand, the finite volume method in two dimensions (using triangles and quadrilaterals as volumes) is easier to apply than conventional FDM. For an introduction to the finite volume method, see Morton (1996).

Binomial and trinomial trees

These methods have their place in the financial engineering Hall of Fame. They are well understood in the financial community. However, they do have their limitations:

- They do not always converge and oscillation solutions appear.
- They have difficulty with certain kinds of exotic options (barriers).
- There are many different implements of the methods, thus making standardisation more difficult.
- They may be difficult for IT people to understand because they are very close to the financial problem domain.

The author has programmed the binomial and trinomial methods for certain kinds of plain options. We prefer using FDM because it is more general, performs better and is more maintainable than binomial or trinomial methods.

Meshless method

The meshless method (Babushka *et al.*, 2002) is a competitor to FDM and FEM because it finds approximate solutions to a PDE, not by using structured meshes (as with FDM) and unstructured meshes (in FEM) but instead it is based on satisfying the PDE at certain points. The meshless method is not so well known but it may prove popular in the future, especially for problems in two and three dimensions and for complicated geometries.

15.5   THE CLASS OF FINITE DIFFERENCE SCHEMES

We now discuss some of the schemes that we use in this book. Let us consider the case of one space variable x and one time variable t for convenience. When working with FDM, we can discretise IBVPs in two different ways:

- As a first iteration, discretise in the x direction only
- Discretise in x and t simultaneously.

The first approach is called the method of lines (MOL) and it produces a system of ODEs that can then be solved by the methods in Chapter 11. The second approach is to discretise in both x and t to get a system of equations at time level $n + 1$ as a function of known quantities at time level n. In both cases we distinguish between explicit and implicit time differencing. With an explicit method the value at level $n + 1$ is calculated in terms of the value at level n without any extra matrix inversion, while with an implicit method the solution at level $n + 1$ is calculated from the known values at level n by solving a linear system of equations.

15.6   SPECIAL SCHEMES FOR SPECIAL PROBLEMS

They say that the devil is in the details. When applying FDM to financial engineering problems things never go as in the numerical cookbooks. Numerical analysis is as much an art as a science and each problem must be examined on its own merits. There is no golden rule or silver bullet.

We shall discuss the following kinds of partial differential equations in this book:

- The one-dimensional and two-dimensional heat equation
- The one-factor Black–Scholes equation
- The two-factor Black–Scholes equation.

Of course, we shall introduce a scale of finite difference schemes that are in fact generalisations of the schemes in Chapter 11:

- Centred-differencing in the space direction
- Explicit and implicit Euler schemes
- Crank–Nicolson
- Exponentially fitted schemes (Il'in, 1969; Duffy, 1980).

These schemes work well in 'normal' circumstances. However, the parameters of the PDE may be defined in such a way that the traditional methods break down and hence the well-known finite difference recipes leave us high and dry. Some of the problems that we encounter in practice are:

- Discontinuous initial conditions (e.g. with binary options)
- Discontinuous boundary conditions (e.g. with barrier options)

- Problems with small volatility, large drift (or both)
- Possible schemes for approximating the Greeks (delta, gamma).

In particular, we discuss at a fundamental level in Chapter 18 why recipe-type schemes do not work. There is a lot of confusion in the literature and some articles tend to 'fudge' in order to improve the accuracy. There is hope: robust algorithms do exist and have been known to engineers and numerical analysts for about 40 years. To this end, we discuss some special and robust schemes:

- Extrapolated Euler (implicit Euler on two consecutive meshes)
- The exponentially fitted scheme for the convection-diffusion equation (Duffy, 1980)
- The Keller Box scheme (Keller, 1971).

15.7   IMPLEMENTATION ISSUES AND THE CHOICE OF PROGRAMMING LANGUAGE

This book is about C++. We could have chosen another language but we did not. In general, one should choose the language that is most appropriate to the problem at hand. If you prefer Java or C#, then that's fine. However, C++ is an ISO standard and we expect it to be around in 20 years' time, just as its ancestor C is still alive and kicking at the moment or writing!

15.8   ORIGINS AND APPLICATION AREAS

The world's most famous mathematicians, engineers and scientists have been working with partial differential equations for at least 200 years. In fact, we could probably state without contradiction that Isaac Newton laid the foundation for all the results with the introduction of his laws of motion, and the world owes a debt of gratitude to him as well as to others such as Gauss, Fourier, Laplace and somewhat more recently Courant and John von Neumann, to mention just a few.

Many physical and natural phenomena can be modelled by parabolic partial differential equations that are then approximated numerically. We give a short summary of some major application areas where such equations (and in particular, the convection–diffusion equation) are everyday occurrences (see Morton, 1996, for further information on these equations and how to approximate them using finite element methods):

- Pollutant dispersion in a river estuary
- Velocity transport in the incompressible Navier–Stokes equation
- Atmospheric pollution
- Fokker–Plank equation
- Semiconductor equations
- Groundwater transport
- Stefan problem
- Turbulence transport
- Viscous incompressible flow past an aerofoil.

In general, partial differential equations for financial engineering applications tend to be simpler to solve than some of the above problems. A classic on the finite difference method is Richtmyer and Morton (1967). It is somewhat dated but well worth reading.

15.9 CONCLUSIONS AND SUMMARY

This chapter was an overview of Part IV of this book in which the chapters are concerned with modelling partial differential equations (aka Black–Scholes) that originate in financial engineering by the finite difference method. We give an introduction to parabolic initial boundary value problems and how to approximate them. Furthermore, we complement traditional finite difference methods by special schemes that are suited to difficult problems in option modelling.

16

Finite Difference Schemes
for Black–Scholes

16.1 INTRODUCTION AND OBJECTIVES

In this chapter we introduce a class of finite difference equations for a number of model parabolic partial differential equations. We extend the finite difference schemes that we developed for the time-independent two-point boundary value problems in Part III (in particular Chapter 13). We shall use centred divided differences to approximate the first and second derivatives in the space direction. Furthermore, we shall discretise the time dimension in the heat and Black–Scholes equations using the finite difference methods that we introduced in Chapter 11; for example, explicit and implicit Euler and Crank–Nicolson. In short, the problem reduces to one of putting the pieces together: the big challenge is to formulate the *fully discrete* problem (that is, both space and time are discretised) and devise suitable algorithms for this problem that we subsequently implement in C++.

We build up the knowledge in this chapter as follows. First, we give our first example of explicit finite difference schemes by looking at the one-dimensional heat equation with Dirichlet boundary conditions. We discuss how to calculate the solution at time level $n + 1$ in terms of the solution at time level n. We then progress to the Black–Scholes equation (which is essentially a heat equation with an appended convection term) and we devise explicit finite difference schemes for it. Of course, we know that the Black–Scholes equation can be transformed to the heat equation by a change of variables (see, for example, Wilmott, 1998).

For those readers who are familiar with the binomial and trinomial methods for pricing options we include a section to show how the trinomial method can be viewed as a special case of an explicit finite difference scheme. Hopefully, this section will show that finite difference schemes are not much more difficult to understand than the lattice methods with which the reader is already accustomed. They are also more stable and reliable than lattice methods. We take a close look at initial conditions for the heat and Black–Scholes equations. In particular, we examine the problems that arise when the initial condition is smooth but has a discontinuity in the first derivative or even where the initial condition itself is discontinuous at a finite number of points. The relationship with *payoff functions* in option pricing theory is explored because it is here that some traditional finite difference schemes show signs of spurious oscillations. We give some examples of the different kinds of payoff functions for a number of exotic option types.

16.2 MODEL PROBLEM: THE ONE-DIMENSIONAL HEAT EQUATION

The heat equation has its roots in physics and is probably the best-known partial differential equation in the whole of mathematics. Many famous people have studied it from a number of perspectives. It is the prototypical example of a *diffusion equation*. Our interest in the heat equation is that we use it as a springboard for more complicated *convection–diffusion* equations, among others the Black–Scholes equation.

In order to motivate the heat equation, think of a one-dimensional metal rod of length L that is being heated in some way. For example, a gas jet may be placed at the middle of the rod at time $t = 0$. We must take account of the ends of the rod. For example, the rod may be insulated or heat may be entering or leaving the rod by means of conduction or radiation. The basic differential equation with Dirichlet boundary conditions is given by

$$\frac{\partial U}{\partial T} = K \frac{\partial^2 U}{\partial X^2}, \quad K = \text{constant}$$

$$U(X = 0) = U(X = L) = 0 \text{ (insulated)} \tag{16.1}$$

$$U(T = 0) = U_0 \text{ (initial condition)}$$

In this case we assume that the rod is insulated (this is why the temperature U is zero at the ends). By using the change of variables

$$t = KT/L^2, \qquad x = X/L, \qquad u = U/U_0 \tag{16.2}$$

we can then transform equation (16.1) to the *non-dimensional* form

$$\frac{\partial u}{\partial t} = \frac{\partial^2 u}{\partial x^2}$$

$$u(x = 0) = u(x = 1) = 0 \tag{16.3}$$

$$u(t = 0) = 1$$

Problem (16.3) is called an initial boundary value problem on the continuous region $(0, 1) \times (0, T)$. In order to approximate the solution of (16.3) by finite differences we must break the space up into discrete meshes, as shown in Figure 16.1. We define so-called *mesh points* where the solution of the finite difference scheme is defined. Note that the approximate solution is **not** *a priori* defined in the area between the mesh points, and some kind of interpolation is used if a value is needed between two mesh points (this is in contrast to other methods, such as the finite element method, where the approximate solution is in principle defined throughout the whole region of interest).

In general, we use one-step methods in the time direction for the heat equation. This can be seen from Figure 16.1, where the dotted mesh points represent known values at time level n (there are three of them) and the crossed mesh points (in this case there is just one of them) represent points where the solution is unknown and hence must be calculated there. To this end, we extend the results from Chapters 11 and 13 to propose the following explicit difference scheme for the heat equation:

$$\left.\begin{array}{l} \dfrac{u_j^{n+1} - u_j^n}{k} = \dfrac{u_{j+1}^n - 2u_j^n + u_{j-1}^n}{h^2} \\[2mm] u_j^{n+1} = u_j^n + r(u_{j+1}^n - 2u_j^n + u_{j-1}^n) \\[2mm] \qquad = ru_{j-1}^n + (1 - 2r)u_j^n + ru_{j+1}^n \quad (r \equiv k/h^2) \end{array}\right\} \tag{16.4}$$

where h is the step size in the x direction and k is the step size in the t direction.

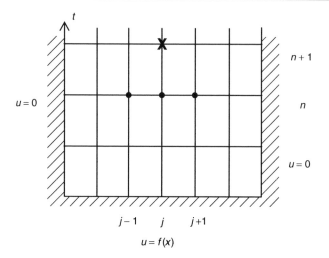

Figure 16.1 Explicit method (1/2)

In this case we see that all values on the right-hand side of (16.4) are known (evaluated at time level n) while the unknown value on the left-hand side of (16.4) can be directly calculated. There is no need to solve a linear system of equations. Sounds great! Unfortunately, there is no free lunch in the land of finite differences and the bad news is that scheme (16.4) is stable (and convergent) **only** under the condition:

$$\text{Valid scheme if } (1 - 2r) \geq 0 \Longleftrightarrow r \leq \tfrac{1}{2} \tag{16.5}$$

We now introduce the fully implicit finite difference scheme for the heat equation. In this case there are three unknown values at time level $n + 1$ and one known value at time level n, as can be seen in Figure 16.2. The corresponding scheme is a generalisation of the results in Chapter 11:

$$\left. \begin{aligned} \frac{u_j^{n+1} - u_j^n}{k} &= \frac{u_{j+1}^{n+1} - 2u_j^{n+1} + u_{j-1}^{n+1}}{h^2} \\ \alpha u_{j-1}^{n+1} + \beta u_j^{n+1} &+ \gamma u_{j+1}^{n+1} = u_j^n \\ \begin{cases} \alpha = -r < 0 \\ \beta = 1 + 2r > 0 \\ \gamma = -r < 0 \end{cases} & \\ U^n = {}^t(u_1, \ldots, u_{j-1}) & \end{aligned} \right\} \tag{16.6}$$

Of course, this problem is more difficult to solve than the explicit scheme (16.4) because we now have to solve a tridiagonal matrix system:

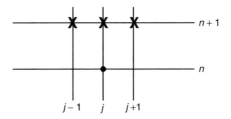

Figure 16.2 Fully implicit method

$$AU^{n+1} = U^n$$

$$A = \begin{pmatrix} \beta & \gamma & & & \\ \alpha & \ddots & \ddots & & 0 \\ & \ddots & \ddots & \gamma \\ 0 & & \ddots & \ddots & \gamma \\ & & & \alpha & \beta \end{pmatrix}$$

(16.7)

Of course, we can use the matrix techniques from Chapter 8 (for example, *LU* decomposition) to solve this system of equations at each time level.

Another implicit scheme for approximating the heat equation is the famous Crank–Nicolson method and it can be motivated by averaging the explicit and implicit schemes in equations (16.4) and (16.6) to give:

$$u_j^{n,1/2} \equiv \tfrac{1}{2}(u_j^{n+1} + u_j^n)$$

$$\frac{u_j^{n+1} - u_j^n}{k} = \frac{u_{j+1}^{n,1/2} - 2u_j^{n,1/2} + u_{j-1}^{n,1/2}}{h^2}$$

(16.8)

$$-ru_{j-1}^{n+1} + (2 + 2r)u_j^{n+1} - ru_{j+1}^{n+1} = ru_{j-1}^n + (2 - 2r)u_j^n + ru_{j+1}^n$$

$$AU^{n+1} = F^n \quad \text{Matrix form}$$

This scheme can also be written as a matrix system in much the same way as in equation (16.7). This scheme corresponds to the mesh, as depicted in Figure 16.3.

It is possible to combine the explicit, implicit and Crank–Nicolson schemes into a single *theta scheme*, as it is called. We introduce a new variable in the range 0 to 1; the resulting scheme is:

$$\frac{u_j^{n+1} - u_j^n}{k} = \frac{u_{j+1}^{n,\theta} - 2u_j^{n,\theta} + u_{j-1}^{n,\theta}}{h^2}$$

$$u_j^{n,\theta} \equiv \theta u_j^{n+1} + (1 - \theta)u_j^n, \ \theta \in [0, 1]$$

$$\theta = 0 \quad \text{Explicit Euler}$$

$$\theta = 1 \quad \text{Fully implicit (backward)}$$

$$\theta = \tfrac{1}{2} \quad \text{(Crank-Nicolson CN)}$$

(16.9)

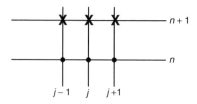

Figure 16.3   Crank–Nicolson scheme (1947)

16.3   THE BLACK–SCHOLES EQUATION

The one-factor Black–Scholes equation is similar to the heat equation but includes an extra convection term. Recall the famous equation once again:

$$-\frac{\partial V}{\partial t} + \frac{1}{2}\sigma^2 S^2 \frac{\partial^2 V}{\partial S^2} + rS\frac{\partial V}{\partial S} - rV = 0 \tag{16.10}$$

The explicit scheme is built on similar lines to the explicit scheme for the heat question:

$$-\frac{V_j^{n+1} - V_j^n}{k} + \frac{1}{2}\sigma^2 S_j^2 \left(\frac{V_{j+1}^n - 2V_j^n + V_{j-1}^n}{h^2}\right)$$

$$+ r S_j \left(\frac{V_{j+1}^n - V_{j-1}^n}{2h}\right) - r V_j^n = 0 \tag{16.11}$$

$$V_j^{n+1} = \alpha_j V_{j-1}^n + \beta_j V_j^n + \gamma_j V_{j+1}^n$$

where the coefficients are given by

$$\alpha, \beta, \gamma : \text{ interpret as probabilities}$$

$$\alpha_j = \frac{k\sigma^2 S_j^2}{2h^2} - \frac{rkS_j}{2h} = \frac{k\sigma^2(jh)^2}{2h^2} - \frac{rk(jh)}{2h} = \frac{k\sigma^2 j^2}{2} - \frac{rkj}{2}$$

$$\beta_j = 1 - \frac{2k\sigma^2(jh)^2}{2h^2} - rk = 1 - \sigma^2 j^2 k - rk \tag{16.12}$$

$$\gamma_j = \frac{k\sigma^2 j^2}{2} + \frac{rkj}{2}$$

It is possible to get incorrect answers (negative values, for example) if the time step k is chosen inappropriately. To motivate what we mean we note that the scheme (16.12) is in fact equivalent to the trinomial method, as can be verified by examining how the meshes compare, as in Figure 16.4. Furthermore, the coefficients in (16.12) correspond to *positive* probabilities in the trinomial method:

α: the probability that the stock price decreases
β: the probability that the stock price remains the same
γ: the probability that the stock price increases.

Of course, these values should be positive if we are to retain any physical or financial meaning in the numerical results. We say that the explicit scheme is *conditionally stable.*

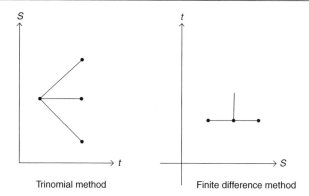

Trinomial method   Finite difference method

Figure 16.4 Comparing meshes

This means that there are restrictions on k and h and there is some kind of inequality between them that must be satisfied at all times if we wish to have a good approximation. The bad news is that the relationship is of the form: the time step must be of the order of the square of the space step as shown in inequality (16.5) in the case of the heat equation (see Thomas, 1998, p. 104).

We shall see in Chapter 18 how to create *uniformly stable* schemes for the Black–Scholes equation where this constraint does not need to be satisfied.

16.4 INITIAL CONDITIONS AND EXOTIC OPTIONS PAYOFFS

It can be proved mathematically that finite difference schemes for a problem in which the initial function and its derivatives are continuous is very close to the solution of the corresponding partial differential equation. It can be shown (see Richtmyer and Morton, 1967) for a certain class of finite difference scheme that if the initial function and its first $(p - 1)$ derivatives are continuous and the pth derivative is normal discontinuous, then the difference between the solution of the partial differential equation and a convergent solution of the difference equation is of the order

$$\frac{p+2}{p+4}$$
$$k$$

for small k (note that k is the time step). Thus, for example $p = 1$ for functions whose first derivative is discontinuous and the expected error is

$$3/5$$
$$k$$

It can also be proved analytically that if boundary conditions are constant the effect of discontinuities in initial values and initial derivatives upon the solution of a parabolic differential equation decreases as the time t increases. This observation has been borne out by experiment.

Another problem that we can encounter is when there is a *compatibility problem* between the initial and boundary conditions for the heat equation. To this end, let us look at the following model problem:

$$\frac{\partial u}{\partial t} = \frac{\partial^2 u}{\partial x^2}, \quad 0 < x < 1$$

$$u(x, 0) = \sin \pi x, \quad 0 < x < 1$$

$$u(0, t) = u(1, t) = 0, \quad t > 0$$

Here see that the initial function and its derivatives are continuous and that the boundary conditions at $(0, 0)$ and $(1, 0)$ remain equal to the initial values at these points. On the other hand, consider the problem

$$u(x, t) = (e^{-\pi^2 t}) \sin \pi x$$

$$\frac{\partial u}{\partial t} = \frac{\partial^2 u}{\partial x^2}, \quad 0 < x < 1, \quad t > 0$$

$$u(x, 0) = 1, \quad 0 < x < 1$$

$$u(0, t) = u(1, t) = 0, \quad t > 0$$

whose exact solution is given by

$$u = \frac{4}{\pi} \sum_{n=0}^{\infty} \frac{1}{2(n+1)} e^{-(2n+1)^2 \pi^2 t} \sin(2n + 1)\pi x$$

In this case we have problems with the solutions at the point $(0, 0)$ because the limiting value of the initial value is unity as x tends to zero. However, the boundary condition at $x = 0$ states that the value of u is zero! We thus have a discontinuity at $(0, 0)$ and its value could equally well have been chosen as 1 or 0.5 instead of 0. The finite difference scheme is thus poor near $x = 0$ for small values of t. It can be shown experimentally however that the accuracy of the finite difference solution improves as t increases. This is characteristic of parabolic equations (in contrast to hyperbolic equations where errors are propagated undiminished). Explicit finite difference schemes are bad in this case while the fully implicit method does not suffer this problem because it does not get its information exclusively from the first row and first column of the finite difference mesh.

It is not possible to compute an accurate solution at a point of discontinuity. The situation can be improved by removing the discontinuity by means of a change of variables. For example, we can change (x, t) to (X, T) where

$$X = \frac{x}{\sqrt{t}}$$

$$T = \sqrt{t}$$

We now discuss initial conditions for exotic options. These are in fact payoff functions.

16.4.1 Payoff functions in options modelling

We give an overview of the role of payoff functions in option theory. These are in fact the *terminal condition* of the option price in the Black–Scholes equation. In general, they are continuous but their first derivative is usually discontinuous. We see a loss in accuracy at the points in the S dimension where the first derivative of the payoff function is discontinuous. In fact, this is where we experience the famous spurious oscillation problem. The oscillations are not so pronounced in the solution itself but they become evident when we calculate the delta and gamma functions. The Crank–Nicolson method, for example, exhibits these problems, which makes it unsuitable as a universal robust method. We discuss improved schemes for approximating the delta and gamma functions in Chapter 18.

The payoff functions for exotic options are more complicated than the payoff for plain European call options:

$$C = \max(S - K, 0)$$

Notice that the derivative of this function is zero if $S \leq K$ and 1 if $S > K$, thus making the latter function discontinuous.

A *binary (digital) option* is one whose payment is determined by whether the underlying is above the strike price. The amount paid is independent of the difference:

$$C = 1 \text{ if } S > K, \qquad C = 0 \text{ if } S \leq K$$

An *asset-or-nothing* option has the following payout: if the stock ends above the strike, the owner of the option gets this stock. If the stock ends under the strike the options ends out of the money:

$$C = S \text{ if } S > K, \qquad C = 0 \text{ if } S \leq K$$

We note that this is a discontinuous function in general.

A *super-share* option is a combination of a long position in an asset-or-nothing at strike K_1 and a short position in an asset-or-nothing struck at K_2. In fact, the holder receives the stock if the option ends in the open range (K_1, K_2):

$$C = S \text{ if } S \text{ is in range } (K_1, K_2)$$
$$C = 0 \text{ if } S \text{ is outside the range } (K_1, K_2)$$

The *step structure* is a long position in a binary option struck at K_1 combined with a short position in a binary option stuck at K_2:

$$C = (K_1 + K_2)/2 \text{ if } S \text{ is in range } (K_1, K_2)$$
$$C = 0 \text{ if } S \text{ is outside the range } (K_1, K_2)$$

The *contingent premium* option is composed of a long position in a call option and a short position in a binary option with the same strike price.

A *shout option* allows a client a single opportunity to fix the price of the option at some time before expiry. Let this time be called H. Then the payoff function is:

$$C = \max\left(S(T) - K, S(H) - K\right)$$

With a shout option the client has to actually call the dealer in order to trigger the option. The act of triggering is called *shouting*.

Options with two or more underlyings can also have payoff functions whose derivatives are discontinuous. A discussion of these cases is, however, outside the scope of this book.

Figure 16.5 is a pictorial representation of some payoff functions.

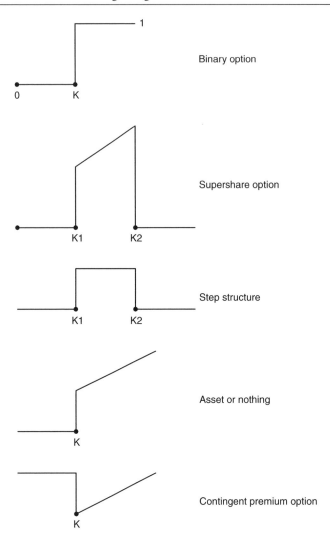

Figure 16.5 Payoff functions

16.5   IMPLEMENTATION

Explicit finite difference schemes are easy to program but, on the other hand, we shall not devote much attention to them because of their inherent lack of stability. Thus, our code on the CD for these schemes has not been designed with reusability or flexibility in mind. In later chapters we shall see how implicit difference methods are implemented and why they are better than explicit methods.

16.6   METHOD OF LINES: A WHIRLWIND INTRODUCTION

Many articles on finite difference methods in the financial literature discretise the Black–Scholes equation in the S and t variables simultaneously. This is fine, but there is another way, namely discretising in the S direction only and keeping t fixed. This process is called semi-discretisation and is quite common in the finite element method (see Strang and Fix, 1973). Let us again take the heat equation in (16.3). Using centred differencing in the space direction gives the following ODE system

$$\frac{du_j}{dt} = \frac{u_{j+1} - 2u_j + u_{j-1}}{h^2}, \quad j = 1, \ldots, J-1$$

(16.13)

$$u_j = u_j(t) \text{ (discrete in } x, \text{ continuous in } t)$$

and its equivalent matrix form

$$\frac{dU}{dt} = AU(t), \quad U(0) = U_0$$

$$A = \frac{1}{h^2} \begin{pmatrix} -2 & 1 & & & \\ 1 & \ddots & \ddots & & 0 \\ 0 & \ddots & \ddots & 1 & \\ & & 1 & -2 \end{pmatrix}$$

(16.14)

The advantages of the method of lines (MOL) are:

- It is easier to understand than the fully discrete scheme.
- The ODE system can be solved by standard schemes such as Runge–Kutta, Crank–Nicolson, Predictor–Corrector and so on.
- Separation of concerns: look at the discretisation of space and then discretisation in time.
- MOL can be applied to non-linear systems.
- There are many robust ODE solvers in the marketplace.

The MOL does not seem to be popular in the financial engineering literature as most authors tend to develop finite difference schemes by simultaneous discretisation in space and time.

16.7 CONCLUSIONS AND SUMMARY

We have introduced some simple finite difference schemes for the one-dimensional heat equation that serves as a baseline example for the Black–Scholes equation. In fact, the one-factor Black–Scholes equation can be transformed to a heat equation by a clever change of variables (see Wilmott, 1993). We focused on explicit schemes in this chapter because they are easy to understand (especially if you have studied Chapters 11 and 13) and to program. Explicit schemes do have their shortcomings because the time step k must be of the order of the square of h (the mesh size in the space direction). However, you could use an explicit scheme to test some new model by letting it run all night or in a low-priority background process. In other words, explicit methods might be useful for Proof-of-Concept (POC) tests and prototypes.

We have taken a critical look at initial and payoff functions for the Black–Scholes equation and in particular we discussed how and why oscillation problems occur when the input function is not very smooth (as is nearly always the case with exotic options). We have given examples of a number of payoff functions for some major exotic option types.

17
Implicit Finite Difference Schemes for Black–Scholes

17.1 INTRODUCTION AND OBJECTIVES

In this chapter we introduce a number of finite difference schemes that are used to approximate the solution of the Black–Scholes equation. We concentrate on *implicit schemes* where the solution of the finite difference equation at time level $n + 1$ is calculated from the solution at time level n by solving a system of linear questions. Since we are using three-point difference schemes for one-factor models, the matrix appearing in the system is tridiagonal. In this case we can apply either the Double Sweep method or *LU* decomposition (discussed in Chapter 8) for the solution at each time level:

$$A^{n+1} U^{n+1} = F^n$$

U^0 given

$$A^n = \begin{pmatrix} b_1^n & c_1^n & & & \\ a_2^n & \ddots & \ddots & & 0 \\ & \ddots & \ddots & \ddots & \\ & & \ddots & \ddots & c_{J-1}^n \\ 0 & & & \ddots & \ddots \\ & & & a_J^n & b_J^n \end{pmatrix} \tag{17.1}$$

This system of equations is generic and we shall discuss two particularly important implicit schemes that lead to such matrix systems:

- The Euler, fully implicit method
- The centred difference (or Crank–Nicolson) method.

The difference between these methods lies is how they calculate values at time level $n+1$ in terms of the solution at level n. Both the fully implicit and Crank–Nicolson methods use centred divided differences to approximate the first and second derivatives of the option price with respect to S while they employ one-step differencing in time t. To this end, the theory and methods that we developed in Chapter 11 (finite difference schemes for initial value problems) will be of help in this chapter. Whereas Chapter 11 dealt with ordinary differential equations, the situation is a bit more complicated in this chapter but the same techniques can be applied to the time variable in the Black–Scholes equation.

Please note that we have cast the Black–Scholes equation as a PDE with *initial conditions* rather than *terminal conditions*. Thus, the values of the solution are known at time level n and we *march* to time level $n + 1$ in order to compute a solution. In the financial literature, we march from a 'terminal' value at level $n + 1$ to the solution at level n.

17.2   FULLY IMPLICIT METHOD

We start with the fully implicit method for the Black–Scholes partial differential equation:

$$-\frac{\partial V}{\partial t} + \frac{1}{2}\sigma^2 S^2 \frac{\partial^2 V}{\partial S^2} + rS\frac{\partial V}{\partial S} - rV = 0 \tag{17.2}$$

Of course, this equation must get auxiliary information, such as initial condition (payoff) and boundary conditions in order to have a unique solution and, furthermore, we must decide how we are going to define numerical approximations to these auxiliary conditions. For the moment, however, we just concentrate on equation (17.2) and its approximation by finite differences. To this end, we discretise (S, t) space in the usual way and approximate (17.2) by the fully implicit scheme

$$-\frac{V_j^{n+1} - V_j^n}{k} + rj\Delta S\left(\frac{V_{j+1}^{n+1} - V_{j-1}^{n+1}}{2\Delta S}\right)$$
$$+ \frac{1}{2}\sigma^2 j^2 \Delta S^2\left(\frac{V_{j+1}^{n+1} - 2V_j^{n+1} + V_{j-1}^{n+1}}{\Delta S^2}\right) = rV_j^{n+1} \tag{17.3}$$

The stencil for this scheme is given in Figure 17.1 and we thus see that the scheme is implicit:

$$a_j^{n+1} V_{j-1}^{n+1} + b_j^{n+1} V_j^{n+1} + c_j^{n+1} V_{j+1}^{n+1} = F_j^{n+1} \tag{17.4}$$

where

$$a_j^{n+1} = \left(\frac{1}{2}\sigma^2 j^2 k - \frac{krj}{2}\right)$$

$$b_j^{n+1} = -(1 + \sigma^2 j^2 k + rk)$$

$$c_j^{n+1} = \left(\frac{1}{2}\sigma^2 j^2 k + \frac{krj}{2}\right)$$

$$F_j^{n+1} = -V_j^n$$

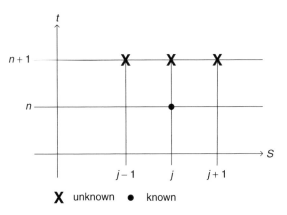

Figure 17.1   Stencil for fully implicit scheme

The fully implicit scheme has a number of desirable features. First, it is stable and there is no restriction on the relative sizes of the time mesh size k and the space mesh size ΔS. Furthermore, no spurious oscillations are to be seen in the solution (as is the case with some other methods). A disadvantage is that it is only first-order accurate in k. On the other hand, this can be rectified by using extrapolation, which results in a second-order scheme. A discussion of how this is done is outside the scope of this book.

17.3 AN INTRODUCTION TO THE CRANK–NICOLSON METHOD

The famous one! In this case we can view Crank–Nicolson (CN) as the averaged scheme by adding the fully explicit and fully implicit schemes together. The stencil in Figure 17.2 attempts to motivate the relationship.

We define the quantity

$$V_j^{n+\frac{1}{2}} \equiv \tfrac{1}{2}(V_j^{n+1} + V_j^n)$$

Then the Crank–Nicolson method is defined as follows:

$$-\frac{V_j^{n+1} - V_j^n}{k} + rj\Delta S \left(\frac{V_{j+1}^{n+\frac{1}{2}} - V_{j-1}^{n+\frac{1}{2}}}{2\Delta S} \right)$$

$$+ \frac{1}{2}\sigma^2 j^2 \Delta S^2 \left(\frac{V_{j+1}^{n+\frac{1}{2}} - 2V_j^{n+\frac{1}{2}} + V_{j-1}^{n+\frac{1}{2}}}{\Delta S^2} \right) = r V_j^{n+\frac{1}{2}}$$

(17.5)

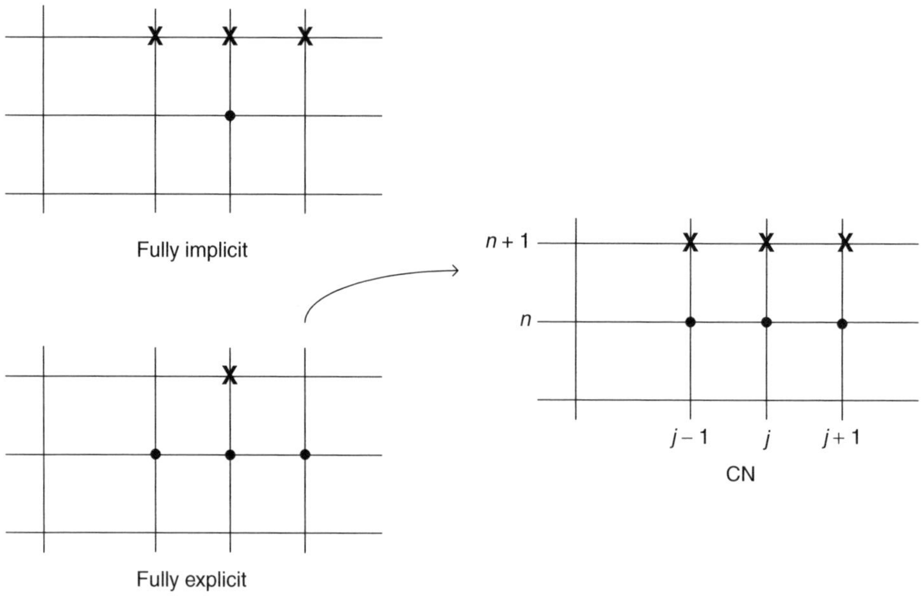

Figure 17.2   Crank–Nicolson stencil

Again, this is a system that can be posed in the forms (17.4) or (17.1) and hence can be solved by standard matrix solver techniques at each time level.

The Crank–Nicolson method has gained wide acceptance in the financial literature and seems to be the *de-facto* finite difference scheme for one-factor and two-factor Black–Scholes equations. It has second-order accuracy in the parameter k and is stable. Unfortunately, it has been known for some considerable time (Il'in, 1969) that centred differencing schemes in space combined with averaging in time (what essentially CN is in this context) leads to spurious oscillations in the approximate solution and in the divided differences for approximating its derivatives. These oscillations have nothing to do with the physical or financial problem that the scheme is approximating. Thus, the scheme is wrong! To make a very bad pun: *CN is not what it is cranked up to be!* We defend this statement in the next section.

17.4   A CRITIQUE OF CRANK–NICOLSON

The Crank–Nicolson method has become a very popular finite difference scheme for solving the Black–Scholes equation. This is an example of a *convection–diffusion* equation and it has been known for some time that centred-difference schemes are inappropriate for approximating it (Il'in, 1969; Duffy, 1980). In fact, many independent discoveries of novel methods have been made in order to solve difficult convection–diffusion problems in fluid dynamics, atmospheric pollution modelling, semiconductor equations, the Fokker–Planck equation and groundwater transport (Morton, 1996). The main problem is that traditional finite difference schemes start to oscillate when the coefficient of the second derivative (the *diffusion term*) is very small or when the coefficient of the first derivative (the *convection term*) is large (or both). In this case, the mesh size h in the space direction must be smaller than a certain value if we wish to avoid these oscillations. This problem has been known since the 1950s (see de Allen and Southwell, 1955). We now discuss the Crank–Nicolson from a number of viewpoints. For convenience and generality reasons, we cast the Black–Scholes equation as a generic parabolic initial boundary value problem in the domain $D = (A, B) \times (0, T)$ where $A < B$:

$$Lu \equiv -\frac{\partial u}{\partial t} + \sigma(x, t)\frac{\partial^2 u}{\partial x^2} + \mu(x, t)\frac{\partial u}{\partial x} + b(x, t)u = f(x, t) \text{ in } D$$

$$u(x, 0) = \varphi(x), \quad x \in (A, B)$$

$$u(A, t) = g_0(t), \quad u(B, t) = g_1(t), \quad t \in (0, T)$$

(17.6)

In this case the time variable t corresponds to increasing time while the space variable x corresponds to the underlying asset price S. We specify Dirichlet boundary conditions on a finite space interval and this is a common situation for several kinds of exotic options, for example barrier options. Actually, the system (17.6) is more general than the original Black–Scholes equation.

17.4.1   How are derivatives approximated?

There are two kinds of independent variables associated with the one-factor Black–Scholes, as can be seen in (17.6). These correspond to the x and t variables. We concentrate on the

x direction for the moment. We discretise in this direction using centred differences at the point (jh, nk):

$$\frac{\partial^2 u}{\partial x^2} \sim \frac{u_{j+1}^n - 2u_j^n + u_{j-1}^n}{h^2}$$

$$\frac{\partial u}{\partial x} \sim \frac{u_{j+1}^n - u_{j-1}^n}{2h} \tag{17.7}$$

Using this knowledge we can apply the Crank–Nicolson method to (17.6) by a generalisation of (17.5), namely:

$$-\frac{u_j^{n+1} - u_j^n}{k} + \sigma_j^{n+\frac{1}{2}} \frac{u_{j+1}^{n+\frac{1}{2}} - 2u_j^{n+\frac{1}{2}} + u_{j-1}^{n+\frac{1}{2}}}{h^2}$$

$$+ \mu_j^{n+\frac{1}{2}} \frac{u_{j+1}^{n+\frac{1}{2}} - u_{j-1}^{n+\frac{1}{2}}}{2h} + b_j^{n+\frac{1}{2}} u_j^{n+\frac{1}{2}} = f_j^{n+\frac{1}{2}} \tag{17.8}$$

A bit of simple arithmetic allows us to rewrite (17.8) in the form:

$$a_j^n u_{j-1}^{n+1} + b_j^n u_j^{n+1} + c_j^{n-1} + c_j^n u_{j+1}^{n+1} = F_j^n \tag{17.9}$$

where F_j^n is a known quantity and

$$a_j^n = \left(\frac{\sigma_j^{n+\frac{1}{2}}}{h^2} - \frac{\mu_j^{n+\frac{1}{2}}}{2h} \right)$$

$$b_j^n = \left(-k^{-1} - \frac{2\sigma_j^{n+\frac{1}{2}}}{h^2} + b_j^{n+\frac{1}{2}} \right) \tag{17.10}$$

$$c_j^n = \left(\frac{\sigma_j^{n+\frac{1}{2}}}{h^2} + \frac{\mu_j^{n+\frac{1}{2}}}{2h} \right)$$

Of course, this system of equations can be posed in the form of a matrix system, as in (17.1). A number of researchers have examined such systems in conjunction with convection–diffusion equations (for example, Farrell et al., 2000; Morton, 1996). A critical observation is that if the coefficient a appearing in (17.10) is not positive, then the resulting solution will show oscillatory behaviour at best or produce non-physical solutions at worst. The requirement that this coefficient is positive reduces to the inequality:

$$h \le \left| \frac{2\sigma}{\mu} \right| \tag{17.11}$$

This means that h must be chosen so as to satisfy this inequality. This will give problems in general for Black–Scholes applications where the volatility is a decaying function of time (see van Deventer and Imai, 1997), for example:

$$\sigma(t) = \sigma_0 \, e^{-\alpha(T-t)} \tag{17.12}$$

where σ_0 and α are given constants.

Furthermore, for the standard Black–Scholes equation, the restriction on h is

$$h \leq \frac{\sigma^2 S}{r} \tag{17.13}$$

The quantity on the right-hand side of (17.13) is sometime called the *Reynolds number* and is a fundamental quantity when dealing with finite difference schemes for convection–diffusion equations.

We speak of a *singular perturbation problem* associated with problem (17.6) when the coefficient of the second derivative is small (see Duffy, 1980). In this case traditional finite difference schemes perform badly at the so-called *boundary layer* situated at $x = 0$. In fact, if we formally set the coefficient to zero in equation (17.8) we get a so-called weakly stable difference scheme (see Peaceman, 1977) that approximate the *first-order hyperbolic equation*

$$-\frac{\partial u}{\partial t} + \mu \frac{\partial u}{\partial x} + bu = f \tag{17.14}$$

This has the consequence that the initial errors in the scheme are not dissipated and hence we can expect oscillations, especially in the presence of rounding errors. We need other *one-sided schemes* in this degenerate case (Peaceman, 1977; Duffy, 1977) and we shall discuss them when we deal with exponentially fitted difference schemes in Chapter 18.

17.4.2 Boundary conditions

In general, we distinguish three kinds of boundary condition:

- Dirichlet (as seen in the system (17.6))
- Neumann
- Robin.

The last two boundary conditions involve the first derivative of the unknown u at the boundaries. We must then decide on how we are going to approximate this derivative. We can choose between first-order accurate one-sided schemes or, instead, use *ghost points* (Thomas, 1998) to produce a second-order approximation to the first derivative. We must thus be aware of the fact that the low-order accuracy at the boundary will adversely impact the second-order accuracy in the interior of the region of interest. To complicate matters, some models have a boundary condition involving the second derivative of u at the boundary, or even a 'linearity' boundary condition (see Tavella and Randall, 2000).

Finally, the boundary conditions may be discontinuous. We may resort to non-uniform meshes to accommodate the discontinuities. This strategy will also destroy the second-order accuracy of the Crank–Nicolson method.

The conclusion is that the wrong discrete boundary conditions adversely affect the accuracy of the finite difference scheme.

17.4.3 Initial conditions

It is well-known that discontinuous initial conditions adversely impact the accuracy of finite difference schemes (see Smith, 1978). In particular, the solution of the difference schemes exhibits 'jumps' and oscillations just after $t = 0$ but the solution becomes more smooth as time goes on. This has consequences for options pricing applications because, in general, the initial condition (this is in fact a payoff function) is not always smooth. For example, the derivative for the payoff function for a plain European call option is:

$$C = \max(S - K, 0) \tag{17.15}$$

where K is the strike price and S is the stock price. Its derivative is given by the jump function:

$$\frac{\partial C}{\partial S} = \begin{cases} 0, & S \leq K \\ 1, & S > K \end{cases} \tag{17.16}$$

This derivative is discontinuous and in general we can expect to get bad accuracy at the points of discontinuity (in this case, at the strike price where at-the-money issues play an important role). It is possible to determine mathematically what the accuracy is in some special cases (Smith, 1978) but numerical experiments show us that other things are going wrong as well.

Of course, if the option price is badly approximated there is not much hope of getting good approximations to the delta and gamma. This statement is borne out in practice. One last remark: another source of annoyance is that the boundary and initial conditions may not be *compatible* with each other. By compatibility, we mean that the solution is smooth at the corners $(A, 0)$ and $(B, 0)$ of the region of interest and we thus demand that the solution is the same irrespective of the direction from which we approach the corners. If we assume that $u(x, t)$ is continuous as we approach the boundaries, then the following should be true:

$$u(A, 0) \equiv \varphi(A) = g_0(0)$$
$$U(B, 0) \equiv \varphi(B) = g_1(0) \tag{17.17}$$

In other words, we must satisfy the compatibility conditions:

$$\varphi(A) \equiv u(A, 0) \equiv g_0(0)$$
$$\varphi(B) \equiv u(B, 0) \equiv g_1(0) \tag{17.18}$$

Failure to take these conditions into account in a finite difference scheme will lead to inaccuracies at the corner points of the region of interest. On the up side, the discontinuities are quickly damped out.

17.4.4 Proving stability

Much of the literature uses the von Neumann theory to prove stability of finite difference schemes (Tavella and Randall, 2000). This theory was developed by John von Neumann, a Hungarian-American mathematician, the father of the modern computer and probably one of the greatest brains of the twentieth century.

Strictly speaking, the von Neumann approach is only valid for constant coefficient, linear initial value problems, and the Black–Scholes equation does not fall under this category. Furthermore, much work has been done in the engineering field to prove stability in other ways, for example using the maximum principle and matrix theory (Morton, 1996; Duffy, 1980).

A discussion of von Neumann stability for the constant coefficient, linear convection–diffusion equation can be found in Thomas (1998).

17.5   IS THERE HOPE? THE KELLER SCHEME

In Chapter 18 we shall show how to resolve the spurious oscillation problem associated with the Crank–Nicolson method when we introduce the so-called exponentially fitted scheme for the one-dimensional convection–diffusion equation based on the work in Duffy (1980). We recall that the Black–Scholes equation is a special case of a convection–diffusion equation.

In this section however, we give a short overview of the Box scheme (Keller, 1971) that resolves many of the problems associated with Crank–Nicolson. In short, we reduce the second-order Black–Scholes equation to a system of first-order equations containing at most first-order derivatives. We then approximate the first derivatives in S *and* t by averaging in a box.

We motivate the Box scheme by examining the generic parabolic initial boundary value problem in the space interval $(0, 1)$:

$$\frac{\partial u}{\partial t} = \frac{\partial}{\partial x}\left(a\frac{\partial u}{\partial x}\right) + cu + S, \quad 0 < x < 1, \quad t > 0$$

$$u(x, 0) = g(x), \quad 0 < x < 1 \tag{17.19}$$

$$\alpha_0 u(0, t) + \alpha_1 a(0, t)u_x(0, t) = g_0(t)$$

$$\beta_0 u(1, t) + \beta_1 a(1, t)u_x(1, t) = g_1(t)$$

Here u is the (unknown) solution to the problem that satisfies the *self-adjoint equation* in (17.19) and it must also satisfy the initial and boundary conditions (note the latter contain derivatives of the unknown at the boundaries of the interval). In general, the coefficients in (17.19) are functions of both x and t.

We now transform (17.19) to a first-order system by defining a new variable v. The new transformed set of equations is given by:

$$a\frac{\partial u}{\partial x} = v$$

$$\frac{\partial v}{\partial x} = \frac{\partial u}{\partial t} - cu - S$$

$$u(x, 0) = g(x) \tag{17.20}$$

$$\alpha_0 u(0, t) + \alpha_1 v(0, t) = g_0(t)$$

$$\beta_0 u(1, t) + \beta_1 v(1, t) = g_1(t)$$

We now see that we have to do with a first-order system of equations with no derivatives on the boundaries! The stencil that we use is shown in Figure 17.3. We now see the reason for the name of the scheme; all calculations are done on a box.

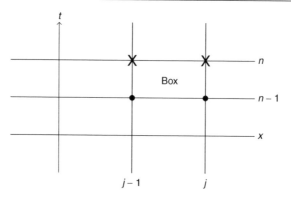

Figure 17.3 Discrete mesh

We now need to introduce some notation. First, we define average values for x and t coordinates as follows:

$$x_{j\pm\frac{1}{2}} = \tfrac{1}{2}(x_j + x_{j\pm1})$$

$$t_{n\pm\frac{1}{2}} = \tfrac{1}{2}(t_n + t_{n\pm1})$$

(17.21)

and for general net functions (in principle the approximations to u and v) by

$$\phi^n_{j\pm\frac{1}{2}} = \tfrac{1}{2}(\phi^n_j + \phi^n_{j\pm1})$$

$$\phi^{n\pm\frac{1}{2}}_j = \tfrac{1}{2}(\phi^n_j + \phi^{n\pm1}_j)$$

(17.22)

Finally, we define notation for divided differences in the x and t directions as follows:

$$D^-_x \phi^n_j = h^{-1}_j(\phi^n_j - \phi^n_{j-1})$$

$$D^-_t \phi^n_j = k^{-1}_n(\phi^n_j - \phi^{n-1}_j)$$

(17.23)

We are now ready for the new scheme. To this end, we use one-sided difference schemes in both directions while taking averages and we thus solve for both u and v simultaneously at each time level:

$$a^n_{j-\frac{1}{2}} D^-_x u^n_j = v^n_{j-\frac{1}{2}}$$

$$D^-_x v^{n-\frac{1}{2}}_j = D^-_t u^n_{j-\frac{1}{2}} - c^{n-\frac{1}{2}}_{j-\frac{1}{2}} u^{n-\frac{1}{2}}_{j-\frac{1}{2}} - S^{n-\frac{1}{2}}_{j-\frac{1}{2}}$$

(17.24)

$$(1 \le j \le J, \quad 1 \le n \le N)$$

The corresponding boundary and initial conditions are:

$$\left.\begin{array}{l} \alpha_0 u^n_0 + \alpha_1 v^n_0 = g^n_0 \\ \beta_0 u^n_J + \beta_1 v^n_J = g^n_1 \end{array}\right\} 1 \le n \le N$$

$$\left.\begin{array}{l} u^0_j = g(x_j) \\ v^0_j = a^0_j \dfrac{dg(x_j)}{dx} \end{array}\right\} 0 \le j \le J$$

(17.25)

A full discussion of how to design algorithms to solve the systems (17.24) and (17.25) is given in Keller (1971).

17.5.1   The advantages of the Box scheme

The Box scheme has a number of very desirable properties:

- It is simple, efficient and easy to program.
- It is unconditionally stable.
- It approximates u and its partial derivative in x with second-order accuracy. For the Black–Scholes equation this means that we can approximate both option price and the option delta without trace of spurious oscillation, as is experienced with Crank–Nicolson.
- Richardson extrapolation is applicable and yields two orders of accuracy improvement per extrapolation (with non-uniform nets!).
- It supports data, coefficients and solutions that are only piecewise smooth. In a financial setting it is able to model piecewise smooth payoff functions. For example, with piecewise continuous initial conditions we define the midpoint of an interval in the x direction as shown in Figure 17.4. We then define the approximate initial condition as follows:

$$v^0_{j-\frac{1}{2}} = a^0_{j-\frac{1}{2}} \frac{\mathrm{d}g\left(x_{j-\frac{1}{2}}\right)}{\mathrm{d}x}, \quad 1 \le j \le J \tag{17.26}$$

For piecewise smooth boundary conditions we use the following tactic:

$$\alpha_0 u_0^{n-\frac{1}{2}} + \alpha_1 v_0^{n-\frac{1}{2}} = g_0^{n-\frac{1}{2}}$$

$$\beta_0 u_J^{n-\frac{1}{2}} + \beta_1 v_J^{n-\frac{1}{2}} = g_1^{n-\frac{1}{2}} \tag{17.27}$$

$$1 \le n \le N$$

Discontinuities at $t = t_n$!

Of course we are assuming that the mesh points are sitting on the discontinuities!
- It can be used for parabolic systems and non-linear parabolic equations.

A full discussion of these issues in relation to option modelling is given in Duffy (2004b).

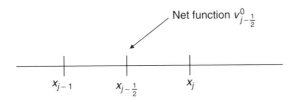

Figure 17.4   Midpoint of an interval

17.6   CONCLUSIONS AND SUMMARY

We have given an overview of three implicit finite difference schemes that approximate the one-factor Black–Scholes equation in conjunction with associated terminal and boundary conditions. The schemes are called

- Fully implicit scheme
- Crank–Nicolson scheme
- The Keller Box scheme.

The fully implicit scheme is unconditionally stable and first-order accurate in time. The Crank–Nicolson scheme is second-order accurate in time on *uniform* meshes but produces spurious oscillations for large convective terms or in the regions of low regularity in the payoff function (for example, near the strike price K for a European option). We have also critically examined the Crank–Nicolson in section 17.4 in order to determine what its weak points are. Finally, the Box scheme produces second-order accuracy to both the option price and its delta on non-uniform meshes.

In the next chapter we shall develop another scheme that produces good approximations to the option price and its delta.

Special Schemes for Plain and Exotic Options

18.1 INTRODUCTION AND OBJECTIVES

In this chapter we introduce a special kind of finite difference scheme that is particularly suited to convection–diffusion equations (among others, the Black–Scholes equation) where the coefficient of the second derivative is small compared with the coefficient of the first derivative. These are called *convection-dominated* problems and such problems have been the focus of much interest in the engineering and scientific community during the last 30 years or so (see Morton, 1996, for an overview of the applications and numerical schemes). In Chapter 17 we introduced the Crank–Nicolson method and we discussed some of its shortcomings when applied to the convection–diffusion equation in general and the Black–Scholes equation in particular. In particular, the solution gave small spurious oscillations that become more pronounced in the delta, thus making the scheme unsuitable for delta hedging applications. A number of numerical analyses and experiments have been carried out in order to determine what the precise problems with Crank–Nicolson were and how the exponentially fitted schemes of the current author managed to resolve these problems (for a thesis on this subject, see Cooney, 1999).

18.2 MOTIVATING EXPONENTIALLY FITTED SCHEMES

18.2.1 A new class of robust difference schemes

We now introduce the class of exponentially fitted schemes for general two-point boundary value problems. Exponentially fitted schemes are stable, have good convergence properties and do not produce spurious oscillations. In order to motivate what an exponentially fitted difference scheme is, let us look at the problem:

$$\sigma \frac{d^2u}{dx^2} + \mu \frac{du}{dx} = 0 \quad \text{in } (A, B) \tag{18.1}$$

$$u(A) = \beta_0, \quad u(B) = \beta_1$$

Here we assume that σ and μ are positive constants for the moment. We now approximate (18.1) by the difference scheme defined as follows:

$$\sigma \rho D_+ D_- U_j + \mu D_0 U_j = 0, \quad j = 1, \ldots, J - 1 \tag{18.2}$$

$$U_0 = \beta_0, \quad U_J = \beta_1.$$

where ρ is a so-called fitting factor (this factor is identically equal to 1 in the case of the centred difference scheme. We now choose ρ so that the solutions of (18.1) and (18.2) are identical at the mesh points. Some easy arithmetic shows that

$$\rho = \frac{\mu h}{2\sigma} \coth \frac{\mu h}{2\sigma}$$

where coth x is the hyperbolic cotangent function defined by

$$\coth x = \frac{e^x + e^{-x}}{e^x - e^{-x}} = \frac{e^{2x} + 1}{e^{2x} - 1}.$$

The fitting factor will be used when developing fitted difference schemes for more general problems. In particular, we discuss the following problem:

$$\sigma(x)\frac{d^2 u}{dx^2} + \mu(x)\frac{du}{dx} + b(x)u = f(x) \tag{18.3}$$

$$u(A) = \beta_0, \quad u(B) = \beta_1$$

where σ, μ and b are given continuous functions, and

$$\sigma(x) \geq 0, \quad \mu(x) \geq \alpha > 0, \quad b(x) \leq 0 \text{ for } x \in (A, B).$$

The fitted difference scheme that approximates (18.3) is defined by:

$$\rho_j^h D_+ D_- U_j + \mu_j D_0 U_j + b_j U_j = f_j, \quad j = 1, \ldots, J - 1 \tag{18.4}$$

$$U_0 = \beta_0, \quad U_J = \beta_1$$

where

$$\rho_j^h = \frac{\mu_j h}{2} \coth \frac{\mu_j h}{2\sigma_j} \tag{18.5}$$

$$\sigma_j = \sigma(x_j), \quad \mu_j = \mu(x_j), \quad b_j = b(x_j), \quad f_j = f(x_j)$$

We now state the following fundamental results (see Il'in, 1969; Doolan *et al.*, 1980; Duffy, 1980):

The solution of scheme (18.4) is uniformly stable, that is

$$|U_j| \leq |\beta_0| + |\beta_1| + \frac{1}{\alpha} \max_{k=1,\ldots,J} |f_k|, \quad j = 1, \ldots, J - 1$$

Furthermore, scheme (18.4) is monotone in the sense that the matrix representation of (18.4)

$$AU = F$$

where $U = {}^t(U_1, \ldots, U_{J-1})$, $F = {}^t(f_1, \ldots, f_{J-1})$ and

$$\mathbf{A} = \begin{pmatrix} \ddots & & \ddots & & & 0 \\ & \ddots & & a_{j,j+1} & & \\ \ddots & & a_{j,j} & & \ddots & \\ & a_{j,j-1} & & \ddots & & \\ 0 & & \ddots & & \ddots & \end{pmatrix} \tag{18.6}$$

$$a_{j,j-1} = \frac{\rho_j^h}{h^2} - \frac{\mu_j}{2h} > 0 \quad \text{always}$$

$$a_{j,j} = -\frac{2\rho_j^h}{h^2} + b_j < 0 \quad \text{always}$$

$$a_{j,j+1} = \frac{\rho_j h}{h^2} + \frac{\mu_j}{2h} > 0 \quad \text{always}$$

produces positive solutions from positive input. Sufficient conditions for a difference scheme to be monotone have been investigated by many authors in the last 30 years; we mention the work of Samarski (1976) and Stoyan (1979). The latter author has used several various fitting factors:

$$\rho_0 = \sigma^{-1}\{1 + q^2/(1 + |q|)\}$$

$$\rho_1 = (1 + q^2)^{\frac{1}{2}} \qquad (18.7)$$

$$\rho_2 = \sigma^{-1}(\gamma)$$

where ρ is the Il'in fitting factor.

Stoyan also produced stable and convergent difference schemes for the convection–diffusion equation producing results and conclusions that are similar to the author's work (see Duffy, 1980):

Let u and U be the solutions of (18.3) and (18.4), respectively. Then

$$|u(x_j) - U_j| \le Mh$$

where M is a positive constant that is independent of h and σ (Il'in, 1969). The conclusion is that the fitted scheme (18.4) is stable, convergent and produces no oscillations for all parameter regimes. In particular, the scheme 'degrades gracefully' to a well-known stable scheme when σ tends to zero.

18.3 EXPONENTIALLY FITTED SCHEMES FOR PARABOLIC PROBLEMS

We now discuss how to apply exponentially fitted schemes to the parabolic initial value problem:

$$Lu \equiv -\frac{\partial u}{\partial t} + \sigma(x,t)\frac{\partial^2 u}{\partial x^2} + \mu(x,t)\frac{\partial u}{\partial x}$$

$$+ b(x,t)u = f(x,t) \text{ in } D \qquad (18.8)$$

$$u(x,0) = \varphi(x), \quad x \in \Omega$$

$$u(A,t) = g_0(t), \quad u(B,t) = g_1(t), \quad t \in (0,T)$$

18.3.1 The fitted scheme in more detail: Main results

We now discuss how to approximate (18.8) by experientially fitted schemes. In particular, we propose an exponentially fitted scheme in the space direction and fully implicit discretisation in the time direction. The results are based on Duffy (1980) where the main theorems are proposed and proven, and these results are valid for coefficients that depend on both x and t.

We discretise the rectangle $[A, B] \times [0, T]$ as follows:

$$A = x_0 < x_1 < \cdots < x_J = B \ (h = x_j - x_{j-1}), \quad h \text{ constant}$$

$$0 = t_0 < t_1 < \cdots < t_N = T \ (k = T/N), \quad k \text{ constant}$$

Consider again the operator L in equation (18.8) defined by

$$Lu \equiv -\frac{\partial u}{\partial t} + \sigma(x, t)\frac{\partial^2 u}{\partial x^2} + \mu(x, t)\frac{\partial u}{\partial x} + b(x, t)u.$$

We replace the derivatives in this operator by their corresponding divided differences and we define the fitted operator L_k^h by

$$L_k^h U_j^n \equiv -\frac{U_j^{n+1} - U_j^n}{k} + \gamma_j^{n+1} D_+ D_- U_j^{n+1} + \mu_j^{n+1} D_0 U_j^{n+1} + b_j^{n+1} U_j^{n+1} \qquad (18.9)$$

Here we use the notation

$$\varphi_j^{n+1} = \varphi(x_j, t_{n+1}) \text{ in general}$$

and

$$\gamma_j^{n+1} \equiv \frac{\mu_j^{n+1} h}{2} \coth \frac{\mu_j^{n+1} h}{2\sigma_j^{n+1}}$$

Having defined the operator L_h^k we now formulate the fully discrete scheme that approximates system (18.8):

Find a discrete function $\{U_j^n\}$ such that

$$L_k^h U_j^n = f_j^{n+1}, \qquad j = 1, \ldots, J - 1, \quad n = 0, \ldots, N - 1$$

$$U_0^n = g_0(t_n), \qquad U_J^n = g_1(t_n), \quad n = 0, \ldots, N \qquad (18.10)$$

$$U_j^0 = \varphi(x_j), \quad j = 1, \ldots, J - 1$$

This is a two-level implicit scheme. We wish to prove that scheme (18.10) is stable and is consistent with the initial boundary value problem. We prove stability of (18.10) by the so-called discrete maximum principle instead of the von Neumann stability analysis. The von Neumann approach is well known but the discrete maximum principle is more general and easier to understand and to apply in practice. It is also the *de-facto* standard technique for proving stability of finite difference and finite element schemes (see Morton, 1996; Farrell *et al.*, 2000).

Lemma 1 *Let the discrete function w_j^n satisfy $L_k^h w_j^n \leq 0$ in the interior of the mesh with $w_j^n \geq 0$ on the boundary Γ. Then*

$$w_j^n \geq 0, \quad \forall j = 0, \ldots, J, \quad n = 0, \ldots, N.$$

Proof: We transform the inequality $L_k^h w_j^n \leq 0$ into an equivalent vector inequality. To this end, define the vector $W^n = {}^t(w_1^n, \ldots, w_{J-1}^n)$. Then the inequality $L_k^h w_j^n \leq 0$ is equivalent to the vector inequality

$$A^n W^{n+1} \geq W^n \tag{18.11}$$

where

$$A^n = \begin{pmatrix} \ddots & & \ddots & & 0 \\ & \ddots & & t_j^n & \\ \ddots & & s_j^n & & \ddots \\ & r_j^n & & \ddots & \\ 0 & & \ddots & & \ddots \end{pmatrix}$$

$$r_j^n = \left(-\frac{\gamma_j^n}{h^2} + \frac{\mu_j^n}{2h} \right) k$$

$$s_j^n = \left(\frac{2\gamma_j^n}{h^2} - b_j^n + k^{-1} \right) k$$

$$t_j^n = \left(-\left(\frac{\gamma_j^n}{h^2} + \frac{\mu_j^n}{2h} \right) \right) k$$

It is easy to show that the matrix A^n has non-positive off-diagonal elements, has strictly positive diagonal elements and is irreducibly diagonally dominant. Hence (see Varga, 1962, pp. 84–85) A^n is non-singular and its inverse is positive:

$$(A^n)^{-1} \geq 0$$

Using this result in (18.11) gives the desired result. □

Lemma 2 *Let $\{U_j^n\}$ be the solution of scheme (18.10) and suppose that*

$$\max_j |U_j^n| \leq m \quad \text{for all } j \text{ and } n$$

$$\max |f_j^n| \leq N \quad \text{for all } j \text{ and } n$$

Then

$$\max_j |U_j^n| \leq -\frac{N}{\beta} + m \quad \text{in } \overline{Q} \quad \text{where } b(x, t) \leq \beta < 0$$

Proof: Define the discrete barrier function

$$w_j^n = -\frac{N}{\beta} + m \pm U_j^n$$

Then $w_j^n \geq 0$ on Γ. Furthermore,

$$L_k^h w_j^n \leq 0$$

Hence $w_j^n \geq 0$ in $\overline{Q}$ which proves the result. $\square$

Let $u(x, t)$ and $\{U_j^n\}$ be the solutions of (18.8) and (18.10), respectively. Then

$$|u(x_j, t_n) - U_j^n| \leq M(h + k) \qquad (18.12)$$

where M is a constant that is independent of h, k and σ.

Remark: This result shows that convergence is assured regardless of the size of σ. No classical scheme (for example, centred differencing in x and Crank–Nicolson in time) have error bounds of the form (18.12) where M is independent of h, k and σ.

Summarising, the advantages of the fitted scheme are:

- It is uniformly stable for all values of h, k and σ.
- It is oscillation-free. Its solution converges to the exact solution of (18.8). In particular, it is a powerful scheme for the Black–Scholes equation and its generalisations.
- It is easily programmed, especially if we use object-oriented design and implementation techniques.

We shall discuss how to program this model using C++ in Chapter 19.

18.4   WHAT HAPPENS WHEN THE VOLATILITY GOES TO ZERO?

In Chapter 17 we saw that the limiting case for the Crank–Nicolson scheme when the volatility goes to zero is a so-called weakly stable scheme. This is not a good state of affairs because rounding errors can affect the solution. In the case of the fitted scheme, however, the news is a bit brighter.

18.4.1   Graceful degradation

We now examine some 'extreme' cases in system (18.10). In particular, we examine the cases

(pure convection/drift) $\sigma \to 0$

(pure diffusion/volatility) $\mu \to 0$

We shall see that the 'limiting' difference schemes are well-known schemes and this is reassuring. To examine the first extreme case we must know what the limiting properties of the hyperbolic cotangent function are:

$$\lim_{\sigma \to 0} \gamma_j^n = \lim_{\sigma \to 0} \frac{\mu_j^n h}{2} \coth \frac{\mu_j^n h}{2\sigma_j^n}$$

We use the formula

$$\lim_{\sigma \to 0} \frac{\mu h}{2} \coth \frac{\mu h}{2\sigma} = \begin{cases} +\dfrac{\mu h}{2} & \text{if } \mu > 0 \\[2mm] -\dfrac{\mu h}{2} & \text{if } \mu < 0 \end{cases}$$

Inserting this result into the first equation in (18.10) gives us the first-order scheme

$$\mu > 0, \quad -\frac{U_j^{n+1} - U_j^n}{k} + \mu_j^{n+1} \frac{(U_{j+1}^{n+1} - U_j^{n+1})}{h} + b_j^{n+1} U_j^{n+1} = f_j^{n+1}$$

$$\mu < 0, \quad -\frac{U_j^{n+1} - U_j^n}{k} + \mu_j^{n+1} \frac{(U_j^{n+1} - U_{j-1}^{n+1})}{h} + b_j^{n+1} U_j^{n+1} = f_j^{n+1}$$

These are so-called implicit upwind schemes and are stable and convergent (Duffy, 1977; Dautray and Lions, 1993). We thus conclude that the fitted scheme degrades to an acceptable scheme in the limit. The case $\mu \to 0$ uses the formula

$$\lim_{x \to 0} x \coth x = 1$$

Then the first equation in system (18.10) reduces to the equation

$$-\frac{U_j^{n+1} - U_j^n}{k} + \sigma_j^{n+1} D_+ D_- U_j^{n+1} + b_j^{n+1} U_j^{n+1} = f_j^{n+1}$$

This is a standard approximation to pure diffusion problems and such schemes can be found in standard numerical analysis textbooks (see, for example, Press et al., 1980).

These limiting cases reassure us that the fitted method behaves well for 'extreme' parameters values.

18.5   EXPONENTIAL FITTING WITH EXPLICIT TIME

18.5.1   An explicit time-marching scheme

It is interesting to investigate the use of fitting in combination with explicit time marching. We do not expect the corresponding scheme to be unconditionally stable. The scheme is:

$$-\frac{U_j^{n+1} - U_j^n}{k} + \gamma_j^n D_+ D_- U_j^n + \mu_j^n D_0 U_j^n + b_j^n U_j^n = f_j^n \qquad (18.13)$$

Rearranging terms in (18.13) gives

$$U_j^{n+1} = A_j^n U_{j+1}^n + B_j^n U_j^n + C_j^n U_{j-1}^n - k f_j^n \qquad (18.14)$$

where

$$A_j^n = k \left(\frac{\gamma_j^n}{h^2} + \frac{\mu_j^n}{2h} \right)$$

$$B_j^n = 1 - \frac{2k\gamma_j^n}{h^2} + kb_j^n$$

$$C_j^n = k \left(\frac{\gamma_j^n}{h^2} - \frac{\mu_j^n}{2h} \right)$$

If each of the coefficients A_j^n, B_j^n and C_j^n are non-negative then the right-hand side of (18.14) will be positive, thus leading us to the conclusion that $U_j^{n+1} \geq 0$. Assume U of $b = 0$. In this case $B_j^n \geq 0$ if

$$k^{-1} - \frac{2\gamma_j^n}{h^2} \geq 0$$

or

$$\frac{\mu_j^n k}{h} \leq \tanh \frac{\mu_j^n h}{2\sigma_j^n}. \tag{18.15}$$

Inequality (18.15) is a variation of the famous Courant–Friedrichs–Lewy (CFL) condition. If we let $\sigma \to 0$ in (18.15) the limiting case of (18.15) becomes

$$\frac{|\mu_j^n| k}{h} \leq 1$$

which is precisely the CFL condition for first-order hyperbolic equations! The corresponding reduced scheme is called the explicit upwind scheme (see Dautray and Lions, 1993, p. 99):

$$\mu > 0, \quad -\frac{U_j^{n+1} - U_j^n}{k} + \mu_j^n \left(\frac{U_{j+1}^n - U_j^n}{h} \right) = 0$$

$$\mu < 0, \quad -\frac{U_j^{n+1} - U_j^n}{k} + \mu_j^n \left(\frac{U_j^n - U_{j-1}^n}{h} \right) = 0$$

18.6   EXPONENTIAL FITTING AND EXOTIC OPTIONS

We have applied the method to a range of plain and exotic European and American type options. In particular, we have applied it to various kinds of barrier options (see Topper, 1998; Haug, 1998), for example:

- Double barrier call options
- Single barrier call options
- Equations with time-dependent volatilities (for example, a linear function of time)
- Asymmetric plain vanilla power call options
- Asymmetric capped power call options.

We have compared our results with those in Haug (1998) and Topper (1998) and they compare favourably (Mirani, 2002). The main difference between these types lies in the specific payoff functions (initial conditions) and boundary conditions. Since we are working with a specific kind of parabolic problem these functions must be specified by us. For example, for a double barrier option we must give the value of the option at these barriers while for a single barrier option we define the 'down' barrier at $S = 0$. For an asymmetric plain vanilla call option

$$\max(S^p - K)$$

where S is the stock price, K is the strike price and p is some factor ($p = 1$ for the plain European case). The final condition is:

$$f(T, S) = \max(S^p - K, 0)$$

Furthermore, no boundary conditions are given in this case and we choose $S = 0$ for the lower boundary and $S = 1000$ for the upper boundary:

$$f(t, 0) = 0$$

$$f(t, 1000) = S^p - K \exp(-(r - d)t)$$

In this case d is the dividend and r is the risk-free interest rate. Finally, asymmetric capped power call options have a payoff of the form

$$\min(\max(S^p, 0), C)$$

and a final condition

$$f(T, S) = \min(\max(S^p, 0), C)$$

where C is the cap value. Summarising, the exponentially fitted finite difference scheme gives good approximations to the option price and delta of the above exotic option types. We have compared the results with Monte Carlo, Haug (1998) and Topper (1998).

18.7 SOME FINAL REMARKS

We now give some examples of output from Crank–Nicolson. We took an 'extreme' case:

$$s = 0.001, \quad r = 0.15, \quad T = 1.0, \quad K = 10$$

Furthermore, the number of sub-divisions in the S direction was 60 (the mesh size h is then 20/60) while the number of time intervals was 2, and thus $k = 0.5$. We examined how the exponentially fitted method, Crank–Nicolson and the exact solution compared and we examined the option price and two of its sensitivities, namely delta and gamma. The option price is a monotonically increasing function of S, the delta is between 0 and 1 and the gamma is highly spiked because of the small value of the volatility σ (of course, we know the exact formulae for these quantities for a European call option). We now examine the Crank–Nicolson scheme. Based on the problems that we discussed in Chapter 17 we expect to see these manifest themselves in the numerical results. First, the payoff function shows 'kinks' around the strike price and, second, since the volatility is very small, we are effectively solving a first-order hyperbolic equation in which we need one boundary condition. Around the strike price $K = 10$ we see small kinks in the price that become progressively more accentuated as we move to the delta and gamma. This is to be expected because we are taking divided differences. We thus conclude that the Crank–Nicolson scheme performs badly for this admittedly extreme set of parameters. For the examples in this section we have taken $k = 0.5$ because $T = 1.0$ and we have two sub-divisions of the interval $(0, T)$. We now take the value $k = 0.1$ and examine the fitted scheme. We note the excellent approximations. The same good levels of accuracy are also achieved with barrier option approximation. In particular, Richardson's Deferred Approach to the Limit can be used to improve the accuracy from first-order to second-order accuracy.

My First Finite Difference Solver

19.1 INTRODUCTION AND OBJECTIVES

In this chapter we develop a fully fledged application in C++ to calculate the price and sensitivities of plain and barrier options. Much of the code is object-oriented in the sense that we model many processing entities as classes. We focus on the exponentially fitted scheme that we introduced in Chapter 18. There are three key classes that are essential to the application:

- ParabolicPDE: A C++ class that models second-order parabolic initial boundary value problems, including operator coefficients, boundary conditions and initial conditions. We model all functions by C++ classes as introduced in Chapter 9.
- ParabolicFDM: A specific class that approximates parabolic initial boundary problems by the use of discrete meshes and exponentially fitted schemes.
- DoubleSweep: The matrix solver that calculates the solution of the finite difference scheme at each time level (this and other solvers are discussed in Chapters 8 and 14).

A generic UML class diagram depicting the relationships between these classes is shown in Figure 19.1. We must complement this figure by showing how work gets done in the application. In other words, we describe the basic information flow by the following activities:

A1: Input for the continuous problem
A2: Input for the discrete problem
A3: Describing the algorithm that implements the exponentially fitted scheme.

We document the information flow by means of the generic UML activity diagram as shown in Figure 19.2. This will be an invaluable aid later when we wish to understand the resulting C++ code (which can be difficult to wade through without a corresponding roadmap as it were). We paraphrase the flow in Figure 19.2 as follows:

We define the functions (as 'flat' C functions) that describe the coefficients, boundary and initial conditions for the activity A1 which creates a PDE object. We discretise this object by defining a mesh (the Discrete Parameters) and activity A2 which then instantiates an FDM object. We are then ready to go because we solve the problem in activity A3 by continuous application of the DoubleSweep matrix solver for each time level. Output is in the form of an ASCII file containing option price, delta and gamma for a range of stock prices.

The code in this chapter is flexible on the one hand and hard-wired on the other. First, you must edit, compile and link all input functions in a separate file while the output is an ASCII file. Second, core processing is reasonably generic. We shall see in Part V how to apply design patterns to help you to improve the code in order to make it more flexible. The objective in this chapter is to introduce a milestone to show how to integrate

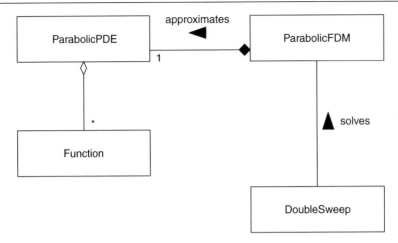

Figure 19.1   UML class structure

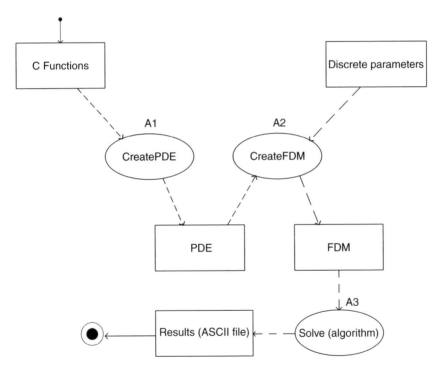

Figure 19.2   Information flow in application

the results to date into a complete application. Having got something up and running we can then extend it to suit even more stringent software requirements. Our motto is:

Get it working
Then get it right
Then get it optimised.

Quoting Jackson (1975, p. 251) we realise that optimising a program costs money and thus a risk-averse strategy should be adhered to:

Rule 1: *Don't do it*
Rule 2: *Don't do it yet.*

The first rule tells us that we need a positive quantified justification before we optimise, and that often the justification simply does not exist. We should remember that there is usually a customer who is out there waiting on the developer to deliver his or her masterpiece!

19.2   MODELLING PARTIAL DIFFERENTIAL EQUATIONS IN C++

We know that a second-order parabolic initial boundary value problem is uniquely identified by the following functions:

- The coefficients of the parabolic operator appearing in the equation
- The region in which the PDE is defined
- The boundary region and the corresponding boundary conditions
- The initial condition.

This chapter discusses problems in one space dimension and one time dimension so that things become simpler than modelling a general *n*-dimensional problem. Thus, we can model everything by real-valued functions having one and two arguments. To this end, we create a separate C++ class for each case and we model the following kinds of real-valued functions:

```
double func(double x)
{ // Real-valued function of a single variable
  // ...
}

double func2(double x, double t)
{ // Real-valued function of two variables
  // ...
}
```

These kinds of function are necessary and sufficient for modelling parabolic equations in one space dimension. However, we modify the signature of functions having two variables by combining the two variables into a single STL `pair` object as the following example shows:

```
double func2(const pair<double,double>& args);
```

This syntax is more verbose than the first prototype for the functions but we shall use the new syntax in what follows and it will soon become clear why we are using this particular form. Furthermore, functions of a single variable will have the following form:

```
double func(const double& s);
```

In general, we shall work with template versions of the above kinds of function.

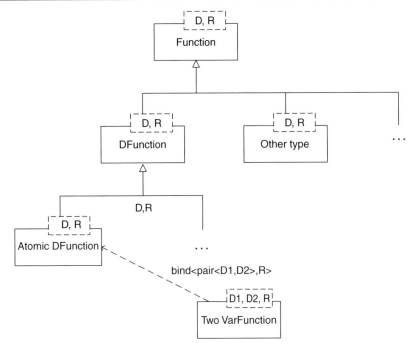

Figure 19.3   Function hierarchy

19.2.1   Function classes in C++

We now discuss how to model C functions by C++ classes (see Chapter 9 where this is discussed in more detail). In short, we create a class by encapsulating a C function as private members. This approach is similar to the Command design pattern (see Gamma *et al.*, 1995). We create a hierarchy of C++ template classes to model functions as shown in Figure 19.3. The root class Function is empty and it represents any mapping from a domain type D to a range type R. Possible specialisations of this class are:

- DFunction: Deterministic continuous function from D to R
- Other types, for example stochastic functions and functions whose arguments and/or return types may be discrete, for example.

Our main interest in this chapter lies in the class DFunction because the functions that we need are specialisations of it. In particular, we use the class AtomicDFunction to model real-valued functions of a single variable, while we use the class TwoVarFuction to model real-valued functions of two variables. The structure can be seen in Figure 19.3 and we show the C++ declarations for completeness:

```
template <class D, class R> class Function
{ // D == Domain, R == Range
private:

public:
   // We try to have as little functionality as possible here
};
```

```
template <class D,class R> class DFunction
  : public Function <D,R>
{ // Abstract base class for all deterministic functions
public:
  DFunction() { }

  // Empty
};

template <class D, class R> class AtomicDFunction
  : public DFunction<D, R>
{

private:
  R (*f)(const D& x);// Hidden classic C-type function
};

template <class D1, class D2, class R> class TwoVarDFunction
  : public AtomicDFunction<pair<D1, D2>, R>
{ // A class representing a function of two variables.

private:

public:
};
```

These classes have constructors that allow us to create instances by providing them with the *appropriate* C functions. Once an object has been instantiated we can then calculate its value by giving values for the formal parameter or parameters. We now give a simple example to show what we mean:

```
// C-style function with 1 parameter
double MyExp(const double& d)

{ // Just a test case, don't read deeper than that ☺

  return (::exp(d));
}

AtomicDFunction<double, double> myfun;
myfun.function(MyExp);          // Set the function

cout << myfun.calculate(1.0) << endl;
```

Using functions with two input parameters reads as follows:

```
TwoVarDFunction<double, double, double> myfun;
myfun.function(add);
cout << myfun.calculate(pair<double, double>(1,1)) << endl;

myfun.function(diff);    // Choose another C function

cout << myfun.calculate(pair<double, double>(2, 1)) << endl;
```

The functions 'add' and 'diff' are defined as follows:

```
double add(const pair<double, double>& p)
{
  return p.first + p.second;
}

double diff(const pair<double, double>& p)
```

```
  {
    return p.first - p.second;
  }
```

The reader may be wondering what the added value of this approach is as compared to using good old function pointers. Well, function classes are first-class entities to which we can apply design patterns, for example. Furthermore, you can add extra state (such as a name or synthetic ID, for example, in order to reference an object), something that cannot be done with function pointers. Furthermore, these are template classes so that you can specialise them to suit your own specific data types.

19.2.2   Function classes for partial differential equations

We now discuss how to model a second-order parabolic initial boundary value problem using sets of `AtomicDFunction` and `TwoVarDFunction` classes. We group the functions that define the differential operator itself and those functions that model boundary and initial conditions. To this end, we propose the following class:

```
class PDE { };

template <class X, class T, class V> class ParabolicPDE
  : public PDE
{

private:
  Range<X> xaxis;                    // Space interval
  Range<T> taxis;                    // Time  interval
  TwoVarDFunction<X, T, V> sig, m, b, f;    // Coeffs
  AtomicDFunction<X, V> ic;          // Initial condition
  AtomicDFunction<t, V> bcl, bcr;    // Boundary conditions
};
```

Thus, the private member data describes the structure of the partial differential equation. The modifier functions that initialise the structure are:

```
// Coefficients of parabolic second order operator
virtual void diffusion(TwoVarDFunction<X,T,V>& new_function);
virtual void convection(const TwoVarDFunction<X,T,V>& new_function);
virtual void zeroterm(const TwoVarDFunction<X,T,V>& new_function);
virtual void RHS(const TwoVarDFunction<X,T,V>& new_function);

// Boundary and initial conditions
virtual void BCL(const AtomicDFunction<T,V>& new_function);
virtual void BCR(const AtomicDFunction<T,V>& new_function);
virtual void IC(const AtomicDFunction<X,V>& new_function);

// The domain in which the PDE is 'played'
virtual void first (const Range<X>& new_range);
virtual void second(const Range<T>& new_range);
```

We have chosen the names of the functions to reflect their mathematical significance. Please note that we also have selector functions that allow us to calculate the value of any function as the following subset shows:

```
// Calculation of functions
virtual V diffusion(const X& xvalue, const T& tvalue) const; // Sigma
```

```
virtual V convection(const X& xvalue, const T& tvalue) const; // Mu
virtual V zeroterm(const X& xvalue, const T& tvalue) const; // b
virtual V RHS(const X& xvalue, const T& tvalue) const;      // f
```

Summarising, we have encapsulated all information pertaining to parabolic initial boundary value problems in a single class. Thus, all client code accesses the PDE object through its public interface!

19.3   FINITE DIFFERENCE SCHEMES AS C++ CLASSES, PART I

We have modelled the Duffy exponentially fitted scheme (as explained in Chapter 18) for parabolic problems as a class:

```
template <class X, class T, class V> class ParabolicFDM
{ // Finite difference method for solving parabolic PDE
  // X == x-direction value; T == t-direction value;
  // V == value space of unknown

private:
  // Lots of stuff here

public:
  // public stuff
};
```

The kinds of member data in this class can be classified as follows:

Group 1: Discrete mesh information
Group 2: Reference to the corresponding PDE object
Group 3: Work arrays for the Double Sweep matrix solver.

The current version of the software is not as flexible as we would like it to be; however, it works! The main challenge in order to make the software more flexible is to filter and encapsulate the code that sets up the linear system of equations at each time level. To this end, a possibility would be to use a Strategy pattern (Gamma *et al.*, 1995). We shall discuss in later chapters how the code can be made more maintainable and portable.

The member data in Group 1 contains information pertaining to the mesh points where the approximate finite difference solution is evaluated:

```
// Input parameters
long J;         // Number of x steps
long N;         // Number of t steps
V theta;        // Time discretisation (Implicit == 1,
                // CN == 0.5, Explicit == 0)

// Dynamic attribute
T current;  // Current time level

// Calculated values (redundant values)
V h;        // Mesh size in x
T k;        // Mesh size in t

Vector<X, long> XARR;   // The array of x (S) values
Vector<T, long> TARR;   // The array of t values
```

The member data in Group 2 is simple. In the finite difference class we embed a copy of a PDE object:

```
ParabolicPDE<X, T, V> pde;
```

We could have modelled the relationship differently, for example by using a reference or a pointer to the PDE object. However, we do not see any added advantage in doing this at the moment.

The data in Group 3 is more problematic because we must define a number of so-called work arrays that hold information needed to solve the linear systems of equations at each time level. Without going into too much detail, the work arrays have to do with administrative duties concerning the solution of the linear systems of equations:

$$A^{n+1}U^{n+1} = F^n \quad (U^0 \text{ given}) \tag{19.1}$$

In this case the tridiagonal matrix A consists of elements based on the coefficients in the original partial differential equation. The basic algorithm for solving the system (19.1) is:

```
Set n = 0;
Next:
  Calculate the vector F at level n
  Calculate the three diagonals of A at time level n+1
  Solve the system AU = F by the Double Sweep method
  If n < N then go to Next
```

The actual code that implements the above algorithm (in the current version) is a bit messy but straightforward. The full source is provided on the accompanying CD.

19.4 FINITE DIFFERENCE SCHEMES AS C++ CLASSES, PART II

We can improve the maintainability and portability of the code for the class Parabol-icFDM by structuring it as an aggregation. In particular, we see opportunities in two

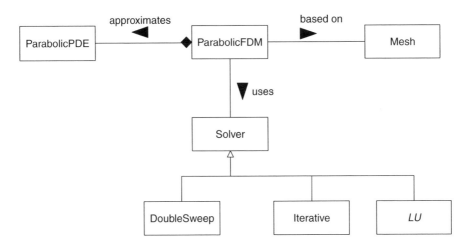

Figure 19.4 Optimised structure

applications of the Information Hiding principle. First, we create a class whose responsibility is to calculate the mesh arrays and mesh sizes that the finite difference scheme uses. Second, and possibly more important, we create a dedicated class whose responsibility is to calculate the solution of the finite difference scheme at time level $n + 1$ in terms of the solution at level n and other given data at time levels n and $n + 1$. The modified UML class diagram (compare Figure 19.1) is shown in Figure 19.4. Please note the presence of the two new façade classes `Mesh` and `Solver`.

These new classes contain the same code, more or less, as before. The difference, however, is that functionality is more evenly distributed among a network of objects rather than being placed in one large monolithic class, in this case the current class `ParabolicFDM`.

19.5   INITIALISATION ISSUES

Of course, we need some way of defining both the continuous and discrete parameters that allow us to compute the price, delta and gamma of plain and exotic options. To this end, we must carry out the following duties:

- Define C functions that model the parabolic initial boundary value problem
- Create function classes based on these C functions
- Define the parameters needed for the Black–Scholes equation
- Create an instance of the class `ParabolicPDE`
- Define the parameters for the class `ParabolicFDM`
- Calculate the price, delta and gamma at each time level
- Output the price, delta and gamma to an ASCII file.

We shall discuss each of these issues in turn.

19.5.1   Functions and parameters

First, place all functions, parameters and constants in one file (which we call `charac-teristics.(hpp, cpp)`), for example:

```
const double r = 0.1;     // interest rate
const double d = 0.0;     // dividend
const double s = 0.3;     // volatility
const double f = 0;       // forcing term, zero for BS
const double K = 10;      // strike price
const double bcl = 0;     // value of left boundary condition
const double bcr = 0;     // value of right boundary condition
double sigma(const pair<double,double>& state); // volatility
double mu(const pair<double,double>& state);       // drift
double forcing(const pair<double,double>& state); // forcing term
double b(const pair<double,double>& state);        // free term
double IC(const double& s);                        // initial condition
double IC_put(const double& s);          // initial condition for a put
double BCR(const double& t);             // right boundary condition
double BCL(const double& t);             // left boundary condition
double BCL_put(const double& d);         // right boundary condition
double BCR_Topper_p10(const double & t); // special right boundary condition
```

```
double BCR_Topper_p11(const double & t);  // special right boundary condition
double IC_PO(const double& s);       // power options: initial condition
double IC_ASCPO(const double & s);   // asymmetric capped power options
double IC_SCPO(const double & s);    // symmetric capped power options
double BCR_PO(const double& t);      // power options
```

These prototypes must be coded of course, and this is to be found in `characteris-tics.cpp`:

```
double sigma(const pair<double,double>& state)
{ return 0.5*s*s*state.first*state.first; }

double mu(const pair<double,double>& state)
{ return (r-d)*state.first; }

double forcing(const pair<double,double>& state)
{ return f; }

double b(const pair<double,double>& state)
{ return -r; }

// initial condition for call
double IC(const double& s)
{ return (s>K) ? s-K : 0; }

// initial condition for put
double IC_put(const double& s)
{ return (s<K) ? K-s : 0; }
```

Continuing with the parameters for the discrete problem, we note the following:

```
  const double Xfrom = 0;  // minimum value of stock-price domain
  const double Xto = 20;   // maximum value of stock-price domain
  const double Yfrom = 0;  // initial time
  const double Yto = .01;  // final time
  const long XINTERVALS = 20;   // number of intervals in S
  const long YINTERVALS = 100;  // number of time-intervals
  const double THETA = 0.5; // Crank Nicolson
```

19.5.2   The main program

We now define the objects corresponding to the parabolic PDE and FDM:

```
  // Set all ranges
  Range<double> X(Xfrom,Xto);
  Range<double> T(Yfrom,Yto);

  // Declare all TwoVarDFunctions
  TwoVarDFunction<double,double,double> Sigma(*sigma);
  TwoVarDFunction<double,double,double> Mu(*mu);
  TwoVarDFunction<double,double,double> Forcing(*forcing);
  TwoVarDFunction<double,double,double> B(*b);

  // Declare all AtomicDFunctions
  AtomicDFunction<double,double> Ic(*IC);
  AtomicDFunction<double,double> Bcr(*BCR_Topper_p11);
  AtomicDFunction<double,double> Bcl(*BCL);
```

```
// Instantiate the pde
ParabolicPDE<double,double,double>
   pde(X,T,Sigma,Mu,B,Forcing,Ic,Bcl,Bcr);

// Declare the finite difference scheme
ParabolicFDM<double,double,double>
   FDM(pde,XINTERVALS,YINTERVALS,THETA);

// Compute option prices
FDM.start();
```

The body of this function is as follows:

```
template <class X, class T, class V> void ParabolicFDM<X,T,V>::start()
{ // Fill in initial data

  // Set initial condition
  for (long j = tmp.MinIndex(); j <= tmp.MaxIndex(); j++)
  {
    tmp[j] = IC(XARR[j]);
  }

  // Compute the results
  while(!finished())      // Checks if t == T
    advance();           // Compute next level
}
```

We are now ready to compute the delta and gamma of the option. To this end, we call the member function `ParabolicFDM::line()` to calculate the option price:

```
// Retrieve and store option prices
long startIndex = 1;
Vector <double,long> C_tmp = FDM.line();
print(C_tmp);
Vector <double,long> C(XINTERVALS+1,startIndex,0.0);
C = C + C_tmp;
C[startIndex] = BCL(T.high());
C[XINTERVALS] = BCR_Topper_p11(T.high());
```

In this case we are calculating the price of a barrier option based on the work in Topper (1998).

Continuing, we calculate the delta and gamma functions by taking divided differences. First, we calculate the vector of stock prices:

```
// Create and fill stock price vector
Vector <double,long> S(XINTERVALS+1,startIndex);
S[S.MinIndex()] = X.low();
double h = (X.high()-X.low())/XINTERVALS;
for (long j = S.MinIndex() + 1; j <= S.MaxIndex(); j++)
{
  S[j] = h + S[j-1];
}
```

Next, we calculate the delta function by taking divided differences of the option price vector C:

```
// Create and fill delta vector
Vector <double,long> Delta(XINTERVALS+1,startIndex);
```

```
long min = Delta.MinIndex();
long max = Delta.MaxIndex();
for (j = Delta.MinIndex() + 1; j<Delta.MaxIndex(); j++)
{
   Delta[j] = (C[j+1] - C[j-1])/(2*h);
}
Delta[min] = (C[min+1] - C[min])/h;
Delta[max] = (C[max] - C[max-1])/h;
```

Next, we calculate the gamma function by taking divided differences of the delta vector:

```
// Create and fill gamma vector
Vector <double,long> Gamma(XINTERVALS+1,startIndex);
for (j = Gamma.MinIndex() + 1; j<Gamma.MaxIndex(); j++)
{
   Gamma[j] = (Delta[j+1] - Delta[j-1])/(2*h);
}
Gamma[min] = (Delta[min+1] - Delta[min])/h;
Gamma[max] = (Delta[max] - Delta[max-1])/h;
```

Finally, we place these three vectors in a nested vector class which is then sent to an object that is responsible for putting this vector in an ASCII file:

```
// Create result vector
Vector<Vector<double,long>,long> result(3,startIndex);
result[1] = C;
result[2] = Delta;
result[3] = Gamma;

// Write results to file
FileClass fileclass;
fileclass.SetFileName("output.dat");
fileclass.SetAxis(S,result);
fileclass.WriteToFile();
```

The contents of the ASCII file "output.dat" are:

```
0.000000     0.000000 0.000000 0.000000
1.000000     0.000000 0.000000 0.000000
2.000000     0.000000 0.000000 0.000000
3.000000     0.000000 0.000000 0.000000
4.000000     0.000000 0.000000 0.000000
5.000000     0.000000 0.000000 0.000000
6.000000     0.000000 0.000001 0.000059
7.000000     0.000001 0.000119 0.005846
8.000000     0.000238 0.011693 0.237640
9.000000     0.023387 0.475400 0.457691
10.000000    0.951037 0.927076 0.220181
11.000000    1.877539 0.915761 -0.016975
12.000000    2.782560 0.893127 -0.023705
13.000000    3.663792 0.868351 -0.025729
14.000000    4.519262 0.841669 -0.027420
15.000000    5.347131 0.813511 -0.022149
16.000000    6.146283 0.797371 0.169031
17.000000    6.941872 1.151572 0.368345
18.000000    8.449427 1.534061 -2.688143
19.000000    10.009995 -4.224714 -5.772028
20.000000    0.000000 -10.009995 -5.785281
```

This file consists of records (space-separated format) and each record consists of the following data:

> Stock Price + Option Price + Delta + Gamma

Incidentally, the original version of this program used the above output for use with the package `gnuplot` under Linux. It is not a big challenge to adopt the program so that it produces XML output. We shall discuss this topic in more detail in Chapters 26 (introduction) and 27 (XML from the programmer's perspective).

19.6   INTERFACING WITH EXCEL

We introduce a forward reference in this section. While producing output in the form of an ASCII file has its uses it is often advantageous to display results in a more user-friendly manner, in this case Excel. We shall deal with this topic in more detail in Chapters 22, 28 and 29, but, for the present, have a look at the following code:

```
// Print each chart separately
printOneExcel(S, C, "Price");
printOneExcel(S, Delta, "Delta");
printOneExcel(S, Gamma, "Gamma");
```

The *magic function* accepts three parameters; first, the vector S that represents the x-axis values, the second vector contains the y-axis values and the third argument is a string that represents the title of the chart. We call the function three times, thus producing three charts in Excel.

This will be further discussed in later chapters. I promise!

19.7   CONCLUSIONS AND SUMMARY

We have given a walkthrough example of how we have created a C++ application that calculates the price, delta and gamma of one-factor plain and barrier options. We discussed how we designed and implemented the foundation classes (such as `ParabolicPDE` and `ParabolicFDM`) and then how they are to construct the final solution. You can use the text in this chapter to help you to understand the corresponding source code on the CD. We have produced a working system that you can extend to suit your own needs. This incremental approach is appealing because you always have a working prototype that can be demonstrated. If the customer is happy you can always ask for more funds to create a more sophisticated system with lots of whistles and bells!

You can study the source code (on the CD) for this problem and adapt it to your own particular application. For example, you can adapt it to suit one-factor models for exotic options and interest-rate problems (for example, callable bonds).

An Introduction to ADI and Splitting Schemes

20.1 INTRODUCTION AND OBJECTIVES

In this chapter we discuss how to apply finite difference schemes to approximate the solution of multidimensional diffusion equations. In general, an exact solution to these problems is not possible to find, and even when an exact solution is known it is complicated to evaluate. Our interest is in applying and extending the schemes from previous chapters in this book to multi-factor problems. Some typical applications are:

- Asian options (payoff depends on the underlying S and the average price of S over some prescribed period)
- Multi-asset options (for example, basket options and options with two underlyings)
- Convertible bonds (bond price is a function of the underlying S and the (stochastic) interest rate r)
- Multidimensional interest rate models.

In general, each of the above models can be subsumed under the general parabolic partial differential equation (Bhansali, 1998)

$$\frac{\partial V}{\partial t^*} + \sum_{j=1}^{n}(r - D_j)S_j\frac{\partial V}{\partial S_j} + \frac{1}{2}\sum_{i,j=1}^{n}\rho_{ij}\sigma_i\sigma_j S_i S_j\frac{\partial^2 V}{\partial S_i\,\partial S_j} = rV \tag{20.1}$$

Here we see that the derivative quantity V is a function of n underlyings. Furthermore, these underlyings may be correlated. As discussed in Bhansali (1998), the rate of change of V with respect to time may be written as the sum of three elements

$$r\left(V - \sum_{j=1}^{n}S_j\frac{\partial V}{\partial S_j}\right) \tag{20.2}$$

$$\sum_{j=1}^{n}D_j S_j\frac{\partial V}{\partial S_j} \tag{20.3}$$

$$-\frac{1}{2}\sum_{i,j=1}^{n}\rho_{ij}\sigma_i\sigma_j\frac{\partial^2 V}{\partial S_i\,\partial S_j} \tag{20.4}$$

Of course, we must provide initial (terminal) and boundary conditions in order to produce a unique solution to (20.1). As there is no explicit formula for the solution in general, we must resort to approximate methods. In this book we look at finite difference methods for such problems and concentrate on *two-factor equations* (that is where $n = 2$ in equation (20.1)). In particular, we first of all discuss discretising all variables in (20.1) simultaneously, and we show the consequences of such an approach. In particular, we encounter the *curse of dimensionality* because solving two-factor equations by a straightforward finite difference scheme leads to large systems of equations that are difficult (but not impossible) to solve. Another approach is to reduce the multidimensional problem to a series of one-dimensional sub-problems where each sub-problem corresponds to one specific underlying variable. For this latter case we discuss two major approaches called Alternating Direction Implicit (ADI) and splitting (or splitting up) methods, respectively.

In this chapter we shall concentrate on the heat equation in a rectangle in order to motivate the ADI and splitting methods. Furthermore, we focus on Dirichlet conditions only. In the next chapter we shall extend the methods to handle convection–diffusion equations in general (and Black–Scholes in particular).

Understanding how ADI and splitting methods work for the heat equation will help you to appreciate similar schemes for convection–diffusion and Black–Scholes equations.

20.2   A MODEL PROBLEM

In this chapter we focus primarily on the two-dimensional heat equation

$$\frac{\partial u}{\partial t} = \frac{\partial^2 u}{\partial x^2} + \frac{\partial^2 u}{\partial y^2} \tag{20.5}$$

that is defined in some region of (x, y, t) space. In this section we extend the finite difference method that we defined in previous chapters to the case where the continuous (x, y) space is replaced by a two-dimensional mesh. To this end, we use some notation for difference operators in the x and y directions:

$$\Delta_x^2 u_{ij} = h_1^{-2}(u_{i+1,j} - 2u_{i,j} + u_{i-1,j})$$
$$\Delta_y^2 u_{ij} = h_2^{-2}(u_{i,j+1} - 2u_{i,j} + u_{i,j-1})$$
$$\Delta_x^+ u_{ij} = h_1^{-1}(u_{i+1,j} - u_{i,j}) \tag{20.6}$$
$$\Delta_x^- u_{ij} = h_1^{-1}(u_{i,j} - u_{i-1,j})$$
$$\Delta_x^0 u_{ij} = (2h_1)^{-1}(u_{i+1,j} - u_{i-1,j})$$

These operators are just the two-dimensional extensions of the one-dimensional discrete operators of previous chapters. Thus, when approximating the heat equation (20.5) we can choose centred differencing in the x and y directions while we can choose the following options for the time direction:

- Explicit Euler (EE)
- Implicit Euler (IE)
- Crank–Nicolson (CN).

For EE, the finite difference scheme becomes (neglecting boundary and initial conditions for the moment)

$$\frac{U_{i,j}^{n+1} - U_{i,j}^n}{k} = \Delta_x^2 U_{i,j}^n + \Delta_y^2 U_{i,j}^n \tag{20.7}$$

Of course, this is an explicit scheme and stability is only conditional. By a von Neumann stability analysis we can prove that (20.7) is stable if

$$r = \frac{k}{h_1^2} = \frac{k}{h_2^2} \le \frac{1}{2} \qquad (20.8)$$

where we assume now that the step sizes in the x and y directions are the same (see Peaceman, 1977).

Rewriting equation (20.7) in a different form allows us to write the approximate solution at time level $n + 1$ in terms of the solution at time level n

$$U_{i,j}^{n+1} = U_{i,j}^n + k(\Delta_x^2 U_{i,j}^n + \Delta_y^2 U_{i,j}^n) \qquad (20.9)$$

It is then easy to develop some C++ code to implement this algorithm without the need to solve a linear system of equations. However, you must keep the constraint (20.8) in mind (you must satisfy it!) otherwise you will get non-realistic results.

The IE scheme for (20.5) is given by

$$\frac{U_{i,j}^{n+1} - U_{i,j}^n}{k} = \Delta_x^2 U_{i,j}^{n+1} + \Delta_y^2 U_{i,j}^{n+1} \qquad (20.10)$$

This is an unconditionally stable scheme (for all values of k and h) but we see that the solution at time level $n + 1$ is defined on both sides of equation (20.10). We must resort to some kind of matrix solver if we wish to find this solution. A good treatment is given in Peaceman (1977). For the heat equation we get a system of the form

$$AU = F \qquad (20.11)$$

If we assume that the x and y regions have been partitioned into N and M intervals, respectively, then the matrix A has N row and M columns if we use Dirichlet boundary conditions.

Thus A has a block form. In general, the vector U will have $N \times M$ elements, where N is the number of sub-divisions of the x dimension and M is the number of sub-divisions of the y dimension.

There are methods for solving systems of the form (20.11) (Peaceman, 1977; Tavella and Randall, 2000) but such a discussion is outside the scope of this book. The methods are very advanced, in my opinion, and there are more effective ways of solving such systems as we shall see in this chapter and the next.

20.3   MOTIVATION AND HISTORY

We now give a short introduction to the origins and history of the ADI and splitting methods. Like much of numerical analysis, many techniques were developed during the 1960s when the digital computer started to be used to model various industrial, scientific and engineering problems. Some examples are:

• Reservoir engineering (Peaceman, 1977)

- Solving the heat equations in several dimensions (Douglas and Rachford, 1955)
- Problems in hydrodynamics and elasticity (Yanenko, 1971).

The ADI method was pioneered in the United States by Douglas, Rachford, Peaceman, Gunn and others. The ADI method has a number of advantages over the methods that are discussed in section 20.2. First, explicit difference methods are rarely used to solve initial boundary value problems due to their poor stability properties. Implicit methods have superior stability properties but unfortunately they are difficult to solve in two or more dimensions. Consequently, ADI methods became an alternative because they can be programmed by solving a simple tridiagonal system of equations in the x and y directions, respectively.

During the period that ADI was being developed, a number of Soviet numerical analysts (most notably Yanenko, Marchuk, Samarskii and D'Yakanov) were developing splitting methods (also known as fractional step or locally one-dimensional (LOD) methods) for solving time-dependent partial differential equations in two and three dimensions.

It would seem that the financial engineering community tends to use the ADI method when solving multi-factor Black–Scholes equations (see Sun, 1999; Wilmott, 1998) although there is evidence to show that it is inferior to splitting methods, especially when cross-derivatives (correlation terms) must be modelled. Furthermore, great leaps of faith have been taken by some authors who think that numerical recipes that work well for the two-dimensional heat equation can be applied with the same success to convection–diffusion equations in two and three dimensions. Unfortunately, there is evidence to show that ADI performs badly for *convection-dominated* systems. We shall discuss this particular topic in the next chapter.

In this chapter we introduce the ADI and splitting methods for the two-dimensional heat equation and shall also pay a fleeting visit to approximating three-dimensional equations using these methods. However, these are the easiest cases and we must also extend our knowledge to include answers for the following problems:

- Approximating cross-derivatives in the multi-factor Black–Scholes equation
- How to handle boundary conditions and determine how their approximation affects accuracy of the scheme
- Approximating multidimensional convection–diffusion problems
- Dealing with convection-dominated problems
- Developing algorithms that we map to C++ code.

In particular, we shall address these issues in the next chapter. We concentrate solely on splitting methods in that chapter for the following reasons: I find them more appealing than ADI methods, they tend to perform better, and it would seem that 'pure ADI' has gone out of fashion.

20.4   BASIC ADI SCHEME FOR THE HEAT EQUATION

We shall now introduce the basic ADI scheme for the two-dimensional heat equation, and for the moment shall neglect boundary and initial conditions. The basic idea behind ADI is to replace a two-dimensional scheme such as (20.10) (which is implicit in the x and y directions) by two simpler equations, each of which is implicit in one direction only. To this end, we devise what is in fact a kind of predictor–corrector scheme (as discussed in Chapter 11) as follows:

$$\frac{\tilde{U}_{ij} - U_{ij}^n}{k/2} = \Delta_x^2 \tilde{U}_{ij} + \Delta_y^2 U_{ij}^n \tag{20.12a}$$

$$\frac{U_{ij}^{n+1} - \tilde{U}_{ij}}{k/2} = \Delta_x^2 \tilde{U}_{ij} + \Delta_y^2 U_{ij}^{n+1} \tag{20.12b}$$

Here we see the introduction of an intermediate value in equation (20.12a). This equation is implicit in x and explicit in y and hence can be solved by LU decomposition or the Double Sweep method that we examined in Chapter 8. Having found the intermediate value we then calculate the value of the approximate solution at time level $n + 1$ using equation (20.12b). This equation is implicit in y and explicit in x and again can be solved using LU decomposition or the Double Sweep method.

It can be shown that the scheme (20.12) is unconditionally stable. Thus there are no restrictions on the mesh size k. The scheme (20.12) is sometimes called the Peaceman–Rachford scheme.

20.4.1   Three-dimensional heat equation

Let us try to extend the Peaceman–Rachford scheme to three dimensions as follows:

$$\frac{U^{n+\frac{1}{3}} - U^n}{k/3} = \Delta_x^2 U^{n+\frac{1}{3}} + \Delta_y^2 U^n + \Delta_z^2 U^n$$

$$\frac{U^{n+\frac{2}{3}} - U^{n+\frac{1}{3}}}{k/3} = \Delta_x^2 U^{n+\frac{1}{3}} + \Delta_y^2 U^{n+\frac{2}{3}} + \Delta_z^2 U^{n+\frac{1}{3}} \tag{20.13}$$

$$\frac{U^{n+1} - U^{n+\frac{2}{3}}}{k/3} = \Delta_x^2 U^{n+\frac{2}{3}} + \Delta_y^2 U^{n+\frac{2}{3}} + \Delta_z^2 U^{n+1}$$

(notice that we have suppressed the space indices in (20.13) for readability reasons). A lengthy stability analysis (see Peaceman, 1977) should be that scheme (20.13) is stable if

$$\frac{k}{h_1^2} \leq \frac{1}{2} \tag{20.14}$$

Thus, the three-dimensional version of the Peaceman–Rachford method is not unconditionally stable.

The first unconditionally stable ADI method for three dimensions was developed by J. Douglas Jr. and H. Rachford and is given by

$$\frac{U^{n+\frac{1}{3}} - U^n}{k} = \Delta_x^2 U^{n+\frac{1}{3}} + \Delta_y^2 U^n + \Delta_z^2 U^n$$

$$\frac{U^{n+\frac{2}{3}} - U^{n+\frac{1}{3}}}{k} + \Delta_y^2 U^n = \Delta_y^2 U^{n+\frac{2}{3}} \tag{20.15}$$

$$\frac{U^{n+1} - U^{n+\frac{2}{3}}}{k} + \Delta_z^2 U^n = \Delta_z^2 U^{n+1}$$

20.5   BASIC SPLITTING SCHEME FOR THE HEAT EQUATION

Splitting schemes are more ruthless than ADI schemes in the sense that they reduce a partial differential equation to a series of one-dimensional equations. Each of the latter equations is then approximated by a suitable one-dimensional finite difference scheme. We can choose between explicit and implicit schemes, whereas ADI uses an implicit scheme only. For the two-dimensional heat equation, for example, we define the splitting scheme by solving two *legs* in one specific direction. In the case of the explicit splitting scheme we get

$$\frac{\tilde{U}_{ij} - U_{ij}^n}{\Delta t} = \Delta_x^2 U_{ij}^n$$

$$\frac{U_{ij}^{n+1} - \tilde{U}_{ij}}{\Delta t} = \Delta_y^2 \tilde{U}_{ij}$$

(20.16)

We assume that the mesh size in both x and y directions is a constant h. Then (20.16) is stable under the condition

$$r \equiv \frac{k}{h^2} \leq \frac{1}{2}$$

(20.17)

(for a proof, see Godunov and Riabenki, 1987). A schematic representation of the above scheme is shown in Figure 20.1 where the explicit nature of the scheme can be clearly seen. The implicit splitting scheme for the two-dimensional heat equation is given by

$$\frac{\tilde{U}_{ij} - U_{ij}^n}{\Delta t} = \Delta_x^2 \tilde{U}_{ij}$$

$$\frac{U_{ij}^{n+1} - \tilde{U}_{ij}}{\Delta t} = \Delta_y^2 U_{ij}^{n+1}$$

(20.18)

and its graphical representation is shown in Figure 20.2.

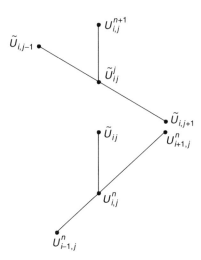

Figure 20.1   Mesh for explicit scheme

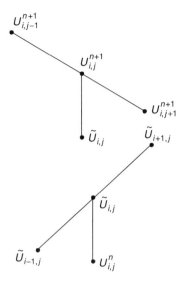

Figure 20.2   Mesh for implicit scheme

20.5.1   Three-dimensional heat equation

Analysis of the stability of ADI methods shows that approximation with an explicit operator reduces the stability of the scheme. This suggests using an implicit operator at each leg or fractional step (Yanenko, 1971). In order to improve the accuracy of this scheme Yanenko proposes using the weighted scheme

$$\frac{U^{n+\frac{1}{3}} - U^n}{k} = \Delta_x^2[\theta U^{n+\frac{1}{3}} + (1-\theta)U^n]$$

$$\frac{U^{n+\frac{2}{3}} - U^{n+\frac{1}{3}}}{k} = \Delta_y^2[\theta U^{n+\frac{2}{3}} + (1-\theta)U^{n+\frac{1}{3}}]$$

$$\frac{U^{n+1} - U^{n+\frac{2}{3}}}{k} = \Delta_z^2[\theta U^{n+1} + (1-\theta)U^{n+\frac{2}{3}}]$$

$$\theta \in [0, 1]$$

(20.19)

For example, in the case $\theta = \frac{1}{2}$, the scheme (20.19) has second-order accuracy in both space and time.

20.6   APPROXIMATING CROSS-DERIVATIVES

In many financial engineering applications we must model cross-derivative terms, for example with various kinds of PDEs for bonds and interest-rate models. To this end, we devise good schemes for handling these terms. The mathematical financial literature is a bit fuzzy on this topic. Let us take the following example:

$$\frac{\partial u}{\partial t} = Lu$$

$$Lu \cong \sum_{i,j=1}^{2} a_{ij} \frac{\partial^2 u}{\partial x_i \, \partial x_j} \tag{20.20}$$

$$a_{11} a_{22} - a_{12}^2 > 0, \quad a_{11} > 0, \quad a_{22} > 0$$

a_{ij} constant

Again, Yanenko states that the ADI method is not applicable to solving (20.20) because its application does not lead to a simple three-point scheme (in fact we get a nine-point scheme). Instead, the following splitting scheme is proposed

$$\frac{\tilde{U}_{ij} - U_{ij}^n}{\Delta t} = a_{11} \Delta_x^2 \tilde{U}_{ij} + a_{12} \Delta_x^0 \Delta_y^0 U_{ij}^n$$

$$\frac{U_{ij}^{n+1} - \tilde{U}_{ij}}{\Delta t} = a_{12} \Delta_x^0 \Delta_y^0 \tilde{U}_{ij} + a_{22} \Delta_y^2 U_{ij}^{n+1} \tag{20.21}$$

(Stable and Convergent)

We conclude our discussion of splitting methods by introducing a predictor–corrector method (compare with Chapter 11) for the three-dimensional heat equation. It consists of four equations, the first three of which are predictors in the x, y and z directions while the last equation is a corrector based on the 'full' discrete operator:

$$\frac{U^{n+\frac{1}{6}} - U^n}{k/2} = \Delta_x^2 U^{n+\frac{1}{6}}$$

$$\frac{U^{n+\frac{2}{6}} - U^{n+\frac{1}{6}}}{k/2} = \Delta_y^2 U^{n+\frac{2}{6}}$$

$$\frac{U^{n+\frac{1}{2}} - U^{n+\frac{2}{6}}}{k/2} = \Delta_z^2 U^{n+\frac{1}{2}} \tag{20.22}$$

$$\frac{U^{n+1} - U^n}{k} = (\Delta_x^2 + \Delta_y^2 + \Delta_z^2) U^{n+\frac{1}{2}}$$

Thus, the predictor is based on a splitting scheme.

20.7 HANDLING BOUNDARY CONDITIONS

Of course, when solving initial boundary value problems for the heat equation (and for any parabolic equation for that matter) we must model the bounded or unbounded region in which the equation is to be valid. In particular, we must describe the conditions on the solution at the boundary of the region. There are five main issues that we must address:

- The shape or geometry of the region
- The kinds of boundary conditions (Dirichlet, Neumann, Robins, linearity)

- How to approximate the boundary conditions
- How to incorporate the boundary conditions into the ADI or splitting equations
- Ensuring that boundary approximation does not adversely affect the stability and accuracy of the difference approximation.

We now give a brief discussion of each of these topics and focus on creating the algorithm for the two-dimensional heat equation in a rectangular region with Dirichlet boundary conditions. In general, it would seem that ADI and splitting methods are better suited to rectangular regions rather than non-rectangular regions because it is more difficult to approximate function values and their derivatives on curved boundaries than on horizontal or vertical boundaries.

In this chapter we concentrate on Dirichlet boundary conditions for the two-dimensional heat equation, how to approximate such conditions and to incorporate them into ADI and splitting schemes. A good discussion of these and other issues can be found in Thomas (1998). In particular, Thomas discusses how to define first-order and second-order approximations to the derivative of the exact solution on the boundary of the region of interest.

We now discuss the case of Dirichlet boundary conditions. To this end, we consider the model problem on a unit square:

$$(1) \quad \frac{\partial u}{\partial t} = a \left(\frac{\partial^2 u}{\partial x^2} + \frac{\partial^2 u}{\partial y^2} \right), \quad (x, y) \in R, \quad t > 0$$

$$(2) \quad u(x, y, t) = g(x, y, t), \quad (x, y) \in \partial R, \quad t > 0$$

$$(3) \quad u(x, y, 0) = f(x, y), \quad (x, y) \in \overline{R}$$

$$R = (0, 1) \times (0, 1)$$

We rewrite the ADI equations (20.12a) and (20.12b) for the two-dimensional heat equation by grouping known terms on the right-hand side of the equations and unknown terms on the left-hand side:

$$\left(1 - \frac{k}{2} \Delta_x^2 \right) \tilde{U}_{ij} = \left(1 + \frac{k}{2} \Delta_y^2 \right) U_{ij}^n \tag{20.23a}$$

$$\left(1 - \frac{k}{2} \Delta_y^2 \right) U_{ij}^{n+1} = \left(1 + \frac{k}{2} \Delta_x^2 \right) \tilde{U}_{ij} \tag{20.23b}$$

In general, there is not much difficulty involved if we wish to calculate the boundary values of the approximate solution at times n and $n + 1$. The real challenge is to determine suitable boundary conditions for the intermediate value in equations (20.23). To this end, we add the left-hand side of equation (20.23a) to the right-hand side of equation (20.23b) and vice versa. This give us a formula for the intermediate solution in terms of the solution at time levels n and $n + 1$:

$$\tilde{U}_{ij} = \frac{1}{2} \left(1 - \frac{k}{2} \Delta_y^2 \right) U_{ij}^{n+1} + \frac{1}{2} \left(1 + \frac{k}{2} \Delta_y^2 \right) U_{ij}^n \tag{20.24}$$

This formula allows us to find the appropriate boundary values. For example, in the x direction these will be:

$i = 0$

$$\tilde{U}_{0j} = \frac{1}{2}\left(1 - \frac{k}{2}\Delta_y^2\right)g(0, jh_2, (n+1)k) + \frac{1}{2}\left(1 + \frac{k}{2}\Delta_y^2\right)g(0, jh_2, nk)$$

(20.25)

$i = M_x$

$$\tilde{U}_{M_x,ij} = \frac{1}{2}\left(1 - \frac{k}{2}\Delta_y^2\right)g(1, jh_2, (n+1)k) + \frac{1}{2}\left(1 + \frac{k}{2}\Delta_y^2\right)g(1, jh_2, nk)$$

Of course, we can find the corresponding boundary conditions in the y direction by plugging in special index values of j in equation (20.24).

Equation (20.25) is a second-order (in time) accurate approximation to the boundary condition. An alternative solution is to use the (again) second-order approximation

$$\tilde{U}_{0j} = g(0, jh_2, (n + \tfrac{1}{2})k)$$

$$\tilde{U}_{M_x,ij} = g(1, jh_2, (n + \tfrac{1}{2})k)$$

(20.26)

Thus, you may choose between (20.25) and (20.26) as each gives second-order accuracy. See Thomas (1998) for a justification.

20.8   ALGORITHMS AND DESIGN ISSUES

We now discuss how to solve ADI systems. First, we set up the system of equations, then we describe the solution using some kind of pseudo-code and, finally, we map this pseudo-code to C++. Since ADI is essentially a method for solving an n-dimensional problem as a series of (simpler) one-dimensional problems we would hope that many of our classes and results from previous chapters can also be used in this chapter. This hope is realistic. In particular, we shall be able to reuse the following artefacts:

- Data structures for vectors and numeric matrices (template classes `Vector` and `Numer-icMatrix`). Furthermore, we will need structures for tridiagonal matrices.
- Code that generates meshes in one and two dimensions.
- Mechanisms that implement divided difference schemes in one and two directions. For example, we wish to implement divided differences for first and second derivatives in the x and y directions.
- Algorithms, schemes and code that solve linear systems of equations, in particular LU decomposition and Double Sweep method (see Chapter 8) in conjunction with tridiagonal matrices.

Using the above artefacts improves the quality of our code for ADI in a number of ways. First, this approach improves reliability because we are using code that has already been written, reviewed and tested, albeit in a possibly simpler context. It is hoped that the same code can be used *as is* in the present context. Second, this approach improves the understandability of the code because we are using the code as façades or black boxes; you do not need to know about the internals of the code because you just need to use the appropriate interfaces. Finally, the resulting code is maintainable. This means that you can change and modify the source code to suit new wants and needs. For example, the C++ code that implements ADI and splitting schemes can be extended to include models for convection–diffusion equations in general and multi-factor Black–Scholes equations in particular. It may even be possible to extend the two-dimensional schemes and corresponding code to three dimensions.

Let's get down to business. We develop the algorithms that describe the ADI scheme (20.12) or its equivalent representation (20.23). We discuss the algorithm that gets us from the solution U at time level n to the solution U at level $n + 1$. We first describe the algorithm in general terms. Once we have done that we then describe the algorithm in more detail so that the *cognitive distance* between this level of detail and C++ is not too great.

The first cut algorithm for solving (20.23) is described by a series of activities:

A1: Calculate the right-hand side (RHS) of equation (20.23a)
A2: Create the stencil (system of equations) for (20.23a)
A3: Solve system of equations (by LU decomposition, for example)

A4: Calculate the right-hand side (RHS) of equation (20.23b)
A5: Create the stencil (system of equations) for (20.23b)
A6: Solve system of equations (by LU decomposition, for example)

This approach is based on the algorithms in Thomas (1998). Each of the above activities has input I and output O. It is useful to motivate the information flow by an activity diagram in UML. We develop a somewhat more top-down approach in the first instance in order to scope the problem. To this end, the major input and output from the top-level activity corresponding to equations (20.23) is given in Figure 20.3. We decompose the main activity into two sub-activities, each one corresponding to a 'leg'(whether it be x or y) in the ADI scheme (20.23). This is shown in Figure 20.4. We now can subsume the activities A1 to A6 above under each leg: Leg 1 consists of activities A1, A2 and A3 while Leg 2 consists of activities A4, A5 and A6.

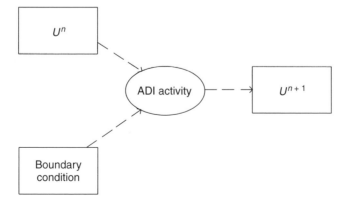

Figure 20.3   ADI main activity

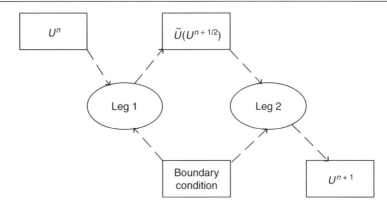

Figure 20.4   Activity decomposition x and y legs

There is a lot of commonality between the eventual code that implements Legs 1 and 2. In fact they share the following common steps:

- Calculate a RHS vector (A1 and A4)
- Create a tridiagonal matrix (A2 and A5)
- Solve the tridiagonal system (A3 and A6).

The steps for these algorithms are given in detail in Thomas (1998) in the form of pseudo-code. In our code we can give C++ as an alternative to this pseudo-code.

20.9   CONCLUSIONS AND SUMMARY

We have given an introduction to Alternating Direction Implicit (ADI) and splitting methods that are used in engineering and science to solve multidimensional partial differential equations. These methods are based on the assumption that a multidimensional problem can be broken down into a series of one-dimensional problems. We then solve each sub-problem using the techniques for one-factor equations, already discussed in earlier chapters of this book.

We have included this chapter for a number of reasons. First, there is growing interest in ADI as can be seen in the financial literature, and it is probably a good idea to present the essence of the method for a simple but important model problem, namely the two-dimensional heat equation. Second, ADI is a bit overhyped and in some cases it is better to use splitting methods. There is some evidence to show that splitting methods give better results than ADI for two-factor Black–Scholes equations. Third, ADI and splitting methods are easy to understand and to implement and they are preferable to direct methods (as discussed in Tavella and Randall, 2000) in this respect. Thus, these methods are easier to understand for a reader with a non-numerical analysis background. Finally, once you have understood how ADI and splitting methods work for diffusion problems it is relatively easy to move to more complex problem such as multidimensional convection–diffusion PDE and multi-factor Black–Scholes equations. This is the content of the next chapter.

Numerical Approximation of Two-Factor Derivative Models

21.1 INTRODUCTION AND OBJECTIVES

In this chapter we discuss how to approximate two-factor derivative models using finite difference schemes. We focus on ADI and splitting methods because they are easy to implement and build on the methods that we developed in Chapter 20. Furthermore, they are easier to understand than directly discretising space and time variables simultaneously (for an introduction to this approach, see Peaceman, 1977, and Tavella and Randall, 2000, for example).

The general two-dimensional Black–Scholes equation is given by

$$-\frac{\partial u}{\partial t} + L_1 u + L_2 u + L_3 u = f$$

$$L_j u \equiv \sigma_j \frac{\partial^2 u}{\partial x_j^2} + \mu_j \frac{\partial u}{\partial x_j} + b_j u, \quad j = 1, 2 \tag{21.1}$$

$$L_3 u = \rho_{12} \frac{\partial^2 u}{\partial x_1 \partial x_2} \text{(Cross-term)}$$

Here we see that there are three main operators, namely two convection–diffusion operators and a cross-term. These correspond to single-factor models and coupling, respectively. There are many special cases of (21.1) in the numerical analysis and financial literature and we give an introduction to some of these cases and how they are approximated using finite difference schemes. There is a vast literature on this subject (dating from the 1950s) and, in particular, the ADI method is also making inroads in the financial literature. The main issue is how to split a two-dimensional problem into simpler problems, proving that the scheme is stable (or not), avoiding spurious oscillation and proving that the schemes are (reasonably) accurate. We do not pretend to have all the answers but we do give some guidelines and results based on a number of successful models for two-factor problems.

21.2 TWO-FACTOR MODELS IN FINANCIAL ENGINEERING

We now give some interesting examples of problems in financial engineering that can be approximated by parabolic partial differential equations in two 'space' variables. These variables will have a specific meaning depending on the context. For example, options based on the maximum or minimum of two stocks have the space variables based on the variation of the two stocks.

21.2.1 Asian options

An Asian option is a contract that gives the holder the right to buy the underlying asset for an average price over some prescribed interval. This kind of option is popular in the currency and commodity markets and there are two ways of averaging the value:

- Arithmetic averaging
- Geometric averaging

If the underlying asset is assumed to be lognormally distributed then the geometric average of the asset will also be lognormally distributed. Arithmetic averaging takes the arithmetic average of the underlying asset.

We must also determine *when* this sampling takes place:

- Discretely averaged samples
- Continuously averaged samples.

The formulae for the averaging scenarios are shown in equations (21.2) and (21.3) and are well documented in the literature (Haug, 1998; Wilmott *et al.*, 1993).

Arithmetic averaging

$$\text{Continuous:} \quad I = \frac{1}{t} \int_0^t S(\tau)\mathrm{d}\tau$$

$$\text{Discrete:} \quad I = \frac{1}{n} \sum_{j=1}^n S_j \tag{21.2}$$

Geometric averaging

$$\text{Continuous:} \quad \exp\left(\frac{1}{t} \int_0^t \log S(\tau)\mathrm{d}\tau\right)$$

$$\text{Discrete:} \quad \left(\prod_{j=1}^n S_j\right)^{\frac{1}{n}} \tag{21.3}$$

The corresponding PDEs are given in equations (21.4) and (21.5):

$$\frac{\partial V}{\partial t} + S\frac{\partial V}{\partial I} + \frac{1}{2}\sigma^2 S^2 \frac{\partial^2 V}{\partial S^2} + (rS)\frac{\partial V}{\partial S} - rV = 0$$

$$I \equiv \int_0^t S(\tau)\mathrm{d}\tau \tag{21.4}$$

Asian option (Arithmetic averaging)

$$\frac{\partial V}{\partial t} + \log S\frac{\partial V}{\partial I} + \frac{1}{2}\sigma^2 S^2 \frac{\partial^2 V}{\partial S^2} + rS\frac{\partial V}{\partial S} - rV = 0$$

$$I = \int_0^t \log S(\tau)\mathrm{d}\tau \tag{21.5}$$

We note that these equations are convection–diffusion in the S variable (thus, of parabolic type) while in the I direction it is essentially a first-order hyperbolic equation:

$$\frac{\partial V}{\partial t} + S\frac{\partial V}{\partial I} = 0$$

$$\frac{\partial V}{\partial t} + \log S\frac{\partial V}{\partial I} = 0 \tag{21.6}$$

and since we only have a derivative of, at most, order one in the I direction we can only accommodate one boundary condition. Furthermore, centred difference schemes are not suitable (they are weakly stable) and we must resort to one-sided (upwinded) schemes (Peaceman, 1977; Duffy, 1977) that take the so-called *characteristic direction* of the first-order equations into account.

21.2.2 Convertible bonds with random interest rates

A convertible bond is like a normal bond except that it may be exchanged for an asset. The exchange is called *conversion*. The corresponding PDE is:

$$
\frac{\partial V}{\partial t} + \frac{1}{2}\sigma^2 S^2 \frac{\partial^2 V}{\partial S^2} + \rho\sigma Sw\frac{\partial^2 V}{\partial S\,\partial r} + \frac{1}{2}w^2\frac{\partial^2 V}{\partial r^2}
$$

$$
+ rS\frac{\partial V}{\partial S} + (u - w\lambda)\frac{\partial V}{\partial r} - rV = 0
$$

$$
\lambda(r, S, t): \text{Market price of risk} \tag{21.7}
$$

$$
-1 \leq \rho(r, S, t) \leq 1: \text{Correlation}
$$

This equation is based on the stochastic differential equations (SDEs) that describe the evolution of the asset and random interest rate:

$$
ds = \mu(S, t)S\,dt + \sigma(S, t)S\,dX_1
$$

$$
dr = u(r, t)\,dt + w(r, t)\,dX_2 \tag{21.8}
$$

Here, dX_1 is a normally distributed random variable with mean 0 and variance dt. The drift μ and volatility σ depend on both the asset price S and time t. For the SDE describing the interest rate, dX_2 is a normally distributed random variable with mean 0 and variance dt.

We note that the convertible bond has an underlying asset of either European or American type. In the latter case we note the existence of a free boundary that depends on both the interest rate r and time t (see Sun, 1999).

Note the presence of the cross-derivative term in equation (21.7) in which the correlation of the random variables in S and r is given by:

$$
E[dX_1, dX_2] = \rho(S, r, t)\,dt \tag{21.9}
$$

In Chapter 20 we discussed a number of finite difference discretisations for approximating this cross-term.

21.2.3 Options with two underlying assets

A general PDE that describes a derivative quantity that depends on two underlying assets is given by:

$$
\frac{\partial V}{\partial t} + \frac{1}{2}\sigma_1^2 S_1^2 \frac{\partial^2 V}{\partial S_1^2} + (r - D_1)S_1\frac{\partial V}{\partial S_1} + \frac{1}{2}\sigma_2^2 S_2^2 \frac{\partial^2 V}{\partial S_2^2}
$$

$$
+ (r - D_2)S_2\frac{\partial V}{\partial S_2} + \rho\sigma_1\sigma_2 S_1 S_2\frac{\partial^2 V}{\partial S_1\,\partial S_2} - rV = 0 \tag{21.10}
$$

(Topper, 1998). The PDE is played out in a general two-dimensional region D having boundary R. On one part of the boundary we can specify Dirichlet boundary conditions while on its complement we specify Neumann boundary conditions. We must also specify terminal conditions:

$$V(S_1, S_2, T) = g_1(S_1, S_2) \text{ in } D$$

$$V(S_1, S_2, t) = g_2(S_1, S_2, t) \text{ on } R_1 \qquad (21.11)$$

$$\frac{\partial V}{\partial \eta}(S_1, S_2, t) = G_3(S_1, S_2, t) \text{ on } R_2$$

When the region D is rectangular we can apply finite differences to approximate the space variable, but if it has a more general form we may need to resort to finite element methods (Strang and Fix, 1973; Topper, 1998). In particular, approximating the derivatives of the option variable on curved boundaries is a challenge if we use finite differences.

21.2.4 Basket options

It is known that there is no known analytical solution to options on baskets and we must thus resort to numerical approximations. A common simplifying technique is to combine the volatilities of the underlying assets and their correlations into a single volatility of the basket. The basket is then treated as a single underlying. In this section we pose the problems as a PDE:

$$\frac{\partial V}{\partial t} + \frac{1}{2}\sigma_1^2 S_1^2 \frac{\partial^2 V}{\partial S_1^2} + (r - D_1)S_1 \frac{\partial V}{\partial S_1} + \frac{1}{2}\sigma_2^2 S_2^2 \frac{\partial^2 V}{\partial S_2^2}$$

$$+ (r - D_2)S_2 \frac{\partial V}{\partial S_2} + \rho\sigma_1\sigma_2 S_1 S_2 \frac{\partial^2 V}{\partial S_1 \partial S_2} - rV = 0 \qquad (21.12)$$

in a bounded domain D, as shown in Figure 21.1.

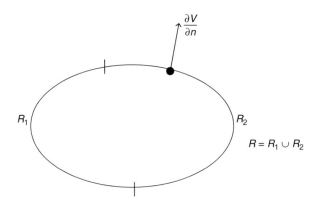

Figure 21.1 Region of integration

The corresponding terminal and boundary conditions are given by:

$$V(S_1, S_2, T) = \max(0, X - (w_1 S_1 + w_2 S_2)) \text{ in } D$$

$$V(S_1, 0, t) = g\left(S_1, \frac{X}{w_2}, t\right)$$

$$V(L, S_2, t) = g\left(S_2, \frac{X}{w_1}, t\right)$$

(21.13)

$$V(L, S, t) = 0$$

$$V(S_1, M, t) = 0$$

(Topper, 1998) where w is a weight corresponding to each of the underlyings.

21.2.5 Fixed-income applications

This section is a short introduction to a two-factor model that links instrument-specific cash flows and random prices to the observed term structure of interest rates. As with convertible bonds we assume the following SDEs:

$$dr \equiv \mu_1(v, \theta, t)\, dt + \sigma\, dt$$

(21.14)

$$d\theta \equiv \mu_2(v, \theta, t)\, dt + \sigma_\theta\, dZ_\theta$$

where v is a special variable. If we apply Ito's lemma we get the following PDE:

$$\frac{\partial P}{\partial t} = -(r + \lambda)P - \mu_1 \frac{\partial P}{\partial r} - \frac{\sigma^2}{2}\frac{\partial^2 P}{\partial r^2} - \mu_2 \frac{\partial P}{\partial v} - \frac{\sigma_\theta^2}{2}\frac{\partial^2 P}{\partial v^2} - c - \lambda$$

(21.15)

where P is the price that we wish to calculate. In general, r, λ and the μ's depend on both r and v (Levin, 2000).

21.3 FINITE DIFFERENCE APPROXIMATIONS

The two main competing finite difference schemes are ADI and splitting. ADI seems to be more popular than splitting methods in the financial literature, and there are historical reasons for this state of affairs, the main one being that splitting methods originated in the former Soviet Union and many of the original articles may have been difficult to access by western researchers in the past. However, there is anecdotal evidence to show that splitting methods give better results than ADI for two-dimensional convection–diffusion problems (Levin, 2000).

We have various choices when approximating a two-factor model:

1: ADI with standard centred differencing
2: Splitting with standard centred differencing
3: ADI with exponential fitting
4: Splitting with exponential fitting.

We stress that we are still developing the above kinds of schemes and these will be dealt with in more detail in Duffy (2004b).

21.4   ADI SCHEMES FOR ASIAN OPTIONS

We rewrite the PDE for an Asian option (21.4) and (21.5) in the slightly more general form:

$$-c\frac{\partial V}{\partial t} + \varepsilon\frac{\partial^2 V}{\partial S^2} + a\frac{\partial V}{\partial S} + \alpha\frac{\partial V}{\partial I} - bV = f \tag{21.16}$$

We apply the ADI by discretising (21.16) in two steps. We first proceed from time level n to $n + \frac{1}{2}$ by using the implicit exponentially fitted scheme (see Chapter 18) in S and centred differencing in the I direction:

$$-c_{ij}^{n+\frac{1}{2}}\frac{V_{ij}^{n+\frac{1}{2}} - V_{ij}^n}{\frac{1}{2}k} + \sigma_{ij}^{n+\frac{1}{2}}\frac{V_{i+1j}^{n+\frac{1}{2}} - 2V_{ij}^{n+\frac{1}{2}} + V_{i-1j}^{n+\frac{1}{2}}}{h^2}$$

$$+ a_{ij}^{n+\frac{1}{2}}\frac{V_{i+1j}^{n+\frac{1}{2}} - V_{i-1j}^{n+\frac{1}{2}}}{2h} + \alpha_{ij}^{n+\frac{1}{2}}\frac{V_{ij+1}^n - V_{ij-1}^n}{2m}$$

$$- b_{ij}^{n+\frac{1}{2}}V_{ij}^{n+\frac{1}{2}} = f_{ij}^{n+\frac{1}{2}} \tag{21.17}$$

where k, h and m are the mesh sizes in the time, and S and I are variables. This equation can also be written in the form

$$A_{ij}^{n+\frac{1}{2}}V_{i-1j}^{n+\frac{1}{2}} + B_{ij}^{n+\frac{1}{2}}V_{ij}^{n+\frac{1}{2}} + C_{ij}^{n+\frac{1}{2}}V_{i+1,j}^{n+\frac{1}{2}} = r_{ij}^{n+\frac{1}{2}} \tag{21.18}$$

which we can solve, for example, by the use of LU decomposition or by the Double Sweep method (see Chapter 8).

The next step is to obtain the solution at level $n + 1$ in terms of the solution at level $n + \frac{1}{2}$ by using explicit fitting (see Chapter 18) and the implicit method in the I direction:

$$-c_{ij}^{n+1}\frac{V_{ij}^{n+1} - V_{ij}^{n+\frac{1}{2}}}{\frac{1}{2}k} + \sigma_{ij}^{n+1}\frac{V_{i+1j}^{n+\frac{1}{2}} - 2V_{ij}^{n+\frac{1}{2}} + V_{i-1j}^{n+\frac{1}{2}}}{h^2}$$

$$+ a_{ij}^{n+1}\frac{V_{i+1j}^{n+\frac{1}{2}} - V_{i-1j}^{n+\frac{1}{2}}}{2h} + \alpha_{ij}^{n+1}\frac{V_{ij+1}^{n+1} - V_{ij-1}^{n+1}}{2m}$$

$$- b_{ij}^{n+1}V_{ij}^{n+\frac{1}{2}} = f_{ij}^{n+1} \tag{21.19}$$

Again, we can write (21.19) as a tridiagonal system:

$$A_{ij}^{n+1}V_{ij-1}^{n+1} + B_{ij}^{n+1}V_{ij}^{n+1} + C_{ij}^{n+1}V_{ij+1}^{n+1} = r_{ij}^{n+1} \tag{21.20}$$

21.4.1   Upwinding

In equations (21.17) and (21.19) we have approximated the first-order derivative with respect to the independent variable I by using centred differences. A better approach is to use a one-sided scheme depending on the sign of the coefficient α appearing in equation (21.16). The correct schemes are:

$$
\text{for } \alpha > 0, \qquad \alpha \frac{\partial V}{\partial I} \sim \alpha_{ij+\frac{1}{2}} \frac{V_{ij+1}^n - V_{ij}^n}{m}
$$

$$
\text{for } \alpha < 0, \qquad \alpha \frac{\partial V}{\partial I} \sim \alpha_{ij-\frac{1}{2}} \frac{V_{ij}^n - V_{ij-1}^n}{m}
$$

(21.21)

Of course, we must augment this problem with Dirichlet boundary conditions.

21.5 SPLITTING SCHEMES

Let us consider the general two-dimensional equation:

$$
\frac{\partial u}{\partial t} + Lu = f \text{ in } D \times (0, T)
$$

$$
u = g \text{ in } D, \quad t = 0
$$

(21.22)

where L is an operator of the form in equation (21.1) and D is some two-dimensional bounded region in which the equation is defined. The function f is a non-homogeneous term defined on $D \times (0, T)$. Let us assume that we have finite difference approximations Λ to the components of the operator L. Then our first splitting method (with $f = 0$) is given by the following sequence of Crank–Nicolson schemes (written in vector form):

$$
\frac{u^{n+\frac{1}{2}} - u^n}{k} + \Lambda_1^n \frac{u^{n+\frac{1}{2}} + u^n}{2} = 0
$$

$$
\frac{u^{n+1} - u^{n+\frac{1}{2}}}{k} + \Lambda_2^{n+\frac{1}{2}} \frac{u^{n+1} + u^{n+\frac{1}{2}}}{2} = 0
$$

(21.23)

This set of equations can be solved by iterated LU decompositions, as discussed in Chapter 20 and Thomas (1998).

The finite difference schemes defined by the discrete operators Λ in system (21.23) can take various forms depending on the peculiarities of the continuous problem:

• Use exponential fitting for convection-dominated flow
• Upwinding for first-order hyperbolic operators
• Traditional finite difference methods (for example, centred differencing).

This represents work in progress. A full discussion is provided in Duffy (2004b).

21.6 CONCLUSIONS AND SUMMARY

We have given a discussion of how to apply ADI and splitting methods to several two-factor derivatives models. In general, these approximate methods replace a two-dimensional problem into a sequence of simpler one-dimensional problems that we solve using tridiagonal solvers at each time level. Of course, we have to incorporate boundary conditions into the finite difference schemes.

We summarise the strengths and weaknesses of the finite difference method. First, the strengths:

- Easy to map a PDE to a FDM scheme (use divided difference)
- Stability and convergence properties known
- Can be applied to a wide range of one-factor and two-factor problems
- Simpler than FEM or finite volume (less mathematical sophistication required)
- Is far superior to the binomial method.

The difficulties are:

- Difficult with non-rectangular domains
- Does not scale well to more than three factors
- Conventional schemes can show spurious oscillations (in fairness, the same holds for FEM)
- Lots of tricks to be learned; it is as much an art form as a science.

Part V

Design Patterns

22

A C++ Application for Displaying Numeric Data

22.1 INTRODUCTION AND OBJECTIVES

Part V is where we start applying design principles to the software that we are going to write. It takes a lot of money to create bad software products so it is in everyone's interest to ensure that our software products are flexible and maintainable. This comes at a price of course. We have to invest up-front in thinking about how our designs will look. To this end, we shall use and apply the established design patterns as documented in Gamma *et al.* (1995) and Buschmann *et al.* (1996).

In this chapter we introduce a fully fledged test application that uses many of the foundation classes from previous chapters. The emphasis is on designing and implementing an application that is easy to understand and maintain. In a sense, the application in this chapter is a non-trivial 'Hello World' example for the financial engineering environment and we paraphrase it as follows:

Draw the line graphs of the Normal (Gaussian) probability distribution and cumulative distribution functions between the lower limit A and the upper limit B. The line graphs should be displayed in the Microsoft Excel spreadsheet program. Then generalise the program to other useful applications in financial engineering.

We develop a solution to this problem by decomposing it into three activities:

A1: Registration
A2: Conversion
A3: Presentation

The core process is to display the two Gaussian functions in Excel and the above three activities A1, A2 and A3 describe how to achieve this end. The *Registration* activity elicits input from the user (using the `iostream` library). What we are interested in here is the range $[A, B]$ where the functions will be displayed and the number of intervals N that we use to sub-divide the interval. The *Conversion* activity accepts the output from *Registration* as well as the definitions of the Gaussian functions as input and produces two instances of the class `Vector` as output. These vectors are then dispatched to the *Presentation* activity whose responsibility is to display them in Excel. A full discussion of how Excel works with our C++ classes and code is given in Chapters 28 (presentation and output issues) and 29 (input issues). Thus, there is a little bit of forward referencing in this chapter, but we describe the Excel C++ driver as a black box in this chapter while the internals will be explained in Chapter 28.

The UML *activity diagram* for the process in this chapter is shown in Figure 22.1. Here we see how work gets done in the sense that we model the workflow or information flow in the system. This diagram is important for at least three reasons. First, it is an aid to understanding the C++ code that we shall discuss in subsequent sections. For example, the code for each activity is localised in a file. Second, the code for this test application

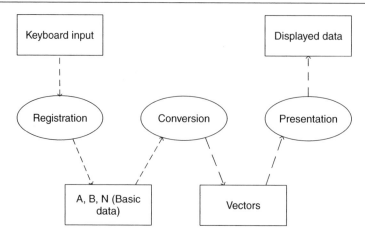

Figure 22.1 Information flow in application

has *extension potential* because we have separated the input, processing and output by designing them as loosely coupled systems. We shall see in later chapters, for example, that the same basic model as in Figure 22.1 can be used to model the Black–Scholes equation using finite differences. In this case the *Conversion* activity will be more complicated than what is presented here but the interfacing with *Registration* and *Presentation* are more or less the same. Finally, the model in Figure 22.1 can be generalised to large system development and to this end the author has documented standard reference models for a range of application areas (see Duffy, 2004a). This model subsumes many applications as special cases. We can then apply and instantiate these reference models to real financial applications, thus improving developer productivity. This application represents the first step on the road to creating large applications in financial engineering. We adopt an incremental approach and we advance in small 'hops'. We also discuss a number of extensions to the code in order to make it more flexible and reusable. The solutions will be the topics of Chapters 23, 24 and 25 where we introduce Design Patterns.

Now is the time to describe each of the activities in Figure 22.1 and how we implement them in C++.

22.2   INPUT MECHANISMS

We are interested in plotting line graphs in Excel. To this end, we need to give some input:

- The range $[A, B]$ on the real line where the graph will be displayed
- The number of sub-intervals N in order to partition $[A, B]$.

Based on the *Registration* activity we create code that produces the necessary information, as follows:

```
#include <iostream>
using namespace std;
void Registration(double& A, double& B, int& N)
{ // Initialise A, B and N with values from user *keyboard*

  cout << "Give lower value of interval: ";
```

```
  cin >> A;
  cout << "Give upper value of interval: ";
  cin >> B;
  cout << "Give number of subdivisions:  ";
  cin >> N;
}
```

This kind of coding style is easy to realise and is useful when we develop new algorithms or when we wish to test and debug our code.

Some applications may wish to produce the above input based on a dialog box, data file or Excel. We then replace the above code by another function having the same signature (input arguments, function name and return type).

22.3   CONVERSION AND PROCESSING MECHANISMS

In this test case we display the Gaussian pdf and cdf functions in Excel. First of all, we must define these functions as ordinary C functions (we have taken the formulae from Haug, 1998):

```
///////////// Gaussian functions ////////////////////////////////////
double NormalPdf(double x)
{ // Probability density function (pdf)
  double A = 1.0/sqrt(2.0 * 3.1415);
  return A * exp(-x*x*0.5);
}

double NormalCdf(double x)
{ // The approximation to the cumulative normal distribution (cdf)

  double a1 = 0.4361836;
  double a2 = -0.1201676;
  double a3 = 0.9372980;

  double k = 1.0/(1.0 + (0.33267 * x));

  if (x >= 0.0)
  {
    return 1.0 - NormalPdf(x) * (a1*k + (a2*k*k) + (a3*k*k*k));
  }
  else
  {
    return 1.0 - NormalCdf(-x);
  }
}
```

Now, we transform these functions by creating vectors that contain the values of the functions at equi-distributed points in the interval [A, B]. Notice how we use the functionality of the class Vector in the resulting code:

```
void Conversion(double& A, double& B, int& N, Vector<double, int> & x,
Vector<double, int> & n_result, Vector<double, int> & N_result)
{
  // Step size.
  double h = (B-A)/N;
  // Calculate input values and call functions.
  double current = A;
```

```
for (int i = x.MinIndex(); i <= x.MaxIndex(); i++)
{
  // Call functions and set values in vectors.
  x[i] = current;
  n_result[i] = NormalPdf(current);
  N_result[i] = NormalCdf(current);
  // Calculate next value.
  current += h;
  }
}
```

Having created both arrays of *x* and *y* values we can then export them to Excel for presentation.

22.4   OUTPUT AND DISPLAY MECHANISMS

We are now ready to display the graphs in Excel. To this end, we shall *use* a class called `ExcelDriver` that encapsulates a lot of functionality to help us interface with our C++ applications. We shall discuss it in more detail in Chapters 28 and 29. For the moment we ask the reader to accept things on face value and use `ExcelDriver` as a black box. To this end, we offer two member functions that create charts:

Option 1: display one vector
Option 2: display a list of vectors

The first option is useful when we wish to display the result of one calculation while the second option is useful when we wish to compare the results of several calculations, for example when we wish to benchmark competing finite difference schemes for ordinary and partial differential equations.

Let us examine Option 2 first. We have created a C function that implements the corresponding activity A3 (*Presentation*) in Figure 22.1. It expects three arrays:

- The array of abscissa points (*x* axis)
- The arrays corresponding the Gaussian pdf and cdf functions

The code is structured as follows:

1. Start Excel as object and make it visible
2. Create two lists, one containing strings and the other containing the array data
3. Call the `CreateChart` member function

The resulting code is as follows:

```
// Create Excel spreadsheet and show values.
void Presentation( const Vector<double, int> & x,
  const Vector<double, int> & n_result,
  const Vector<double, int> & N_result)
{
  try
  {
    // Excel is invisible initially.
    cout << "Creating Excel output, please wait a moment...";
```

```
// Create and initialise Excel.
ExcelDriver & excel = ExcelDriver::Instance();
excel.MakeVisible(true);       // Default is INVISIBLE!

cout << " instance \n";

// Create list with function + derivatives + labels.
list<Vector<double, int> > functions;
list<string> labels;
functions.push_back(n_result);
functions.push_back(N_result);

labels.push_back("pdf");
labels.push_back("cdf");

cout << "chart I\n";

// Display list of function + derivatives in single chart.
excel.CreateChart(x, labels, functions, "Combined Functions");
// Create other charts on another sheet
excel.CreateChart(x, n_result, "n", "X", "Y");
excel.CreateChart(x, N_result, "N (integrated)");
}
catch( string error )
{
cout << error << endl;
}
}
```

It is also possible to display individual functions without having to put them into a list (as in the above code). Instead, we can create charts by calling another *overloaded member function*, as the following specific code shows:

```
excel.CreateChart(x, n_result, "n", "X", "Y");
excel.CreateChart(x, N_result, "N (integrated)");
```

This function has the following signature:

```
void CreateChart(
const Vector<double, int> & x, const Vector<double, int> & y,
const std::string& chartTitle,
const std::string& xTitle = "X", const std::string& yTitle = "Y")
```

Notice the presence of the default values for the text that annotates the x and y axes of the corresponding charts.

22.4.1   Ensuring that Excel is started only once

The reader may have noticed the following code in the previous section:

```
ExcelDriver & excel = ExcelDriver::Instance();
```

In this case we have implemented a so-called *Singleton* pattern in order to ensure that Excel gets started only once during the application. We have implemented this pattern by defining a static object as follows:

```
static ExcelDriver& Instance()
{
```

```
    static ExcelDriver singleton;
    return singleton;
}
```

There are no public constructors in the class ExcelDriver, thus the only way to instantiate Excel is by calling this static member function. This approach improves reliability and efficiency.

We introduce the Singleton pattern in Chapter 23.

22.5   PUTTING IT ALL TOGETHER

Having discussed how the individual activities are implemented we now bring all the pieces together in a main program. The code is easy to follow because we have partitioned the problem into smaller, understandable pieces.

```
int main()
{
  double A, B;
  int N;

  // Run Registration activity A1
  Registration(A, B, N);

  cout << "A etc " << A << ", " << B << ", " << N << endl;

  // Create vectors.
  Vector<double, int> x(N+1);
  Vector<double, int> n_result(N+1);
  Vector<double, int> N_result(N+1);

  // Run Conversion activity A2
  Conversion(A, B, N, x, n_result, N_result);

  cout << "display " << endl;
  // Run Presentation activity A3
  Presentation(x, n_result, N_result);

  // Wait for input.
  cout << "Press ANY key to continue: ";

  string abc;
  cin >> abc;

  return 0;
}
```

22.6   OUTPUT

We now show some examples of output that Excel produces. We first show the chart that is produced by sending a list of Vector object to the Excel driver (Figure 22.2).

Of course, it is possible to display each function as a separate Excel chart as the examples in Figures 22.3 and 22.4 show.

This concludes the main steps in the execution of the activities A1, A2 and A3 in Figure 22.1. We can modify the code to suit to our needs.

22.7   OTHER FUNCTIONALITY

There are many applications that can benefit from the Excel driver class. We discuss two particular examples, namely using Excel to read and write matrices and using Excel in

X	pdf	cdf	X	n	X	N (integrated)
−4	0.000134	3.2E-05	−4	0.000134	−4	3.2E-05
−3.6	0.000612	0.00016	−3.6	0.000612	−3.6	0.00016
−3.2	0.002384	0.00069	−3.2	0.002384	−3.2	0.00069
−2.8	0.007916	0.002562	−2.8	0.007916	−2.8	0.002562
−2.4	0.022395	0.008208	−2.4	0.022395	−2.4	0.008208
−2	0.053992	0.022759	−2	0.053992	−2	0.022759
−1.6	0.110922	0.054798	−1.6	0.110922	−1.6	0.054798
−1.2	0.194189	0.115061	−1.2	0.194189	−1.2	0.115061
−0.8	0.289696	0.211861	−0.8	0.289696	−0.8	0.211861
−0.4	0.368276	0.344592	−0.4	0.368276	−0.4	0.344592
−5.55E-16	0.398948	0.500007	−5.55E-16	0.398948	−5.55E-16	0.500007
0.4	0.368276	0.655408	0.4	0.368276	0.4	0.655408
0.8	0.289696	0.788139	0.8	0.289696	0.8	0.788139
1.2	0.194189	0.884939	1.2	0.194189	1.2	0.884939
1.6	0.110922	0.945202	1.6	0.110922	1.6	0.945202
2	0.053992	0.977241	2	0.053992	2	0.977241
2.4	0.022395	0.991792	2.4	0.022395	2.4	0.991792
2.8	0.007916	0.997438	2.8	0.007916	2.8	0.997438
3.2	0.002384	0.99931	3.2	0.002384	3.2	0.99931
3.6	0.000612	0.99984	3.6	0.000612	3.6	0.99984
4	0.000134	0.999968	4	0.000134	4	0.999968

Figure 22.2   Combined output display

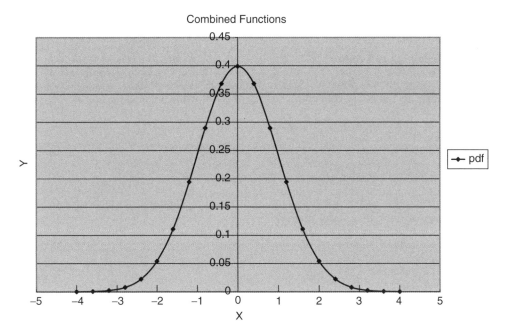

Figure 22.3   Chart display of results for finite difference scheme

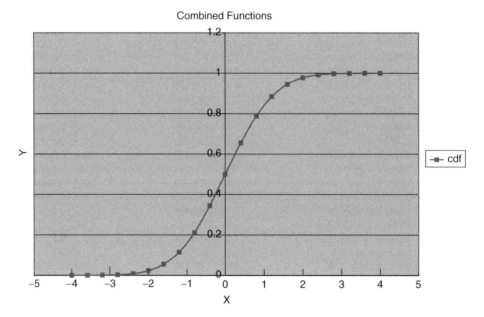

Figure 22.4   Cell data of results for finite difference scheme

order to print the results from finite difference schemes for ordinary and partial differential equations.

22.7.1 Accessing cell data

We now discuss another kind of output in Excel. We can use the Excel driver class to write a matrix to Excel. To this end, consider the following matrix:

```
// 2 rows, 4 columns, start indices = 1
NumericMatrix<double> matrix(2, 4, 1, 1);
matrix(1, 1) = 1; matrix(1, 2) = 2; matrix(1, 3) = 3;
matrix(1, 4) = 4; matrix(2, 1) = 5;  matrix(2, 2) = 6;
matrix(2, 3) = 7; matrix(2, 4) = 8;
```

We now prepare the matrix for presentation in Excel by defining the labels for the rows and columns of the Excel-based matrix:

```
// Create matrix labels.
list<string> rowLabels;
rowLabels.push_back("R1");
rowLabels.push_back("R2");

list<string> columnLabels;
columnLabels.push_back("C1");
columnLabels.push_back("C2");
columnLabels.push_back("C3");
columnLabels.push_back("C4");
```

We now create the cell data structure by calling the appropriate function in the Excel driver class:

```
// Display matrix in Excel.
excel.AddMatrix("MyMatrix", matrix, rowLabels, columnLabels);
```

The output from this effort is:

```
            C1   C2   C3   C4
        R1   1    2    3    4
        R2   5    6    7    8
```

22.7.2   Cell data for functions

Instead of plotting functions as charts (as in section 22.6, for example) it is possible to display the data in matrix form, as the following example shows:

X	pdf	cdf	X	n	X	N (integrated)
−5	1.49E-06	2.92E-07	−5	1.49E-06	−5	2.92E-07
−4.75	5.03E-06	1.03E-06	−4.75	5.03E-06	−4.75	1.03E-06
−4.5	1.6E-05	3.45E-06	−4.5	1.6E-05	−4.5	3.45E-06
−4.25	4.77E-05	1.08E-05	−4.25	4.77E-05	−4.25	1.08E-05
−4	0.000134	3.2E-05	−4	0.000134	−4	3.2E-05
−3.75	0.000353	8.92E-05	−3.75	0.000353	−3.75	8.92E-05
−3.5	0.000873	0.000234	−3.5	0.000873	−3.5	0.000234
−3.25	0.002029	0.00058	−3.25	0.002029	−3.25	0.00058
−3	0.004432	0.001355	−3	0.004432	−3	0.001355
−2.75	0.009094	0.002987	−2.75	0.009094	−2.75	0.002987
−2.5	0.017529	0.00622	−2.5	0.017529	−2.5	0.00622
−2.25	0.03174	0.012236	−2.25	0.03174	−2.25	0.012236
−2	0.053992	0.022759	−2	0.053992	−2	0.022759
−1.75	0.086279	0.040062	−1.75	0.086279	−1.75	0.040062
−1.5	0.12952	0.066803	−1.5	0.12952	−1.5	0.066803
−1.25	0.182652	0.105641	−1.25	0.182652	−1.25	0.105641
−1	0.241974	0.158651	−1	0.241974	−1	0.158651
−0.75	0.301142	0.226636	−0.75	0.301142	−0.75	0.226636
−0.5	0.352071	0.308553	−0.5	0.352071	−0.5	0.308553
−0.25	0.386674	0.401297	−0.25	0.386674	−0.25	0.401297
0	0.398948	0.499993	0	0.398948	0	0.499993

In this way we can (mis)use Excel as a persistent datastore for matrices and vectors.

22.7.3   Using Excel with finite difference schemes

In Chapter 11 we introduced quite a few finite difference schemes for scalar, linear initial value problems (IVP). The results were in the form of Vector objects and we used the `iostream` library to print the results. The disadvantage in this case is that it is difficult to visualise if the answers are good or not or how to compare the different schemes. What we would like to do is to display the results of different schemes in one Excel chart! To this end, we use the following function in the Excel driver to display a list of vectors:

```
void CreateChart(
  const Vector<double, int>& x, const list<string>& labels,
  const list<Vector<double, int> > & vectorList,
  const std::string& chartTitle, const std::string& xTitle = "X",
  const std::string& yTitle = "Y")
```

Applying this function in practice is easy, as the following code shows. First, we define a function that displays a list of vectors in Excel:

```
void printInExcel(const Vector<double, int>& x, // X array
  const list<string>& labels,               // Names of vectors
  const list<Vector<double, int> >& functionResult)
                                            // The list of Y values
{ // Print a list of Vectors in Excel.

  cout << "Starting Excel\n";

  ExcelDriver & excel = ExcelDriver::Instance();

  excel.MakeVisible(true);            // Default is INVISIBLE!

  // Don't make the string names too long!!
  excel.CreateChart(x, labels, functionResult,
    string("FDM Scalar IVP"),
    string("Time Axis"), string ("Value"));
}
```

We now use this function in the code that approximates the solutions of initial value problems (IVP) using finite difference schemes (see Chapter 11 for the full details). We first of all define an initial value problem and then approximate it using several schemes. The results from each scheme are placed in a list that is then offered to the Excel driver chart function.

The following function defines the right-hand side of the IVP:

```
double RHS(const double& d)
{ // Right hand side function in IVP
  return ::sin(d);
}
```

The following function defines the coefficient of the zero-order term in the IVP:

```
double a(const double& d)
{ // Coefficient of zero derivative term in IVP
  return 5.0;
}

// The continuous problem
Range<double> r(0.0, 1.0);
ScalarIVP<double> ivp1(r, 1.0);
ivp1.Rhs(RHS);
ivp1.Coeff(a);
```

Having defined the continuous problem, we use several finite difference schemes. First of all we must define the data structures for the chart function:

```
// Stuff for Excel output
Vector<double, int> x = r.mesh(N);   // Length N+1, start index 1
list<string> labels;                 // Names of each vector
list<Vector<double, int> > functionResult;// The list of Y values
```

We now define the object that represents the IVP solver (notice that N is the number of divisions of the interval of integration). In this case we commence with the explicit Euler scheme:

```
ScalarIVPSolver<double, int> ivpSol(ivp1, EEuler);
ivpSol.steps(N);
```

We now add the necessary information to the lists:

```
labels.push_back("EEuler");
Vector<double, int> res = ivpSol.result();
functionResult.push_back(res);
```

We now set the finite difference scheme type to other values and add the resulting output to the list:

```
ivpSol.setType(Fitted);
labels.push_back(string("Fitted"));
res = ivpSol.result();
functionResult.push_back(res);

ivpSol.setType(IEuler);
labels.push_back(string("IEuler"));
res = ivpSol.result();
functionResult.push_back(res);

ivpSol.setType(PC);
labels.push_back(string("PredCorr"));
res = ivpSol.result();
functionResult.push_back(res);
```

Having done all this work, we now call the function to display the list in the Excel driver:

```
printInExcel(x, labels, functionResult);
```

Finished! The output from these endeavours is shown in Figure 22.5 and the corresponding numeric output is:

Time Axis	EEuler	Fitted	IEuler	PredCorr
0	1	1	1	1
0.1	0.509983	0.622165	0.679911	0.637429
0.2	0.274859	0.400618	0.472976	0.418136
0.3	0.166981	0.273632	0.341278	0.288194
0.4	0.122432	0.203694	0.259481	0.213828
0.5	0.109159	0.16798	0.21063	0.17386

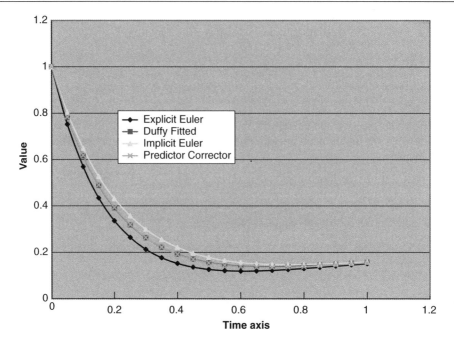

Figure 22.5   FDM scalar IVP

0.6	0.111044	0.152581	0.183368	0.15499
0.7	0.119944	0.148997	0.170069	0.148842
0.8	0.131707	0.152014	0.165601	0.150126
0.9	0.144186	0.15842	0.166499	0.155486
1	0.15624	0.166219	0.170413	0.162776

22.8   USING EXCEL AND PROPERTY SETS

The code in this chapter can be made a bit more flexible by working with `Property` and `SimplePropertySet` classes instead of hard-coded parameters as seen in the `Registration` function in section 22.2 above. In the current strategy we let the implementation of the activities in Figure 22.1 communicate via properties. We focus on one specific example, namely, inputting the following parameters:

- The range $[A, B]$ where the graph will be displayed
- The number of sub-intervals N to partition $[A, B]$

There are two objectives in this section. First, we wish get our input from Excel itself and, second, the data should be placed in a `SimplePropertySet` object. To this end, we create a function to extract appropriate information from Excel:

```
// Initialise A, B and N with values from user.
void GetInput(SimplePropertySet<string, double> & input)
{
```

```
  try
  {
    ExcelDriver & excel = ExcelDriver::Instance();

    // Add property set.
    excel.AddPropertySet(input);
    excel.MakeVisible();

    // Wait...
    cout << "Enter values in Excel spreadsheet." << endl;
    cout << "When done, make sure cursor is not blinking and
      type a letter followed by Enter.";
    string abc;
    cin >> abc;

    // Get property set.
    excel.GetPropertySet(input);
  }
  catch( string & error )
  {
    cout << error << endl;
  }
}
```

The cell data structure in this case is given by:

$$
\begin{array}{ll}
A & -4 \\
B & 4 \\
N & 10
\end{array}
$$

Using this function in client code goes as follows:

```
// Declare variables.
SimplePropertySet<string, double> input;
input.add( Property<string, double>("A", 0.0) );
input.add( Property<string, double>("B", 1.0) );
input.add( Property<string, double>("N", 10.0) );

// Run Registration activity.
GetInput(input);
```

We can then use this property set in other functions if, for example, we need to calculate vectors:

```
void Calculate( const SimplePropertySet<string, double> & input,
  Vector<double, int> & x, // etc.)
```

Thus, if we can define a standard representation for the data structures in an application we shall be in a position to incrementally improve the interoperability and flexibility of our code.

22.9 EXTENSIONS AND THE ROAD TO DESIGN PATTERNS

In the next three chapters we shall show how design patterns are applied to enhance the flexibility of our software applications – for example, the code in this chapter. In particular, we shall concentrate on three categories of patterns that model the lifetime of any object in C++:

- Creating objects based on data from different sources (Creational patterns)
- Structuring objects and networks of objects (Structural patterns)
- How messages are propagated in networks of objects (Behavioural patterns).

The added value of design patterns is that we can customise an application to suit different customer needs.

22.10   CONCLUSIONS AND SUMMARY

We have developed a mini-application that allows us to display functions and vector data in Excel. You can reuse and modify the code to suit your own particular needs. In particular, we have use the class `ExcelDriver` to map C++ structures to Excel:

- Create a chart for a function or vector
- Create a chart for a list of vectors
- Export and import Property Sets to and from Excel
- Store matrices in Excel.

As an example, we showed how to display the results in Excel from various finite difference schemes for initial value problems. The results are easier to visualise than with basic `iostream` operations.

We shall discuss interfacing between C++ and Excel in more detail in Chapters 28 and 29.

23

Object Creational Patterns

'To make the building live, its patterns must be generated on the site, so that each one takes its own shape according to its context.'

CHRISTOPHER ALEXANDER

23.1 INTRODUCTION AND OBJECTIVES

In this and the next two chapters we introduce the reader to Design patterns and what they mean for the quality of software in general and for financial engineering software in particular. During the early 1990s the object-oriented paradigm began to make small inroads into mainstream software circles. Several developers and designers discovered that the same kinds of problems kept recurring during the software development process and some time later they managed to document their findings in the form of Design patterns. In a sense a Design pattern is a method for solving a problem in a given context (Gamma *et al.*, 1995; Buschmann *et al.*, 1996). It is peculiar that the software Design patterns movement was influenced by the work of the architect Alexander (see Alexander, 1979).

In this chapter we introduce those patterns that have to do with the first phase of the object life cycle. We wish to develop software systems where we have some choice in the kinds of objects that we can create at configuration time or at run-time. In other words, we try to avoid as much hard-wired constructor calls as possible in our code. Of course, objects are created by calling their constructors as the following simple example shows. To start us on our journey, let us consider creating an instance of a Uniform statistical distribution that we introduced in Chapter 10:

```
int main()
{
  // Uniform distribution on interval [0, 2]
  Uniform<double> linseg(0.0, 1.0);

  // Gamma distribution
  Gamma<double> g(2.0, 3.9);

  return 0;
}
```

This piece of code creates two instances of continuous distribution classes and we have created it in order to test the classes `Uniform` and `Gamma`. There is nothing wrong with this code as such but it is highly inflexible because any desired modifications will force us to edit and modify the source code. We must then link the code into our application. This is unacceptable for many applications where a higher level of flexibility is desired. In particular, we may wish to adapt the code in some way in order to accommodate the following requirements:

• Source data: in the above code the data that is used in the constructors is hard-coded in the main program. We wish to define arbitrary data sources, for example the command line, as ASCII file, XML or a relational database. The choice of data source should be transparent to the client code; in other words, client code receives its data from some object that points to an abstract base class at run-time.

- The address space of the newly created objects: in the above code the instances of the two distributions are created on the stack. In some cases we wish to create these instances on the heap (free store), for example. This level of flexibility is not possible with the current code without modifying it.

```
Uniform<double>* unif = new Uniform<double>(0.0, 1.0);
```

In this case the object is placed on the heap and an explicit delete is needed to remove it.

- We would like to create 'global' instances of distribution classes: this is equivalent to saying that we would like to create classes that have only one instance and, furthermore, this instance should be accessible from all points in our application code. For example, we would like to create 'canonical' distribution instances such as a standard uniform or normal distribution. We would only have to create these instances once, they would be unique and you can make copies of them for later use.
- We would like to have a mechanism to create a copy or clone of an object. This is the prototype mechanism and is based on the assumption that there is an instance of a class that is a good representative for the class of which it is an instance (a bit like saying that John Wayne is the prototype of the Cowboy). You can then modify the cloned object's member data if the 'default' values in the prototype object are not to your liking.
- In general, we model hierarchies of classes (for example, discrete and continuous probability distributions) using the C++ inheritance mechanism and would like to have a set of standard interfaces that specify how to create instances of those classes. It must then be possible for developers to implement these interface functions.

Having understood what the challenges are when creating objects we then embark on developing C++ code based on the GOF creational patterns (see Gamma *et al.*, 1995) that allow us to achieve the desired level of flexibility. In other words, our objective is to have as little (as possible) hard-coded constructors, data initialisation code or hard-coded switch statements in *client code*. Of course, hard-coded stuff does have to be created somewhere and at some time but this is hidden in façades and black boxes. The client sees a pointer to a base class only.

The above attention points will be resolved by the four major object creational patterns:

- *Singleton*: Create a unique instance of a class. In other words, we wish to create a class that has only one instance. Any deliberate or accidental attempts to create another instance of the class are intercepted.
- *Prototype*: Create an object as a deep copy or clone of another 'representative' object of a given class. This is a competitor to the classical C++ technique of creating an object as an instance of some class. In this sense we see the Prototype as a pattern for 'classless' objects. We don't need classes in order to create objects; instead we clone new objects from other existing objects.
- *Factory Method*: Define an interface for creating an instance (object) of a single class. Derived classes decide how to actually implement the creation function.
- *Abstract Factory*: Create an interface that specifies how to create families of related or dependent classes (for example, classes in some inheritance structure). Derived classes must implement the interface.

We have used the word 'interface' in some of the above definitions. An interface in C++ is essentially an abstract (base) class containing one or more pure virtual functions. You can implement these functions by defining a derived class and implementing these pure virtual functions in the derived class.

We now discuss these creational patterns in some detail. The focus is on describing what these patterns are without worrying about how they are used in conjunction with other patterns (this is a common situation). In short, we describe each pattern as follows:

- The intent of the pattern: why is it needed?
- A small example in C++ to show how the pattern works
- Documenting the patterns using UML
- A more extensive set of examples in C++.

Furthermore, we devote a section to describing where creational patterns can be used in financial engineering applications.

23.2   THE SINGLETON PATTERN

The goal of the Singleton pattern is to define a class that has only one instance. In other words, we wish to define a class having a unique instance and, furthermore, we should provide a global point of access to it. In simple terms, we wish to create a unique object that is known to all other objects in our application. The main reason for applying this pattern is reliability, because clients can always be assured that they are accessing the unique instance of the given class. There is only one way to create the singleton object and any deliberate or accidental attempts to instantiate the Singleton class will be thwarted.

The description of the singleton is very simple yet its implementation is somewhat more complicated. In fact, the implementation of the pattern in Gamma *et al.* (1995) is incorrect on at least two counts. First, the singleton object that is created on the heap does not get deleted (its destructor does not get called) and, second, Gamma uses inheritance to specialise a base Singleton class. We prefer to use template classes and in fact our class will be called `Singleton<SomeType>` to denote that it can later be instantiated to create singletons having *any* underling class.

It is not our wish to go into all the nitty-gritty details of this pattern but we note some of the issues associated with designing and implementing various singleton variants in C++ (Alexandrescu, 2001):

- The difference between a singleton and a global object
- Better enforcement of the singleton's uniqueness
- Destroying the singleton
- Advanced lifetime management of the singleton object
- Multi-threading issues.

In this section we concentrate on implementing the Singleton pattern by using C++ templates and introducing a so-called destroyer object that takes care of Singleton destruction (incidentally, there is no 'best' way of implementing a singleton).

23.2.1   The templated Singleton solution

We now describe the implementation of the Singleton pattern. We require that singletons be created by specific functions only. For example, it must not be possible to create a singleton using constructors or assignment operators. Furthermore, once you have created the singleton for the first time all new attempts to create the object should be intercepted. In this case the returned object will be the singleton object itself! Finally, our design is based on the fact that a destroyer object deletes the singleton when the latter is no longer needed. We propose the following interface for the Singleton class (this is actually a generic form of the solution in Gamma *et al.*, 1995):

```
template<class Type>
  class Singleton
  { // Templated Singleton class

  private:
    static Type* ins;
    static Destroyer<Type> des;

  protected:
    Singleton();
    Singleton(const Singleton<Type>& source);
    virtual ~Singleton();
    Singleton<Type>& operator = (const Singleton<Type>& source);

  public:
    static Type* instance();
  };
```

Here we see that there is only one (static) public member function `instance()` that clients may use. All other functions are private. The body of `instance()` as well as the initialisation of the static entities is:

```
// Templated Singleton code
template<class Type> Type* Singleton<Type>::ins=0;
template<class Type> Destroyer<Type> Singleton<Type>::des;

template<class Type>
  Type* Singleton<Type>::instance()
  { // Return the singleton instance

    if (ins == 0)
    {
      ins=new Type;
      des.doomed(ins);
    }

    return ins;
  }
```

Here we see how the singleton is instantiated and that it registers itself with the destroyer as it were. The interface for the Destroyer class is:

```
template<class Type>
  class Destroyer
  { // Class which is responsible for the destruction

    friend class Singleton<Type>;

  private:
    Type* doomed_object;

    // Prevent users doing funny things (e.g. double deletion)
    Destroyer();
```

```
  Destroyer(Type* t);
  Destroyer(const Destroyer<Type>& source);
    Destroyer<Type>& operator = (const Destroyer<Type>& source);

  // Modifier
  void doomed(Type* t);

 public:
   virtual ~Destroyer();
   Destroyer();
 };
```

When the destroyer goes out of scope it will then delete the singleton as the following code shows:

```
template<class Type>
void Destroyer<Type>::doomed(Type* t)
{ // Set the doomed object

  // doomed_object will be the singleton
  doomed_object=t;
}

template<class Type>
Destroyer<Type>::~Destroyer()
{ // Destructor

  delete doomed_object;
}
```

We have now finished with the details of the implementation. As a client of Singleton you do not have to know or worry about the above internal details. All you need to know is how to use its public interface function. In particular, you create singleton objects by using template specialisation. For example, each of the following declarations gives us a pointer to a unique object of the corresponding instantiated template class:

```
  Uniform* u = Singleton<Uniform>::instance();
  Gamma* g = Singleton<Gamma>::instance();
  Uniform* uList = Singleton<list<Uniform> >::instance();

  cout << u -> expected() <<  endl;
  cout << g -> pdf(3.0) << endl;
```

The third example is interesting because it is a model for a singleton *repository*, that is a singleton object that contains a collection of Uniform instances (in this case it is a list). Of course, we realise that the code may be a bit difficult to understand so we document the new classes using UML notation (see Rumbaugh, 1999, p. 175). In this case we can model both template classes and their instance classes using the usual notation in UML; see Figure 23.1. In this case we see that the class SingletonUniform is a so-called binding in the sense that the generic template argument *T* has been replaced by a real class Uniform. The corresponding C++ looks something like:

```
class  SingletonUniform: public Singleton<Uniform>
{

  // put your specialised functions here
};
```

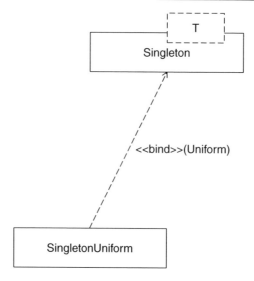

Figure 23.1 Documenting singletons

23.2.2 An extended example

In Part I of this book we saw how to create classes for options by modelling them using
the `Property` and `SimplePropertySet` classes, for example:

```
ExactEuropeanOption futureOption("C", "Future Option");
futureOption.U(105.0);
futureOption.K(100.0);
futureOption.T(0.5);
futureOption.r(0.10);
futureOption.sig(0.36);
futureOption.b( 0.0);

// Calculate all interesting values
SimplePropertySet<string,double> r = futureOption.propertylist();

// Iterate over the result and print the values
SimplePropertySet<string,double>::const_iterator it;

cout << "\nDump the parameters, call prices ... \n";
for (it=r.Begin(); it!=r.End(); it++)
{
   cout << (*it).name() << ", " << (*it)() << endl;
}
```

Instead of having to key in all the parameters each time we create an option, we define
a singleton object that contains these 'default' parameters and clone this object. To this
end, we carry out the following steps:

- Create a class as a specialisation of `Singleton<EuropeanOption>` and add some
  new member functions to it. This class will have one unique instance.
- Show how the unique object can be modified by assigning new values to its parameters.
- Use the unique object as a prototype for 'normal' European objects.

For the sake of the example in this section we consider a stripped-down class defined as follows:

```
class EuropeanOption
{ // For test cases only. Real class is more extensive
public:
  EuropeanOption ()
  {
    attributes = SimplePropertySet<string, double>();
  }
  SimplePropertySet<string, double> attributes;      // Member data
  void setProperties (const SimplePropertySet<string,double>& pset)
  {
    attributes = pset;
  }
  void print()
  {
    SimplePropertySet<string,double>::const_iterator it;
    cout << "\nPrinting normal option\n";
    for (it = attributes.Begin(); it!= attributes.End(); it++)
    {
      cout << (*it).name() << ", " << (*it)() << endl;
    }
  }
};
```

We now wish to define a `Singleton` containing only one instance of `EuropeanOption`:

```
class UniqueOption: public Singleton<EuropeanOption>
{ // Singleton class this is a prototype for all European options
public:
  static void configure(const
  SimplePropertySet<string,double>& pset)
  { // Function to customise the member data of unique option
    (instance() -> attributes) = pset;
  }
  static void print()
  {
    SimplePropertySet<string,double>::const_iterator it;
    EuropeanOption* eo = instance();
    cout << "\nPrinting Unique option\n";
    for (it = eo -> attributes.Begin();it!=eo -> attributes.End(); it++)
    {
      cout << (*it).name() << ", " << (*it)() << endl;
    }
  }
};
```

Notice that the new class is derived from `Singleton<EuropeanOption>` and has its functions for defining properties and printing them. We have created two functions to define sets of option properties. The only difference between these two functions is that they have different property names:

```
void myPset(SimplePropertySet<string,double>& myDefaultSet)
{ // My property set that is default for my European Option class
  // You can customise this to suit your own needs and wants
```

```
    Property<string, double> r;            // Interest rate
    Property<string, double> sig;          // Volatility
    Property<string, double> K;            // Strike price
    Property<string, double> T;            // Expiry date
    Property<string, double> U;            // Current underlying price
    Property<string, double> b;            // Cost of carry

    r = Property<string, double> ("Interest rate", 0.08);
    sig = Property<string, double> ("Volatility", 0.30);
    K = Property<string, double>("Strike Price", 65.0);
    T = Property<string, double>("Expiry date", 0.25);
    U = Property<string, double>("Underlying Asset", 60.0);
    b = Property<string, double>("Cost of carry rate", r());
    myDefaultSet.add(r);  myDefaultSet.add(sig); myDefaultSet.add(K);
    myDefaultSet.add(T); myDefaultSet.add(U); myDefaultSet.add(b);
}
void yourPset(SimplePropertySet<string,double>& myDefaultSet)
{ // Another property set that is default for my European Option class
    // You can customise this to suit your own needs and wants

    Property<string, double> r;            // Interest rate
    Property<string, double> sig;          // Volatility
    Property<string, double> K;            // Strike price
    Property<string, double> T;            // Expiry date
    Property<string, double> U;            // Current underlying price
    Property<string, double> b;            // Cost of carry

    r = Property<string, double> ("R", 0.08);
    sig = Property<string, double> ("V",0.30);
    K = Property<string, double>("S", 65.0);
    T = Property<string, double>("E", 0.25);
    U = Property<string, double>("U", 60.0);
    b = Property<string, double>("B", r());

    myDefaultSet.add(r); myDefaultSet.add(sig); myDefaultSet.add(K);
    myDefaultSet.add(T); myDefaultSet.add(U); myDefaultSet.add(b);
}
```

We now show how to use the new singleton as a prototype object containing default properties that can be copied into normal objects.

```
int main()
{ // All options are European

    // Fill the singleton with first property set
    SimplePropertySet<string,double> myDefaultSet; myPset(myDefaultSet);
    UniqueOption::configure(myDefaultSet);
    UniqueOption::print();

    // Now choose the second property set
    SimplePropertySet<string,double> yourDefaultSet; yourPset(yourDefaultSet);
    UniqueOption::configure(yourDefaultSet);
    UniqueOption::print();

    // Now copy all default parameters to a 'normal' object
    EuropeanOption eo;
    eo.setProperties(yourDefaultSet);
    eo.print();

    return 0;
}
```

The output from the `main()` programs is given as follows:

```
Printing Unique option
Interest rate, 0.08
Volatility, 0.3
Strike Price, 65
Expiry date, 0.25
Underlying Asset, 60
Cost of carry rate, 0.08

Printing Unique option
R, 0.08
V, 0.3
S, 65
E, 0.25
U, 60
B, 0.08

Printing normal option
R, 0.08
V, 0.3
S, 65
E, 0.25
U, 60
B, 0.08
```

This simple example should show how powerful templates are when used in conjunction with the Singleton pattern. This example could be extended to create a configuration class for plain and exotic options, their properties and other related information (such as the payoff functions, for example). In the future, we could use standard names in standards for instruments (see FpML, 2003).

23.2.3 Applications to financial engineering

You should use the Singleton pattern in applications where it is logical and correct to define well-known unique objects that can be accessed by other objects. Furthermore, you may need to use a singleton in cases where you want to be absolutely sure that you are working with objects containing reliable data. Singletons could be used as prototypes for configuring various kinds of entities in financial engineering applications:

- Standard properties for plain and vanilla options: you can define singleton `SimplePropertySet` objects that you can clone and use in your option calculator applications.
- Standard instruments: for each kind of financial instrument we can create a representative prototype object that the developer can use as a reliable representative containing all necessary member data.
- Standard distributions: you can create a singleton for the standard normal distribution $N(0, 1)$ for example without having to recreate it every time you work with this distribution.
- Other objects in an application that represent patterns can be singletons. For example, in this book we have created a class called `ExcelDriver` whose responsibility it is to present data in Excel charts. This is a Singleton class because we only want one

instance of Excel to be up and running at any given moment in time. For some details, see Chapter 22 where we discussed an Excel-based application.

● A repository object that contains settings for our application.

23.3   THE PROTOTYPE PATTERN

The intent of the Prototype pattern is to create an object, not by instantiating a class but by cloning or making a copy of a special object that we call the prototype. In other words, there is an assumption that we can create an object as a deep copy of some other prototypical object. This latter object is highly representative of its class. All member data and values are copied to the new object. Of course, you can modify the new object thereafter but the original object will be unchanged.

At a very basic level we see an example of the Prototype pattern in the copy constructor. This is a hard-coded constructor that creates an instance of a class from another instance, for example:

```
Point pt1(1.0, 2.0);
Point pt2(pt1);            // Calls copy constructor
```

This code is a bit too hard-wired for our liking because we usually work with lists of pointers to objects and we wish to have some means of polymorphically creating copies of these pointers without having to worry about the actual object types. Let us take an example to show what we mean. Suppose that we create a class called ShapeComposite that is implemented as follows:

```
class ShapeComposite: public Shape
{ // A Shape is a base class for all 2d things like
  // Point, Line, Circle

  private:
  // The shapelist using the STL list
  std::list<Shape*> sl;

  public:
  // ...
  ShapeComposite(const ShapeComposite& source);
};
```

Here we see that this class represents a heterogeneous list of Shape pointers. The copy constructor is interesting because we must copy a heterogeneous list to another heterogeneous list and hard-coded constructors will not do the job. Instead, we must create a function

```
virtual Shape* Clone() const;       // Create a copy of the shape
```

This function creates a deep copy of the current object and is declared as pure virtual in the base class Shape and each of its derived classes must implement it. Returning to the copy constructor in the composite shape class, what we need to do is to iterate over its elements and recursively call the clone function on each of its elements as the following code shows:

```
ShapeComposite::ShapeComposite(const ShapeComposite& source)
  : Shape(source)
```

```
{ // Copy constructor
  sl=std::list<Shape*>();

  // Create STL list iterator
  std::list<Shape*>::const_iterator it;

  for (it=source.sl.begin(); it!=source.sl.end(); it++)
  { // Copy the whole list
    // Add a copy of the shape to our list
    sl.push_back((*it)->Clone());
  }
}

Shape* ShapeComposite::Clone() const
{ // Create a copy of the shape
  return new ShapeComposite(*this);
}
```

This code shows the essence of cloning in C++ and how to apply the Prototype pattern. The pattern can be directly applied to other class hierarchies.

23.3.1   The Prototype pattern: Solution

We now describe what needs to be done in order to implement the Prototype pattern. In general, it is most useful when we have a hierarchy of C++ classes. We are only interested in single inheritance hierarchies at this moment. To take a generic example, let us assume that we have a base class B and two derived classes D1 and D2. Then the procedure for the application of the Prototype pattern is:

- Create a pure virtual clone() function in B
- Create the implementations of the clone function in D1 and D2.

We show the code for the classes B and D1:

```
Class B
{
public:
  // ...
  virtual B* Clone() const = 0;
};

class D1 : public B
{
public:
  B* Clone() const { return new D1(*this);}
};
```

For composite classes we can apply the techniques that we used for the Shape hierarchy. It is of course important that the developer has created the code for the copy constructor for every class in the hierarchy in order to avoid unexpected results!

23.3.2   Applications to financial engineering

The Prototype pattern and its applications seem to be a well-kept secret. Many early Computer Aided Design (CAD) systems used this pattern as a means of letting users create objects and then use them to create more complex objects. In fact, the first example of a prototype was in Ivan Sutherland's Sketchpad system. Another example is the Visual Basic environment where the user can create sophisticated controls (such as buttons, text boxes and dialog boxes) by copying them onto a form and changing the values of the properties of the newly created objects.

So where could we use the Prototype pattern in financial engineering applications? In general, you can create *default objects* for a range of artefacts, such as:

- Plain and exotic option properties
- Plain and exotic option classes (and of course other classes for financial instruments)
- Default vectors for cash flow dates
- Default function classes for option payoffs (we discussed functions in Chapter 9)
- Default exact option price and sensitivity formulae.

A discussion of these specific topics is outside the scope of this book.

23.4 FACTORY METHOD PATTERN (VIRTUAL CONSTRUCTOR)

This pattern defines an interface for creating an instance of a given class but the actual implementation is deferred to derived classes. A synonym for this pattern is *virtual constructor* because it eliminates the need to bind application-specific classes into your code. In other words, there is no need to have hard-wired constructors in your application code. In short, we define an interface that creates an instance of some class and its derived classes implement this interface. Let us take the generic example, as shown in Figure 23.2. Here we have a Product class with two derived classes CP1 and CP2 ('CP' stands for ConcreteProduct). There are two major varieties of factory method (see Gamma *et al.*, 1995):

- The ProductFactory class is an abstract class and does not provide an implementation for the factory method. This option requires that derived classes implement the factory method because there is no reasonable default.
- The ProductFactory class is a concrete class which provides a default implementation for the factory method.

We now give some code to show how this pattern works. The code is very easy to understand and once you get the idea you can then apply the patterns to more complex

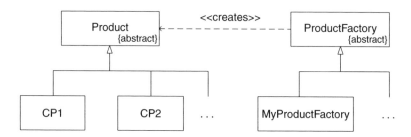

Figure 23.2 Documenting the Factory Method pattern

and interesting applications. First of all, the product hierarchy is as follows:

```
class Product
{
  // Your stuff
};
class CP1 : public Product
{
  // Your stuff
};
class CP2 : public Product
{
  // Your stuff
};
```

The base class for the product factory is (notice the presence of the pure virtual function):

```
class ProductFactory
{
public:
  virtual Product* createProduct() = 0;
};
```

The code for the two specific factory classes is (notice that all code is inline):

```
class MyProductFactory : public ProductFactory
{
public:
  Product* createProduct()
  {
    cout << "CP1 just made\n";
    return new CP1;
  }
};
class YourProductFactory : public ProductFactory
{
public:
  Product* createProduct()
  {
    cout << "CP2 just made\n";
    return new CP2;
  }
};
```

We now create a function that allows us to select a *specific* factory. This is the only place in the application that has to know about derived factory classes. If you add a new kind of factory, this is the function in which this action should be carried out:

```
ProductFactory* getFactory()
{
  cout << "1. My Factory, 2. Your factory: " << endl;
  int k; cin >> k;
  if (k == 1)
    return new MyProductFactory;
  if (k == 2)
```

```
    return new YourProductFactory;
  // Default or future extensions here
    return new MyProductFactory;
}
```

Finally, we test our classes in the following test program (notice that it does not have any knowledge of derived factory classes):

```
int main()
{
  ProductFactory* currentFactory = getFactory();
  Product* myProduct = currentFactory -> createProduct();
  delete myProduct;
  return 0;
}
```

Another variation is to use *parametrised factory methods.* In this case the factory method takes a parameter that identifies the kind of object to be created. See Gamma *et al.* (1995) for further details.

23.4.1   An extended example

We now discuss a specific problem, namely creating instances of European and executive options. An executive option is similar to a plain option except that it has an extra parameter, the so-called *jump rate* (Haug, 1998). The class hierarchy is shown in Figure 23.3. We shall now describe how we create the factory code.

The C++ classes have the following structure (notice the polymorphic Price() member function):

```
class Option
{ // Abstract base class for the options in this book
public:
  virtual double Price() const = 0;
};

class ExactEuropeanOption : public Option
{
  virtual double Price() const;
};

class ExecutiveOption : public Option
{
  virtual double Price() const;
};
```

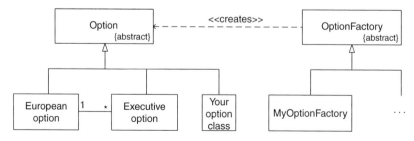

Figure 23.3 Creating a factory method for option classes

The factory classes are:

```
class OptionFactory
{
public:
  virtual Option* createOption() = 0;
};

class MyOptionFactory : public OptionFactory
{
public:
  virtual Option* createOption()
  {    // In practice this code will be 'more'
    return new ExactEuropeanOption;
  }
};

class YourOptionFactory : public OptionFactory
{
public:
  virtual Option* createOption()
  {
    return new ExecutiveOption;
  }
};
```

We now give the code that lets the user choose an option factory type. We then create a pointer to `Option` and calculate the option's price.

```
int main()
{
  cout << "1. European, 2. Executive: ";
  int k;
  cin >> k;

  OptionFactory* of;
  if (k == 1)
    of = new MyOptionFactory;
  else
    of = new YourOptionFactory;

  Option* option = of -> createOption();
  double d = option -> Price();
  cout << "Price is: " << d << endl;
  return 0;
}
```

You can modify the hierarchy in Figure 23.3 for new option and factory types.

23.5   ABSTRACT FACTORY PATTERN

This pattern can be compared to an extended Factory Method pattern because it defines an interface, not just for one particular object or product but for families of related or dependent objects without specifying their concrete classes. Thus the Abstract Factory pattern contains Factory Method entries, one for each kind of class in a class hierarchy. Let us take the example. Consider again the product hierarchy as shown in Figure 23.4 where

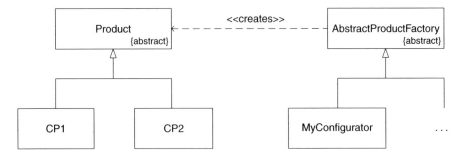

Figure 23.4   Abstract Factory pattern

we now have a class called `AbstractProductFactory` that contains two factory methods, namely for classes `CP1` and `CP2`:

```
class AbstractProductFactory
{ // One particular interface for use in Abstract Factory pattern

public:
  virtual Product* createCP1() = 0;
  virtual Product* createCP2() = 0;
};
```

Derived classes must implement these member functions. For example, we have created a factory class that creates default instances of `CP1` and `CP2`:

```
class MyConfigurator: public AbstractProductFactory
{ // One particular interface for use in Abstract Factory pattern

public:
  Product* createCP1() { return new CP1; }
  Product* createCP2() { return new CP2; }
};
```

The next issue to be addressed is to use this factory class in an application. Here comes the crux. Each factory method in `MyConfigurator` returns a pointer to the base class `Product`; thus, you must cast the pointer to the correct `Type` as the following code shows:

```
  AbstractProductFactory* myF = new MyConfigurator;
  CP1* cp1;
  Product* prodA = myF -> createCP1();
  cp1=dynamic_cast<CP1*>(prodA);
  if (cp1!=0)
  {
    cout << "OK, RTTI works, this is a CP1 thing\n";
  }
```

If this casting approach is not to your liking, you could define the interface in the abstract factory class to return the pointer to the specific derived class of `Product`:

```
class AbstractProductFactory2
{ // One particular interface for use in Abstract Factory pattern
```

```
public:
  virtual CP1* createCP1() = 0;
  virtual CP2* createCP2() = 0;
};

class MyConfigurator2: public AbstractProductFactory2
{ // One particular interface for use in Abstract Factory pattern

public:
  CP1* createCP1() { return new CP1; }
  CP2* createCP2() { return new CP2; }
};
```

Using the factory class in an application allows us to get a real product without the need for casting:

```
// Abstract Factory stuff, alternative 2
AbstractProductFactory2* myF2 = new MyConfigurator2;
CP1* prodA2 = myF2 -> createCP1();
CP2* prodB2 = myF2 -> createCP2();
```

23.5.1   The abstract factory: Solution

In general, we use this pattern when we are interested in creating product families (as modelled in class hierarchies) using different creational processes. We thus assume that we have a context class hierarchy in place. We then create an abstract class that contains a number of pure virtual functions. Each virtual function is a factory method that specifies the interface for one class in the context hierarchy. There are different possibilities for specifying the signature of this function. Then we create derived factory classes that actually implement the interface in the abstract factory class.

23.5.2   An extended example

In Chapter 10 we introduced a C++ class hierarchy that models discrete and continuous probability distributions. In this section we discuss how we have applied the Abstract Factory pattern to the family of continuous distributions and in order to reduce the scope we have focused on the classes Uniform, Gamma and Exponential. The interface is:

```
class CnsDistFactory
{
private:
public:
// Usual stuff
virtual ContinuousDistribution<double,double>*
CreateUniform() = 0;
virtual ContinuousDistribution<double,double>*
CreateGamma() = 0;
virtual ContinuousDistribution<double,double>*
CreateExponential() = 0;
};
```

We notice, first, that we are working with instantiated template classes and, second, that the factory method returns a pointer to the base class. This means that we can switch between distributions at run-time while at the same time retaining polymorphic behaviour.

We have created a class called `CommandFactory` that has functions for creating continuous distributions from the command line. The interface function that shows how to implement one of the functions is:

```
virtual ContinuousDistribution<double, double>*
    CommandFactory::CreateGamma()
{
  double r, a;
  cout << "Creating a Gamma distribution" << endl;
  cout << "Input r: ";
  std::cin >> r;
  std::cout << "Input a: ";
  std::cin >> a;
  return new Gamma<double> (r, a);
}
```

The other functions for the `Uniform` and `Exponential` classes can be programmed in a similar vein.

The power of the pattern can be seen in applications because we can switch between distributions while at the same time retaining access to the polymorphic functions for the mean, variance, pdf and cdf.

First, we create a function that lets the user decide which factory to use. This function only needs to be written once and that is where all references to specific factories are placed; client code is thus shielded from these context-dependent issues:

```
CnsDistFactory* CreateFactory()
{
  // Normally you would have to make a choice which factory
  // to instantiate, for example in a GUI radio button box
  // This is the function where the real choice is made.
  return new CommandFactory();
}
```

We will need a function to print some details about any continuous distribution:

```
void print(const ContinuousDistribution<double, double>& dis)
{
  cout << "Mean value: " << dis.expected() << "Variance: " << dis.variance()
  << endl;
}
```

Finally, we can use the factory class in our applications as shown by the following example code:

```
void main()
{
  // Create the current factory
  CnsDistFactory* myFactory = CreateFactory();
  // Pointer to current continuous distribution
  ContinuousDistribution<double, double>* myDist;
  myDist = myFactory->CreateGamma();

  print (*myDist); // We have no knowledge of derived classes!
  delete myDist;
  delete myFactory;
}
```

Notice that this code has no knowledge of the specific factory object; all it gets is a pointer to the base factory. Thus, adding new factories has no effect on the client code!

23.6   APPLICATIONS TO FINANCIAL ENGINEERING

The Abstract Factory pattern is very powerful and it is useful for configuring related or dependent objects. In general, we wish to create instances of objects in a class hierarchy and this pattern is a good candidate. Examples where it can be used are:

- Discrete and continuous probability distributions
- Class hierarchies representing financial instruments
- Class hierarchies for partial differential equations
- Class hierarchies that model finite difference schemes

... and many more. For example, let us suppose that we have developed classes that model finite difference schemes for some partial differential equation. The class hierarchies are shown in Figure 23.5. Each hierarchy could have its own factory hierarchy. For example, for the class FDM, we could create its instances using the following devices:

- From an XML source file
- From a dialog box or menu option
- By sending data from Excel to the C++ application.

The third option will be developed in more detail in Chapters 28 and 29 when we show how to create two-way interfaces between C++ and Excel.

23.7   CONCLUSIONS AND SUMMARY

We have discussed four major creational patterns in this chapter, namely Singleton, Prototype, Factory Method and Abstract Factory. These patterns have one thing in common: they create instances of classes and are an improvement over using hard-coded constructors. The Singleton pattern allows us to create a class that has only one instance. Any attempts to create another instance of the class are thwarted. The Prototype pattern is based on the idea that we create an object as a deep copy or clone of another *prototypical object*. This is an important feature in some object-based languages where we do not create an object as an instance of a class (as in most languages such as C++, Java and C#) but objects are copied from other objects and modified as desired. The Factory

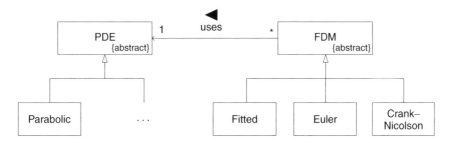

Figure 23.5   Class hierarchies

Method pattern defines an interface for creating an instance of a class. Specific factory classes implement the interface and they also determine the specific derived class instance that you return. Finally, the Abstract Factory pattern defines an interface for creating instances of various classes. These classes are usually part of a C++ context class hierarchy. Each method in the interface describes how to create an instance of one specific context class. In fact, the Abstract Factory pattern can be described as an extended Factory Method pattern because each method in the former pattern is a factory method.

Object Structural Patterns

'Within this process, every individual act of building is a process in which space gets differentiated. It is not a process of addition, in which pre-formed parts are combined to create a whole; but a process of unfolding, like the evolution of an embryo, in which the whole precedes its parts, and actually gives birth to them, by splitting.'

CHRISTOPHER ALEXANDER

24.1 INTRODUCTION AND OBJECTIVES

After having created an object (by applying one or more of the creational patterns in Chapter 23, for example) we must introduce the object to other objects. This means that we create structural relationships between the newly created object and other objects in our application. To this end, we introduce the reader to the major structural relationships in the object-oriented paradigm and we document these relationships using the Unified Modeling Language (UML). We then describe a number of special object structural patterns based on the results in GOF (Gamma *et al.*, 1995) and POSA (Buschmann *et al.*, 1996). In particular, we focus on the following patterns:

- Whole–Part pattern (complex objects)
- Composite pattern (nested objects and tree structures)
- Bridge pattern (allow an object to have several implementations)
- Façade pattern (creating a unified interface to a logical grouping of objects).

These are the patterns we shall discuss in this chapter. Of course, these are not the only object structural patterns available, but they are probably the most important ones. In particular, we are able to give several good applications of these patterns to financial engineering. For a discussion of object structural patterns, we again refer the reader to Gamma *et al.* (1995). It is not possible in this book to discuss all the GOF patterns and their applications.

24.2 KINDS OF STRUCTURAL RELATIONSHIPS BETWEEN CLASSES

Creating well-designed, correct and robust object-oriented applications demands more than just drawing pretty pictures in UML. We must first discover the most important classes in the domain of discourse and then we define the semantic relationships between these classes. Gone are the days when objects were for the picking; objects are not intuitive and the object-oriented paradigm does not always reflect the way people think. Some people think in terms of processes, others in terms of functional and non-functional requirements. A discussion of the issues involved when analysing and designing software systems using object technology can be found in Duffy (2004a).

The main semantic relationships in this chapter are:

• Aggregation
• Association
• Generalisation.

Large applications can be built by the use of these relationships. Of course, we are building a *model* of reality and not reality itself. It is possible (and inevitable) that your class diagrams many undergo several revisions before they stabilise. In the immortal words of Demming, 'All models are wrong, some are useful'.

24.2.1 Aggregation

Aggregation relationships (also known as Whole–Part relationships) are central to many applications and it is important to identify such relationships. The common feature of these relationships is that one object (the so-called Whole) is composed of, or consists of, other objects (the components or Parts). The Whole has its own attributes and operations and these are distinct from those of its parts. Thus, the object-oriented analyst must take note of the following issues when modelling aggregation structures:

• The interface of the Whole
• How the Whole is structured in terms of its parts
• How the Whole and its parts communicate (possibly in both directions).

In general, the Whole consists of zero or more parts (and the parts need not necessarily belong to the same class), but a part (when viewed as an object) cannot simultaneously belong to more than one Whole. Some initial (and specific) examples of aggregations are shown in Figure 24.1 and we paraphrase the aggregations and their corresponding multiplicity as follows:

• A `Spread` consists of two `Options`
• A `BullSpread` object consists of a long and a short position (Hull, 2000)
• A `Portfolio` consists of `Options` (one or more `Options`)

In general, a portfolio will contain instruments other than just options, as we shall see later. A spread is a special kind of portfolio that consists of two (or more) options. Each

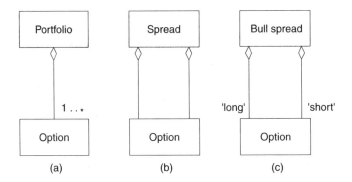

Figure 24.1 Examples of aggregation

option plays a role in the portfolio. For example, in a bull spread one option is long and the other is short. We discuss spreads and other option strategies in more detail in Chapter 30 and, in particular, we show how to implement these classes in C++.

We discuss aggregation relationships in some more detail in section 24.3. Like rock music, there are several kinds.

In general, aggregation structures are important in financial engineering applications because we can use them to model various kinds of instruments, portfolios and other structured products. Some possibilities are:

- Various kinds of option trading strategies (spreads, straddles, strangles)
- A diversified portfolio
- Options based on two or more underlying assets.

24.2.2   Association

In contrast to aggregation relationships (where there is a clear 'parent–child' or 'whole–part' metaphor), associations describe possible relationships between 'independent' classes. Associations represent the 'glue' in object-oriented systems. There are various kinds of association but we focus on two main types because they are important for real applications.

Binary associations

A binary association represents a relationship between two different classes. The classic example is given in Figure 24.2, and this summarises that a person can work for zero or more companies and that a company can give employment to zero or more persons. Here we introduce the notion of a role in UML; in this association the person plays the role of 'employee' while the company plays the role of 'employer'. We shall also need to model roles in a financial engineering context. Some typical examples are:

- Long and short roles for an option
- The derivative role and the underlying role.

In general, there is a many-to-many relationship between roles and objects. An object can have several roles, and several objects can play a role. For example, an option can play the roles of 'derivative' for an asset (which plays the role of 'underlying') while the same option can be an underlying for another option; in this case the derivative role is called a *compound option* (or option on an option).

It is possible to let the following assets play the role of underlying (Haug, 1998):

- Stock (with or without cash dividend)
- Stock indexes
- Futures

Figure 24.2   My first binary association

- Currency
- Swap (cash flow exchange between two companies).

In general, we can define a large class of derivative roles for the above underlyings:

- Options on stock
- Options on future
- Currency options
- Options on options
- Options on swaps (options on interest-rate swaps).

We can describe some of the above relationships by an initial association using UML notation, as shown in Figure 24.3. In this case we have a class called `Option` and a class called `Asset` (in fact, we shall see that `Asset` is an abstract class and has classes such as `Future` as specialisations). In this case, we have a one-to-many relationship between `Option` and `Asset`: an option has to do with one or more assets while an asset has to do with one option. This is a simplifying assumption in this book. In real applications the multiplicity will be many-to-many.

In Part I of this book we imagined an option as having a number of properties such as volatility, interest rate and so on. Real life is a bit more complicated because we see that an option may have several underlyings in general. In this case the C++ classes from Part I are not up to the job and we must model the option differently. For example, we could model the `Option` class as follows:

```
class Option:
{
private:
  list<Asset*> underlying;
public:

  // Public interface here
};
```

Unary associations

A unary (or recursive) association represents a relationship between two instances of the same class. A simple example is given in Figure 24.4 where we describe how people

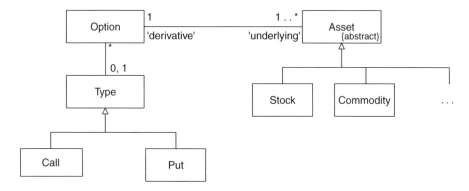

Figure 24.3   Derivatives and underlying

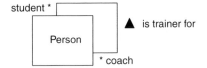

Figure 24.4 My first unary association

relate to each other in a particular use case: a person (who plays the role of 'coach') manages zero or more persons (who play the 'student' role).

There are several possible applications of unary associations in financial engineering. Let us take the particular example of the class `Instrument` that subsumes all financial products. This is an abstract class because it is not possible to create objects from it. Typical specialisations of instruments are:

- Assets of all kinds
- Options of all kinds
- Swaps
- Bonds

... and so on. In general (and in principle) it should be possible to define one instrument as the derivative quantity and another instrument (or instruments) as the underlying. We document this as shown in Figure 24.5 and here we see that any instrument can have any other instrument as underlying. This is very flexible and is an improvement on the initial class structure that the author created in Duffy (1995). At that time object technology was an emerging technology and the market was just starting to learn this new way of thinking.

Finally, ternary, quaternary and high-order association can be modelled in UML but they are difficult to understand and to implement, and we refer the reader to the UML specifications.

Associations are well documented in the UML literature. This is the reason why we do not discuss them in great detail as it would be like bringing coals to Newcastle! For more information on UML, see Rumbaugh (1999).

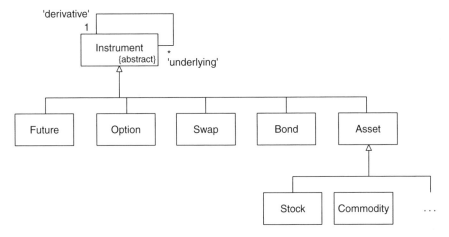

Figure 24.5 Unary association and instrument

24.2.3   Generalisation/specialisation

We now come to the third and final kind of relationship that we define between classes. We say that a class D (sometimes called a derived class or subclass) is a specialisation of a class B (called a base class or superclass) if an instance of D is in every respect an instance of the class B. This means that an instance of D 'inherits' all the attributes and operations from B. It thus behaves as an instance of B but it may also add its own extra attributes and operations. The derived class may even redefine operations from the base class.

Saying that D is a specialisation of B is equivalent to saying that B is a generalisation of D. Object-oriented languages such as C++, Java and C# support the Gen/Spec relationship (as it is conveniently called) by the use of the inheritance mechanism.

Abstract classes and concrete classes

An abstract class is, by definition, a class that has no instances. A concrete class, on the other hand, is one that does have and may have instances. An abstract class represents a root or base class for other classes sharing similar interfaces.

In order to denote that a class is abstract we use the constraint symbol {abstract}. An example is shown in Figure 24.5 where Instrument is the abstract base class for all more specific classes. To convince yourself that Instrument is indeed abstract, answer the following question: When is the last time that you traded an Instrument?

Generalisation health warnings

Too much generalisation can damage the understandability and maintainability of your software if it is carried to excess. Each new generation of object-oriented programmers (and we appear to be in the third generation at the moment) seems to apply inheritance in much the same way as the previous generations. We are referring to the incorrect use of inheritance and many of the problems have been reported in the annals of the OO masters. We mention some of the ways that inheritance is misused:

- Creating deep inheritance hierarchies
- Using inheritance to model roles (roles are really objects and not classes)
- Implementation inheritance instead of interface inheritance
- Using multiple inheritance incorrectly in C++.

The application of inheritance using one or more of the above scenarios is a major source of risk in object-oriented projects. It is a symptom of a bad design.

A full discussion of the dangers and opportunities when applying inheritance is beyond the scope of this book.

24.3   WHOLE–PART PATTERN

We introduce a special kind of aggregation relationship in this section and the results are based on the work in Buschmann *et al.* (1996) where such relationships are used in documenting design and system patterns. We apply them to analysing classes in the problem domain itself. Quite a lot of work has been done in this area during the 1990s (see, for instance, the *Journal of Object Oriented Programming* (JOOP)). As always, the Whole consists of several parts but it is possible to specialise the pattern to include more precise information on the types and multiplicities of the parts and the Whole's interface functions. The three main types are:

- Assembly parts
- Container contents
- Collection members.

An *assembly parts* structure is the most rigid of the three types in the sense that the Whole consists of a predetermined number of parts of predefined types. These parts are created when the Whole is created. A *container contents* relationship models loosely coupled parts; the Whole does not have a well-developed interface as such but is a 'wrapper' for its contents. It may be likened to a white box through which clients can peek. The parts in this type may be heterogeneous. The *Collection Members* pattern is an aggregation in which all the parts are essentially of the same type. Which specific Whole–Part pattern you should use in an application depends on the level of flexibility desired and the structure of the objects that your are modelling. Some general remarks and conclusions are (for more, see Buschmann *et al.*, 1996):

- In general, the interface of the Whole is different from that of its parts; in fact, the Whole is more than just the sum of the parts.
- The parts in an assembly–parts relationship are added to the Whole at initialisation time; it is not possible to add or remove parts at run-time. Container contents or collection members do not suffer from this restriction.
- The interface of the Whole in the container–contents relationship tends to be fairly 'lightweight'.
- The interface of the Whole in the Collection–Members relationship contains functionality for iterating over its parts; for example, a portfolio has an operation `Payoff ()` that calculates the payoff function and is calculated by iterating over its parts (in this case, options).

Composition: a special kind of aggregation

We discuss another special type of aggregation that is supported in UML. It is called Composition and is for all intents and purposes the same as the assembly–parts relationship already referred to. The defining characteristic of a composition is that the Whole and its parts have coincident lifetimes. In other words, the parts are added to the Whole when the latter is created. It is not possible to add or remove parts as long as the Whole exists. The parts are destroyed when the Whole dies. UML depicts the composition relationship by a filled diamond. We give an example in Figure 24.6 where we state that a `Spread` instance is composed of two `Option` instances. It is, strictly speaking, more accurate than the drawing in Figure 24.1(b).

In general, the author is not very concerned with the niceties of filled or unfilled diamonds during the analysis phase of the software life cycle. We have included a short discussion of composition because students tend to ask the questions: What is composition; what's that filled diamond doing there?

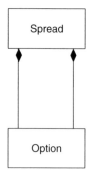

Figure 24.6   Modelling a spread as a composition

24.4   THE COMPOSITE PATTERN

We discuss an interesting pattern (by the way, it is not the same as Composition), namely aggregate objects that consist of objects of the same class. In general, we call these *nested objects*. Some examples of nested objects are:

- Directories consist of other directories and files
- A dialog box may consist of other dialog boxes
- A portfolio may contain other portfolios.

We model these and other nested objects by application of the famous Composite pattern (see Gamma *et al.*, 1995). The general UML structure is given in Figure 24.7. We paraphrase the diagram as follows:

'A Composite class is a derived class of B and it consists of zero or more references to B'.

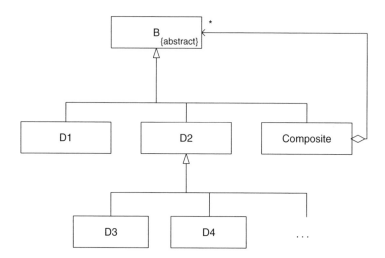

Figure 24.7   Atomic and Composite class

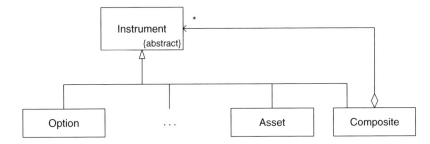

Figure 24.8   Composite pattern with instruments

Many developers who meet this pattern for the first time have difficulty in visualising how it would be implemented in an object-oriented language. In order to help those people we give a specific example of Composite GUI controls (for example, dialog boxes). The C++ code is given as follows:

```
class Control{}
class TextBox : public Control {};
class Composite : public Control
{
private:
  list<Control*> elements; // Use STL library templates
public:
  // Public functions here
};
```

An example of a Composite class in financial engineering is shown in Figure 24.8. Here we see that it is possible to create complex new instruments to any level of complexity. Whether this is a good thing or not depends on the context.

We give several examples of the C++ code for this pattern on the accompanying CD. The Composite is very powerful because it allows us to nest objects to any depth. The reader can find more details on the Composite pattern in Gamma *et al.* (1995).

24.5   THE FAÇADE PATTERN

In general, clients of an aggregation structure cannot access the parts of a Whole directly. In this sense we see that the Whole is the parent or owner of its parts. It may choose whether to expose or hide its parts to outside clients. In this context we speak of *white box* and *black box* structures. In other words, in the white box case the clients can peek into the internal structure of the Whole while in the case of a black box the clients see an impenetrable interface and are unable to determine the Whole's internal structure. White boxes and black boxes represent design decisions and, of course, we must accept the consequences of these decisions. In general, the designer must choose between short-term gains and long-term maintainability benefits. In general, design by the white box approach is easier than the black box approach.

The white box approach introduces undesirable coupling between objects. In particular, badly designed and/or runaway object-oriented applications are networks whose complexity can be objectively measured.

If you discover that your UML class diagrams are *becoming* too complex, it is then time to stop and think! The author has once seen a diagram containing 2000 classes and it took almost 30 minutes to load the corresponding file from disk when using a particular CASE tool. This is a ridiculous state of affairs and the problem should be redressed as soon as possible (actually, the problem should not have occurred in the first place). In order to reduce the complexity of classes themselves and coupling between classes, we can consider grouping closely related classes into so-called façades and defining new unified interfaces for these Façade classes. This technique is discussed in Gamma *et al.* (1995).

24.6   THE BRIDGE PATTERN

This object structural pattern is very powerful. Its main intent is to separate a class into two distinct parts by using a *separation mechanism*. In precise term, we divide a class into two other classes. The first class contains the code that is in principle invariant and does not change while the second class contains code that is implementation or context-dependent. Since the classes are now disjoint we can switch between implementations at configuration-time or even at run-time. There are very many situations where we can apply this pattern in financial engineering and we shall discuss some of them now.

Some examples of the Bridge pattern in numerical analysis are:

- Structuring a matrix as a full matrix or as a sparse matrix.
- Solving the linear system $AU = F$ by Double Sweep, LU decomposition or iterative techniques.
- Integrating functions using various quadrature techniques (e.g. Newton–Cotes).
- Various finite difference schemes for ordinary and partial differential equations.

Some other examples closer to financial engineering are:

- Modelling stochastic differential equations by Wiener and other processes.
- Calculating option price and sensitivities by Monte Carlo, finite differences or finite element methods.
- Calculating option price and sensitivities depending on whether it is a call option or a put option.

Desiring flexibility in switching from one regime to another is the reason for using a Bridge pattern in the first place. Each of the above descriptions can be posed in the same general form and we discuss this form now. In general, we create two hierarchies: the first contains invariant code while the second contains implementation-dependent or context-dependent code, as shown in Figure 24.9. In general, clients call member functions in classes in the *application hierarchy* and these classes then *forward* the request to a specific class in the *implementation hierarchy*. The UML sequence diagram that shows the flow of control is shown in Figure 24.10. In more specific cases, the message names with have particular significance in a given application.

24.6.1   An example of the Bridge pattern

We now give a concrete example of the Bridge pattern. In this case we wish to integrate real-valued functions of a single variable using a variety of numerical integration rules. In some cases the functions may be well behaved but they may also have nasty discontinuities

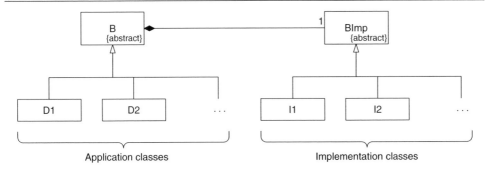

Figure 24.9 Bridge pattern

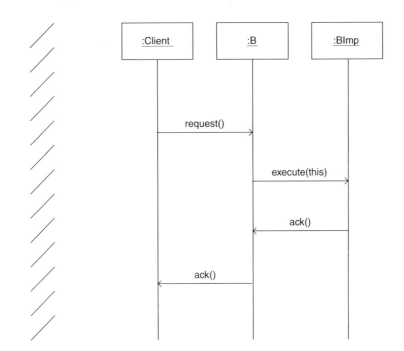

Figure 24.10 Information flow in Bridge pattern

either on the boundary or in the region where the function is to be integrated. To this end, we wish to create numerical integrators that can switch between specific numerical integration regimes. The UML class structure is shown in Figure 24.11. In this case the class NumIntegrator plays the role of the abstraction and the classes TanhRule and the well-known midpoint rule defined by the class MidpointRule play the roles of the Bridge implementations. Mathematically, these integration rules are given by

$$\int_a^b f(x)\mathrm{d}x \approx 2\tanh\left(\frac{h}{2}f\left(\frac{a+b}{2}\right)\right), \quad h = b - a$$

$$\int_a^b f(x)\mathrm{d}x \approx hf\left(\frac{a+b}{2}\right), \quad h = b - a$$

(24.1)

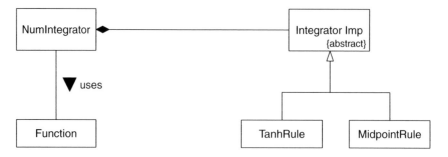

Figure 24.11   Bridge and numerical integration

Incidentally, the Tanh rule was discovered in Duffy (1980) as a by-product of the work
on exponentially fitted difference schemes, and the rule is suitable for difficult functions
for which traditional rules do not always work. In principle, `NumIntegrator` delegates
all requests to the bridge but, in the current test case, we have concentrated just on the
function that actually calculates the approximate value of the integral.

```
class NumIntegrator
{ // The Application class (implementation-independent)

private:
  int nSteps;              // Number of subdivisions of interval
  Range<double> interval;  // Interval of interest
  double (*f)(double x);   // C style function
  IntegratorImp* imp;      // The 'real' integrator

public:
  NumIntegrator(double (*fp)(double x), const Range<double>& myRange,
      IntegratorImp& implementor, int numSteps = 30);
  // Modifiers
  void function(double (*fp)(double x));
  void range (const Range<double>& myRange);

  // Selectors
  int numberSteps() const;
  Range<double> getInterval() const;
  double calculate(double x) const;  // Value at value == x

  // Calculating the integral of the function. Functions that are
  // delegated to the Bridge implementation.

  double value() const;
};
```

The Bridge implementations are very easy and are based on the formulae in equation (24.1)
above. The corresponding code is:

```
class IntegratorImp
{
public:
virtual double value(const NumIntegrator& f) const = 0;
};
```

```
class TanhRule: public IntegratorImp
{ // Rule for integrating nasty functions; based on Duffy 1980
public:
  virtual double value(const NumIntegrator& f) const;
};

class MidpointRule: public IntegratorImp
{ // The Midpoint integration rule
public:
  virtual double value(const NumIntegrator& f) const;
};
```

The code for evaluating the integral using the Tanh rule and Midpoint rule is:

```
double TanhRule::value(const NumIntegrator& f) const
{
  // Get all the stuff from the client in order to do my job
  Range<double> r = f.getInterval();
  double A = r.low();
  double B = r.high();

  int N = f.numberSteps();
  double res = 0.0;
  double nd = double(N);
  double h = r.spread() / nd;
  for (double x = A + (0.5 * h); x < B; x += h)
    res += tanh(f.calculate(x) * 0.5 * h);

  return 2.0 * res;
}
double MidpointRule::value(const NumIntegrator& f) const
{
  // Get all the stuff from the client in order to do my job
  Range<double> r = f.getInterval();
  double A = r.low();
  double B = r.high();

  int N = f.numberSteps();
  double res = 0.0;
  double nd = double(N);
  double h = r.spread() / nd;
  for (double x = A + (0.5 * h); x < B; x += h)
    res += f.calculate(x);
  return res*h;
}
```

Of course, there are opportunities for *refactoring* in the above two functions; common and invariant code could be placed in the base class `IntegratorImp`.

How do we use the classes? Here is a test program:

```
double myfuncx (double x)
{ // Nasty function
  return log(x) / (1.0 - x);
}

int main()
{
  // Choose your specific integrator
```

```
IntegratorImp* imp = new TanhRule;

// Build NumIntegrator function
Range<double> r(0.0, 1.0);          // Region of integration
int N = 200;                        // Number of subdivisions

NumIntegrator context(myfuncx, r, (*imp), N);
double result = context.value();
cout << "And the value is: " << result << endl;

// Choose another specific integrator
IntegratorImp* imp2 = new MidpointRule;
context = NumIntegrator(myfuncx, r, (*imp2), N);
result = context.value();
cout << "And the value is: " << result << endl;

delete imp;
delete imp2;
return 0;
}
```

The output from this program is:

```
And the value is: -1.64319
And the value is: -1.64321
```

This example of a Bridge pattern can be used as a springboard for other similar problems. For example, we could envisage more functionality for class `NumIntegrator`:

- Numerical differentiation of functions
- Displaying functions in different media

and many more. To this end, we use a Visitor class (more about this in Chapter 25) that is coupled with a Bridge to help us to achieve the desired level of flexibility. The UML class diagram for this problem is shown in Figure 24.12.

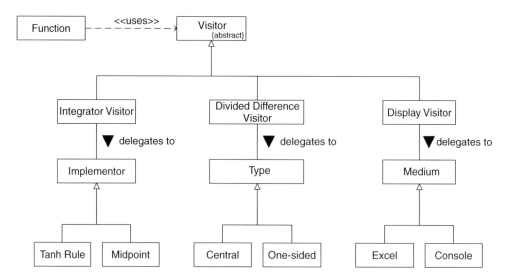

Figure 24.12 Central Visitor pattern for functions

24.7 CONCLUSIONS AND SUMMARY

We have discussed a number of ways to help us to structure classes and define relationships between them. These relationships are called *aggregation, association* and *generalisation*. It is possible to define some well-defined and recurring structural patterns that we can use in financial engineering applications, namely Whole–Part, Composite, Bridge and Façade. Many object networks can be described as a combination of these basic patterns. We use the Unified Modeling Language (UML) to document all structural relationships because it is unambiguous and is a *de-facto* standard in the IT industry.

Having defined the structural interclass relationships, we now need to model how instances of these classes exchange information by message passing. This is the subject of Chapter 25 when we introduce Object Behavioural Patterns.

Object Behavioural Patterns

'In order to define this quality in buildings and in towns, we must begin by understanding that every place is given its character by certain patterns of events that keep on happening there.'

CHRISTOPHER ALEXANDER

25.1 INTRODUCTION AND OBJECTIVES

In this chapter we introduce the patterns that come into play after an object has been created and structured. In other words, we are interested in how objects communicate in a network, tree or other dependency graph. In particular, behavioural patterns deal with a number of issues whose resolution dramatically increases the flexibility of your software:

- Creating flexible and interchangeable member data
- Creating flexible and interchangeable member functions
- Extending the functionality of a class without having to touch its source code
- Preserving data integrity in an object graph.

In general, behavioural patterns have to do with member data and member functions. As developer, you must decide if the application of a design pattern is worth the effort; the return on investment may not be commensurate with the effort expended.

Behavioural patterns are very important in financial engineering applications. Some of the reasons are:

- *Suitability for various user groups*: We can customise object methods to suit various needs. For example, some clients may wish to choose a specific algorithm that implements a member function, others may wish to extend the functionality of a class to include interfaces to Excel and XML (to take two examples) while others may be satisfied with minimal functionality.
- *Interoperability*: We may wish to create applications that can share data and information with other applications. For example, we could develop an option calculator program in C++. This program could get its input data from a C# or Java program in another process. Both programs can read and write XML data, thus ensuring interoperability between the programs even though they are in different address spaces and have different byte orderings.
- *Efficiency*: We can choose algorithms and data structures that allow us to achieve desired levels of time and resource efficiency. For example, we could customise our application to allow us to work with two algorithms to calculate the price of an option (for example, an Asian option); one algorithm could be time efficient (for example, the exact solution or using finite difference techniques) while the other algorithm would be very reliable but also very time consuming (for example, the Monte Carlo method).

    Furthermore, there are different ways to model member data. For example, you could model member data by hard-coded types or you could use the Property pattern.

- *Maintainability*: It is estimated that at least 70% of the effort spent in IT is devoted to keeping applications up and running. We do not go into the details of describing why this percentage is so high but we do give one major reason:

C++ programs tend to become more complex

In other words, C++ applications tend to evolve into monolithic monsters. One way to avoid this situation is to create a stable architecture for an application by breaking the problem into smaller manageable pieces (see Duffy, 2004a). At the level of design patterns we try to *separate concerns* by a suitable application of patterns such as Strategy, Mediator, State and Visitor. The upside is that your software becomes easier to modify and to change than monolithic applications. The downside is that you have to invest in learning how these patterns work and how to apply them to financial engineering.
- *Portability*: By encapsulating hardware and software specific code in special objects you can shield your application code from changes in the environment. For example, you can use patterns to encapsulate the following specific features:

  – Different kinds of relational database systems (Oracle, SQL/Sever)
  – Different user interfaces (GUI, command line, direct manipulation)
  – Presentation issues (MS Excel, OpenGL, GDI, VRML, MS Word)
  – Coupling with other systems (for example, market data feed systems)

  Again, we encapsulate specific code in special objects.
- *Usability*: Code that is based on design patterns tends to be easier to understand than code that is based on some undocumented and idiosyncratic solution (however clever it might be). An important proviso in this regard is that if you use design patterns in your code you **must** document your design blueprints using UML class diagrams and sequence diagrams, otherwise it will be almost impossible to determine what is happening.

25.2   KINDS OF BEHAVIOURAL PATTERNS

There are 11 documented behavioural patterns in GOF (Gamma *et al.*, 1995). They are all concerned with the member functions of existing objects and the 11 patterns can be differentiated on the basis of their intent. There are three main sub-categories:

Variational patterns

These are patterns that describe behaviour in an object that may have different implementations. No new functionality is added to the object. The main variational patterns are:

- *Strategy*: Define a family of algorithms and model them using objects. This makes the algorithms interchangeable because client code and algorithms can vary independently of each other. For example, we could create strategies for calculating the price and sensitivities for call and put options.
- *Iterator*: An iterator is an object that provides access to the elements of an object aggregate. In particular, we can navigate in aggregates without exposing their underlying representations. In general, all the iterators in our own development work are based on the STL iterators.

- *Command*: This is a pattern to encapsulate a request or function as an object. Thus, no hard-wired functionality resides in client code but client and command are independent. The Command pattern is similar to the notion of function object or functor in STL.

Extension patterns

These are patterns that allow us to add functionality to a class or object without necessarily having to modify the source code of the class. In Gamma *et al.* (1995) there is (only) one such pattern:

- *Visitor*: This is a pattern that allows us to extend the functionality of the classes in a (context) class hierarchy without having to modify the structure of the classes in the context hierarchy. This is a very useful pattern because different customer groups can extend a class hierarchy without having to modify or pollute the source code in the context.

There are other ways to extend the functionality of classes and objects, for example using Role patterns and a form of component-based programming, but a discussion of these interesting topics is outside the scope of this book.

Notification patterns

These are patterns that model the interactions in graphs or networks of objects. In particular, we are interested in keeping the data in an object network synchronised and consistent. The most important patterns are:

- *Observer*: Define a one-to-many dependency relationship between one object (called the publisher) and a number of other objects (called the subscriber). Subscribers are notified of changes in the state of the publisher. As a result of this pattern, we can be sure that data in a network remains consistent and synchronised.
- *Mediator*: Define an object that acts as a coordinator between a set of objects. Objects receive and send messages through the mediator. This pattern promotes loose coupling by preventing any object from referring to another.

Other patterns

There are other, less critical behavioural patterns in Gamma *et al.* (1995) that we do not document in this book. Our feeling is that if you are able to understand and apply the most important patterns then you are in a position to write flexible code.

We now begin on our journey in the behavioural pattern landscape. We give several examples from financial engineering. The **full source code** can be found on the accompanying CD. In this chapter we give the essential code that is needed for an understanding of the appropriate pattern.

25.3 ITERATOR PATTERN

The Iterator pattern described in Gamma *et al.* (1995) is a pointer-type mechanism that allows us to navigate sequentially in a composite structure. There are various kinds of iterators (sequential, random and so on) and it is indeed possible to create your own iterator classes but this is probably overkill in C++ because the Standard Template Library (STL) already provides us with most of the iterators that we need. However, we must show how to integrate STL iterators with our application code. To this end, we show how to do this using composite two-dimensional graphics objects.

25.3.1 Iterating in composites

A good way to learn how to implement iterators is to look at the work of other developers. We use the classes that model two-dimensional shapes as a springboard. The full source code can be found on the accompanying CD. In particular we define a base class Shape that has derived classes such as Point, Circle, Polyline and so on. The technique for creating iterators can be applied to other class hierarchies. The relevant interface is:

```
class ShapeComposite: public Shape
{ // N.B. Stripped down version
private:
  // The shapelist using the STL list
  std::list<Shape*> sl;
public:
  // User can use the STL iterator
  typedef typename std::list<Shape*>::iterator iterator;
  typedef typename std::list<Shape*>::const_iterator
const_iterator;

  // Iterator functions
  iterator Begin();              // Return iterator at begin
  const_iterator Begin() const; // Return const iterator at begin
  iterator End();                // Return iterator after end
  const_iterator End() const;   // Return const iterator after end

  // Remove functions
  void RemoveAll();              // Remove all shapes from the list
};
```

We now discuss the code that implements this functionality. We wish to define iterators than are read-only as well as iterators that are read and write and, furthermore, we wish to model the following features:

- Go to the beginning of the list
- Go to the end of the list
- Remove all elements in the list by iterating in the list
- Copy one list to another list.

The source code now follows.

```
// Iterator functions
ShapeComposite::iterator ShapeComposite::Begin()
{ // Return iterator at begin of composite

  return sl.begin();
}

ShapeComposite::const_iterator ShapeComposite::Begin()
```

```
const
{ // Return const iterator at begin of composite

  return sl.begin();
}

void ShapeComposite::RemoveAll()
{ // Remove all shapes from the list

  // Create STL list iterator
  std::list<Shape*>::iterator it;

  for (it=sl.begin(); it!=sl.end(); it++)
  { // Delete every shape in the list

    delete (*it);   // Delete shape
  }

  // Remove the shape pointers from the list
  sl.clear();
}

void ShapeComposite::Copy(const ShapeComposite& source)
{ // Copy the source composite to this shape composite

  // Create STL list iterator
  std::list<Shape*>::const_iterator it;

  for (it=source.sl.begin(); it!=source.sl.end(); it++)
  { // Copy the whole list

    // Add a copy of the shape to our list
    sl.push_back((*it)->Clone());
  }
}
```

25.3.2 Iterating in property sets

A bit closer to home, we now define a class that represents a list of `Property` instances and the corresponding iterators for it. To this end, we examine the class:

```
template <class N, class V> class SimplePropertySet
{ // N.B. Stripped down version

private:
  N nam;          // The name of the set
  // The SimplePropertySet list using the STL list
  list<Property<N,V> > sl;

public:
  // User can use the STL iterator
  typedef typename list<Property<N,V> >::iterator iterator;
  typedef typename list<Property<N,V> >::const_iterator const_iterator;

  // Iterator functions
  iterator Begin();
  const_iterator Begin() const;
  iterator End();
  const_iterator End() const;

  // Add and remove functions (mixin or embedded inheritance)
  void add(const Property<N,V>& p);
  void add(const SimplePropertySet<N,V>& p);
```

```
  void remove(const N& value);   // Remove all elements with 'value'

  // + more
};
```

This class can then be used in other classes, for examples classes for options. To motivate, let use consider a class for European options and let us suppose that we wish to code a member function that returns the parameters of the option as a property set. The code for this is:

```
SimplePropertySet<string, double>
ExactEuropeanOption::propertylist() const
{
  SimplePropertySet<string, double> result;

  result.add(Property<string, double> ("Option Value", Price() ) );
  result.add(Property<string, double> ("Delta",Delta() ) );
  result.add(Property<string, double> ("Gamma",Gamma() ) );
  result.add(Property<string, double> ("Vega",Vega() ) );
  result.add(Property<string, double> ("Vega",Theta() ) );
  result.add(Property<string, double> ("Rho",Rho() ) );
  result.add(Property<string, double> ("Cost of Carry",Coc() ) );

  return result;
}
```

Finally, how do we use iterators in code? Here is an example that creates an option and prints its value on the console:

```
ExactEuropeanOption indexOption3("P", "Index Option");
SimplePropertySet<string, double>
  allprops = indexOption.properties();

// Now iterate in the list
SimplePropertySet<string,double>::const_iterator ci;

cout << "\nDump the values \n";
for (ci=allprops.Begin(); ci!=allprops.End(); ci++)
{
  cout << (*ci).name() << ", " << (*ci)() << endl;
}
```

25.4   THE VISITOR PATTERN

This pattern is a so-called extension pattern because it allows us to extend the functionality of the classes in a class hierarchy (the *context*) without actually having to change the context's source code. We can then speak of non-intrusive extensions. The advantage of this pattern is that different customers and clients can choose which Visitor functionality they wish to obtain. In other words, you do not pay for what you do not use.

We have already had an example of a Visitor pattern in Chapter 24 in which the functionality of a class that encapsulates a real-valued function with one argument can be extended by the use of Visitor. In fact there were three main Visitor specialisations that extend the functionality in some way, namely:

- Numerical integration
- Numerical differentiation
- 'Displaying' functions in different environments.

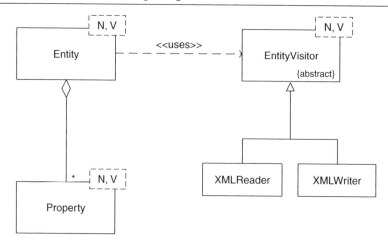

Figure 25.1   Entities and XML Visitor classes

We saw from Figure 24.12 that we can construct a specific Visitor class for each desired piece of functionality. The Function class sends requests to a specific Visitor class. The actual mechanics for setting up this structure is described in GOF (Gamma *et al.*, 1995). On the other hand, the CD in this book gives several examples describing how we have implemented the Visitor pattern in C++. Furthermore, we also describe how we have used Visitor in order to create XML representation of Property objects (and vice versa).

The advantages of the Visitor pattern are:

- Separation of Concerns: Each Visitor class is dedicated to a specific feature. We can concentrate on one thing at a time and it is possible to keep features independent of each other.
- Flexibility: You can extend the functionality of a class or class hierarchy almost at will.

We shall now give a specific example of the Visitor pattern.

25.4.1   Visitors and the Extensible Markup Language (XML)

Suppose that we have defined a template class representing entities. An entity has a name or ID and consists of a collection of Property objects. The UML class diagram is shown in Figure 25.1. In general terms we see that clients of an Entity receive a request to perform a specific Visitor function. The entity then delegates to the specific Visitor class. To this end, we need the following Entity function:

```
template <class N, class V>
  void Entity<N, V>::accept(EntityVisitor<N, V>& visitor)
{ // The delegation function in the Visitor

  visitor.visit(*this);
}
```

Thus, we see that Visitors must implement the visit() function. In fact, the classes Property and SimplePropertySet implement the accept() function as well. This leads us to the following interface specification for EntityVisitor:

```
template <class N, class V> class EntityVisitor
{
public:
  // Visit functions.
  virtual void visit(Property<N, V>& property) = 0;
  virtual void visit(SimplePropertySet<N, V>& pset) = 0;
  virtual void visit(Entity<N,V>& entity) = 0;
};
```

Derived classes of `EntityVisitor` must implement these pure virtual member functions. In order to reduce the scope we concentrate on the Visitor class that writes the properties in an Entity to an XML file. Its interface specification is:

```
template <class N, class V> class XMLWriter : public
EntityVisitor<N,V>
{
private:

  // Member data. Microsoft-specific libraries!
  MSXML2::IXMLDOMDocument2Ptr m_pXMLDoc;  // XML document
  MSXML2::IXMLDOMElementPtr pRoot;

  // No copy-constructor and assignment operator for now
  XMLWriter( const XMLWriter<N,V> & ) { }
  XMLWriter & operator = ( const XMLWriter<N,V> & ) { }

  // Private Visit functions
  virtual void visit(Property<N, V>& property);
  virtual void visit(SimplePropertySet<N, V>& pset);

public:
  // Constructor and destructor
  XMLWriter();
  virtual ~XMLWriter();

  // Public Visit functions
  virtual void visit(Entity<N,V>& entity);

  // Saves XML nodes to file
  void Save( const string & name );

  // Write XML nodes to string
  string ToString();
};
```

In this class we have defined three functions that visit properties, property sets and entities. Without going into the gory details, we can state the following general rules:

- Writing a property to XML entails writing the property using Microsoft's implementation of the Document Object Model (DOM).
- Writing a property set entails iterating over its properties and calling the `visit()` function for each of its properties. This occurs in a roundabout way:

```
template <class N, class V>
    void XMLWriter<N,V>::visit(SimplePropertySet<N, V>& pset)
{
  pset.accept(*this);
}
```

```
template <class N, class V>
  void SimplePropertySet<N,V>::accept (EntityVisitor<N,V>& v)
{
  // We iterate over the list and visit each element
  iterator it;
  for (it=sl.begin(); it!=sl.end(); it++)
  {
    v.visit(*it);
  }
}
```

- Writing an entity entails creating a new node in the DOM hierarchy and then writing its encapsulated property set:

```
template <class N, class V> void
XMLWriter<N,V>::visit(Entity<N,V>& entity)
{ // Write an entity to XML document

    // 1. Write name as the root of the XML document
    // 2. Write property set
    try
    {
      // Create root
      string N = entity.name.name();
      _bstr_t root = N.c_str();
      pRoot = m_pXMLDoc->createElement( root );

      // Add root to document element.
      m_pXMLDoc->appendChild( pRoot );
    }
    catch( _com_error & error )
    {
      bstr_t description = error.Description();
      throw string(description);
    }
    visit(entity.properties);
}
```

Finally, we show how to use the class. To this end, we create a program that does the following:

- Creates an option as an entity
- Writes the entity to XML (using XMLWriter)
- Reconstructs the option by reading the XML file (using XMLReader)
- Iterates over the option properties and prints their properties.

Here is the source code.

```
int main()
{
  XMLWriter<string, double> xmlW, xmlW2;

  // Names in properties may not contain spaces/funny characters
  Property<string, double> K("StrikePrice", 100.0);
  Property<string, double> r("InterestRate", 0.06);
  Property<string, double> T("Expiry", 1);
  Property<string, double> S("Stock", 120);
```

```
Property<string, double> U("UnderlyingAsset", 134.2);
Property<string, double> b("CostOfCarry", 12.0);

Entity<string, double> option("EuropeanOption");
option.AddProperty(K);     option.AddProperty(r);
option.AddProperty(T);     option.AddProperty(S);
option.AddProperty(U);     option.AddProperty(b);

xmlW.visit(option);
xmlW.Save ("Option.xml");

// Now read the file back in
XMLReader<string, double> xmlR;
xmlR.Load("Option.xml");

Entity<string, double> option2;
xmlR.visit(option2);

SimplePropertySet<string, double>
  optionParams = option2.properties;

// Iterate over the result and print the values
SimplePropertySet<string,double>::const_iterator it;

cout << "\nDump the parameters, call prices ... \n";

for (it=optionParams.Begin(); it!=optionParams.End(); it++)
{
   cout << (*it).name() << ", " << (*it)() << endl;
}

return 0;
}
```

The output from this program is:

```
<?xml version="1.0"?>

<EuropeanOption><StrikePrice>100</StrikePrice><InterestRate>0.06
</InterestRate><Expiry>1</Expiry><Stock>120</Stock><UnderlyingAsset>134.2
</UnderlyingAsset><CostOfCarry>12</CostOfCarry></EuropeanOption>

Dump the parameters, call prices ...
StrikePrice, 100
InterestRate, 0.06
Expiry, 1
Stock, 120
UnderlyingAsset, 134.2
CostOfCarry, 12
```

25.5 NOTIFICATION PATTERNS

We give a brief overview of the sub-category of behavioural patterns that have to do with keeping the data in an object-oriented application consistent. For example, in a hedging application we would like to support the following features:

- Update a portfolio when an important event takes place.
- Recalculate option price and delta when a stock parameter changes.
- Display new values in Excel when an instrument has been modified.
- Advise on what to do.

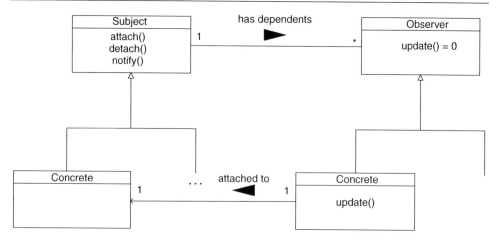

Figure 25.2 Structure of Observer pattern

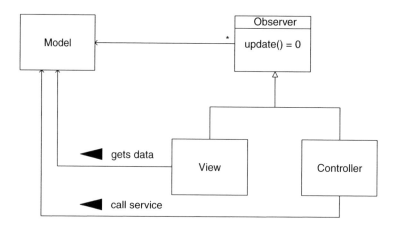

Figure 25.3 MVC structure

In general, object-oriented systems are graphs or networks of objects. For each object (called the Subject or Publisher) there may be zero or more other objects (that play the role of Observer or Subscriber) that must be notified of changes in the former objects. There are a number of very important design patterns in this category:

- *Observer*: Define a $1:N$ dependency relationship between a Subject and its Observers. Observers register/unregister themselves with the subject. When some interesting event occurs in the subject it will then update its associated observers. The structure of the Observer pattern is shown in Figure 25.2.
- *Mediator*: In this case we define an object that acts as a central hub or coordinator between other loosely coupled objects. All communication takes place via the mediator.
- *Model-View-Controller MVC (Buschmann et al., 1996)*: This is an extended version of the Observer pattern and was built with interactive applications in mind. In general, interactive applications have three main components:

- Model (the functional core of the application)
- View (the presentation/output component)
- Controller (in the input component)

The structure of the MVC is shown in Figure 25.3.

A full discussion of these patterns is outside the scope of this book. However, we provide some examples on the CD.

In Duffy (2004a) we have developed reference architectures for enterprise systems and these subsume and use many of the more basic patterns in GOF (Gamma *et al.*, 1995) and POSA (Buschmann *et al.*, 1996).

25.6   CONCLUSIONS AND SUMMARY

We have introduced behavioural patterns in this chapter. These are needed because a typical object-oriented application is essentially a graph of dependent objects. There are a number of scenarios involved with such graphs and they are all concerned with object methods (member functions):

- *Variational*: Choose between different implementations of a method.
- *Extensions*: The ability to add/remove methods and properties in an object or class.
- *Notification*: Changes in one part of an object graph should propagate to other dependent objects in the graph.

We introduced three very important notification patterns, namely Observer, Mediator and Model-View-Controller. For a full discussion of these patterns, see Gamma *et al.* (1995) and Buschmann *et al.* (1996). There are also several examples on the CD.

Part VI

Design and Deployment Issues

26
An Introduction to the Extensible Markup Language

26.1 INTRODUCTION AND OBJECTIVES

In this chapter we give an introduction to the Extensible Markup Language (XML). XML is a so-called markup language and it describes rules for encoding text for human and computer processing. In general terms, we can say that XML allows different software systems to exchange data in a uniform and standard manner. In fact, XML is a universal standard as specified by the World Wide Web Consortium (W3C). XML is free and no royalties need be paid if you use it in your applications.

Our interest in XML is that it allows instrument properties and data to be exchanged between different software systems. It is no longer necessary to define proprietary data formats that only work with a specific compiler or network byte protocol. Instead, diverse applications can exchange data once they understand its structure and semantics.

We now describe the contents of this chapter. In section 26.2 we give a brief overview of XML. Section 26.3 introduces the reader to the basics of XML and describes how an XML document is structured. In section 26.4 we introduce Document Type Definition (DTD). The DTD defines the allowed structure for XML documents and, in general, we say that it describes the semantics of an XML document. We describe how to model UML-like relationships (such as groups, sequences and multiplicities) using DTDs. DTDs are a part of the XML standard. We discuss XML stylesheets in section 26.5.

Section 26.6 discusses the application of XML to financial applications.

This chapter is a self-contained and compact introduction to XML and the focus is on understanding the most important syntax in this language and learning how to read XML files with the same ease as you would read the morning newspaper.

26.1.1 What's the big deal with XML?

This book is concerned with numerical methods (in particular, finite differences) for option pricing. We use C++ for all calculations, classes and algorithms. C++ is ideal for this kind of work but we must have some way of getting data into our C++ applications by means of a User Interface (UI) component. We could write this component in C++ (using the MFC or OWL graphics libraries, for example). However, in large system development a part of an application may be written in Java, another part in C++ while the UI could be written in Visual Basic. We then experience major problems with data interoperability because each language has its own way of representing data. Also, the situation is exacerbated when the components in an application are in different address spaces. XML resolves data format problems between different applications. Would it not be better if there were a single data standard that all systems could understand without the necessity of having to write dedicated code? Well, the good news is that XML resolves these problems. Furthermore, you can start using it now in your applications.

26.2   A SHORT HISTORY OF XML

The term 'markup' has its roots in the printing industry and refers to how documents are formatted. In this case notes or marks were placed in a piece of text for a typist or printer in order to indicate that the text should be made bold, italic and so on. The objective of markup is to make the interpretation of text explicit. The grand daddy of all markup languages is the Standard Generalised Markup Language (SGML), an ISO standard dating from 1986. XML is a subset of SGML but is simpler and has stricter rules than the latter. XML was designed specifically for use in Internet applications but it is not restricted to such applications. The standards body W3C has created specifications to improve Internet interoperability and promote standardisation.

26.3   THE XML STRUCTURE

In this section we give a gentle introduction to XML syntax by examining a simple example. We consider documenting two-dimensional points using XML. Each point has an x coordinate and a y coordinate as well as corresponding values. For example, the syntax

```
<X>23</X>
```

denotes a so-called *element* in XML. An element is a means of structuring text. In this case <X> denotes the *begin tag* of the element and </X> is the *end tag*. The *element name* is 'X'. The value '23' denotes the *contents* of the element. In short, the above syntax could describe a point's x coordinate. But how would we describe a point in XML? In short, we define a new element called 'Point' that contains two simpler elements as follows:

```
<Point>
  <X>2</X>
  <Y>6</Y>
</Point>
```

We thus see that elements can be nested and we shall discuss this in more detail at a later stage.

26.3.1   XML files

In general, we store XML data in so-called *XML documents*. An XML document is a unit of data storage and has the file extension '.xml'. It must conform to some rules (which we shall discuss at a later stage) and in general contains instantiated data. It is possible to have multiple elements with the same name in a single XML document as the following example shows:

```
<Shapes>
  <Point>
    <X>1</X>
    <Y>4</Y>
  </Point>
  <Point>
    <X>6</X>
    <Y>7</Y>
  </Point>
</Shapes>
```

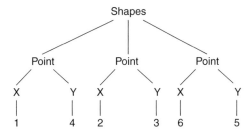

Figure 26.1   Tree structure

In this example we see that two `Point` elements are embedded in a root element called `Shapes`. We could represent this structure as a tree that highlights the nesting, as shown in Figure 26.1.

We now give another example to show how to document the properties of a European option. We create a root element and each property is modelled as a nested element:

```
<EuropeanCallOption>
  <Name>EuropeanCallOption</Name>
  <T>1</T>
  <K>15</K>
  <sigma>0.01</sigma>
  <r>0.15</r>
  <Dividend>0.03</Dividend>
  <S>20</S>
</EuropeanCallOption>
```

This structure is similar to the member data of the class for European options in Appendix 1 of this book.

We shall encounter more examples from financial engineering in Chapter 27, but the above example should give you a feeling for what XML syntax is for this domain.

26.3.2   XML syntax

The first line in each XML document must contain the following:

```
<?xml version="1.0" encoding="UTF-8" ?>
```

Furthermore, you can create structures containing parent and child elements. Child elements must be completely defined within the scope of their parent, as the following correct example shows:

```
<Course>
  <Name>C++ and Design Patterns</Name>
  <Body>
    <Module>
      <Title>Structural Patterns</Title>
      <Bullet>Bridge</Bullet>
      <Bullet>Decorator</Bullet>
    </Module>
    <Module>
      <!-- and more stuff -->
```

```
    </Module>
  </Body>
</Course>
```

This structure describes part of a course on design patterns: the course has a title and a body. The body consists of a number of modules. However, the following XML structure is incorrect because the element 'Module' is closed after the scope of the element 'Body':

```
<Course>
  <Name>C++ and Design Patterns</Name>
  <Body>
    <Module>
      <Title>Structural Patterns</Title>
      <Bullet>Bridge</Bullet>
      <Bullet>Decorator</Bullet>
  </Body>
    </Module>
</Course>
```

It is possible to include text in an XML document without having to define a corresponding element as the following example shows:

```
<Module>
  <Title>Structural Patterns</Title>
  Structural patterns are concerned with how
    classes and objects are composed to form
    larger structures. Examples of these patterns
    Bridge, Composite, Proxy, Facade (see Gamma et al., 1995)
    <Bullet>Bridge</Bullet>
    <Bullet>Decorator</Bullet>
</Module>
```

26.3.3 Attributes in XML

An attribute in XML is a description of a specific element but it does not refer to the element's contents. An attribute provides metadata information about an element. It provides extra information about the contents of the element in which it appears. A given element may have several attributes and these are serialised inside the start tag for the element.

In general, an attribute is a name–value pair and is similar to the Property pattern in Part I of this book. Some simple examples are:

```
<Person name = "Abraham" age = "250">

<Point Colour = "Blue" Name='p1'>
  <X>7</X>
  <Y>3</Y>
</Point>
```

You can use either single quotes or double quotes to denote literal strings, as the above example shows.

Finally, you can place comments in XML documents as the following example shows:

```
<!-- (C) Datasim Education BV 2002 -->
<!-- This is a collection of shapes. -->
```

```
<Shapes>
<!-- Point element. -->
  <Point>
    <X>2</X>
    <Y>7</Y>
  </Point>
</Shapes>
```

26.4   DOCUMENT TYPE DEFINITION

Whereas XML documents contain information pertaining to objects or instances, they do not contain information pertaining to the allowed structure of these objects. To this end, we need syntax for describing and constraining the logical structure of an XML document; in particular, we would like to address the following issues:

- What elements are allowed in a document?
- What attributes are allowed?
- What are the restrictions on the values of an attribute?
- How is element nesting defined and what is allowed?

These issues and considerations are taken care of in the Document Type Definition (DTD) and it should be seen as a kind of Data Definition Language (DDL). It is part of the official XML and it is usually referenced from an XML document; in other words, an XML document may know about its DTD but not the other way around. The DTD information is defined in a separate ASCII file having the file extension '.dtd'. It is not mandatory to create a DTD file (the XML document is sufficient) but if you do create one and reference it from the XML document then all elements used must be referenced in the DTD. In general, multiple XML documents refer to a given DTD file.

26.4.1   DTD syntax

Defining the element names and their contents in DTD can be difficult to understand. It is very compact but once you get used to it you will find it quite easy and will be in a position to create your own DTD files.

We discuss the following topics:

- Defining element types and element contents
- Special elements: sequence, choice and group
- Multiplicity issues
- Attribute list declaration and value types
- Identifiers and references
- Entity declarations.

This is quite a list, but we shall discuss each topic in turn and give illustrative examples for each. XML uses a number of keywords that we use in the following discussion.

Element types

In this case we define the name of an element and the allowed contents. The data type of the contents is one of the following:

```
#PCDATA (free-form text)
EMPTY (an element with no contents)
ANY (unspecified, a combination of text and elements).
```

The EMPTY type is used for elements that do not have contents (or that do not need contents) and they can be likened to control data in applications. An example is the page break control element in HTML.

Some examples of element using the above types now follow (note that these are defined in the .dtd file):

```
<!ELEMENT A (#PCDATA)>
<!ELEMENT Scale (#PCDATA)>
<!ELEMENT br EMPTY>
<!ELEMENT X ANY>
<!ELEMENT Scale (#PCDATA)>
```

Note the presence of the keyword !ELEMENT in the above examples.

Some examples of how these elements are correctly instantiated in XML documents are:

```
<A>Hello XML</A>

<Scale>23</Scale>
<BR/>
<X>
   32
   <Scale>2</Scale>
</X>
```

Special elements

We can model the following special elements (we take a set with three elements A, B and C for convenience):

- Sequence (A, B, C): choose an element from a list of candidate elements
- Choice $(A|B|C)$: choose an element from a mutually exclusive set of candidate elements
- Group $(A|(B, C))$: nest a group of elements.

We now give some examples of these special elements by giving the entries in the .dtd file as well as some instances in the XML document.

An example of the Sequence specifier is:

```
<!ELEMENT Point (X, Y)>
<!ELEMENT X (#PCDATA)>
<!ELEMENT Y (#PCDATA)>

<Point>
   <X>1.2</X>
   <Y>3.4</Y>
</Point>
```

An example of the Choice specifier is:

```
<!ELEMENT Answer (Choice_A|Choice_B)>
<!ELEMENT Choice_A (#PCDATA)>
```

```
<!ELEMENT Choice_B (#PCDATA)>

<Answer>
  <Choice_B>Apple</Choice_B>
</Answer>
```

An example of the Group specifier is:

```
<!ELEMENT Point ((X, Y)|(Angle, Length))>
<!ELEMENT X (#PCDATA)>
<!ELEMENT Y (#PCDATA)>
<!ELEMENT Angle (#PCDATA)>
<!ELEMENT Length (#PCDATA)>

<Point>
  <X>1</X>
  <Y>1</Y>
</Point>

<Point>
  <Angle>45</Angle>
  <Length>1.1</Length>
</Point>
```

This example shows how a DTD can generate multiple XML instances; the first one is a point in Cartesian space while the second example is a point in polar coordinates.

Multiplicity

This option is concerned with the number of child elements within a parent element. This is achieved by appending a special sign or marker to the child element. The options are:

- '?' zero or 1 time (an optional multiplicity in UML terms)
- '*' zero or more times
- '+' 1 or more times
- No sign signifies just once.

The following example is an element representing an e-mail message. The message must be sent to at least one recipient, it is from exactly one sender, there are zero or more 'cc' addresses, the subject is optional and the body is also optional:

```
<!ELEMENT EMail (To+, From, CC*, Subject?, Body?)>
<!ELEMENT To (#PCDATA)>
<!ELEMENT From (#PCDATA)>
<!ELEMENT CC (#PCDATA)>
<!ELEMENT Subject (#PCDATA)>
<!ELEMENT Body (#PCDATA)>
```

An example of an XML document corresponding to this DTD is:

```
<EMail>
  <To>Ilona</To>
    <To>Brendan</To>
    <From>Danny</From>
    <Subject>Anyone for tennis?</Subject>
    <Body>3 o'clock next Wednesday</Body>
</EMail>
```

Attribute lists and value types

It is possible to declare one or more attributes of an element. To this end, we use the
ATTLIST keyword and define a list of attributes where each attribute is in essence a
name–value pair in conjunction with the value type of the attribute. The allowed value
types are:

- CDATA (text)
- ID (this is a document-specific identifier)
- IDREF (identifier reference, a reference to a document-specific identifier)
- IDREFS (multiple references to document-specific identifiers)
- NMTOKEN (a name composed of characters but no white space)
- NMTOKENS (multiple NMTOKEN names)
- Enumerations

Identifiers must be unique in a given document. No duplicates are allowed. Furthermore,
it is possible to assign default values to an attribute. Thus, when no value is given the
default value is assumed.

Let us take an example of a point with two attributes: the first attribute is the name of
the point (default value 'P') while the second attribute is the geometry type (default is
'Cartesian'). Both attributes are text types.

```
<!ELEMENT Point (X, Y)>
<!ELEMENT X (#PCDATA)>
<!ELEMENT Y (#PCDATA)>

<!ATTLIST Point
 Name CDATA "P"
 Geometry CDATA "Cartesian">
```

An example of use in an XML document is as follows:

```
<Point Name = "P1">
  <X>1.2</X>
  <Y>3.4</Y>
</Point>
```

In this case the default coordinate system is 'Cartesian'.

Identifiers and references

An ID is similar to a primary key from database theory and it is a unique identifier for
an element. An IDREF is a pointer to a unique ID. The following example shows how
these are used:

```
<All>
  <Point Id = "P1">
    <X>1</X>
    <Y>2</Y>
  </Point>
  <Reference IdRef="P1"/>
</All>
```

Concluding with our discussion of attributes, we note that are three ways to control the values of attributes. First, we can demand that a value is mandatory (#REQUIRED), in which case the attribute value must be defined for each element instance. Second, the value may be optional (#IMPLIED), in which case no attribute value is given. Finally, the value may be fixed (#FIXED), which in fact says that the attribute is a constant. The following example shows the usage:

```
<!ELEMENT Point (X, Y)>
<!ELEMENT X (#PCDATA)>
<!ELEMENT Y (#PCDATA)>
<!ATTLIST Point
 Name CDATA #IMPLIED
 Dimensions CDATA #FIXED "2">
```

Entity declarations

We now come to the important issue of defining entities and referencing them from an XML document. There are two kinds of entity:

- Internal entity
- External entity.

An internal entity is a text string while an external entity is a file. There are three good reasons for using entities: first, they avoid text duplication; second, we can compose XML documents from multiple files; and, finally, we can use reserved or special characters. We concentrate on internal entities in this chapter. We take an example. In a .dtd file we define

```
<!ELEMENT X (#PCDATA)>
<!ENTITY CopyRight2002 "(c) 2002 Datasim">
```

while we refer to the copyright entity by using a reference to it from an XML document as follows:

```
<!DOCTYPE X SYSTEM "x.dtd">
<X>&CopyRight2002;</X>
```

We conclude with a short discussion of parameter entities. These are entities that are used only inside the DTD itself. The general form is:

```
<!ENTITY % entity_name "entity_type">
```

Having defined a parameter entity we can reference it in other parts of the DTD document using the notation (%entity_name;).

26.4.2   Validation issues

In general we use the DTD file to validate the structure of an XML document. In fact, the XML document should refer to its corresponding .dtd file, as shown in the following example:

```
<!DOCTYPE Point SYSTEM "point.dtd">
<Point>
  <X>2</X>
  <Y>6</Y>
</Point>
```

In this case the first line defines the location of the .dtd file. We use the keyword 'DOCTYPE'. The other parameters have the following meaning:

Point (the root element)
SYSTEM (this indicates that the next item is the file location)
"point.dtd" (the file location itself).

Finally, we can draw analogies between the object paradigm and XML. A class is similar to a DTD because it is abstract and describes the allowed structure of instances of the DTD, for example objects or XML documents. In short, DTD is the class and the XML document contains instances of the class.

The uses of DTDs can be summed up as follows:

- They document the structure of a markup language or application (for example, FpML, MathML).
- They provide default attribute values.
- They can check the structure of hand-written XML documents.
- They are used as input to XML-editing tools in order to automatically generate XML elements.

26.4.3   Limitations of DTDs

DTDs do have some limitations. First, they have support for attribute data types but they have no data types for element values. Furthermore, they have limited support for child element multiplicity constraints and it is not possible to validate an XML document that combines elements from different markup languages. This poses serious problems for enterprise B2B applications.

We shall see in the next chapter how XML schemas overcome some of these limitations.

26.5   EXTENSIBLE STYLESHEET LANGUAGE TRANSFORMATION (XSLT)

The Extensible Stylesheet Language (XSL) is used to present XML data over the Internet. It is an XML application language and it is used to transform an input document to an output document. The output document can be any one of a number of types:

- HTML document displaying XML data
- An XML document containing a subset of XML data
- An XML document using some other markup language.

XSL uses a fixed set of tags (vocabulary) used to define presentation templates called *stylesheets*. Stylesheets are used to manipulate the data and they describe formatting information in an XML document. In short, we say that XSL provides a language for

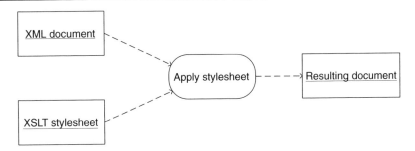

Figure 26.2   Applying a stylesheet

creating stylesheets that describe how XML documents should be rendered. The main advantages of using stylesheets are (see Ceponkus and Hoodbhoy, 1999):

- Reuse of data
- Standardisation of presentation style
- Separation of concerns: data and presentation are in distinct files
- Transform a source document to multiple output formats.

The basic UML activity diagram for the transformation is shown in Figure 26.2. There are two input files, namely the XML document and the XSL stylesheet containing transformation rules (please note that a stylesheet is also an XML document). The output can be Text (RTF), XML or HTML, for example.

We wish to give a more detailed account of XSL but before we do that we need to introduce the concept of a namespace in XML.

26.5.1   Namespaces in XML

The main reason for using namespaces is to avoid name collisions. Thus, it is possible to define an element name more than once provided it is defined in different namespaces. By the way, if you know how namespaces work in C++ you will not have much problem understanding the XML namespace concept.

A namespace is identified by a Universal Resource Locator (URL) and the URL is in essence the location of a file on the Web. There are two ways to identify a namespace. The first way is by means of a namespace prefix. You can define your own namespaces while XML has a reserved keyword 'xmlns' that identifies an URL. Let us take an example:

```
<crs:Point
   xmlns:crs="http://www.datasim.nl/cartesian">
   <crs:X>1.2</crs:X>
   <crs:Y>5.8</crs:Y>

</crs:Point>
```

In this case we see that two namespaces are defined. In fact, 'crs' is declared as a new namespace in this example.

A default namespace uses just one namespace, that is 'xmlns'. Let us take an example. The elements Point, X and Y are in the namespace identified by

```
xmlns="http://datasim.nl/cartesian"
```

The full structure is

```
<Point xmlns="http://datasim.nl/cartesian">
  <X>5.1</X>
  <Y>3.5</Y>
</Point>
```

It is possible to use elements from different namespaces in an XML document. We give an example again to show what we mean. Let us suppose that we have representations for a Point in both Cartesian and polar formats and we wish to initialise the data accordingly. The following code shows how:

```
<All xmlns:crs="http://www.datasim.nl/cartesian"
     xmlns:plr="http://www.datasim.nl/polar">

  <crs:Point>
    <crs:X>1</crs:X>
    <crs:Y>1</crs:Y>
  </crs:Point>

  <plr:Point>
     <plr:Angle>45</plr:Angle>
     <plr:Length>1.14</plr:Length>
  </plr:Point>

</All>
```

26.5.2 Main concepts in XSL

A stylesheet consists of one or more *templates*. Each template matches a *pattern* that specifies a set of XML elements. A pattern is a very simple query language. XSL defines a limited set of XML elements under the XSL namespace that XSL processors interpret as executable functions. A full description of these elements can be found in Ceponkus and Hoodbhoy (1999). We concentrate on three specific elements:

- xsl:stylesheet (root node containing templates that we apply to the source document)
- xsl:template (define a series of transformations or formatting options)
- xsl:output (define how output is to be serialised)
- xsl:value-of (insert the string value of a specified node).

The xsl:stylesheet element is used once for every XSL stylesheet and is the root node of every stylesheet. It informs the XSL processor that the document is an XSL stylesheet and houses all templates:

```
<xsl:stylesheet
xmlns:xsl="http://www.w3.org/1999/XSL/Transform"
version="1.0">
```

The xsl:output element describes the output format of the transformed document. Possible output types are XML, HTML, text and qualified names. (A qualified name consists of a namespace and a local part. The namespace name selects the namespace while the local part is the local document element or attribute name.) An example is:

```
<xsl:output method="text"/>
```

The `xsl:template` element is used to create a template in which formatting and transforming actions are specified, as shown in the following example:

```
<xsl:template match="/Shapes/Point">
   P( <xsl:value-of select="./X"/> ,   <xsl:value-of select="./Y"/> )
</xsl:template>
```

In this example we match `X` and `Y` elements in the pattern `"/Shapes/Point"` and we show literal text in bold. The input file for this code is:

```
<Shapes>
  <Point>
    <X>1</X>
    <Y>2</Y>
  </Point>
</Shapes>
```

and the transformed document has the following form:

```
P( 1 , 2 )
```

We conclude this section with a discussion of the `xsl:value-of` element. This element is used to insert the text/string value of the node indicated by a pattern. It can be used any number of times. Let us take an example of an XML input document containing points:

```
<Shapes>
  <Point>
    <X>1</X>
    <Y>2</Y>
  </Point>
  <Point>
    <X>3</X>
    <Y>4</Y>
  </Point>
  <Point>
    <X>5</X>
    <Y>6</Y>
  </Point>
</Shapes>
```

and let us suppose that we wish to print these values in the following way:

```
P( 1 , 2 ) P( 3 , 4 ) P( 5 , 6 )
```

The code that realises this output is:

```
<xsl:template match="/Shapes/Point">
   P( <xsl:value-of select="./X"/>, <xsl:value-of select="./Y"/>   )
</xsl:template>
```

Again, we show literal text in bold.

26.6   AN APPLICATION OF XML: FINANCIAL PRODUCTS MARKUP LANGUAGE

The Financial products Markup Language (FpML) is a protocol enabling e-commerce activities in the field of financial derivatives (see FpML, 2003). It establishes the industry protocol for sharing information on, and dealing in, financial swaps, derivatives and structured products over the Internet. One of the objectives of FpML is to support many kinds of products such as portfolios for risk management and over-the-counter (OTC) derivatives. FpML is an *application* of XML.

We include a discussion of FpML in this chapter because of its relevance to XML and to financial engineering. FpML supports XML definitions for the following kinds of products:

- Interest rate cap
- Interest rate floor
- Interest rate swaption
- FX resetable cross-currency swap
- Equity derivatives

This list is only a snapshot in time and many other products are being added. For an up-to-date account, please refer to the FpML website www.fpml.org. For example, FpML deals with Equity Options and other derivative products.

26.6.1   Product architecture overview

FpML adopts a structured approach by grouping related elements into so-called components. A component describes one particular feature of a trade. Components are recursive in the sense that they may contain, and be contained in, other components. Components may also contain primitive types such as strings and dates. Thus, all these features allow components to be used as building blocks for a flexible and extendible model. Each component serves a particular semantic purpose and is typically represented as an entity in an XML DTD. However, most new development work centres on XML Schema. Arbitrarily complex financial products can be created by combining a few simple ideas in a variety of different ways.

Some primitive components in FpML are:

```
FpML_Money
FpML_Interval
FPML_BusinessCenters
FPML_BusinessDayAdjustments
```

Some examples of entries in the FpML DTD are:

```
<!ENTITY % FpML_MONEY "currency, amount">
<!ENTITY % FpML_Strike "strikeRate, buyer?, seller?">
<!ENTITY % FpML_BusinessCenters "businessCenter+">
```

Higher-level components are built from simpler components as the following examples show:

```
<!ENTITY % FpML_ProductSelection "bulletPayment |
capFloor | fra | swap | swaption">
```

FpML uses a graphical notation to display an XML entity definition. The representation is similar to UML (see FpML, 2003). In this section however, we prefer to use UML because it is a well-accepted standard and is highly expressive (see www.omg.org for the UML specification).

We begin our discussion of FpML architecture by looking at core `trade` components. A trade is a top-level component with the root element `FpML`. A trade is an agreement between two parties to enter into a financial contract and the `trade` component contains all the economic information necessary to execute and confirm that trade. A trade has the following parts:

- `tradeHeader` (common to all kinds of trades, for example, dates and trade parties)
- `product` (abstract concept, base class for all specific products, for example, fra)
- `party` (holds information about a party involved in the trade)
- `otherPartyPayment` (additional payment to third parties, for example, brokers).

The UML diagram for a trade is shown in Figure 26.3. Each of the classes in this diagram is also an aggregate containing parts. The corresponding DTD entry is:

```
<!ENTITY % FpML_Trade "tradeHeader,
%FpML_ProductSelection; , party+ ,
otherPartyPayment*">
```

The product entity in Figure 26.3 is abstract and has a number of specialisations. For example, the swap entity is documented in the FpML specification as a complex aggregate entity, as shown in Figure 26.4.

A swap contains one or more instances of the `swapStream` component, zero or more instances of the `additionalPayment` component as well as an optional `cancelableProvision` component, Furthermore, it contains an optional `extendibleProvision` component and an optional `earlyTerminationProvision` component

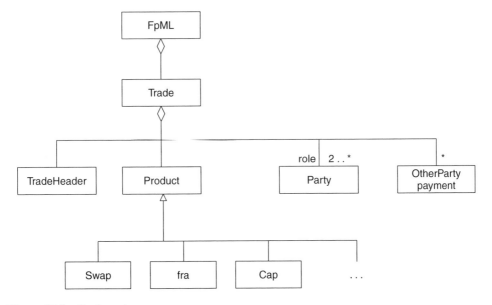

Figure 26.3   Trade entity

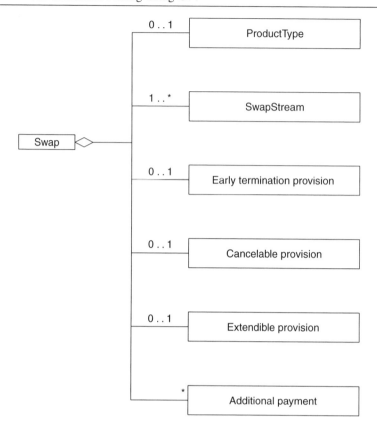

Figure 26.4 Interest rate swap

Finally, the swapStream contains the elements required to define an individual swap leg. Each of these entities has its corresponding DTD entry in the FpML specification. We give the structure for swaps:

```
<!ENTITY % FPML_Swap "%FpML_Product; , swapStream+ ,
earlyTerminationProvision? , cancelableProvision? ,
extendibleProvision? , additionalPayment*">
```

The reader might like to check that this structure and the UML structure in Figure 26.4 are two representations of the same information.

26.6.2 Example: Equity derivative options product architecture

FpML has support for a range of put and call options with European or American exercise styles. These options can be based on single stocks or indices and delivery can be either cash or physical stock. FpML has support for the following:

- Bermudan exercise style
- Basket underlyings
- Forward starts

- Quantos and composites
- Averaging; knock-in, knock-out and binary (digital) options.

FpML models options by the `equityOption` entity that contains approximately 15 parts! We discuss a few of them to motivate the structure:

```
underlyer
equityExercise
equityOptionFeatures
```

The `underlyer` component specifies the asset(s) on which the option is granted, for example a `singleUnderlyer` or basket and it may consist of equity, index or convertible bond components or some combination of these. FpML supports three styles of `equityExercise`: European, American and Bermudan. Each of these styles is represented by its own component.

26.7   CONCLUSIONS AND SUMMARY

We have given an introduction to the Extensible Markup Language (XML). XML is a universal information exchange format. In particular, it is a vehicle for exchanging information over the Web. With XML we can structure data in almost any way we wish and it can be accessed by a variety of programming languages, for example, C++, Java, Visual Basic and C#.

In this chapter we introduced you to the most important syntax in XML and described how to read and understand XML documents. We also gave an overview of Document Type Definition (DTD). DTD gives us the syntax we need for describing and constraining the logical structure of an XML document; in particular, it addresses the following issues:

- What elements are allowed in a document?
- What attributes are allowed?
- What are the restrictions on the values of an attribute?
- How is element nesting defined and what is allowed?

We use the DTD to validate XML documents.

Finally, we gave an introduction to Financial products Markup Language (FpML), an application of XML. FpML is a protocol enabling e-commerce activities in the field of financial derivatives (see FpML, 2003). It establishes the industry protocol for sharing information on, and dealing in, financial swaps, derivatives and structured products over the Internet.

We expect to see growing interest in applications of XML for financial engineering in the years to come.

27

Advanced XML and Programming Interface

27.1 INTRODUCTION AND OBJECTIVES

We continue with our discussion of XML. Chapter 26 was devoted to the major syntax issues in XML and we gave numerous examples to give the reader some feeling for the subject. We also gave an introduction to the FpML, an application based on XML that is used to represent financial instruments in a vendor-neutral and language-neutral manner. In this chapter we concentrate on the programming aspects of XML and its environment. In particular, we wish to read and write XML documents using C++ and to this end we employ a set of interface implementations of the Document Object Model (DOM). We first develop code to show how to use the individual methods and we then hide this rather low-level code in easy to use Visitor classes (recall that Visitor is a design pattern, see Chapter 25 of this book and Gamma *et al.*, 1995). We then extend our results to financial instruments, in particular plain and exotic options.

We include a discussion on XML Schema, the 'next generation' DTD. We describe its essential features and how it differs from DTD.

27.2 XML SCHEMA

The XML Schema serves the same purpose as DTD, namely to define the allowed structure and value types for specific XML documents. XML Schema offers more functionality than DTD.

As with DTD, we need two files: one file for the schema and a file that represents the XML document.

Some features of XML Schema are:

- XML schemas are XML documents and we can thus use the same tools as with normal XML documents. No new tools are needed.
- Support for at least 40 built-in data types.
- It is possible to create both user-defined primitive and complex data types.
- XML namespace support.

Some of the types are primitives while others are derived types that we describe in a schema. Both primitive and derived types are available to schema authors to use in their current form, or from which to derive new types.

We can group the data types into four main categories (see Skonnard and Gudgin, 2002):

- *Numeric types* (the usual stuff that you would expect)
  ```
  decimal
  integer
  int, long
  ```

```
byte
float, double
etc.
```

- *Date and time types*
```
date
time
dateTime
duration
etc.
```

- *XML types*
Types as with DTD (ID, ENTITY, ...)
```
NOTATION
```

- *Name and string types*
```
string
```
`token` (string with normalised white space)
`QName` (an XML Name)
```
etc.
```

All XML Schema elements are in the namespace defined by the URL, as can be seen in the example

```
<xsd:schema
xmlns:xsd="http://www.w3.org/2001/XMLSchema">
  <!-- Types and declarations go here. -->
</xsd:schema>
```

Please note that 'schema' is a keyword in this context.

27.2.1 Element declaration

We now discuss how to declare the name and type of an element. To this end, we use the keywords 'element' and 'type' to specify the name and data type of the element, respectively. The following simple example shows how to define an element called 'X' of type double:

```
<?xml version="1.0"?>
<xsd:schema
xmlns:xsd="http://www.w3.org/2001/XMLSchema">

<!-- Declare element 'X' which has built-in -->
<!-- type 'double'.                          -->

<xsd:element name="X" type="xsd:double"/>
</xsd:schema>
```

For example, the following data is correct according to the schema

```
<!-- Valid according to XML Schema. -->
<X>
  2.4
</X>
```

while the following example is incorrect because we are attempting to put text in an element whose type is `double`

```
<!-- Invalid according to XML Schema. -->
<X>
  Hi there!
</X>
```

27.2.2 User-defined simple and complex types

We create a user-defined simple type based on a built-in type and we can place user-defined constraints on the new type (for example, range checking, length, format and so on). To this end, we use the 'simpleType' element and 'restriction' to specify the appropriate constraints. We take an example of defining a PO box number that consists of four decimals, then a space and two letters. The user-defined type then looks like the following:

```
<xsd:schema
xmlns:xsd="http://www.w3.org/2001/XMLSchema">
<xsd:simpleType name="PoBoxNLType">
  <xsd:restriction base="xsd:string">
    <xsd:pattern value="\d\d\d\d\s\D\D"/>
</xsd:restriction>
</xsd:simpleType>
  <xsd:element name="PoBox" type="PoBoxNLType"/>
</xsd:schema>
```

What have we done here? In essence, we have wrapped the standard string data type with another user-defined string element having a defined structure.

We can also create so-called complex user-defined data types by composing them from other elements and attributes. XML Schema do not have any complex types so you must create your own. In order to create such a type we use the keyword 'complexType'. The resulting element may contain both attribute and element declarations by nesting them. As with DTDs, we can define the following element declaration groups

*   sequence: elements must appear in the given order
*   all: elements may appear in any order
*   choice: only one of the elements may appear.

We now give an example of a two-dimensional Cartesian point.

```
<xsd:schema
  xmlns:xsd="http://www.w3.org/2001/XMLSchema">

  <xsd:complexType name="PointType">
    <xsd:sequence>
      <xsd:element name="X" type="xsd:double"/>
      <xsd:element name="Y" type="xsd:double"/>
    </xsd:sequence>
    <xsd:attribute name="Name" type="xsd:string"/>
  </xsd:complexType>
  <xsd:element name="Point" type="PointType"/>
</xsd:schema>
```

The reader might like to compare the above structure with the way we have done this in DTD (see Chapter 26). Recall

```
<!ELEMENT Point (X, Y)>
<!ELEMENT X (#PCDATA)>
<!ELEMENT Y (#PCDATA)>
<!ATTLIST Point
Name CDATA "P"
Geometry CDATA "Cartesian">
```

We now define what is meant by local and global element declarations. An element declaration with a complex type is called a local element declaration. The elements X and Y in the above XML Schema code are typical examples. An element that is directly nested in the (root) schema element is called a global element declaration. In this case we use the element as a root element. Again, the following example shows the distinction (not all details have been filled in):

```
<xsd:schema
  xmlns:xsd="http://www.w3.org/2001/XMLSchema">
  <xsd:complexType name="PointType">
    <xsd:sequence>
      <xsd:element name="X" .../>
      <xsd:element name="Y" .../>
    </xsd:sequence>
    <xsd:attribute name="Name" type="xsd:string"/>
  </xsd:complexType>
  <xsd:element name="Point" .../>
</xsd:schema>
```

27.2.3 Multiplicity issues

In general, a parent element consists of a number of child elements. We wish to specify upper and lower bounds using two keywords:

- minOccurs: the minimal allowed occurrence
- maxOccurs: the maximal allowed occurrence.

The default value in both cases is 1, which will be the value if these keywords are absent in the element declaration.

We now take an example to show how this works. We return to the e-mail example from section 26.4.1. The XML Schema is:

```
<?xml version="1.0"?>
<xsd:schema
xmlns:xsd="http://www.w3.org/2001/XMLSchema">
  <xsd:complexType name="EmailType">
    <xsd:sequence>
      <xsd:element name="To" type="xsd:double" maxOccurs="unbounded"/>
      <xsd:element name="From" type="xsd:double"/>
      <xsd:element name="CC" type="xsd:double"
          minOccurs="0" maxOccurs="unbounded"/>
```

```
    <xsd:element name="Subject" type="xsd:double"
        minOccurs="0" maxOccurs="1"/>
    <xsd:element name="Body" type="xsd:double"
        minOccurs="0" maxOccurs="1"/>
    </xsd:sequence>
  </xsd:complexType>
  <xsd:element name="EMail" type="EmailType"/>
</xsd:schema>
```

An XML document that conforms to the above schema is:

```
<EMail
xmlns:xsi=
"http://www.w3.org/2001/XMLSchema-instance"
xsi:noNamespaceSchemaLocation="EMail.xsd">
  <To>Mary</To>
  <To>Peter</To>
  <From>John</From>
  <Subject>Hi</Subject>
  <Body>What's up?</Body>
  </EMail>
```

27.2.4   An example

We take an example from two-dimensional geometry. The UML class diagram is shown in Figure 27.1 and we have four classes that we wish to model using XML Schema. There are three main steps in general:

1. Create the complete UML class diagram
2. Translate the UML class diagram to an XML Schema (manually/visually)
3. Create an XML document and validate it against the XML Schema.

In general, we define a complex type for each class and the attributes in the class are mapped to the corresponding attributes in the complex type. We first define `Point` and

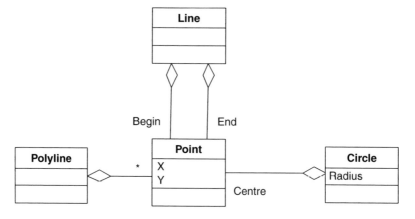

Figure 27.1   UML class diagram

Circle. Notice that `Point` is reused as it were in `Circle` because we model a `Circle` as having a centre point and radius:

```
<?xml version="1.0"?>

<xsd:schema
xmlns:xsd="http://www.w3.org/2001/XMLSchema">

  <xsd:complexType name="PointType">
    <xsd:attribute name="X" type="xsd:double"/>
    <xsd:attribute name="Y" type="xsd:double"/>
  </xsd:complexType>

  <xsd:complexType name="CircleType">
  <xsd:sequence>
    <xsd:element name="CentrePoint" type="PointType"/>
  </xsd:sequence>
  <xsd:attribute name="Radius" type="xsd:double"/>
```

We now define the elements for `Line` and `Polyline`. Notice how we have implemented multiplicity in `Polyline` (note that `minOccurs` is absent, thus default is 1 and `maxOccurs` is unbounded):

```
...
  <xsd:complexType name="LineType">
    <xsd:sequence>
      <xsd:element name="BeginPoint" type="PointType"/>
      <xsd:element name="EndPoint" type="PointType"/>
    </xsd:sequence>
  </xsd:complexType>

  <xsd:complexType name="PolylineType">
    <xsd:sequence>
      <xsd:element name="Point" type="PointType"
        maxOccurs="unbounded"/>
    </xsd:sequence>
  </xsd:complexType>
...
```

Finally, we create an element that represents a `Shape` composite; this corresponds to a class consisting of a list of arbitrary `Shape` objects:

```
...
  <xsd:complexType name="ShapesType">
    <xsd:choice minOccurs="0" maxOccurs="unbounded">
      <xsd:element name="Point" type="PointType"/>
      <xsd:element name="Circle" type="CircleType"/>
      <xsd:element name="Line" type="LineType"/>
      <xsd:element name="Polyline" type="PolylineType"/>
    </xsd:choice>
  </xsd:complexType>
  <xsd:element name="Shapes" type="ShapesType"/>
</xsd:schema>
```

We can use this example as a benchmark for other applications in financial engineering. For example, we can model complex financial products such as straddles, strangles or delta hedges using similar elements.

27.2.5 Comparing DTDs and the XML Schema

We compare DTDs and XML Schemas because they are competitors. In the future the industry standard will be XML Schemas but in a transition period we shall have to support DTDs as well.

We summarise some facts on DTDs and XML Schemas:

- DTDs tend to be small and simple.
- DTDs are good enough for (reasonably) unstructured text-oriented applications.
- Existing markup languages and applications based on XML already use DTDs; thus, developers are and will be confronted with legacy problems.
- XML Schemas use XML syntax; no new editors or software tools are needed in order to process schema files.
- XML Schemas have rich and extensible data type support; this feature eliminates validation code in applications. The validation rules are part of a schema.
- XML Schemas are suitable for data-driven (for example, B2B) applications.

27.2.6 XML Schemas and FpML

Eventually, DTDs will be replaced by XML Schemas as the tool for creating future FpML specifications. There are compelling business and technological reasons for wishing to migrate in the first place (see FpML, 2002, for a more detailed discussion):

- DTDs are dead-end technology
- XML Schemas have better support for defining reusable structures in an object-oriented fashion.
- XML Schemas have direct support for extensions.
- XML Schemas support separation of concerns: independent and decoupled development groups can work on different parts of a specification with minimal cross-group interaction.
- XML Schemas are expressed in XML itself while DTDs are expressed in their own specific language.
- XML Schemas will enjoy better tool support than DTDs in the future.

In the short term, DTDs and XML Schemas must coexist and it may take some time before DTDs completely disappear from the scene.

27.3 ACCESSING XML DATA: THE DOCUMENT OBJECT MODEL

The Document Object Model (DOM) is a set of abstract programming interfaces (as defined in IDLs) that map the data structures in an XML document onto a tree of nodes. These interfaces form a layer of abstraction between the application and the XML document. In other words, the programmer does not have to know about the internal structure of the document but instead states what he or she wants from the document without knowing how it should be done (this is called *information hiding* in computer science jargon).

DOM mirrors XML constructs and elements. Each construct in XML is represented by a DOM *node*. The major interfaces are given below.

- *Node*: This is the base interface for all more specific node types. It is similar to an abstract class in C++, for example. It has methods that manage and manipulate nodes. Furthermore, it has functionality for traversing the tree. A node has properties such as name and value.
- *Document*: This is a representation of the document as a whole. It can be seen as the root of the DOM tree and it is also a factory for other node types. Of course, it has methods to allow us to search in the document.
- *Element*: This is a mirror-image of the XML element construct. It has methods to access and modify attributes and child elements as well as some methods that can retrieve properties of an element.
- *Attr (Attributes)*: This is a node that models the attributes in an XML attribute. It provides access to an attribute's properties. This interface does not have many methods because we can use the methods of the attribute's 'parent' element node.
- *CharacterData*: This is the base interface for various kinds of data, for example Text, Comment and CDATASection. This interface is never used directly.
- *Text*: This contains unstructured text (thus, no elements). This is usually a child of an Element node.

27.3.1 DOM in a programming environment

DOM has been designed in such a way that it works with more than one programming language. You can use DOM with your own favourite language, for example C++, Java, C#, Visual Basic, JavaScript and VBScript. Each language will have its own instance for accessing the DOM nodes. In this book we use the C++ parser from Microsoft.

27.4 DOM AND C++: THE ESSENTIALS

We now discuss how DOM with C++ as language is used in order to create an XML document. The code is placed in one main() program to enable you to see the steps that are needed. Later we shall hide much of the detail in several design patterns; therefore you do not need to learn the function calls. The implementation is under Windows and use is made of COM (Component Object Model) to implement the interfaces.

The example in this section generates the following XML document:

```
<?xml version="1.0" cncoding="UTF-8"?>
<Point><X Name="X coordinate">2.71</X>
<Y Name="Y coordinate">2.71</Y></Point>
```

We now go through the steps that realise this output. All comments and code are interleaved. This part is fairly detailed and you may skip it on a first reading.

```
// Simple demo of creating an XML document with MS' XML parser using
// the DOM interface.
//
// In this case we create an XML document for a two-dimensional point
// having X and Y coordinates.
//
// Required parser: MSXML 2.0 (Microsoft)
```

```
//
// (C) Datasim Education BV 2003

// Step 0
// Include/import for XML component. We must work in this way because
// we are usually a COM library and not 'normal' C library (in the
// latter it is sufficient to include the header file and to link the
// .lib file)

#import "msxml2.dll"
#include <msxml2.h>

// Standard stuff.
#include <string>
#include <iostream>

using namespace std;

void Demo()
{
  // Initialise COM library (don't forget :)).
  CoInitialise(NULL);

  try
  {
  /////////////////////////////////////////////////////////
      // Step 1. Create instance of XML COM class.
      // COM smart pointers.
      MSXML2::IXMLDOMDocument2Ptr doc;        // XML document.
      // Create document object.
      doc.CreateInstance("Msxml2.DOMDocument.4.0");

  /////////////////////////////////////////////////////////
      // Step 2. Create processing instruction.

      // Create the Processing Instruction
      MSXML2::IXMLDOMProcessingInstructionPtr header = NULL;
      header = doc->createProcessingInstruction("xml",
      "version='1.0' encoding='UTF-8'");

      // Add processing instruction.
      _variant_t nullVal;
      nullVal.vt = VT_NULL;
      doc->insertBefore(header, nullVal);

  /////////////////////////////////////////////////////////
      // Step 3. Create root element.

      // Create root.
      _bstr_t root = "Point";
      MSXML2::IXMLDOMElementPtr pRoot = doc->createElement(root);

      // Add root to document element.
      doc->appendChild( pRoot );

      // Step 4. Create child element.
      // Create new child (The X coordinate of the point)
      _bstr_t Xcoord = "X";
      MSXML2::IXMLDOMElementPtr pXcoord;
      pXcoord = doc->createElement(Xcoord);

      // Set value.
      _variant_t value = 2.71;
```

```
        value.ChangeType(VT_BSTR);
        pXcoord->nodeTypedValue = value;

        // Create first attribute.
        pXcoord->setAttribute( "Name", "X coordinate" );

        // Add child to root element.
        pRoot->appendChild(pXcoord);

        // Create another new child (The Y coordinate of the point)
        _bstr_t Ycoord = "Y";
        MSXML2::IXMLDOMElementPtr pYcoord;
        pYcoord = doc->createElement(Ycoord);

        // Set value.
        _variant_t value2 = 2.71;
        value2.ChangeType(VT_BSTR);
        pYcoord->nodeTypedValue = value2;

        // Create first attribute.
        pYcoord->setAttribute( "Name", "Y coordinate" );

        // Add child to root element.
        pRoot->appendChild( pYcoord );

        // Step 5. Create output.

        // Save XML document.
        doc->save( "point.xml" );

        // Show XML on console.
        string xml = doc->Getxml();
        cout << xml << endl;
    }
    catch( _com_error & error )
    {
        // Get pointer to error description.
        bstr_t description = error.Description();

        // If no error description, try error message.
        if( !description )
        {
            description = error.ErrorMessage();
        }

        // Display error.
        cout << (const char*) description << endl;
    }

    // Uninitialise COM library.
    CoUninitialise();
}
```

We now describe this code in some detail. Our approach is to paraphrase each of the above steps.

Step 0: We include the header file needed for the MS XML parser and we must import the corresponding DLL. The precise details may change in the future. Since the parser is implemented as a set of Component Object Model (COM) interfaces, we must initialise COM by calling `CoInitialise()`.

Step 1: Having initialised COM, we then create an instance of the XML COM class by calling the `CreateInstance()` function.

Step 2: We create an XML document in two steps. First, we must create processing instructions (this step) and the root element with children (step 3).

Step 3: We use the `createElement()` function and we add the root element to it. Notice that this element is a child of the XML COM object. Notice that the root's tag is called 'Point'.

Step 4: We create a point with two coordinates. To this end, we create two elements with tags named 'X' and 'Y' and we let them be children of 'root'. Furthermore, these elements both have an attribute called 'Name'.

Step 5: We are almost there! It now remains to save the in-memory tree structure to a file with extension '.xml'. We also print the output on the screen.

Finally, we call `CoUninitialise()` to close down COM.

The main program is:

```
int main()
{
  Demo();
  return 0;
}
```

The code in this section is the basis for a Visitor class that allows us to read and write XML data for financial engineering applications. We discuss this problem in section 27.5.1.

27.5   DOM, ENTITIES AND PROPERTY SETS

The example in section 27.4 was very specific and the main objective there was to show how to apply the DOM interfaces in C++ to produce an XML output document. In this section we wish to produce code that writes *and* reads XML documents. In order to reduce the scope we concentrate on a specific class of entities that we find useful for financial engineering applications. In particular, we are interested in modelling entities that consist essentially of properties. For example, an option entity consists of a number of properties. The UML class diagram for the current discussion is shown in Figure 27.2. The template classes `Property` and `SimplePropertySet` have already been discussed in Chapter 5. The template class `Entity` is essentially a container for a logically related group of attributes. From Figure 27.2 we see that an `Entity` consists of a `Property` (this will play the role of the entity's root element in the XML documentation) and a

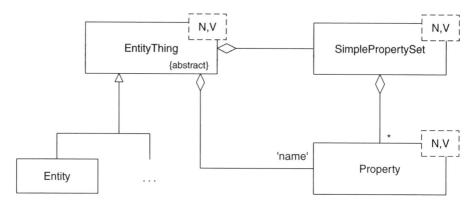

Figure 27.2   Entity and Property classes

`SimplePropertySet` (and its properties will be child elements in the XML document). We now view some sample output based on the following C++ code:

```
Property<string, double> K("StrikePrice", 150.0);
Property<string, double> r("InterestRate", 0.06);
Property<string, double> T("Expiry", 1);
Property<string, double> S("Stock", 120);
Property<string, double> U("UnderlyingAsset", 134.2);
Property<string, double> b("CostOfCarry", 12.0);

Entity<string, double> option("EuropeanOption");
option.AddProperty(K);
option.AddProperty(r);
option.AddProperty(T);
option.AddProperty(S);
option.AddProperty(U);
option.AddProperty(b);
```

The XML output is:

```
<?xml version="1.0" encoding="UTF-8"?>
<EuropeanOption>
  <StrikePrice>150</StrikePrice>
  <InterestRate>0.06</InterestRate>
  <Expiry>1</Expiry>
  <Stock>120</Stock>
  <UnderlyingAsset>134.2</UnderlyingAsset>
  <CostOfCarry>12</CostOfCarry>
</EuropeanOption>
```

The question of course is: How did we do this? We answer this question in section 27.5.1 where we apply the Visitor pattern (see Chapter 25 of this book and the definitive GOF (Gamma *et al.*, 1995)).

To avoid any misunderstandings, we define the scope of the XML readers and writers and the things to watch out for. The features are:

- We support entities consisting of properties. There is no support for nested entities (portfolios, straddles and so on) or nested properties.
- Names of entities and properties should not contain blank spaces or funny characters (such as @, # and so on)
- The classes for reading and writing XML data are templated with two underlying data types, for example `Entity <Name, Value>` where `Name` is a type that can be converted to a string and `Value` is of type `double` or `string`.

In later exercises and chapters we shall discuss how to extend this setup to more complex applications. We first of all wish to get it working and not shower the reader with loads of 'grunge' C++ code.

The interface for `EntityThing` is:

```
template <class N, class V> class EntityThing
{ // N == Name field, V == Value field
private:
public:
  EntityThing();
  EntityThing(const N& t);
```

```
EntityThing(const EntityThing<N,V>& source);
EntityThing<N,V>& operator = (const EntityThing<N,V>& source);
virtual ~EntityThing();

// Member data modelled as a property and a property set
Property<N, V> name;                    // Entity ID
SimplePropertySet<N, V> properties; // Entity properties

// Add property and property set to Entity
virtual void AddProperty(const Property<N, V>& prop);
virtual void AddProperty(const SimplePropertySet<N, V>& pset);
virtual EntityThing<N,V>* Clone() const = 0;  // Prototype copy

// Design patterns extensions (Visitor)
virtual void accept(EntityVisitor<N,V>& visitor) = 0;
};
```

The interface for `Entity` is:

```
template <class N, class V> class Entity : public
EntityThing<N,V>
{
private:
public:
  // Constructors and destructor
  Entity();
  Entity(const N& ename);
  Entity(const Entity<N,V>& source);
  virtual ~Entity();

  // Copy on heap (Prototype pattern)
  virtual EntityThing<N,V>* Clone() const;
  // Assignment operator
  Entity<N,V>& operator = (const Entity<N,V>& source);
  // Design patterns extensions (for Visitor)
  void accept(EntityVisitor<N,V>& visitor);
};
```

27.5.1 XML readers and writers

Our entity class has no provision for writing its contents to an XML document nor can its instances be created from an XML document. We do not wish to embed XML-specific

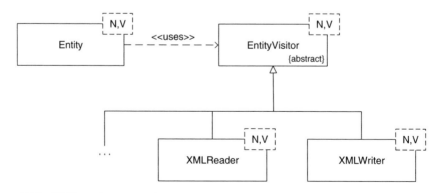

Figure 27.3 XML readers and writers

code in this class because it makes the class less portable and not every customer wishes to have XML functionality. We extend the functionality by creating Visitor classes as shown in Figure 27.3. XMLWriter creates an XML document for an entity while XMLReader creates an entity from an XML document. We concentrate on XMLWriter (the structure of XMLReader being similar). The interface is:

```
template <class N, class V> class XMLWriter : public
EntityVisitor<N,V>
{
private:
  // Member data. Microsoft-specific stuff. See CD for details
  // Private Visit functions.
  virtual void visit(Property<N, V>& property);
  virtual void visit(SimplePropertySet<N, V>& pset);

public:
  // Constructor and destructor.
  XMLWriter();
  virtual ~XMLWriter();

  // The visit() does the real work
  virtual void visit(Entity<N,V>& entity);

  void Save(const string& name);                 // Saves nodes to file.
  string ToString();                             // Write to string.
};
```

Notice that clients can only write entities, and not properties or property sets, to XML. This is a design decision and it keeps things understandable. In general, the detailed work is done in visit(Property<N,V>&) while we use the *double dispatch* mechanism (see Gamma *et al.*, 1995) for property sets:

```
template <class N, class V>
  void XMLWriter<N,V>::visit(SimplePropertySet<N, V>& pset)
  {
    pset.accept(*this);
  }
```

Finally, the code for writing an entity is:

```
template <class N, class V>
  void XMLWriter<N,V>::visit(Entity<N,V>& entity)
  { // Write an entity to XML document
    // 1. Write name as the root of the XML document
    // 2. Write property set

    // Create root element, This is the name of the Entity
  try
  {
    // Create root.
    string N = entity.name.name();
    _bstr_t root = N.c_str();
    pRoot = m_pXMLDoc->createElement( root );

    // Add root to document element.
    m_pXMLDoc->appendChild( pRoot );

  }
```

```
catch( _com_error & error )
{
  bstr_t description = error.Description();
  throw string(description);
}

visit(entity.properties); // Call visit of entity's props
}
```

The reader can consult the CD for the complete source code.

27.5.2   Examples and applications

Using the Visitor classes for reading and writing XML documents is very easy because all low-level code has been hidden in constructors and `visit()` functions. Let us take an example of creating an entity that contains the attributes of an option, writing the entity to XML and then reading the file back in. We take the entity that we already created in this section. It only remains to show how to use the visitors:

```
XMLWriter<string, double> xmlW;
xmlW.visit(option);
xmlW.Save ("Option.xml");

// Now read the file back in
XMLReader<string, double> xmlR;
xmlR.Load("Option.xml");
Entity<string, double> option2;
xmlR.visit(option2);

SimplePropertySet<string, double> optionParams = option2.properties;
// Iterate over the result and print the values
SimplePropertySet<string,double>::const_iterator it;
cout << "\nDump the parameters, call prices ... \n";
for (it = optionParams.Begin(); it!=optionParams.End(); it++)
{
  cout << (*it).name() << ", " << (*it)() << endl;
}
```

The output from this code is:

```
Dump the parameters, call prices ...
StrikePrice, 150
InterestRate, 0.06
Expiry, 1
Stock, 120
UnderlyingAsset, 134.2
CostOfCarry, 12
```

27.6   XML STRUCTURES FOR PLAIN AND BARRIER OPTIONS

The first part of this section is an introduction to plain and barrier options and may be skipped if you are already familiar with the subject.

An option is a so-called financial derivative (see Hull, 2000). There are two types of option: first, a call option gives the holder the right to buy the underlying asset by a certain date for a certain price. A put option gives the holder the right to sell the underlying asset by a certain date for a certain price. The price in the contract is called the strike price or exercise price. The date in the contract is known as the expiry date, maturity or exercise date. American options can be exercised at any time up to maturity while European options can only be exercised at maturity.

There are two sides to every option contract. First, there is the investor who has taken the long position, by which we mean that he or she has bought the option, while on the other side we have the investor who has taken the short position, that is the person who has sold or written the contract. The writer of the option receives cash up-front but has potential liabilities later. To this end, we define the payoff as the amount of money to be made at maturity. In principle, the payoff is between zero and plus infinity for the long position while it is potentially minus infinity for the short position. This means that the writer is exposed.

The above option types are called plain or vanilla options. This is in contrast to so-called exotic options where the payoff is somewhat more complicated. Exotic options are designed to suit particular needs in the market. For example, barrier options are options where the payoff depends on whether the underlying asset's price reaches a certain level during a certain period of time before the expiry date (Haug, 1998). Barrier options are the most popular of the exotic options. There are two kinds of barrier that are defined as a particular value of the underlying asset (whose value we denote by H):

- *In barrier*: This is reached when the asset price S hits the barrier H before maturity. In other words, if S never hits H before maturity, then the payout is zero.
- *Out barrier*: This is similar to a plain option except that the option is knocked out or becomes worthless if the asset price S hits the barrier H before expiration.

Furthermore, there are four variations on each of these two main categories; for in barrier options they are:

Down-and-in call (knockin) option
Up-and-in call option
Down-and-in put option
Up-and-in put option

For out barriers the combinations are:

Down-and-out (knockout) call option
Up-and-out call option
Down-and-out put option
Up-and-out put option

We would like to model both plain and barrier options using XML. Of course, FpML has a number of structures for these option types but you can create your own XML documents that you can use in your own specific applications. For example, we have used XML in the Datasim Option Calculator Program as the communication channel between the User Interface (written in C#) and the C++ number-crunching code. In this way we have the best of both worlds, namely C# is very good for creating dialog boxes and input screens while C++ is the language of choice for numerical analysis in our opinion. In the examples to date we implicitly assumed that tag values were of `double` types. We can extend the code to add type information to an element, for example:

```
<?xml version="1.0" encoding="UTF-8" ?>
  <!-European Call Options -- >
  <EuropeanCallOption type="propertySet">
    <Name type="string">EuropeanCallOption</Name>
    <T type="double">1</T>
    <K type="double">15</K>
    <sigma type="double">0.01</sigma>
    <r type="double">0.15</r>
    <Dividend type="double">0.03</Dividend>
    <S type="double">20</S>
  </EuropeanCallOption>
```

Furthermore, we can include dividends, rebates and boundary conditions in barrier options:

```
  <DoubleBarrierCallOption type="propertySet">
    <Name type="string">DoubleBarrierCallOption</Name>
    <T type="double">1</T>
    <K type="double">15</K>
    <sigma type="double">0.01</sigma>
    <r type="double">0.15</r>
    <Dividend type="double">0.03</Dividend>
    <RebateLeft type="double">10</RebateLeft>
    <RebateRight type="double">20</RebateRight>
    <UpAndOutBarrier
type="double">20</UpAndOutBarrier>
    <DownAndOutBarrier
type="double">10</DownAndOutBarrier>
  </DoubleBarrierCallOption>

  <SingleBarrierCallOptionUpAndOut type="propertySet">
    <Name
type="string">SingleBarrierCallOptionUpAndOut</Name>
    <T type="double">1</T>
    <K type="double">15</K>
    <sigma type="double">0.01</sigma>
    <r type="double">0.15</r>
    <Dividend type="double">0.03</Dividend>
    <RebateRight type="double">20</RebateRight>
      <UpAndOutBarrier
type="double">20</UpAndOutBarrier>
  </SingleBarrierCallOptionUpAndOut>

  <SingleBarrierPutOptionDownAndOut type="propertySet">
    <Name
type="string">SingleBarrierPutOptionDownAndOut</Name>
    <T type="double">1</T>
    <K type="double">15</K>
    <sigma type="double">0.01</sigma>
    <r type="double">0.15</r>
    <Dividend type="double">0.03</Dividend>
    <RebateLeft type="double">10</RebateLeft>
    <DownAndOutBarrier
type="double">10</DownAndOutBarrier>
    <S type="double">20</S>
```

```
  </SingleBarrierPutOptionDownAndOut>

  <SingleBarrierPutOptionUpAndOut type="propertySet">
    <Name
type="string">SingleBarrierPutOptionUpAndOut</Name>
    <T type="double">1</T>
    <K type="double">15</K>
    <sigma type="double">0.01</sigma>
    <r type="double">0.15</r>
    <Dividend type="double">0.03</Dividend>
    <RebateRight type="double">20</RebateRight>
    <UpAndOutBarrier
type="double">20</UpAndOutBarrier>
  </SingleBarrierPutOptionUpAndOut>
```

To this end, we need to extend the code that adds a node in DOM to the XML document. In this case we create a method we create an element having a value and a given attribute called 'type'.

```
// Add new element to current parent. Code taken out of a larger context
void XmlWriter::AddElement(string key, variant_t& value, string& type )
{
  // Create element.
  RemoveIllegalChars(key);
  _bstr_t bstrKey = key.c_str();
  MSXML2::IXMLDOMElementPtr pEelem=doc->createElement(bstrKey );
  // Set type attribute.
  _bstr_t bstrType = type.c_str();
  pElem->setAttribute( _T("type"), bstrType );

  // Set value.
  value.ChangeType(VT_BSTR);
  pElem->nodeTypedValue = value;
  // Add to current node.
  m_pCurrentParent->appendChild( pNewElement );
}
```

The possibilities are endless. You can customise the code to suit your own specific needs.

27.7   CONCLUSIONS AND SUMMARY

We have looked at XML from the viewpoint of the developer in this chapter. In particular, we discussed the Visitor classes XMLWriter and XMLReader that write and read XML documents, respectively. The code in these classes uses low-level XML interfaces from an XML parser but the developer does not have to worry about the gory details. Instead, he or she calls well-known Visitor functions to read and write XML data. We also gave an introduction to XML Schema and its applications to FpML. DTDs will disappear from the scene in time and we thought that the inclusion of XML Schema would be a good addition. Finally, since XML Schema uses the same syntax as XML it is possible to use XMLWriter and XMLReader to write and read XML Schema documents. This is a big bonus. It means that we can operate at class or meta level in our applications.

Interfacing C++ and Excel

28.1   INTRODUCTION AND OBJECTIVES

In this chapter we introduce a number of design principles to help to improve the flexibility of our financial engineering applications. First, we define C++ classes that interface to the extremely popular spreadsheet program Microsoft Excel. We create an environment that allows us to use Excel as an input dialog to our applications and as well as functionality to display the results of calculations in the form of cells, charts and line charts. Since Excel is very popular in the financial world we hope that the reader will find this chapter useful. We discuss the essentials of the technicalities of the two-way interface between C++ and Excel.

The main topics of concern in this chapter are:

- The object model in Excel
- Accessing Excel objects from C++
- Getting data into C++ from Excel
- Display vector and matrix data in Excel
- Displaying functions in Excel.

The software has been written in such a way that developers can use it without having to worry about low-level C++ code. Unfortunately, a lot of the low-level interfacing to Excel is not well documented.

28.2   OBJECT MODEL IN EXCEL: AN OVERVIEW

We examine Excel from a programmer's point of view in this section and, in particular, we discuss those Excel objects that are of direct relevance to us in our projects to integrate Excel with our financial engineering applications. Of course, the focus is on C++ interoperability in this book and to this end we shall access Excel by means of COM interfaces. What we access is described in the Excel object model, a part of which we show in Figure 28.1. A *workbook* is a file in which we work and where we store data. A *worksheet* is used to list and analyse data. A *chart* displays data from a worksheet in some form, for example as a line chart, bar chart, pie chart or surface chart. A workbook consists of a number of worksheets and charts. (It is possible to embed a chart in a worksheet but we shall not discuss this feature here.) Each sheet has a so-called sheet tab that appears on tabs at the bottom of the workbook window.

A *cell* is an atomic entity in Excel and is a placeholder for data. We address a cell giving its row and column position in a worksheet. In general, a worksheet consists of cells. A *range* is a collection of cells. A range can be a one-dimensional array or a two-dimensional array. Finally, we remark that an Excel application may contain several workbooks.

We shall show in the rest of this chapter how to create and access these objects from our C++ code. To this end, we encapsulate the implementation of the COM interfaces for

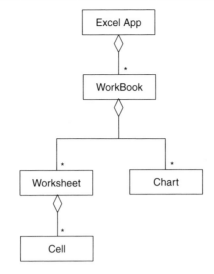

Figure 28.1   UML model for Excel

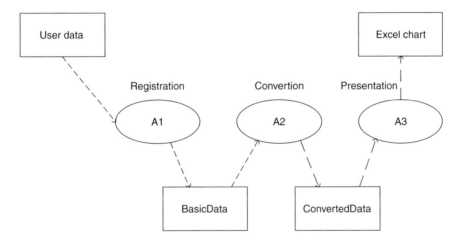

Figure 28.2   Information flow in Excel applications

Excel in a class that clients can use without having to learn low-level functions. In general, we are interested in using Excel as a tool where we can enter data into our applications and where the calculated results can be displayed. This core process is realised by a number of activities as shown in the UML activity diagram in Figure 28.2. Each activity has well-defined input and output data. The activity 'Registration (A1)' converts raw data from some external data source to an internal format that our application can understand. Examples of sources and their formats are:

- Command line
- Dialog box
- XML document
- Excel itself (this is the subject of Chapter 29).

Examples of `BasicData` from A1 are:

- Properties
- Vectors
- Matrices and numeric matrices.

The second activity 'Conversion (A2)' is responsible for coupling `BasicData` with some algorithm or function that calculates some kind of data set such as:

- Vectors
- Lists of vectors
- Lists of two-dimensional points.

Finally, activity 'Presentation (A3)' transforms and formats `ConvertedData` to a form that allows us to display it in Excel. We are interested in the following cases:

- Line diagrams for equally spaced data
- Scatter (smoothed) diagrams for unequally spaced data
- 3D surface diagrams.

In particular, the objects and activities are a fertile ground for an application of the Gamma design patterns (see Gamma *et al.*, 1995). In this chapter, however, we consider a simpler case:

- We use the `iostream` for `Registration` (data input)
- We use Excel cells for `Registration` (data input) (see Chapter 29)
- We use C function pointers whose values in a certain range will be displayed in a chart
- We develop a (medium) reusable class `ExcelDriver`.

The `ExcelDriver` class will be used in activity A3, as we shall see in the coming sections.

28.3 UNDER THE BONNET: TECHNICAL DETAILS OF C++ INTERFACING TO EXCEL

Before we discuss the details of Figure 28.2 and how we have programmed activities and objects we give an introduction to some low-level and fundamental code that we need in later sections.

28.3.1 Startup

We describe the 'life cycle' of the Excel application by a number of activities:

1. Initialise COM (otherwise we cannot start Excel)
2. Create an instance of the Excel application
3. Optional: you can make Excel visible or invisible at start up time
4. Make a workbook the (current) active workbook
5. Access a given worksheet in a workbook
6. Rename a worksheet.

In the `ExcelDriver` class the following steps are executed in its default constructor by the following code:

```
try
{
  // Initialise COM Runtime Libraries.
  CoInitialise(NULL);
  // Start Excel application.
  xl.CreateInstance(L"Excel.Application");
  xl->Workbooks->Add(Excel::xlWorksheet);

  // Rename "Sheet1" to "Chart Data".
  Excel::_WorkbookPtr pWorkbook = xl->ActiveWorkbook;
  Excel::_WorksheetPtr pSheet=pWorkbook->Worksheets->GetItem("Sheet1");
  pSheet->Name = "Chart Data";
}
catch( _com_error & error )
{
  ThrowAsString(error);
}
```

Furthermore, we can toggle Excel to be visible or invisible by calling the function:

```
void ExcelDriver::MakeVisible( bool b = true )
{
  // Make excel visible.
  xl->Visible = b ? VARIANT_TRUE : VARIANT_FALSE;
}
```

We have thus encapsulated several low-level functions in the default constructor. We use it as follows:

```
ExcelDriver excel;
```

This ensures that Excel is created and initialised properly. Furthermore, it is invisible by default.

28.3.2   Creating charts and cell values

Having completed the first round, we must discuss a number of other features that we will need later, namely:

- Getting data into cells (writing)
- Getting data out of cells (reading)
- Defining the titles of axes and charts
- Creating charts and adding them to a workbook.

Most of the code for these features can be found on the accompanying CD. An important function is for creating a chart. Its function prototype is:

```
void CreateChart(
    const Vector<double, int>& x,
    const list<string>& labels,
    const list<Vector<double, int> > &
```

```
vectorList,
  const std::string& chartTitle,
  const std::string& xTitle = "X",
  const std::string& yTitle = "Y")
```

In general terms, this function creates a line chart whose input values in the vector 'x'; this corresponds to the abscissa values. The variable 'labels' are the string values for the output values while 'vectorList' is the desired output. It is a list of vector values. It is also possible to create a chart using a matrix using row and column labels, as the following function prototype shows:

```
void AddMatrix(
    string name,
    const NumericMatrix<double, int> & matrix,
    const list<string> & rowLabels,
    const list<string> & columnLabels)
```

28.3.3   Interoperability with the SimplePropertySet

It would be useful if we could produce code to let properties interface with Excel in both directions. Why should we wish to do that? First, properties have both string names and values and they can be imported into Excel, thus preserving the semantics of the applications. For example, all the properties of an option

r, 0.6 T, 1 K, 120.0   sigma, 0.2

can be imported into Excel cells in a form that is understandable to the user of that application. In a near future, we could envisage XML data (for example, the schemas in FpML) being exchanged in a similar way. The function prototypes for Property to Excel (and back) interfacing are:

```
void AddPropertySet(const SimplePropertySet<string, double>& pset)
void GetPropertySet(SimplePropertySet<string, double> & pset)
```

We include the source code for AddPropertySet() to show how to use the low-level C++ functionality in Excel:

```
void AddPropertySet(const SimplePropertySet<string, double> & pset)
{
  // Add sheet.
  Excel::_WorkbookPtr pWorkbook = xl->ActiveWorkbook;
  Excel::_WorksheetPtr pSheet = pWorkbook->Worksheets->Add();
  pSheet->Name = L"Input";

  // Add properties to cells.
  Excel::RangePtr pRange = pSheet->Cells;
  long row = 1;
  for(SimplePropertySet<string, double>::const_iterator
  it = pset.Begin(); it != pset.End(); ++it, row++)
  {
    // Set name and value.
    pRange->Item[row][(long)1] = it->name().c_str();
    pRange->Item[row][(long)2] = (*it) ();
  }
}
```

In this piece of code we first of all add a worksheet to the current active workbook because it is on this sheet that the values from the property set instance will be placed. In particular, we access all the cells in the worksheet but we start at the first row in the sheet and iterate in the property set, thereby calling the range Item() function twice, first for the name of the current property in the set and then for its value.

We now give the source code that shows how to extract a property set from an Excel sheet.

```
void GetPropertySet(SimplePropertySet<string, double> & pset)
{ // NOTE: THERE ARE SOME MAGIC NUMBERS AND HARD-WIRED CODE HERE
  // Get input sheet.
  Excel::_WorkbookPtr pWorkbook = xl->ActiveWorkbook;
  Excel::_WorksheetPtr pSheet=pWorkbook->Worksheets->GetItem("Input");

  // Get values from cells as long as there are no BLANKS
  Excel::RangePtr pRange = pSheet->Cells;
  long row = 1;
  while(true)
  {
    // Get name from first column.
    _bstr_t bstrName = pRange->Item[row][1];
    string name = bstrName;
    if( name != "" )
    {
      // Get value from second column.
      double value = (double)pRange->Item[row][2];
      pset.set(name, value);
    }
    else
    {
      break;
    }
    row++;
  }
}
```

Finally, when an ExcelDriver goes out of scope its destructor is automatically called of course and COM is shut down:

```
  virtual ~ExcelDriver()
  {
    CoUninitialise();
  }
```

This function ensures that all dangling pointers are cleaned up.

28.4   IMPLEMENTING THE CORE PROCESS

We now take a very special case to show how the ExcelDriver class can be used in an application. In this particular case, we display the graphs of the Gaussian (normal) pdf and cdf on a given interval $[A, B]$. We employ a smooth (scatter graph) by sub-dividing the interval into N pieces.

To this end, we create a `main()` program containing the three functions:

- `Registration()`: Get the values A, B and N
- `Conversion()`: Create two vectors for the `pdf` and `cdf` functions
- `Presentation()`: Display the functions as charts in Excel.

We now discuss the details of each of these functions and we give a test program to show how to tie them in together.

28.4.1 Registration: Getting basic input

This function is responsible for getting the interval of interest (lower value A and upper value B) and the number of sub-divisions N of that interval. We use the standard `iostream` to get these values:

```
void Registration(double& A, double& B, int& N)
{
  // Version 0.01, lots of opportunity for improvement
  cout << "Give lower value of interval: ";
  cin >> A;
  cout << "Give upper value of interval: ";
  cin >> B;
  cout << "Give number of subdivisions:  ";
  cin >> N;
}
```

Of course, this function is very simple and real-life applications would be much more complex. For example, we would use Graphical User Interfaces (GUI) or even XML documents to get data into the application.

28.4.2 Calculations

We are interested in plotting the values of the Gaussian pdf and cdf functions in Excel. To this end, we create an array of x values and we then calculate the values of the above functions at each of the abscissae values and place the results in another array. Recall the Gaussian functions:

```
double n(double x)
{
  double A = 1.0/sqrt(2.0 * 3.1415);
  return A * exp(-x*x*0.5);
}

double _N(double x)
{
  double a1 = 0.4361836;
  double a2 = -0.1201676;
  double a3 = 0.9372980;

  double k = 1.0/(1.0 + (0.33267 * x));

  if (x >= 0.0)
  {
    return 1.0 - n(x) * (a1*k + (a2*k*k) + (a3*k*k*k));
```

```
  }
  else
  {
    return 1.0 - _N(-x);
  }
}
```

We now use these two functions in the following function that produces two arrays n_result and N_result:

```
void Conversion(double& A, double& B, int& N,
      Vector<double, int> & x,
      Vector<double, int> & n_result,
      Vector<double, int> & N_result)
{
  // Step size.
  double h = (B-A)/N;
  // Calculate input values and call functions.
  double current = A;
  for (int i = x.MinIndex(); i <= x.MaxIndex(); i++)
  {
    // Call functions and set values in vectors.
    x[i] = current;
    n_result[i] = n(current);
    N_result[i] = _N(current);

    // Calculate next value.
    current += h;
  }
}
```

28.4.3 Displaying the results of the calculations

We have now done all the necessary calculations, namely the array of abscissa values and the arrays of functions values. These are now used in code to produce the Excel charts.

```
void Presentation(const Vector<double, int> & x,
    const Vector<double, int> & n_result,
    const Vector<double, int> & N_result)
{
  // Excel is invisible initially.
  cout << "Creating Excel output, please wait a moment...";

  // Create and initialise Excel.
  ExcelDriver & excel = ExcelDriver::Instance();
  excel.MakeVisible(true); // Default is INVISIBLE!

  // Create list with the Gaussian pdf and cdf functions
  list<Vector<double, int> > functions;
  list<string> labels;
  functions.push_back(n_result);
  functions.push_back(N_result);
  labels.push_back("pdf");
  labels.push_back("cdf");

  // Display both cdf and pdf function in one chart
  excel.CreateChart(x, labels, functions, "Combined Functions");
```

```
  // Create other charts
  excel.CreateChart(x, n_result, "n", "X", "Y");
  excel.CreateChart(x, N_result, "N (integrated)");
}
```

This code should give you insights into how to present arrays information in Excel in chart form. You can generalise it to other applications.

28.4.4 The application (main program)

This is the easy part of the code as it entails calling the three core functions in succession.

```
int main()
{
  double A, B;
  int N;

  // Run Registration activity.
  Registration(A, B, N);

  cout << "A etc " << A << ", " << B << ", " << N << endl;

  // Create vectors.
  Vector<double, int> x(N+1);
  Vector<double, int> n_result(N+1);
  Vector<double, int> N_result(N+1);

  // Run Conversion activity.
  Conversion(A, B, N, x, n_result, N_result);

  // Run Presentation activity.
  Presentation(x, n_result, N_result);

  return 0;
}
```

28.5 EXTENSIONS

In this chapter we have used the standard `iostream` as the mechanism for data entry. Another interesting possibility is to use Excel itself! We shall not deal with this at any great length but we take an example that shows how the variables in section 28.4.1 can be initialised using cells. To this end, we create a registration function based on Excel:

```
void Registration(SimplePropertySet<string, double> & input)
{
  try
  {
    ExcelDriver & excel = ExcelDriver::Instance();

    // Add property set.
    excel.AddPropertySet(input);
    excel.MakeVisible();

    // Wait...
    cout << "Enter values in Excel spreadsheet." << endl;
    string abc;
    cin >> abc;

    // Get property set.
```

```
    excel.GetPropertySet(input);
  }
  catch( string & error )
  {
    cout << error << endl;
  }
}
```

Notice that the return value is a property set instance and this is an improvement on the hard-wired variables *A*, *B* and *N* in section 28.4.1.

The `Conversion` function based on the new `Registration` function uses the methods in `Property` to extract the raw data:

```
// Get values from input.
double A = input.value("A")();
double B = input.value("B")();
int N = (int) input.value("N")();
```

28.6   APPLICATION AREAS

The code in this chapter can be used, extended and generalised to applications whose results need to be displaced in numerical or graphical form. In this book, we are interested in displaying the numerical solutions of the following kinds of scalar differential equations:

• Ordinary and stochastic differential equations
• Boundary value problems
• One-factor Black–Scholes equation
• Multi-factor Black–Scholes equation.

Other applications are:

• Displaying function values and their derivatives (using divided differences)
• As a storage mechanism for vectors and matrices (a simple database)
• As a front-end and back-end to the Datasim Option Calculator application.

Excel is equipped to deal with this challenge. We must take care to determine how we wish to present the data, how the titles of charts and the names of their axes are initialised, and so on. Chapter 29 deals with this design issue.

28.7   CONCLUSIONS AND SUMMARY

We have given an introduction to the COM programming interface in Excel. In particular, we have shown how to display array and matrix information in Excel charts. The class `ExcelDriver` encapsulates much of the functionality needed for your development work and we have shown how it can be used by taking a simple example: displaying the graph of the normal distribution function and cumulative distribution functions in Excel charts.

We have included appropriate C++ code in this chapter to show how things work. You can study this code and modify it to you own needs. In Chapter 29 we give some examples of what we mean by this statement.

29

Advanced Excel Interfacing

(Daniel Duffy and Robert Demming)

29.1 INTRODUCTION AND OBJECTIVES

In this chapter we discuss how we can use Excel's input mechanisms in combination with its *Add-In* facility. An add-in corresponds to functionality that you can use to manipulate and access the data in Excel sheets. The main objective is to show you how to create new functions in C++ and integrate them with Excel by converting them to add-ins. We take the `ArrayMechanism` package as a test case and extrapolate to show how to apply the knowledge to your own specific situation. This chapter does not explain how to analyse, design and implement medium and large-sized applications. Such topics have been dealt with in Duffy (2004a) but are unfortunately beyond the scope of this chapter.

We have written this chapter in a 'how-do' fashion and is a step-by-step account of getting C++ applications and Excel to talk to each other.

The devil is in the details. You can use this chapter to write your own Excel add-ins.

29.2 STATUS REPORT AND NEW REQUIREMENTS

When embarking on a C++/Excel project we must realise that there is very little documentation and very few worked examples. We must then resort to our investigative skills and a lot of dogged persistence to find out how it all works. Excel has a so-called object model (again, not very well documented in C++ but well documented for Visual Basic) that can be accessed via COM interfaces. In general, the author and colleagues have fathomed the Excel COM depths and have encapsulated specific functionality in easy to use classes. In fact, we have seen several examples of this encapsulation process in Chapter 28.

We focus on using C++ to create Add-Ins and we try to avoid discussing Visual Basic and VBA. This is not to say that we do not find them interesting or that they should not be used in real-life applications, but they are outside the scope of this book. The main requirements for us in this chapter are:

- *Interoperability*: The add-ins should work seamlessly with Excel and with the C++ classes that we have described in this book. In particular, it is important that the add-ins can interoperate with the classes `Array`, `AssociativeArray`, `Matrix`, `AssociativeMatrix` and the Property pattern. Ideally, communication should be in both directions. In future versions we see XML and Excel interoperability as a business opportunity.
- *Usability*: The developer should not have to worry about the fine details of COM or nasty little details of interfacing.
- *Efficiency*: The add-ins should perform almost as well as native C++ applications.

29.3   A GENTLE INTRODUCTION TO EXCEL ADD-INS

An Add-In is a piece of functionality that is written in some programming language and uses the input and output facilities of Excel. We concentrate on the functionality that the various options offer, in which languages they can and cannot be written, and a short note on the limitations of each option.

29.3.1   What kinds of add-ins are there?

There are four main options that allow us to create Excel add-ins.

XLL add-ins

These are the oldest form of add-in. These are written in C using the Microsoft XLL API and are compiled to a DLL library having the extension `.xll`. They can be used to create Excel worksheet functions or functions that we call by means of a menu.

The main advantage of XLL is that it is fast and works with all versions of Excel from Excel 95. The main disadvantage is that development work has ceased. Do not expect XLL to move with the times.

XLL add-ins are managed from the `Tools/Add-ins` menu in the Excel user interface.

XLA add-ins

This option is based on the Visual Basic for Applications (VBA) development environment from the time of Excel 97. We must use VBA to write these add-ins. In essence, an XLA add-in is just a workbook with VBA code that we save with the `.xla` file extension. They can be used to create Excel worksheet functions or functions that we call by means of a menu.

It is possible to protect your code (from Excel 2000!) by using a password, but it is fairly easy to crack (especially, if you really want to crack it!). A major disadvantage is that the code is interpreted (instead of compiled) and hence we shall expect performance degradation in practice.

XLA add-ins are managed from the `Tools/Add-ins` menu in the Excel user interface.

COM add-ins

These have been available since Excel 2000 and are based on a generic COM interface for add-ins. This interface is used by all Office Products as well as Visual Studio and VBA development environments.

On a technical level, we say that COM add-ins must implement the `IDTExtensibility2` COM interface. The most important methods that you implement are:

- *OnConnection event*: This is called when you load an add-in. The add-in initialises itself and a menu item is loaded in the host application. The event has an argument that is the object reference to the host application. You can query the type of this object (for example, Excel or Word) and adjust your add-in behaviour accordingly.
- *OnDisconnection event*: This is called when the add-in is being unloaded. The add-in uninitialises itself and this includes removing installed menu items, for example.

Some other points should be noted. First, the COM add-in must also register itself in the registry for each host application that it supports. This allows the host application to find it. Second, when loading we can specify the desired load behaviour. This means that a COM add-in can be loaded when the host application is loaded or only when it is needed (*on-demand loading*).

When using VB or VBA there exists a so-called add-in designer that makes life easier for the programmer. It takes care of registration and other housekeeping chores.

A feature of COM add-ins is that they cannot be used to create Excel worksheet functions directly. If you wish to do this, you must call the COM add-in function through an XLA add-in worksheet function.

COM add-ins cannot be found in the **Tools/Add-ins** menu. Instead you have to manually add the **COM Add-ins** button to the toolbar using the **Tools/Customise** menu.

Automation add-ins

This is an advanced option and has been available since the introduction of Excel XP. This option uses COM objects whose public functions can be used as worksheet functions. Menus are not supported. An automation add-in is always loaded on demand.

Automation add-ins are managed from the **Tools/Add-ins** menu in the Excel user interface.

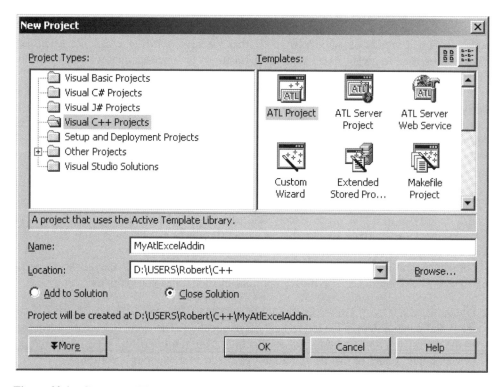

Figure 29.1 Create an ATL project

29.4   AUTOMATION ADD-IN IN DETAIL

We start with an Automation add-in. An Automation add-in can be any COM object with an **IDispatch** interface and we can easily create such an object with the aid of the ATL wizard in Visual Studio .NET.

In Visual Studio create a new C++ project, select an **ATL Project** as project type and give it the name **MyAtlExcelAddin**. See Figure 29.1.

In the **ATL Project Wizard** screen, select **Application Settings** and de-select the **Attributed** checkbox. See Figure 29.2.

The **Attributed** option is new in Visual Studio .NET. It uses attributes instead of macros and IDL to help you to create COM objects from C++ classes. The code for registering the COM object is replaced by attributes. If we create a COM add-in we must make additional changes to the registry when registering the add-in. Since we cannot change the registration code in the attributed version, we must deselect this option so that normal register functions are generated.

When you create the project you will see that a workspace **MyAtlExcelAddin** is created with a **MyAtlExcelAddin** project in which we write our code and a **MyAtl-ExcelAddinps** project that generates Proxy/Stub dlls.

In the **MyAtlExcelAddin** project we must add our COM/Automation object. Do this by right mouse clicking on the **MyAtlExcelAddin** project and selecting **Add Class**. In the following dialog box select **ATL Simple Object**. See Figure 29.3.

In the next dialog box type in the short name **MyExcelFunctions**. All the other fields will be filled automatically. See Figure 29.4.

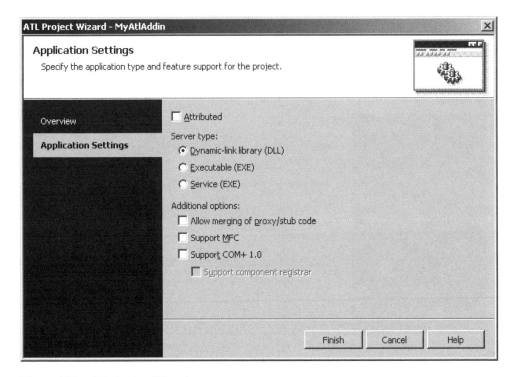

Figure 29.2   ATL Project Wizard

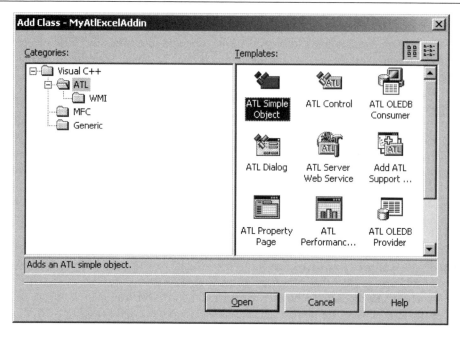

Figure 29.3   Add a ATL Simple Object

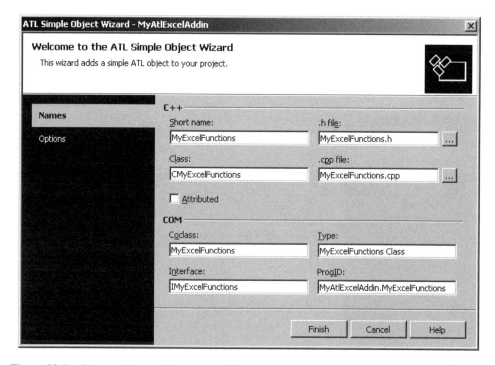

Figure 29.4   Create a MyExcelFunctions COM object

After selecting **Finish** the wizard will create a COM object with a dual interface. This is an interface that supports the **IDispatch** interface that is required for Automation add-ins.

Now we can add an Excel worksheet function to our Automation object. Do this by right clicking on the **IMyExcelFunctions** interface in the class view and selecting **Add Method**. First we create a function that always returns the same value, in this case PI. Enter **MyPI** as method name and add a **MyPIArg** parameter of the type **DOUBLE*** as **retval** type. See Figure 29.5.

The wizard now adds the function to the interface in the .IDL file and will also add an empty implementation to the **CMyExcelFunctions** class. Implement the **MyPI()** function in the following way:

```
STDMETHODIMP CMyExcelFunctions::MyPI(DOUBLE* MyPIArg)
{
  // Return the value PI
  *MyPIArg=3.14;

  // No errors
  return S_OK;
}
```

Now we can use this function in Excel. First we must add the Automation add-in to Excel. On the **Tools** menu select **Add-ins**. In the **Add-ins** dialog box select the **Automation** button. In the list of Automation objects you should select the Automation object we just created. It is shown under the name we entered in the **Type** textbox when we added the **ATL Simple Object**. In this case it was **MyExcelFunctions Class**. See Figure 29.6.

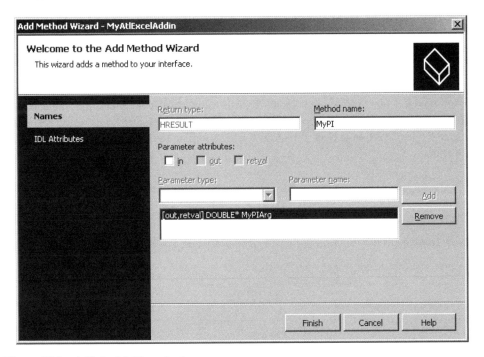

Figure 29.5 Add the MyPI method

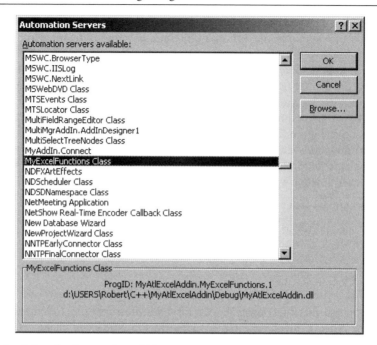

Figure 29.6   Select the Automation add-in

We can now use the Automation add-in functions on the worksheet. Select a cell in which to use the function and select **Insert Function**. In the **Insert Function** dialog box select the **MyAtlExcelAddin.MyExcelFunctions** category. Now you can select the **MyPI()** function. See Figure 29.7. Now the value of PI will be shown in the selected cell.

29.4.1   Functions with two parameters

We now extend our Automation add-in with a function that subtracts the value of one cell from the value of another cell. On the **IMyExcelFunctions** interface, right click and select **Add method**. Create a function called **MySubtract** with the following parameters:

```
[in] DOUBLE* arg1
[in] DOUBLE* arg2
[out, retval] DOUBLE* result
```

This is also shown in Figure 29.8.

Now implement the function in the **CMyExcelFunctions** class in the following way:

```
STDMETHODIMP CMyExcelFunctions::MySubtract(DOUBLE* arg1,
    DOUBLE* arg2, DOUBLE* result)
{
  // Subtract two values
  *result=*arg1-*arg2;

  return S_OK;
}
```

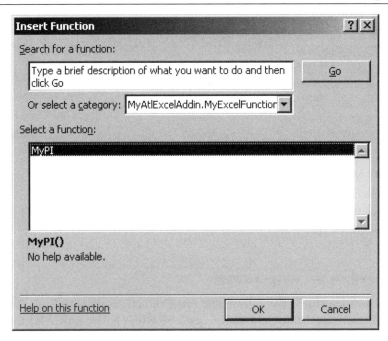

Figure 29.7   Select the MyPI() function

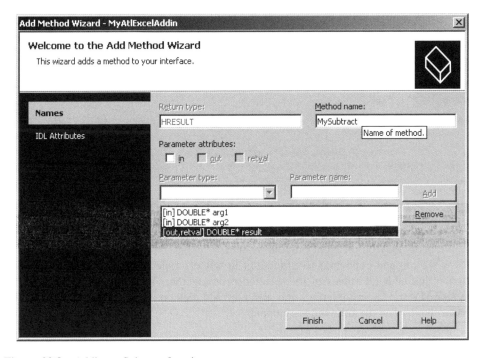

Figure 29.8   Adding a Subtract function

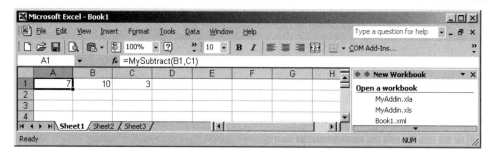

Figure 29.9   My subtract function in action

The result of this function is shown in Figure 29.9. Here the value of cell A1 is the value of cell B1 minus C1.

29.4.2   Functions that accept a range

Creating a function that accepts a variable range of cells is more difficult than working with cells. In this case the function must accept a VARIANT. The VARIANT then contains an Excel range object. To use the Excel objects we have to import the Excel/Office COM libraries. To import the COM libraries of Excel XP/2002 add the following lines of code to the `stdafx.h` file below the `#include` statements (each import must be on one line and not spread over multiple lines as shown here):

```
// Office XP (2002)
#import
"C:\Program Files\Common Files\Microsoft Shared\office10\mso.dll"
rename("DocumentProperties", "DocumentPropertiesXL")
rename("RGB", "RBGXL")

#import
"C:\Program Files\Common Files\Microsoft Shared\VBA\VBA6\vbe6ext.olb"

#import "C:\Program Files\Microsoft Office\Office10\EXCEL.EXE"
rename("DialogBox", "DialogBoxXL") rename("RGB", "RBGXL")
rename("DocumentProperties", "DocumentPropertiesXL")
rename("ReplaceText", "ReplaceTextXL")
rename("CopyFile", "CopyFileXL")
no_dual_interfaces
```

The file paths may be different on your system.

Now we can add our worksheet function. In this example we shall create a worksheet function that adds all values of the selected cells together. To do that right click on the **IMyExcelFunctions** interface and select the add method. Now create a function called **MyAdd**, which has the following arguments:

```
[in] VARIANT* range
[out, retval] DOUBLE* result
```

This is also shown in Figure 29.10.

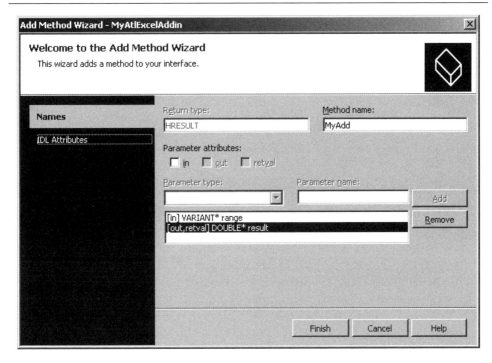

Figure 29.10   Adding a function that accepts a range of cells

Now implement the function in the **CMyExcelFunctions Class** in the following way:

```
STDMETHODIMP CMyExcelFunctions::MyAdd(VARIANT* range, DOUBLE* result)
{
  // Check if a range object was passed
  if (range->vt!=VT_DISPATCH)
  {
    // No range passed so just return the double value
    *result=range->dblVal;
    return S_OK;
  }

  // Retrieve the Excel range object from the variant
  Excel::RangePtr pRange=range.pdispVal;

  // Get the number of rows and columns in the range
  int columns=pRange->Columns->Count;
  int rows=pRange->Rows->Count;

  // Temporary result
  double tmp=0.0;

  // Iterate the rows and columns
  for (int r=1; r<=rows; r++)
  {
    for (int c=1; c<=columns; c++)
    {
      // Get the value of the current cell as double and
```

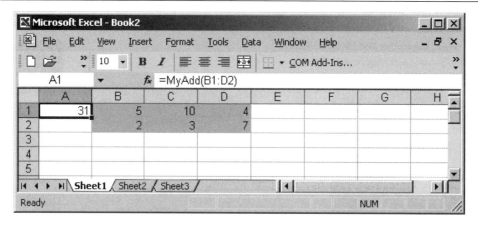

Figure 29.11   Adding a range of cells

```
        // add to running result
        tmp+=(((Excel::RangePtr)pRange->Item[r][c])->Value).dblVal;
    }
  }
  // Return the result
  *result=tmp;
  return S_OK;
}
```

The result of this function is shown Figure 29.11, where the value of A1 is the sum of the cells B1:D2.

29.4.3   Using the Vector template class

The Vector template class is **our** standard in this book. We now use it in order to communicate with Excel. In particular, we use it to simplify the usage of ranges in Excel. Before we can use the **Vector** class, we need to convert the input VARIANT to a **Vector** of doubles. To this end, we have created two static functions in a **COMUtils** class that does this for us and can be reused by other Excel worksheet functions. The two functions are shown below:

```
// Convert a variant to our vector template class
Vector<DOUBLE> COMUtils::ExcelRangeToVector(VARIANT* range)
{
  // Check if a range object was passed
  if (range->vt!=VT_DISPATCH)
  {
    // No range passed so just return the double value in a vector
    Vector<DOUBLE> v(1);
    v[v.MinIndex()]=range->dblVal;
    return v;
  }

  // Retrieve the Excel range object from the variant
  // and convert it to a Vector<DOUBLE>
  Excel::RangePtr pRange=range->pdispVal;
```

```
  return COMUtils::ExcelRangeToVector(pRange);
}

// Convert an Excel range to our vector template class
Vector<DOUBLE> COMUtils::ExcelRangeToVector(Excel::RangePtr pRange)
{
  // Get the number of rows and columns in the range
  int columns=pRange->Columns->Count;
  int rows=pRange->Rows->Count;

  // Create the vector with the correct size
  Vector<DOUBLE> v(columns*rows);

  // Iterate the rows and columns
  int i=v.MinIndex();
  for (int r=1; r<=rows; r++)
  {
    for (int c=1; c<=columns; c++)
    {
      // Add each element in the range to our vector
      v[i++]=(((Excel::RangePtr)pRange->Item[r][c])->Value).dblVal;
    }
  }

  // Return the vector
  return v;
}
```

Now we can use the above functions from our worksheet function. The following example uses the `ExcelRangeToVector()` function to convert the range passed by Excel to a `Vector` of doubles. The vector is then passed to a template function that calculates the sum of the values.

```
STDMETHODIMP CMyExcelFunctions::MySum(VARIANT* range, DOUBLE* result)
{
  // Convert input to vector
  Vector<DOUBLE> v=COMUtils::ExcelRangeToVector(range);

  // Calculate sum
  *result=sum(v);

  return S_OK;
}
```

29.5   CREATING A COM ADD-IN

We now extend the Automation add-in we created earlier so that it is also usable as a COM add-in. COM add-ins must implement the **IDTExtensibility2** interface. This can be done using the wizards in Visual C++. In the class view, right click on the **CMyExcelFunctions** class and select **Implement Interface**. In the **Implement Interface Wizard** dialog box select the **Microsoft Add-In Designer** type library and add the **_IDTExtensibility2** interface to the interface to be implemented. This is shown in Figure 29.12.

The wizard will now add the **IDTExtensibility2** interface functions to the **CMyExcelFunctions** class. Open the header file of the **CMyExcelFunctions** class. You will see that the five interface functions have a default implementation that returns

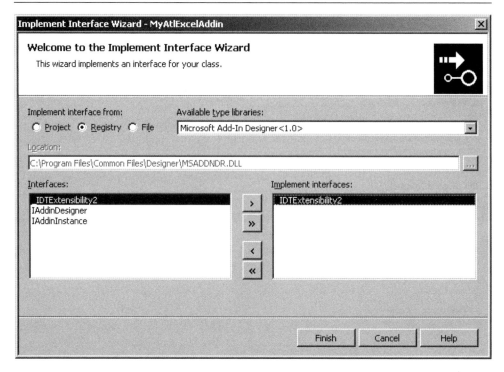

Figure 29.12   Selecting an interface to implement

E_NOTIMPL. Change this return code to S_OK or the add-in will not load. If you now try to use the add-in as Automation add-in, the worksheet functions will not be recognised because adding the interface has changed the binding of the **IDispatch** interface to the **IDTExtensibility** interface instead of the **IMyExcelFunctions** interface. In the header file of the **CMyExcelFunctions** class, search the following piece of code:

```
BEGIN_COM_MAP(CMyExcelFunctions)
  COM_INTERFACE_ENTRY(IMyExcelFunctions)
  COM_INTERFACE_ENTRY2(IDispatch, _IDTExtensibility2)
  COM_INTERFACE_ENTRY(_IDTExtensibility2)
END_COM_MAP()
```

Change the binding of **IDispatch** to **IMyExcelFunctions** so that it works again as Automation add-in. The code now likes like this:

```
BEGIN_COM_MAP(CMyExcelFunctions)
  COM_INTERFACE_ENTRY(IMyExcelFunctions)
  COM_INTERFACE_ENTRY2(IDispatch, IMyExcelFunctions)
  COM_INTERFACE_ENTRY(_IDTExtensibility2)
END_COM_MAP()
```

Next we have to register the COM add-in to enable Excel to find it. Registering the COM add-in takes place at the same time as registering the COM component itself. Registering the COM add-in is putting some things in the registry. For that we have made a general register function that can be found in the **COMUtils** class. Add this class to your project.

Next open the **MyExcelAddin.cpp** file. At the top of the file include the **COMUtils.hpp** header file and add the following two variables:

```
// Strings for registering my COM add-in
LPSTR pszProgID = "MyAtlExcelAddin.MyExcelFunctions";
LPSTR pszFriendlyName = "My First Excel Add-in!";
```

The first variable is the add-in ProgID to register. This is the same as the ProgID text field in the dialog shown in Figure 29.4. The second variable is the description of the add-in, as shown in the **Add-in** dialog box of Excel.

Next find the **DllRegisterServer()** function. Add to this function a call to the **COMUtils::RegisterCOMAddin()** function. The finished function will look like this:

```
// DllRegisterServer - Adds entries to the system registry
STDAPI DllRegisterServer(void)
{
  // Register this COM add-in for Excel
  COMUtils::RegisterCOMAddin("Excel", pszProgID, pszFriendlyName, 3);

  // registers object, typelib and all interfaces in typelib
  HRESULT hr = _AtlModule.DllRegisterServer();
  return hr;
}
```

The value '3' in the function call determines the start-up mode of the add-in. The value '3' means that the add-in is always loaded at start-up. The value '9' is on-demand load and the value '16' is load only the first time at start-up, after which it reverts to load on demand.

Finally find the **DllUnRegisterServer()** function. Add to this function a call to the **COMUtils::UnRegisterCOMAddin()** function. The finished function will look like this:

```
// DllUnregisterServer - Removes entries from the system registry
STDAPI DllUnregisterServer(void)
{
  // Unregister this COM add-in
  COMUtils::UnRegisterCOMAddin("Excel", pszProgID);

  HRESULT hr = _AtlModule.DllUnregisterServer();
  return hr;
}
```

If you now compile the add-in, it will be registered and will be shown in the **COM Add-in** dialog of Excel. However it still does nothing. For that we need to create a menu or button for Excel in the **IDTExtensibility2::OnConnection()** function that calls our add-in function.

We now add a menu item to the Excel **Tools** menu. For that we have made two static functions in the **COMUtils** class named **AddMenuItem()** and **RemoveMenuItem()**. We create and remove the menu item in the functions **OnConnection()** and **OnDisconnection()**, respectively. These are member functions of the **CMyExcelFunctions** class.

To this end, we first create a private variable in the **CMyExcelFunctions** class to hold a reference to a **CommandBarButton** object and then we create a variable that holds a reference to the Excel instance that loaded our add-in. We then initialise these variables to NULL in the constructor.

```
private:
  // The Excel instance the add-in communicates with
  Excel::_ApplicationPtr m_xl;

  // The menu item added by the add-in
  Office::_CommandBarButtonPtr m_menuItem;
```

In the **OnConnection()** method of the **CMyExcelFunctions** class we store the Excel host application and create a menu item in the Excel **Tools** menu. The **OnConnection()** function will look like this:

```
STDMETHODIMP CMyExcelFunctions::OnConnection(LPDISPATCH Application,
            ext_ConnectMode ConnectMode, LPDISPATCH AddInInst,
            SAFEARRAY * * custom)
{
  // Store reference to the Excel host application.
  // Exit if host application is not Excel.
  m_xl=Application;
  if (m_xl==NULL) return S_OK;

  // If an AddInInst object given of the type COMAddin then
  // loaded as COM Add-in.
  // If AddInInst is the same object as myself then I'm loaded
  // as Automation Add-in.
  Office::COMAddInPtr cai=AddInInst;
  if (cai!=NULL)
  {

    // Attach myself to the add-in object
    // In that way I can call functions of this object from VBA
    // using the add-in collections
    void* id;
    this->QueryInterface(IID_IDispatch, &id);
    cai->put_Object((IDispatch*)id);

    // Now install menu item
    m_menuItem = COMUtils::AddMenuItem(m_xl, cai, CComBSTR("Tools"),
        CComBSTR("My ATL Add-in"), CComBSTR("MyATLAddin"));
  }

  return S_OK;
}
```

In the **OnDisconnection()** function we shall remove the installed menu item:

```
STDMETHODIMP CMyExcelFunctions::OnDisconnection(
            ext_DisconnectMode RemoveMode, SAFEARRAY * * custom)
{
  if (m_menuItem!=NULL)
  {
    // Remove the menu item
    COMUtils::RemoveMenuItem(m_xl, RemoveMode, CComBSTR("Tools"),
      CComBSTR("My ATL Add-in"));
  }
  return S_OK;
}
```

When you now compile the add-in and start Excel you see that a **MyATL Add-in** menu item is added to the **Tools** menu. However, if we select it nothing will happen. For that we have to register an event sink to the menu item.

ATL provides several techniques for implementing an event sink. The simplest to use is the **IDispEventImpl** base class. So the first step is to add the **IDispEventImpl** class as base class for the **CMyExcelFunctions** class:

```
class ATL_NO_VTABLE CMyExcelFunctions :
  public CComObjectRootEx<CComSingleThreadModel>,
  public CComCoClass<CMyExcelFunctions, &CLSID_MyExcelFunctions>,
  public IDispatchImpl<IMyExcelFunctions, &IID_IMyExcelFunctions,
    &LIBID_MyAtlExcelAddinLib, /*wMajor =*/ 1, /*wMinor =*/ 0>,
  public IDispatchImpl<_IDTExtensibility2,
    &__uuidof(_IDTExtensibility2), &LIBID_AddInDesignerObjects,
    /* wMajor = */ 1, /* wMinor = */ 0>,
  public IDispEventImpl</*nID*/ 1, CMyExcelFunctions,
    &__uuidof(Office::_CommandBarButtonEvents),
    &__uuidof(Office::__Office), /*wMajor*/ 2, /*wMinor*/ 2>
{
  // Rest of the class definition
}
```

The **IDispEventImpl** class is a template class. The first argument is a unique identifier for this event sink. If you have to handle events of other objects you derive multiple times from **IDispEventImpl**, each with its own identifier.

The second argument is the class that derives from the **IDispEventImpl** class. In this case it is the **CMyExcelFunctions** class.

The third argument is the GUID of the event class to handle. In this case we handle the events declared by the **_CommandBarButtonEvents** COM class.

The fourth, fifth and sixth arguments specify the GUID of the type library and its version where the events to be handled are declared. In this case the events are declared in the **Office 2.2** type library. The version number must be the same as the type library registered. So specifying version 1.0 will not work on a machine with Office XP.

The next step is to specify the function we want to call when an event occurs. The button generates a click event that has, as arguments, a reference to the object that generated the event and a Boolean that can be set in case you want to override a built-in button with the same name.

In our handler we fill the range A1:B2 of the active worksheet with the text Add-in called.

```
// Handle the Click event of the menu item
void __stdcall CMyExcelFunctions::OnButtonClick(
  Office::_CommandBarButtonPtr Ctrl, VARIANT_BOOL * CancelDefault)
{
    m_xl->GetRange("a1:b2")->Value2="Add-in called";
}
```

Next we must add an event sink map to the **CMyExcelFunctions** header file that couples the click event with the event handler function.

```
BEGIN_SINK_MAP(CMyExcelFunctions)
  SINK_ENTRY_EX(/*nID =*/ 1,
    __uuidof(Office::_CommandBarButtonEvents),
    /*dispid =*/ 1, OnButtonClick)
END_SINK_MAP()
```

The first argument of the SINK_ENTRY_EX is the id of the event sink. This must be the same number as specified as the first template argument of the **IDispEventImpl** base class. The second argument is the GUID of the event class to handle. In this case it is the **_CommandBarButtonEvents** COM class. The fourth argument is the dispatch id of the event we want to handle. The dispatch id of the **Click** event of the **Command-BarButton** is 1. You can find this information in the type library. The last argument is the function to call when the event occurs.

The final step is to register our event sink with the menu item we have created. So in the **OnConnection()** function of the **CMyExcelFunctions** class add the following line of code after the call to **COMUtils::AddMenuItem()**:

```
// And add our event sink to the menu item
return DispEventAdvise(m_menuItem);
```

To unregister our event handler when the add-in is unloaded, add the following line of code just before the call to **COMUtils::RemoveMenuItem()** in the **OnDisconnec-tion()** function of the **CMyExcelFunctions** class:

```
// Remove our event sink from the menu item
DispEventUnadvise(m_menuItem);
```

When we now compile the add-in and start Excel, we shall see the **MyATL Add-in** menu item in the **Tools** menu. When we click on it the cells A1:B2 will be filled with the text Add-in called.

As last we give the implementation of the static **AddMenuItem()** and **RemoveMe-nuItem()** functions:

```
// Add a menu item to Excel
Office::_CommandBarButtonPtr COMUtils::AddMenuItem(
  Excel::_ApplicationPtr xl, Office::COMAddInPtr addin,
  CComBSTR menuName, CComBSTR menuItemCaption, CComBSTR menuItemKey)
{
  Office::CommandBarPtr cmdBar;
  Office::_CommandBarButtonPtr button;

  // Get the "menuName" dropdown menu
  cmdBar=xl->GetCommandBars()->GetItem(CComVariant(menuName));

  // If not found then end of exercitation
  if (cmdBar==NULL) return NULL;

  // Try to get the "menuItemCaption" menu item
  button=cmdBar->FindControl(vtMissing, vtMissing,
      CComVariant(menuItemKey), vtMissing, vtMissing);

  // If not found, add it
  if (button==NULL)
  {
    // Add new button
    Office::CommandBarControlsPtr controls;
    cmdBar->get_Controls(&controls);
    button=controls->Add(Office::msoControlButton, vtMissing,
        CComVariant(menuItemKey), vtMissing, vtMissing);

    // Set button's Caption, Tag, Style, and OnAction properties.
    button->put_Caption(menuItemCaption);
    button->put_Tag(menuItemKey);
```

```
  button->put_Style(Office::msoButtonCaption);

  BSTR progId;
  addin->get_ProgId(&progId);

  // Use addin argument to return reference to this add-in.
  CComBSTR str("!<");
  str.AppendBSTR(progId);
  str.Append(">");
  button->put_OnAction(str);
  }

  // Return the created button
  return button;
}
// Remove the installed menu item
void COMUtils::RemoveMenuItem(Excel::_ApplicationPtr xl,
      ext_DisconnectMode removeMode, CComBSTR menuName,
      CComBSTR menuItemCaption)
{
  Office::CommandBarPtr cmdBar;

  // If user unloaded add-in, remove button. Otherwise, add-in is
  // being unloaded because application is closing; in that case,
  // leave button as is.
  if (removeMode == ext_dm_UserClosed)
  {
   // Get the "menuName" dropdown menu
   cmdBar=xl->GetCommandBars()->GetItem(CComVariant(menuName));

   // Delete the "menuItemCaption" menu item
   cmdBar->Controls->GetItem(CComVariant(menuItemCaption))->Delete();
  }
}
```

29.6 FUTURE TRENDS

Future releases of Excel will support XML. In general, XML is a perfect language for defining structured data in a standardised form that all applications can use. Once we agree on a standard format we can import and export data between applications. To this end, Excel (at the moment of writing) has functionality for the following:

- Create a workbook and attach a custom XML Schema to the workbook.
- Identify and extract specific pieces of business data from ordinary business documents.
- Import and export XML data into and out of mapped cells.

In short, we define the structure of our data once in an XML Schema and Excel can then create XML data based on this schema. We see many business opportunities for this new feature in Excel.

29.7 CONCLUSIONS AND SUMMARY

We have given a **detailed** introduction to the problem of getting data into Excel by defining add-in functionality. There are four main options for achieving this end but we are interested mainly in the *Automation interface* because of its support for C++. In particular, we provided a step-by-step procedure for defining your own add-ins and we applied it to defining add-in functionality for some of the functions in the `ArrayMechanisms` package. The CD gives the full source code for the examples in this chapter.

30

An Extended Application: Option Strategies and Portfolios

30.1 INTRODUCTION AND OBJECTIVES

This short chapter discusses how to model a number of option trading strategies as C++ classes. In fact, we create aggregations that consist of two or more simpler types (mostly options). We pay particular attention to spreads, straddles and strangles. Furthermore, we give a short introduction to portfolio hedging.

We propose a simple portfolio hierarchy, as shown in Figure 30.1. A number of the classes will be discussed in some detail while we give some tips and guidelines to help you to develop your own code for the other classes.

30.2 SPREADS

A spread trading strategy involves taking a position in two or more options on the same underlying asset and with the same expiry date. There are three major kinds of spread (Hull, 2000):

- *Bull spreads*: We buy a call option with strike price X_1 and we sell a call option with strike price X_2, where $X_2 \geq X_1$. The investor with this strategy will gain if the underlying asset *rises* in value.
- *Bear spreads*: We buy a call option with strike price X_1 and we sell a call option with strike price X_2, where $X_2 \leq X_1$. The investor with this strategy will gain if the underlying asset *falls* in value.

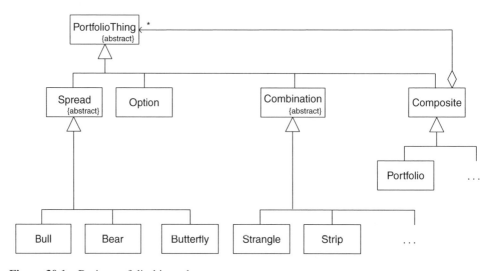

Figure 30.1 Basic portfolio hierarchy

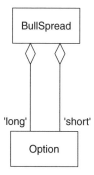

Figure 30.2   Bull spread structure

- *Butterfly spread*: This strategy uses three options with different strikes. The investor buys a call option with relatively low strike price X_1, buys a call option with a relatively high strike price X_3 and sells two call options with strike price X_2, determined by the formula:

$$X_2 = (X_1 + X_3)/2$$

These trading strategies are well documented in, for example, Hull (2000), and it is our objective to show how to model them as Assembly Parts classes in C++ (see Chapter 24 and Buschmann *et al.*, 1996, for a discussion). In particular, we concentrate on modelling bull spreads in C++ and we wish to write the following functions:

- Calculate the payoff for a given underlying asset price
- Calculate the 'payoff curve' for a range of underlying asset prices
- Display the payoff curve in Excel, for example.

An UML class diagram for a bull spread is shown in Figure 30.2.

30.3   COMBINATIONS: STRADDLES AND STRANGLES

A combination is an option trading strategy that involves taking a position in both calls and puts on the same underlying asset. The main types are:

- *Straddle*: In this case we buy a call and a put with the same strike price (call it X) and expiry date (long positions). The total payoff for a straddle is:

$$X - S \quad \text{if } S \leq X$$
$$S - X \quad \text{if } S > X$$

This particular straddle is called a *bottom straddle* or *straddle purchase*.
- *Strip*: A strip consists of a long position in one call and two puts with the same strike price and expiration date.
- *Strap*: This consists of a long position in two calls and one put with the same strike price and expiration date.

- *Strangle*: An investor buys a put with strike price X_1 and a call with strike price X_2 with the same expiration date. The total payoff is:

$$X_1 - S \quad \text{if } S \leq X_1$$
$$S - X_2 \quad \text{if } S \geq X_2$$
$$0 \qquad \text{otherwise, that is in the open interval } (X_1, X_2)$$

As far as C++ is concerned, it is possible to model these strategies in much the same way as we have done for spreads.

30.4   DESIGNING AND IMPLEMENTING SPREADS

We shall model option strategies and spreads in C++. The class hierarchy has already been given in Figure 30.1. We shall now discuss how to program these items. We shall take a minimalist viewpoint and implement those functions that are essential for a working class. We shall concentrate on bull spreads.

The basic hierarchy in C++ is:

```
class PortfolioThing
{ // Base class for all derivative products
};
```

This is the (abstract) base class for all derivative products. At the moment of writing it has neither member data nor member functions.

```
class OptionStrategy: public PortfolioThing
{
public:
  Vector<double, int> payoffGraph(const Range<double>& interval,
      int numberIntervals);
  virtual double payoff(double StockPrice) const = 0;

};
```

This class is the base class for all trading strategy classes. Notice that it has two member functions: first, a function that creates the vector object that represents the total payoff curve in a given range and, second, a pure virtual member function (PVMF) that calculates the payoff for a particular value of the stock price. Derived classes must implement this function. In fact, the function `payoffGraph` is an application of the Template Method patterns (see Gamma *et al.*, 1995) because it represents an algorithm, some of whose steps are delegated to derived classes:

```
Vector<double, int> OptionStrategy::payoffGraph(
    const Range<double>& interval, int numberIntervals)
{
  // This is an application of the Template Method pattern because
  // the graph is calculated at each Stock value by calling the
  // payoff() function in the derived classes (the so-called
  // variant part of the algorithm).
  // The invariant part of the algorithm is the looping in the
  // interval.

  // The vector of stock prices
  Vector<double, int> SArr = interval.mesh(numberIntervals);

  // The vector containing payoff for each stock price
```

```
Vector<double, int> result (SArr.Size(), SArr.MinIndex());

// Now calculate the payoff array
for (int j = result.MinIndex(); j <= result.MaxIndex(); j++)
{
  result[j] = payoff(SArr[j]);
}
return result;
}
```

The classes derived from `OptionStrategy` have the following prototype definitions:

```
class Spread: public OptionStrategy
{ // Take a position in two or more options of the same type

private:

protected:        // This has been done for convenience only
    EuropeanOption * f;
    EuropeanOption * s;
public:
  Spread(EuropeanOption& first, EuropeanOption& second);
};

class BullSpread: public Spread
{ // One long call and one short call

private:
  // Redundant data
  double X1;         // Smaller strike price
  double X2;         // Larger strike price
public:
  BullSpread(EuropeanOption& first, EuropeanOption& second);

  double payoff(double StockPrice) const;
};
```

It is interesting to show how we have coded the constructor for the bull spread class. Notice in particular how we have determined the strike prices:

```
BullSpread::BullSpread(EuropeanOption& first, EuropeanOption& second)
  : Spread(first, second)
{
  X1 = f -> K;
  X2 = s -> K;
}
```

The code for the payoff function is very easy and is based on the formulae in Hull (2000):

```
double BullSpread::payoff(double S) const
{ // Based on Hull's book
  if (S >= X2)
    return X2 - X1;
  if (S <= X1)
    return 0;
  // In the interval [X1, X2]
  return S - X1;
}
```

We shall give an example of the use of bull spreads in section 30.6.

30.5   DELTA HEDGING

We know that the *delta* of a derivative security is the rate of change of its price with respect to the price of the underlying asset. We also know how to calculate the delta of plain European options because there is an exact formula for the calculation. For exotic options, we must resort to numerical schemes in general to calculate the delta. For example, the exponentially fitted finite difference scheme produces a good approximate to the delta while the Keller Box scheme gives second-order accurate approximations to it.

Let P denote the value of a portfolio consisting of one long option position and a short position in some quantity Δ (called **delta**) of the underlying:

$$P = V(S, t) - \Delta S \tag{30.1}$$

We can show that the portfolio change is given by (Wilmott, 1998):

$$
\begin{aligned}
dP &= \frac{\partial V}{\partial t} \, dt + \frac{\partial V}{\partial S} \, ds + \frac{1}{2}\sigma^2 S^2 \frac{\partial^2 V}{\partial S^2} \, dt - \Delta dS \\
&= \left(\frac{\partial V}{\partial t} + \frac{1}{2}\sigma^2 S^2 \frac{\partial^2 V}{\partial S^2} \right) dt + \left(\frac{\partial V}{\partial S} - \Delta \right) dS
\end{aligned}
\tag{30.2}
$$

This equation has a deterministic term (the coefficient of dt) and a random term (the coefficient of dS). Thus everything is known on the right-hand side of (30.2) with the exception of the random term. We can eliminate this term and a corresponding source of risk by defining the delta as follows:

$$\Delta = \frac{\partial V}{\partial S} \tag{30.3}$$

Any reduction in randomness is called **hedging**. In the current situation, in which we exploit correlation between an instrument and its underlying, it is called **delta hedging**. We now turn our attention to finding the delta of a portfolio consisting of a number of options. In this case, define the following variables:

$$\Delta_j = \text{delta of option } j$$

$$w_j = \text{number of options for option } j \tag{30.4}$$

$$\Delta \ = \text{delta of the portfolio}$$

Then since the delta of the portfolio is a linear functional, we know that its delta is the sum of the deltas of the individual options times the number of options:

$$\Delta = \sum_{j=1}^{n} w_j \Delta_j \tag{30.5}$$

Of course, we can calculate the deltas of the individual options by exact or approximate methods.

We now discuss how to implement a portfolio class. We concentrate on a special case of Figure 30.1. In this case we document the class as in Figure 30.3. We note the following:

- A 'basic' portfolio consists of options
- A composite portfolio consists of other portfolios.

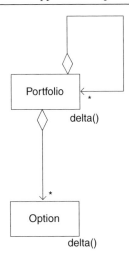

Figure 30.3   Test case: Portfolio class

The basic C++ interface for this class is:

```
class Portfolio: public PortfolioThing
{
private:
  list<pair<int, Option*> > contents;

public:
  // Usual stuff

  double delta() const;
};
```

We have given an exercise to let you program this class in C++.

30.6   AN EXAMPLE

We give an example of a bull spread and how to calculate and display its payoff function.

```
// All options are European; Bull spread

// Buy a call option
EuropeanOption futureOption("C");
futureOption.U = (32.0);
futureOption.K = (30.0);
futureOption.T = (0.5);
futureOption.r = (0.10);
futureOption.sig = (0.36);
futureOption.b = ( 0.0);

// Sell a call option
EuropeanOption futureOption2("C");
futureOption2.U = (32.0);
futureOption2.K = (35.0);
futureOption2.T = (0.5);
futureOption2.r = (0.10);
futureOption2.sig = (0.36);
```

```
futureOption2.b = ( 0.0);

BullSpread spr1(futureOption, futureOption2);
double pay = spr1.payoff (32.0);
cout << "pay off at 32 is: " << pay << endl;
```

We now wish to print the total payoff graph in Excel. The corresponding code is:

```
Range<double> r(20.0, 40.0);
Vector<double, int> payoffGraph = spr1.payoffGraph(r, 20);
print(payoffGraph);

Vector<double, int> x = r.mesh(20);
printOneExcel(x, payoffGraph, "Bull Spread (Call)");
```

For completeness, we include the actual code that presents the vector in Excel:

```
void printOneExcel(const Vector<double, int> & x,
    const Vector<double, int>& functionResult,
    const string& title)
{
  // N.B. Excel has a limit of 8 charts; after that you get a
  // run-time error
  cout << "Starting Excel\n";
  ExcelDriver & excel = ExcelDriver::Instance();

  excel.MakeVisible(true);        // Default is INVISIBLE!
  excel.CreateChart(x, functionResult, title, "Stock S", "Profit");
}
```

The output is given in Figure 30.4.

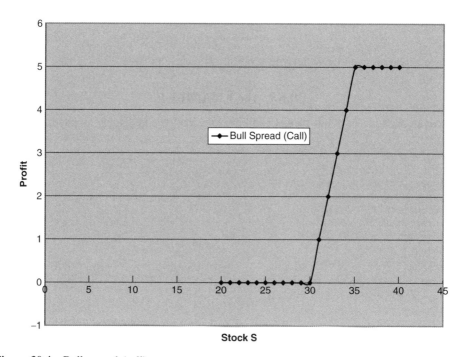

Figure 30.4   Bull spread (call)

30.7   TIPS AND GUIDELINES

We give some ideas on extending the functionality in this chapter.

1. Create a C++ class for a bear spread. The total payoff is (Hull, 2000):

```
double BearSpread::payoff(double S) const
{ // Based on Hull's book
  if (S >= X2)
    return -(X2 - X1);
  if (S <= X1)
    return 0;
  // In the interval [X1, X2]
  return -(S - X1);
}
```

2. Create a class for a butterfly spread. The total payoff is:

```
double ButterflySpread::payoff(double S) const
{ // Based on Hull's book
  if (S < X1)
    return 0.0;
  if (S > X3)
    return 0.0;
  if (X1 < S & S < X2)
    return S - X1;
  if (X2 < S & S < X3)
    return X3 - S;
}
```

The graph of the total payoff for a butterfly spread is shown in Figure 30.5.

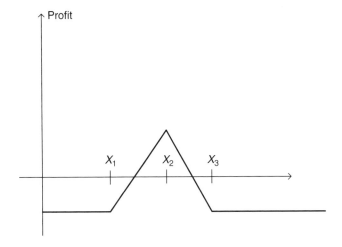

Figure 30.5   Total payoff for butterfly spread

3. Create a software environment in which it is possible to display both the total payoff of a spread as well as its parts. The display should be done in Excel with the function we used for initial value problems:

```
void printInExcel(const Vector<double, int>& x,     // X array
    const list<string>& labels,      // Names of each vector
    const list<Vector<double, int> >& functionResult)  // The list of Y
                                                        // values
{ // Print a list of Vectors in Excel. Each vector is the output of
  // a finite difference scheme for a scalar IVP

    cout << "Starting Excel\n";

    ExcelDriver & excel = ExcelDriver::Instance();
    excel.MakeVisible(true);        // Default is INVISIBLE!
    excel.CreateChart(
    x, labels, functionResult, string("FDM Scalar IVP"),
    string("Time Axis"), string ("Value"));
}
```

You can adapt this function to suit your current needs. To give a hint, for a bull spread you should have three lines in the graph, one for the payoff from the long call option, one for the payoff from the short call option and one for the total payoff.

4. Write the C++ code that implements the Portfolio class in section 30.5. Create a test program and check your answer with the results from a standard reference book on option theory (for example, Hull, 2000).

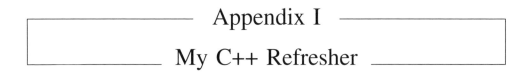

Appendix I
My C++ Refresher

A1.1 SUMMARY

This appendix is meant as a C++ refresher. If the material is new for you it is probably an idea to study an introductory text on the subject before proceeding. Of course, a good way to learn C++ is to study the examples on the CD accompanying this book.

We develop a class in C++ that models the price and sensitivities of European options.

A1.2 WHAT IS C++ AND WHY IS IT IMPORTANT?

The C++ language was born some time around 1980. Its inventor was Dr Bjarne Stroustrup, a researcher at AT&T labs. Since then the language has become one of the major programming languages and it is being used in many business, industrial and scientific domains. C++ has its roots in the C language and it supports the so-called object-oriented paradigm. One of the central features of this paradigm is 'encapsulation'. Encapsulation is the ability to group data and its related functionality into one coherent whole that we call a class. For example, a plain vanilla option has data for strike price, expiry data and so on while there are functions for the calculation of its price and sensitivities. Encapsulation is very powerful and it helps the developer to integrate related data and functionality. It is safe to say that C++ is the language of choice for many applications. We hope to see it being used more for financial engineering applications in the coming years.

Encapsulation is not the only feature in C++ that makes it a great language for software development in financial engineering. This appendix deals with one particular example, namely creating C++ classes for plain vanilla options. We have applied the object-oriented paradigm and C++ to analysing, designing and implementing other problems such as:

- Finite difference methods for one-factor and two-factor models
- Creating reusable foundation classes (statistics, trees, arrays and matrices)
- C++ classes for binomial and trinomial trees
- Monte Carlo simulations and parallel processing.

We see C++ as the *de-facto* programming language for financial engineering applications.

A1.3 THE DATASIM C++ SELF-TEST

This section consists of a number of key questions to test your knowledge of C++. If you answer the questions correctly then your background is OK, if not you should brush up on your C++ skills. In general, you should be able to give on-the-spot answers to these questions. Then you can be sure that you have a good knowledge of basic C++. *Discuss* your answers to the 10 questions below based on the following viewpoints:

- What is the topic (for example, *virtual destructors*)?
- Why do you need it?
- How do you implement it?
- What are the consequences if you don't use it?

The questions are:

1. The minimal class interface that is needed in C++ (the so-called *canonical header file*).
2. Call-by-value versus call-by-reference.
3. *const* member functions, *const* input arguments and *const* return types. The relationship between call-by-reference and *const*.
4. The two different ways to apply *operator overloading* in C++. Advantages and disadvantages of each approach.
5. How to implement the operator '=' (*assignment* in a class). Consider also how dynamic memory is organised in the body of this operator.
6. What is a *friend* function/operator?
7. Let *B* be a base class and *D* is a derived class of *B*. What is inherited and what is **not** inherited from *B* to *D*? How do you (re)implement these members in *D*?
8. How is memory implemented in *D*? What is a *virtual destructor*?
9. What is an *abstract* (base) class?
10. What is *polymorphism*?

A1.4   THE ESSENTIALS OF A C++ CLASS: THE CANONICAL HEADER FILE

We assume that you know how to program the following special member functions when creating header and code files for a class:

- Default constructor
- Copy constructor
- Assignment operator
- Destructor (must be virtual!).

This is called the *canonical header file* and each class must have these functions. Do you know why? Why must the destructor always be `public` but the constructors may either be `private` or `public`? (By the way, we never use the `protected` specifier in our code; life is difficult enough as it is without introducing multiple access specifiers.)

A1.5   AN OVERVIEW OF OBJECT-ORIENTED PROGRAMMING IN C++

C++ is an example of a class-based object-oriented language. A class is a description of a group of related attributes and operations. In C++ we use the synonyms 'member data' for attributes and 'member functions' for operations. The member data and member functions are closely related. This feature is called *encapsulation*. In short, the 'class' functions know which attributes to use. Let us take an example of a class implementing European options for stocks. The defining parameters for the European option will be designed in C++ as the following member data:

The risk-free interest rate: r
The volatility of the relative price change: σ
The strike price: K
The time to expiration (in years): T
The stock price: S (or U depending on the underlying)
The cost-of-carry: b.

The cost-of-carry for the Black–Scholes model has the same value as r but will have different values depending on the type of underlying asset (for example, $b = 0$ for a futures option, see Haug, 1998). We must define the data types of the member data. In this case we usually design them as double precision numbers although C++ allows us to design classes with so-called *generic data types*. This means that the member data can be customised with different *specific data types* depending on programmer preference.

Having defined the member data we now must decide what to do with the data. To this end, we introduce the concept of *object* (or *instance* of a class). A class is abstract in the sense that its member data has not been instantiated (they are just abstract description) while an object is tangible and all its member data has been initialised. For example, the following assignments describe a European put option on an index (Haug, 1998, p. 15):

Underlying value (stock price index), $U = 500$
Volatility, $\sigma = 0.15$
Strike price, $K = 490$
Time to expiry, $T = 0.25$ (3 months)
Risk-free interest rate, $r = 0.08$
Cost-of-carry, $b = 0.03$.

Having discussed member data we now describe the functionality of classes and objects. In general, a class has member functions that model the life cycle of an object. The main categories in general are:

- Member functions (*constructors*) for creation of objects
- Member functions that modify the member data (*modifiers*)
- Member functions that perform calculations on the member data (*selectors*)
- A member function (*destructor*) that deletes an object when no longer needed.

There are various ways to create an object using constructors. For example, it is possible to create an instance of a European option class by initialising its member data. Two other constructors deserve mention: first, the default constructor creates an object with default member data values while the copy constructor creates an object as a deep copy of some other object. The destructor is the other extreme; it removes the object from memory when the object is no longer needed. We note that the names of constructors and the destructor are the same as the names of their corresponding class.

We now discuss the member functions that operate on an object after it has been constructed but before it is destructed. We concentrate on the class for European options in order to be precise and look at the following categories:

- Modifying the object's member data (modifiers)

- Getting the values of the member data (selectors)
- Calculating the option price and its sensitivities (selectors).

C++ is based on the message-passing paradigm. This means that client code sends a message to an object by calling its member functions. For example, here is a piece of code that calculates the price of the index put option (we assume that the member data have been initialised):

```
ExactEuropeanOption myobject ("P", "Index Option");

// ...

double d = myObject.Price();
```

The value d will now contain the price of the put on the index option. Notice that there was no need to include parameters in the function Price() because of the tight binding between data and functions in C++. This is in contrast to procedural languages (such as Visual Basic and Cobol) where the coupling between data and functions is looser.

A1.6   THE EUROPEAN OPTION IN C++: THE DETAILS

We now dissect the code to show how we have used C++ for European options. In particular, there are three separate issues to be discussed in detail:

- Designing the member functions in the class
- Implementing the bodies of each member function
- How client code uses the class.

Once the reader has understood this section he or she should then be in a position to appreciate how larger classes are created, tested and used in applications.

In general, all the code that is needed for a complete description of a class in C++ is contained in two files: first, the so-called header file (this section), which contains the formal descriptions of the member data and member functions in the class. Second, the so-called code file, which contains the implementation of each declared member function as seen in the header file. In other words, each member function declaration in the header file must have a corresponding entry in the code file.

We now discuss the details of the header file. First, there are two regions or parts called *private* or *public*, respectively. Both parts may contain member data and member functions. Members that are declared in the private part are not accessible from outside the class and may only be accessed by members in the class itself, while public members may be accessed by any C++ code. In general, all data should be declared in the private part because this data tends to change; however, in this article we place the data that represents the structure of an option in the public area. This is for convenience only. The public member functions in the options class can be categorised as follows (see the code below):

- Constructors: The different ways of creating instances of the option class.
- Destructor: Deleting an object when it is no longer needed.
- Assignment operator: The ability to assign one object to another object (this is a 'deep' copy).

- 'Core business' functions: These are the functions that calculate the price and the delta for the option.
- Other functions: For example, it is possible to switch a call option to a put option (and vice versa). Of course, the price and delta will be different!

The full interface for the option class is now given.

```cpp
// EuropeanOption.hpp

#include <string>

class EuropeanOption
{
private:
  void init();        // Initialise all default values
  void copy(const EuropeanOption& o2);

  // 'Kernel' functions for option calculations
  double CallPrice() const;
  double PutPrice() const;
  double CallDelta() const;
  double PutDelta() const;

public:
  // Public member data for convenience only
  double r;          // Interest rate
  double sig;        // Volatility
  double K;          // Strike price
  double T;          // Expiry date
  double U;          // Current underlying price
  double b;          // Cost of carry

  string optType;    // Option name (call, put)
public:
// Constructors
EuropeanOption();  // Default call option
EuropeanOption(const EuropeanOption& option2);   // Copy constructor
EuropeanOption (const string& optionType);       // Create option type

// Destructor
virtual ~EuropeanOption();

// Assignment operator
EuropeanOption& operator = (const EuropeanOption& option2);

// Functions that calculate option price and (some) sensitivities
double Price() const;
double Delta() const;

// Modifier functions
void toggle();            // Change option type (C/P, P/C)

};
```

Having discussed the function prototypes for the options class, we need to describe how to fill in the body of the code for these functions. To this end, there are two major issues to be addressed. First, we must include the header file and the headers of libraries that are needed by the code. In this case, this leads to:

```
#include "EuropeanOption.hpp" // Declarations of functions
#include <math.h>             // For mathematical functions, e.g. exp()
```

Second, each function body must be specified. This is where C++ differs somewhat from non-object-oriented languages, namely function overloading. This means that it is possible to define several functions having the same name but differing only in the number and type of arguments. Furthermore, each function is 'scoped' or attached to its class by use of the so-called *name resolution operator* '::' as shown in the following typical code:

```
double EuropeanOption::PutPrice() const
{

  double tmp = sig * sqrt(T);

  double d1 = (log(U/K) + (b + (sig*sig) * 0.5) * T)/ tmp;
  double d2 = d1 - tmp;

  return (K * exp(-r * T) * N(-d2)) - (U * exp((b-r)* T) * N(-d1));

}
```

This function calculates the price of a put option. Note that the function returns a double value (the price of the put option) while all needed parameters (such as the volatility, interest rate and so on) are none other than the member data of the object which of course has already been initialised in a constructor!

We now give the full code of the code file.

```
// EurpeanOption.cpp
//
// Author: Daniel Duffy
//
// (C) Datasim Education BV 2003

#include "EuropeanOption.hpp" // Declarations of functions
#include <math.h>             // For mathematical functions, e.g. exp()

// Kernel Functions
double EuropeanOption::CallPrice() const
{

  double tmp = sig * sqrt(T);

  double d1 = (log(U/K) + (b + (sig*sig) * 0.5 ) * T )/ tmp;
  double d2 = d1 - tmp;

  return (U * exp((b-r) * T) * N(d1)) - (K * exp(-r * T) * N(d2));

}
double EuropeanOption::PutPrice() const
{

  double tmp = sig * sqrt(T);

  double d1 = (log(U/K) + (b + (sig*sig)*0.5 ) * T)/ tmp;
  double d2 = d1 - tmp;

  return (K * exp(-r * T) * N(-d2)) - (U * exp((b-r) * T) * N(-d1));
}
double EuropeanOption::CallDelta() const
{
```

```
  double tmp = sig * sqrt(T);

  double d1 = (log(U/K) + (b + (sig*sig)*0.5) * T )/ tmp;

  return exp((b-r)*T) * N(d1);
}
double EuropeanOption::PutDelta() const
{
  double tmp = sig * sqrt(T);

  double d1 = (log(U/K) + (b + (sig*sig)*0.5) * T )/ tmp;

  return exp((b-r)*T) * (N(d1) - 1.0);
}
void EuropeanOption::init()
{ // Initialise all default values

  // Default values
  r = 0.08;
  sig= 0.30;
  K = 65.0;
  T = 0.25;
  U = 60.0;          // U == stock in this case
  b = r;             // Black and Scholes stock option model (1973)

  optType = "C";     // European Call Option (the default type)

}
void EuropeanOption::copy(const EuropeanOption& o2)
{

  r    = o2.r;
  sig = o2.sig;
  K    = o2.K;
  T    = o2.T;
  U    = o2.U;
  b    = o2.b;

  optType = o2.optType;

}
EuropeanOption::EuropeanOption()
{ // Default call option

  init();
}
EuropeanOption::EuropeanOption(const EuropeanOption& o2)
{ // Copy constructor

  copy(o2);
}
EuropeanOption::EuropeanOption (const string& optionType)
{ // Create option type

  init();
  optType = optionType;

  if (optType == "c")optType = "C";
}
EuropeanOption::~EuropeanOption()
```

```
{ // Destructor

}

EuropeanOption& EuropeanOption::operator = (const EuropeanOption& opt2)
{ // Assignment operator (deep copy)

  if (this == &opt2) return *this;

  copy (opt2);

  return *this;
}

// Functions that calculate option price and sensitivities
double EuropeanOption::Price() const
{
  if (optType == "C")return CallPrice();
  else return PutPrice();
}

double EuropeanOption::Delta() const
{
  if (optType == "C")return CallDelta();
  else return PutDelta();
}

// Modifier functions
void EuropeanOption::toggle()
{ // Change option type (C/P, P/C)

  if (optType == "C")optType = "P";
  else optType = "C";
}
```

The code file is compiled and syntax errors should be resolved. We then need to write a program to test the class. The corresponding file is then compiled and linked with the other code to form an executable unit.

In this section we give an example of a test program. The object-oriented paradigm is based on the *message-passing metaphor*. Here we mean that client software sends messages to an object (by means of member function calls) by using the so-called dot notation. For example, to calculate the price of an existing option instance we code as follows:

```
double option_price = myOption.Price();
```

Here myOption is an object and Price() is one of its member functions.

The following code is an example of how to use the option class. Please note that we create four instances of the class EuropeanOption.

```
// TestEuropeanOption.cpp
//
// Test program for the solutions of European option pricing
// problems.
//
// (C) Datasim Education Technology BV 20003

#include "EuropeanOption.hpp"
#include <iostream>              // I/O stuff like cout, cin
int main()
```

```
{ // All options are European

  // Call option on a stock
  EuropeanOption callOption;
  cout << "Call option on a stock: " << callOption.Price() << endl;

  // Put option on a stock index
  EuropeanOption indexOption;
  indexOption.optType = "P";
  indexOption.U = 100.0;
  indexOption.K = 95.0;
  indexOption.T = 0.5;
  indexOption.r = 0.10;
  indexOption.sig = 0.20;

  double q = 0.05;          // Dividend yield
  indexOption.b = indexOption.r - q;

  cout << "Put option on index: " << indexOption.Price() << endl;

  // Call and put options on a future
  EuropeanOption futureOption;
  futureOption.optType = "P";
  futureOption.U = 19.0;
  futureOption.K = 19.0;
  futureOption.T = 0.75;
  futureOption.r = 0.10;
  futureOption.sig = 0.28;

  futureOption.b = 0.0;

  cout << "Put option on future: " << futureOption.Price() << endl;

  // Now change over to a call on the option
  futureOption.toggle();
  cout << "Call on future: " << futureOption.Price() << endl;

  return 0;
}
```

The output from this program is:

```
Call option on a stock: 2.13293
Put option on an index: 2.4648
Put option on a future: 1.70118
Call option on a future: 1.70118
```

These numbers are the same as those found in the benchmark examples in Haug (1998).

Having described most of the structure, functionality and behaviour of our benchmark option class, we could ask ourselves what the added value is of approaching the pricing problem in this object-oriented way and the benefits we gain by programming it the way we do. To answer these questions we need to base our answers on objective software quality characteristics. In our case we base them on the ISO 9126 standard, which consists of six independent measures:

- *Functionality*: Is the software suitable for certain customers and applications?
- *Reliability*: How robust is the software?
- *Efficiency*: What is the performance of the calculations?
- *Portability*: Does the software run in various software and hardware environments?

- *Maintainability*: Can we easily modify, correct and extend the software?
- *Usability*: Is the software easy to understand and to learn?

These are very important issues that we must address if we wish to produce applications that satisfy the requirements of this particular business domain, namely financial engineering. The more attention we pay to these quality characteristics the more effective we shall be as developer and organisation. It is also more cost-effective in the medium to long term. Remember the old saying: 'It takes a lot of money to make bad products!'? We now discuss each of the above quality characteristics, with particular emphasis on the software solution in this article.

A1.7.1   Functionality

The option class implements the generalised Black–Scholes option pricing formula for a number of common asset types. Both call and put options are supported and the class has functionality for each of the major 'greeks'. We have tested the code with a number of examples and we conclude that the answers agree with the literature.

It is well known that plain vanilla options are used as 'building blocks' for more exotic and complicated financial instruments. To this end, we wish to realise this feature in the software as well. For example, chooser options give the holder the right to choose whether the option is to be a put or a call at some time (Haug, 1998). The payoff in this case is the larger of the call price and put price. Our software can handle this situation; all we have to do is 'toggle' the option object. Other uses of plain vanilla options in other instruments can be found in Tavella and Randall (2000).

A1.7.2   Reliability

All source code is written in C++ and is compiled into machine-readable code. Run-time errors are reduced to a minimum because all data types and assignments are checked at compile time rather than at run-time. Furthermore, no VARIANT or void* types are used so that there is no danger of mixing inconsistent data types in the code.

A1.7.3   Efficiency

C++ is a highly efficient language. All source code is compiled and the resulting executable files are machine-readable. Thus, C++ code runs almost as fast as (and sometimes faster than) C code. Compared with languages such as Java, C# and Visual Basic we see C++ as the language of choice for financial engineering applications, especially in the code that is responsible for calculations and core processing. As far as efficiency of our own code is concerned, the Option class uses standard data types and access methods and we conclude that processing time and the amount of resources needed to perform the calculations are acceptable.

A1.7.4   Portability

Portability refers to the ability of software to function in different software and hardware environments. In the present case, since all of the code is written in C++ (an ISO standard) there will be no problems porting the software from, let's say, a Windows environment to Linux or Unix. Even the Standard Template Library (STL) is now part of the C++ language and *its* ability to function with different compilers is also assured. One of our objectives with the Option class is to produce displays of option prices and their greeks using applications such as Excel, GDI+ (Graphics Device Interface) and OpenGL. To this end, we must ensure that our software does not use any of the code from these libraries otherwise it will be less portable than desired. In order to ensure portability and at the same time have the ability to display in the various output media we must resort to the use of the so-called design patterns (see Gamma *et al.*, 1995).

A1.7.5   Maintainability

The code that we have written is easy to modify. For example, we can easily define new property types as member data and new member functions to suite new needs.

A1.7.6   Last but not least, Usability

Usability refers to the ability to understand the code and learn how it works. Usability is one of our objectives in general. Code that is not easy to understand leads to more errors, more maintenance costs and degraded programmer productivity. Our advice is to use standard libraries, use C++ template class whenever possible and when the time comes apply the proven design patterns (see Gamma *et al.*, 1995) that promote flexible designs in C++.

Appendix II
Dates and Other Temporal Types

A2.1 SUMMARY

In financial engineering applications is it vital to model time-dependent data structures. In none of the chapters in this book did we model any such structures. In this appendix we model data structures for dates, times, timestamps and their extensions. The full source code is to be found on the accompanying CD.

A2.2 THE DATE CLASS

The class DatasimDate is an encapsulation of dates. A date consists of a day, month and year. Internally, these three values are mapped to the equivalent Julian format (a single number).

We support the following date types:

```
STD,        // d[d]-mon-yy[yy]
EUROPEAN,   // d[d]-m[m]-yy[yy]
ANSI,       // yy[yy]-m[m]-d[d]
AMERICAN    // m[m]-d[d]-yy[yy]
```

What do we wish to do with dates? We have created the following functionality:

- Creating dates (using different specifiers)
- Comparing dates ($<$, $>$, $==$, $!=$ etc.)
- Adding days/months/years to a date
- Subtracting days/months/years from a date
- Converting dates to an appropriate string format
- Printing dates.

The main constructors are:

```
// Constructors
DatasimDate();    // Default constructor = Date today
DatasimDate(const DatasimDate& d2); // Copy constructor
DatasimDate(const julTy& days);    // Date from Julian days
DatasimDate(int days);             // Date from Julian days
DatasimDate(int day, int month, int year); // Day, month, year
```

Date comparison operators are:

```
// Comparison functions
bool operator==(const DatasimDate& date2);
bool operator!=(const DatasimDate& date2);
bool operator>(const DatasimDate& date2);
bool operator<(const DatasimDate& date2);
bool operator>=(const DatasimDate& date2);
bool operator<=(const DatasimDate& date2);
```

Adding and subtracting goes as follows:

```
DatasimDate operator-(int days);
DatasimDate operator-(const julTy& days);
DatasimDate operator++();
DatasimDate operator--();
DatasimDate operator+=(const julTy& days);
DatasimDate operator+=(int days);
DatasimDate operator-=(const julTy& days);
DatasimDate operator-=(int days);
DatasimDate add_months(long months);
DatasimDate add_years(long years);
DatasimDate sub_months(long months);
DatasimDate sub_years(long years);
DatasimDate add_period(julTy days,
    julTy months = 0, const julTy years = 0);
DatasimDate sub_period(julTy days,
    julTy months = 0, julTy years = 0);
```

We also have two functions for finding the number of days between two dates:

```
long difference (const DatasimDate& DatasimDate_2);
long operator - (const DatasimDate& d2);
```

Finally, we have conversion and output utilities:

```
// Conversion and output functions
string toString(string formatString = 0);
```

In this case the format string has the following form:

```
%D     insert day (1..31) in 1 digit if possible, otherwise 2 digits
%DD    insert day (1..31) in 2 digits, first digit may be 0
%M     insert month (1..12) in 1 digit if possible, otherwise 2
%MM    insert month (1..12) in 2 digits, first digit may be 0
%YY    insert year number in 2 digits (year in century)
%YYYY  insert full year number in 4 digits
any other character will be copied to the output string.
for example:
  date d("31-1-1977");
  char* str = d.toString("[%D]-[%MM]-[%YY]");
will result str to be:
  "[31]-[01]-[77]"

void print();
friend ostream& operator << (ostream& os, const DATE& dat);
```

A2.3   THE TIME CLASS

We also provide a `DatasimTime` class that represents the time (number of seconds) since midnight. The interface is similar to that of `DatasimDate`.

A2.4   EXTENSIONS

We can use the above classes directly when creating new classes and containers that need temporal types. Furthermore, we can use them in different ways, for example:

- In combination with STL
- We can apply design patterns to them.

In the first case we envisage sets, lists and maps of dates with the corresponding algorithms while we see many opportunities for creational, structural and behavioural patterns, especially in applications that model interest rates, fixed income and the like. A discussion of these topics is outside the scope of this book.

A2.5   A SIMPLE EXAMPLE

We finish with an example to show how to generate an array of dates. The source code is:

```
DatasimDate d1(1, 1, 92);
cout << "First DatasimDate: " << d1 << endl;
DatasimDate d2(1, 3, 92);
cout << "Second DatasimDate: " << d2 << endl;
DatasimDate tod;  // today
cout << "Today is: " << tod << endl;

int diff = d2.difference(d1);
cout << "Difference in days is: " << diff << endl;

// Looping over numbers
DatasimDate fixed(1, 1, 94);
DatasimDate current(1, 1, 94);

int interval = 30;

for (int j = 0; j < 12; j++)
{
   current = fixed - (j*interval);
   cout << current << endl;
}

   return 0;
}
```

The output from this file is:

```
First DatasimDate: 1/1/92
Second DatasimDate: 1/3/92
Today is: 4/1/2004
Difference in days is: 60
1/1/94
2/12/93
2/11/93
3/10/93
3/9/93
4/8/93
5/7/93
5/6/93
6/5/93
6/4/93
7/3/93
5/2/93
```

Remark: I ran this program on January 4, 2004.

References

Aho, A., Kernighan, B. and Weinberger, P. (1988) *The AWK Programming Language*. Addison-Wesley, Reading, MA.

Alexander, C. (1979) *The Timeless Way of Building*. Oxford University Press.

Alexander, C., Ishikawa, S. and Silverstein, M. (1977) *A Pattern Language*. Oxford University Press.

Alexandrescu, I. (2002) *Modern C++ Design*. Addison-Wesley, Reading, MA.

Ayres, F. (1965) *Theory and Problems of Modern Algebra*. Schaum's Outline Series. McGraw-Hill, New York.

Babushka, I., Banerjee, U. and Osborn, J. E. (2002) *Survey of meshless and generalised finite element methods: A unified approach*. Working Paper.

Barraquand, J. and Pudet, T. (1996) Pricing of American path-dependent contingent claims. *Mathematical Finance*, **6** (No. 1, January), 17–51.

Bhansali, V. (1998) *Pricing and Managing Exotic and Hybrid Options*. McGraw-Hill, Irwin Library Series, New York.

Bobisud, L. (1968) Second-order linear parabolic equations with a small parameter. *Arch. Rational Mech. Anal.*, **27**.

Breymann, U. (1998) *Designing Components with the C++ STL*. Addison-Wesley, Harlow, England.

Bronson, R. (1989) *Theory and Problems of Matrix Operations*. Schaum's Outline Series. McGraw-Hill, New York.

Buschmann, F. *et al.* (1996) *Pattern-Oriented Software Architecture: A System of Patterns*. John Wiley & Sons, Chichester, UK (POSA 1996).

Ceponkus, A. and Hoodbhoy, F. (1999) *Applied XML*. John Wiley & Sons, New York.

Cooney, M. (1999) *Benchmarking numerical solutions of European options to the Black–Scholes partial differential equation*. MSc Thesis, Trinity College, Dublin, Ireland.

Cox, J. C. and Rubinstein, M. (1985) *Options Markets*. Prentice Hall, Englewood Cliffs, NJ.

Crank, J. and Nicolson, P. (1947) A practical method for numerical evaluation of solutions of partial differential equations of the heat-conduction type. *Proc. Cambridge Philos. Soc.*, **43**, 50–67; re-published in: John Crank 80th birthday special issue, *Adv. Comput. Math.*, **6** (1997), 207–226.

Cryer, C. (1979) *Successive overrelaxation methods for solving linear complementarity problems arising from free boundary value problems*. Paper presented at a seminar held in Pavia (Italy) September–October, Rome.

Dahlquist, G. (1974) *Numerical Methods*. Prentice-Hall, Englewood Cliffs, NJ.

Dautray, R. and Lions, J. L. (1993) *Mathematical Analysis and Numerical Methods for Science and Technology*, Volume 6. Springer-Verlag, Berlin.

de Allen, D. and Southwell, R. (1955) Relaxation methods applied to determining the motion, in two dimensions, of a viscous fluid past a fixed cylinder. *Quart. J. Mech. Appl. Math.*, 129–145.

Doolan, E. P. *et al.* (1980) *Uniform Numerical Methods for Problems with Initial and Boundary Layers*. Boole Press, Dublin, Ireland.

Douglas, J. and Rachford, H. H. (1955) On the numerical solution of heat conduction equations in two and three dimensions. *Trans. Am. Math. Soc.*, **82**, 421–439.

Duff, I., Erisman, A. and Reid, J. (1990) *Direct Methods for Sparse Matrices*. Clarendon Press, Oxford.

Duffy, D. (1977) *Finite elements for mixed initial boundary value problems for hyperbolic systems of dissipative type*. MSc Thesis, Trinity College, Dublin, Ireland.

Duffy, D. (1980) *Uniformly convergent difference schemes for problems with a small parameter in the leading derivative*. PhD Thesis, Trinity College, Dublin, Ireland.

Duffy, D. (1995) *From Chaos to Classes: Software Development in C++*. McGraw-Hill, London, UK.

Duffy, D. (2004a) *Domain Architecture: Models and Architectures for UML Applications*. John Wiley & Sons, Chichester, UK.

Duffy, D. (2004b) *Numerical Methods for Instrument Pricing*. John Wiley & Sons, Chichester, UK.

Emel'yanov, K. V. (1975) A difference method for solving the third boundary value problem for a differential equation with a small parameter in its leading derivative. *Zh. Vychisl. Mat. mat. Fiz.*, **15** (6), 1466–1481.

Emel'yanov, K. V. (1978) A difference scheme for an ordinary differential equation with a small parameter. *Zh. Vychisl. Mat. mat. Fiz.*, **18** (5), 1146–1153.

Farrell, P. *et al.* (2000) *Robust Computational Techniques for Boundary Layers*. Chapman and Hall/CRC Bota Raton.

FpML (2002) FpML Architecture Working Group Technical Note: Migration to XML Schema (see http://www.fpml.org/spec/XMLSchemaRec).

FpML (2003) FpML Version 4.0 (see www.fpml.org).

Gamma, E., Helm, R., Johnson, R. and Vlissides, J. (1995) *Design Patterns, Elements of Reusable Object-Oriented Software*. Addison-Wesley, Reading, MA (GOF 1995).

Godunov, S. and Riabenki, V. S. (1987) *Difference Schemes: An Introduction to the Underlying Theory*. North-Holland, Amsterdam.

Haug, E. (1998) *The Complete Guide to Option Pricing Formulas*. McGraw-Hill, New York.

Hochstadt, H. (1964) *Differential Equations*. Dover Publications Inc., New York.

Hsu, H. (1997) *Probability, Random Variables and Random Processes*. Schaum's Outline Series. McGraw-Hill, New York.

Hull, J. (2000) *Options, Futures and other Derivative Securities*. Prentice-Hall, Englewood Cliffs, NJ.

Hunter, J. (1964) *Number Theory*. Oliver & Boyd, Edinburgh.

Il'in, A. M. (1969) Differencing scheme for a differential equation with a small parameter affecting the highest derivative. *Mat. Zametki*, **6**, 237–248.

Isaacson, E. and Keller, H. (1966) *Analysis of Numerical Methods*. John Wiley & Sons, New York.

Jäckel, P. (2002) *Monte Carlo Methods in Finance*. John Wiley & Sons, Chichester, UK.

Jackson, M. (1975) *Principles of Program Design*. Academic Press, London.

Keller, H. (1968) *Numerical Methods for Boundary-Value Problems*. Blaisdell Publishing Company, Waltham, MA.

Keller, H. (1971) A new difference scheme for parabolic problems. In B. Hubbard (ed.), *Numerical Solution of Partial Differential Equations–II*. Synspade.

Kitchenham, B. and Pfleeger, S. L. (1996) Software quality: The elusive target. *IEEE Software*, January.

Kloeden, P., Platen, E. and Schurz, H. (1994) *Numerical Solution of SDE through Computer Experiments*. Springer, Berlin.

Levin, A. (2000) *A two-factor model for default risk*. Working Paper.

Lofton, T. (1997) *Getting Started in Futures*. John Wiley & Sons Inc., New York.

Marchuk, G. I. and Shaidurov, V. V. (1983) *Difference Methods and their Extrapolations*. Springer-Verlag, New York.

Meyer, P. L. (1970) *Introductory Probability and Statistical Applications*. Addison-Wesley, Reading, MA.

Mirani, R. (2002) *Application of Duffy's finite difference method to barrier options*. Working Paper, Datasim BV.

Morton, K. (1996) *Numerical Solution of Convection-Diffusion Equations*. Chapman & Hall, London, UK.

Mun, J. (2002) *Real Options Analysis*. John Wiley & Sons, New Jersey.

Musser, D. R. and Saini, A. (1996) *STL Tutorial and Reference Guide*. Addison-Wesley, Reading, MA.

Peaceman, D. (1977) *Numerical Reservoir Simulation*. Elsevier.

Pilipović, D. (1998) *Energy Risk*. McGraw-Hill, New York.

Press, W., Flannery, B., Teukolsky, S. and Vetterling, W. (1980) *Numerical Recipes*. Cambridge University Press.

Richtmyer, R. D. and Morton, K. W. (1967) *Difference Methods for Initial-Value Problems*. Interscience Publishers (John Wiley & Sons), New York.

Rumbaugh, J. (1999) *Unified Modeling Language Reference Manual*. Addison-Wesley, Reading, MA.

Samarski, A. A. (1976) Some questions from the general theory of difference schemes. *Trans. Amer. Math. Soc.*, **105** (2).

Schuss, Z. (1980) *Theory and Applications of Stochastic Differential Equations*. John Wiley & Sons, New York.

Seydel, R. (2003) *Tools for Computational Finance*. Springer, Berlin.

Shephard, G. C. (1966) *Vector Spaces of Finite Dimension*. Oliver & Boyd, Edinburgh.

Skonnard, A. and Gudgin, M. (2002) *Essential XML Quick Reference*. Addison Wesley, Boston.

Smith, G. D. (1978) *Numerical Solution of Partial Differential Equations: Finite Difference Methods*. Oxford University Press.

Spiegel, M. (1959) *Theory and Problems of Vector Analysis*. Schaum's Outline Series. McGraw-Hill, New York.

Spiegel, M. (1992) *Theory and Problems of Statistics*. Schaum's Outline Series. McGraw-Hill, New York.

Steele, J. (2001) *Stochastic Calculus and Financial Applications*. Springer, New York.

Stoyan, G. (1979) Monotone difference schemes for diffusion–convection problems. *ZAMM*, **59**, 361–372.

Strang, G. and Fix, G. (1973) *An Analysis of the Finite Element Method*. Prentice-Hall, Englewood Cliffs, NJ.

Stroustrup, B. (1997) *The C++ Programming Language* (3rd edition). Addison-Wesley, Reading, MA.

Sun, Y. (1999) *High order methods for evaluating convertible bonds*. PhD Thesis, University of North Carolina.

Tavella, D. and Randall, C. (2000) *Pricing Financial Instruments: The Finite Difference Method*. John Wiley & Sons, New York.

Thomas, J. W. (1998) *Numerical Partial Differential Equations*, Volume I: *Finite Difference Methods*. Springer, New York.

Topper, J. (1998) *Finite Element Modeling of Exotic Options*. Internal Report, University of Hannover. ISSN (0949)–(9962).

van Deventer, D. R. and Imai, K. (1997) *Financial Risk Analytics*. McGraw-Hill, Chicago.

Varga, R. S. (1962) *Matrix Iterative Analysis*. Prentice-Hall Inc., Englewood Cliffs, NJ.

Wilmott, P. (1998) *Derivatives*. John Wiley & Sons, Chichester, UK.

Wilmott, P., Dewynne, J. and Howison, S. (1993) *Option Pricing*. Oxford Financial Press, UK.

Yanenko, N. N. (1971) *The Method of Fractional Steps*. Springer-Verlag, Berlin.

Index

WILEY COPYRIGHT INFORMATION AND TERMS OF USE

CD supplement to *Financial Instrument Pricing Using C++*

by **Daniel J. Duffy**

ISBN 0-470-85509-6

CD-ROM Copyright © 2004 Datasim Education BV

Published by John Wiley & Sons Ltd, The Atrium, Southern Gate, Chichester, West Sussex, PO19 8SQ. All rights reserved.